Modern Business Cycle Theory

Modern
Business Cycle
Theory.

EDITED BY

Robert J. Barro

Harvard University Press

Cambridge, Massachusetts   1989

Copyright © 1989 by Harvard University Press and Basil Blackwell
All rights reserved
Printed in the United States of America
10 9 8 7 6 5 4 3 2 1

This book is printed on acid-free paper, and its binding materials
have been chosen for strength and durability.

Library of Congress Cataloging in Publication Data

Modern business cycle theory/edited by Robert J. Barro.
   p. cm.
   Bibliography: p.
   Includes index.
   Contents: Real business cycle models/by Bennett T. McCallum—
Capital accumulation in the theory of long-run growth/by Paul M.
Romer—Rational expectations and the informational role of prices
/by Sanford J. Grossman—Consumption/by Robert E. Hall—The
neoclassical approach to fiscal policy/by Robert J. Barro—
Reputation, coordination, and monetary policy/by Kenneth Rogoff—
Time consistency and policy/by V. V. Chari, Patrick J. Kehoe, and
Edward C. Prescott—Some alternative monetary models and their
implications for the role of open-market policy/by Neil Wallace.
   1. Business cycles. I. Barro, Robert J.
HB3711.M548 1989   ⋀88-28303
338.5′42—dc19   CIP
   ISBN 0-674-57860-0 (alk. paper)

To Josh, a remarkable kid

Contents

Modern Business Cycle Theory

Introduction

Robert J. Barro

The new classical macroeconomics, sometimes referred to as rational expectations macroeconomics or the equilibrium approach to macroeconomics, began in the early 1970s. Although many of the methods and results remain controversial, the general approach—especially the modeling of expectations—has produced significant and long-lasting (and, I would argue, desirable) changes in the way macroeconomists do their research. As a consequence, the new classical macroeconomics has also become part of the core program for students of economics. The teaching of this subject, however, has been hampered by the absence of material that is well exposited and reasonably comprehensive. Some of the major contributors to the research literature have now prepared survey essays of various aspects of the new classical macroeconomics, with an emphasis on developments in the 1980s. These essays, contained in this volume, are designed especially for economics courses at the first-year graduate and advanced undergraduate levels.

From its inception in the early 1970s, the new classical macroeconomics used as its guiding principle the assumption that economic agents acted rationally within their environments. This assumption implied that people assembled and used information in an efficient manner. Although the approach stressed fully worked out equilibrium theories, the analysis was directed at explaining real-world business fluctuations. The basic viewpoint implied that it would be unsatisfactory to "explain" these fluctuations by easily correctable market failures, such as those present in the existing Keynesian models. Hence fluctuations had to reflect real or monetary disturbances, whose dynamic economic effects depended on costs of obtaining information, costs of adjustment, and so on.

The biggest challenge to the new classical approach was to explain why money was nonneutral and, in particular, why monetary disturbances played a major role in business cycles. This area was a challenge for two reasons. First, it appeared to be empirically important; and second, the equilibrium framework with flexible prices has a strong tendency to generate a close approximation to monetary neutrality. (I abstract here from deadweight losses from the inflation tax, administrative costs of changing prices, and so on, because these elements seem to be quantitatively minor in business fluctuations.)

Initially, the theory seemed to achieve notable successes, as described in my earlier survey article (Barro, 1981a). On a theoretical level, short-term real effects of monetary disturbances could arise from imperfect information about money and the general price level (Lucas, 1972, 1973; Sargent, 1973; and Barro, 1976). Monetary disturbances, which affected the general price level in the same direction, could be temporarily viewed as shifts in relative prices, a misperception that led to adjustments in the supply of labor and other quantities. These real effects vanished in the long run but could persist for a short period because of information lags and costs of adjusting the quantities of factor inputs. Conversely, anticipated monetary changes—which include systematic monetary policies— would not matter, because they did not lead to informational confusions (Sargent and Wallace, 1975; but see also Weiss, 1980; and King, 1982a).

On an empirical level, some evidence appeared to support the new classical macroeconomics. Monetary disturbances seemed to be major sources of business fluctuations; and there was some evidence that it was mainly the unanticipated or surprise part of monetary movements that mattered for real variables (see Sargent, 1976; Barro, 1981b; Attfield and Duck, 1983; and Kormendi and Meguire, 1984). The theory was also consistent with the absence of substantial long-run relationships between real economic performance and the growth rates of money or prices, that is, with the absence of long-run Phillips curve–type relations.

But further consideration cast doubt on these successes. First, the informational lag in observing money and the general price level did not seem to be very important (as Sandy Grossman notes in Chapter 3). If information about money and the general price level mattered much for economic decisions, people could expend relatively few resources to find out quickly about money and prices.

Second, the predicted positive effect of surprise money on output and employment was sensitive to changes in specification. Although the belief that a current price or wage is temporarily high represents a perceived profit opportunity for suppliers of goods and labor, it represents a correspondingly bad deal for demanders. Hence a benchmark, symmetric model implies that surprises in money and prices—even if they are substantial because of imperfect information—leave output and employment unchanged (see Barro and King, 1984).

Third, the theory stresses that a shock to money produces a surprise increase in the price level and thereby affects real variables. But the relation between price shocks and output or employment, which is a version of the Phillips curve, turns out to be weak or nonexistent in the post–World War II United States (Sargent, 1976; Fair, 1979). That is, monetary aggregates do much better in "explaining" output than does the price level.

Fourth, the data indicate that a broad monetary aggregate that includes aspects of financial intermediation, such as M1 or M2, is more closely correlated with output than is a narrow aggregate, such as the monetary base or currency. Since financial intermediation is endogenous to economic activity, this finding suggests, as argued by King and Plosser (1984), that reverse causation may be important. The observed positive correlation between money and output may reflect primarily the impact of economic activity on the quantity of money, rather than vice versa.[1] Under some forms of monetary policy—for example, when the central bank targets nominal interest rates (as central banks often claim to do)— even a positive correlation between the monetary base and output could reflect the endogenous response of money (see Barro, 1989).

Finally, the theory has embarrassing implications for other macroeconomic variables. Because the theory relies on a higher expected real rate of return to stimulate labor supply during a boom, it is hard to reproduce the strong procyclical behavior of investment (which tends to fall when real interest rates rise). King (1982b) extended the framework—by allowing the real rate of return pertinent to investment decisions to differ from that for labor supply—to make the model possibly consistent with the observed behavior of investment. It is also difficult to explain why consumption and leisure move in opposite directions during business cycles, that is, why consumption and work are both procyclical (see Grossman, 1973; and Barro and King, 1984). To account for the observed pattern, the model needs a major procyclical movement in real wage rates: if the real wage rises in a boom, work can rise while consumption increases. But the theory cannot generate this response of the real wage solely from a monetary disturbance; some supply shock that affects the productivity of labor is required. The need for a procyclical pattern for the real wage is awkward, because the data indicate that this pattern is weak at best (see Geary and Kennan, 1982).

According to these arguments, the new classical approach does not do well in accounting for an important role of money in business fluctuations. But this failing may not be so serious, because the empirical evidence for the role of money in business fluctuations also seems to have been overstated. In other words, the accounting for major short-run nonneutralities of money was a misplaced priority for the new classical approach. Some of the evidence mentioned earlier supports this conclusion; for example, the observation that the correlation of real economic activity with broad monetary aggregates is greater than that with the monetary base or the price level. This pattern suggests that endogenous responses of money may account for most of the correlations between money and real economic activity.

Consequently, over the past five to ten years, most proponents of the new classical approach have moved away from analyses that emphasize monetary shocks and toward those that rely on real disturbances as sources of business fluctuations. As Ben McCallum points out in Chapter 1, these models stress shocks to technology as the central driving force but allow an important role for the dynamic elements that influence the ways in which shocks propagate. The models are "equilibrium" in style and feature cleared, competitive markets; optimizing agents who are typically modeled as representative households with infinite horizons; and neoclassical production functions that are subject to stochastic disturbances. Although the models deemphasize monetary shocks, the analysis of propagation mechanisms would apply to monetary models as well as to real models. In the real business cycle (RBC) framework, any positive correlation between output and money reflects the endogenous response of monetary aggregates.

A number of authors have simulated versions of these models in which the underlying parameters of preferences and technology are calibrated to be consistent with findings from cross-sectional studies. In many respects the results accord with observed characteristics of business cycles. For example, extended versions of RBC models can accurately predict the relative variances of consumption, investment, capital stocks, and worker hours and also account for the procyclical behavior of these variables. But the models tend to overstate the procyclical patterns of hours, productivity, real interest rates, and real wage rates. In addition, to explain the standard deviation of output growth, the models require a standard deviation for technological disturbances that may be excessive. So far, however, such judgments are based solely on introspection.

The main RBC models generate results that are Pareto optimal. Hence the results demonstrate that observed fluctuations in aggregate business activity are an insufficient reason for advocating government intervention in the form of stabilization policies. The models can be extended, however, to include external effects, such as those implied by public goods and taxation. In these extended models the outcomes are generally not Pareto optimal. But the distortions are of the classical, excess-burden variety rather than of the Keynesian type—that is, they involve triangles instead of gaps. Thus desirable policy in these models gets more from public finance theory than from traditional macroeconomics.

Overall, the real business cycle approach has generated many new insights and techniques that assist in modeling the macroeconomy. But it is not yet clear how much the models contribute to an understanding of actual business cycles or to the construction of useful government policies.

Macroeconomists have also developed new approaches to the theory of economic growth and to the interactions between growth and fluctuations. In Chapter 2 Paul Romer writes, "One of the major themes of this chapter is that the substantive contribution of growth theory has so far been quite small but the methodological impact has been far reaching and fundamental . . . The second theme developed here is that the tools have developed to the point where growth theory is on the verge of having something interesting to say about growth."

Romer summarizes some empirical regularities that a useful theory of growth would replicate, including the persistence of growth in output and capital per worker, but at rates that differ substantially across countries. The rate of growth of factor inputs is typically insufficient to explain the growth of output; that is, growth accounting finds an important "residual." Furthermore, there is little tendency for output per worker to converge across countries, and skilled and unskilled labor tend to migrate toward the places with higher incomes. Other regularities involve the relation of growth and trade, the behavior of population growth, and the patterns in factor shares and factor returns.

Romer's discussion of the methodological contributions revolves around the Kuhn-Tucker theorem. ("All of the theory of growth can be understood in terms of the application of this theorem to models with tractable functional forms for preferences and the technology.'') In a context where the equilibria are Pareto optimal, he shows how to deal with transversality conditions and with discrete and continuous time. Then he applies the techniques to simple growth models of the Ramsey-Solow-Cass-Koopmans type and deals with issues of dynamics and stability. He also discusses models with externalities, for which the equilibria are not Pareto optimal. His examples include distorting taxation, spillover effects from the accumulation of knowledge, and imperfect competition in a model with increasing returns.

Romer argues that increasing returns associated with knowledge are vital for understanding technological progress and, hence, economic growth. He discusses Arrow's analysis of learning by doing and then reviews his own contributions to the positive theory of technological change. He also summarizes the related work of Lucas, which focuses on the external effects associated with the accumulation of human capital. In this model the returns to physical capital can be equalized across countries, while the remaining differentials in wages motivate migration from less- to more-developed countries.

These theories of economic growth stress external effects, which can reflect spillovers of knowledge or the returns from specialization. The suboptimal nature of the decentralized equilibria in these models may allow a role for the government's ''industrial policy.'' Because of second-best interactions, it is possible to generate surprising results, in which countries can benefit from shortages of labor or raw materials or from some types of restrictions on international trade.

Another evolving line of research (associated with King and Rebelo and with Becker and myself) shows that steady-state growth can arise endogenously without external effects when individual production is subject to constant returns to scale. The absence of diminishing returns becomes plausible when one allows for investments in human capital and—in a family context—for accumulation of more bodies through choices about population growth. These models have noninterventionist implications for government policy and do not generate paradoxical, second-best results.

While the choice between the two lines of endogenous growth theories is presently unclear, it is clear that growth theory has become an exciting area of research. The field shows promise for providing an understanding of the forces, including government policies, that influence economic performance over the long term. Considering the significance of this topic, the recent progress and promise are very favorable developments.

Much of macroeconomic theory in the last fifteen years has used the concept of rational expectations, and Sanford Grossman explores the foundations of this concept in Chapter 3. An individual's expectations are rational if they utilize efficiently the information that the individual possesses. This information includes any private knowledge that someone acquires directly, such as facts about a company's productivity, plus the information contained in publicly observed prices. Thus, in elaborating the "micro foundations" of rational expectations, Grossman points out that an equilibrium takes account of the information that market prices convey to traders. In a rational expectations equilibrium, excess demands are zero, given that these demands apply at going prices and are subject to the information implied by these prices being market clearing. In this sense a rational expectations equilibrium is an extension of the Walrasian system to contexts where information is imperfect, and, more important, is dispersed among the market participants.

Grossman shows how markets can aggregate information, in that the equilibrium price guides each person to act as if he obtained directly everyone's private information. This result obtains when there is a complete set of speculative markets—that is, a full array of Arrow-Debreu securities with payoffs contingent on the state of the world. More generally, the result requires people to observe at least as many independent signals (market prices) as there are independent pieces of private information that matter for the market. In these situations the decentralized outcomes are Pareto optimal. Therefore, a social planner who observed directly everyone's private information could not improve on the allocations in a Pareto sense. Markets possess an informational efficiency along the lines suggested by Hayek (1945).

When information is costly for individuals to collect, the outcomes are generally not Pareto optimal. That is, a planner could do better if he unrealistically obtained all the information for free. In this case equilibrium prices contain enough noise to allow the people who invest in the acquisition of knowledge to retain a fair private return from this activity.

Grossman goes on to apply the rational expectations framework to macroeconomic problems. He argues that the models from the early 1970s, which assumed incomplete knowledge about money and the general price level, did not isolate a significant aspect of incomplete information. However, he gets some interesting results in a model of implicit contracts, when firms have private information about productivity shocks. Because of this informational asymmetry, employment fluctuations serve partly as a screening device to regulate firms' incentives to misrepresent their information. In these models, employment fluctuates more and is utilized less than in a setting where all information is public.

As Bob Hall points out in Chapter 4, no area of research has been affected more by the rational expectations revolution than has the study of consumption. After the development of the permanent-income and life-cycle models in the 1950s, the analysis of consumer behavior remained largely dormant until the late 1970s. Then applications of the rational expectations theory showed how the path of consumption would relate to other variables, such as innovations in income, attitudes toward risk and time preference, and expected real rates of return. Under some conditions, including constant expected real interest rates, changes in consumption would be unpredictable—the famous random-walk model of consumption initiated by Hall in 1978. The relation between innovations in consumption and innovations in income depends on the nature of the income process. By implication, the theory rejects the consumption function as a structural relation—a result that illustrates Lucas's well-known critique of policy evaluation. When expected real interest rates vary, the theory predicts a positive relation between the expected real interest rate and the growth rate of consumption. But the coefficients that govern this relation combine parameters of intertemporal substitution with attitudes toward risk.

The theoretical findings about consumption generated a large amount of empirical research, which used time series and cross-sectional data. The results were mixed in terms of their relation to the theoretical hypotheses. The basic random-walk idea captures a good deal of reality but can be rejected as a precise prediction. Some departures from the theory can be explained by liquidity constraints or the durability of consumer goods, with some preference for the latter explanation. But little is known about the empirical relation between real interest rates and the path of consumption.

With the advent of large U.S. budget deficits since the early 1980s, fiscal policy has been at the center of public debate. Fortunately, as I discuss in Chapter 5, the new classical approach has also provided a good deal of recent research into fiscal aspects of macroeconomics. My chapter summarizes the theoretical and empirical developments in this area.

Chapter 5 starts with a basic framework, which analyzes the consumption and saving choices for a representative family with an infinite horizon. Competitive firms produce the single type of good with a neoclassical production function. The government purchases goods to provide a flow of public services to households and firms. The government's expenditures, as well as its transfers, are financed by income or other types of taxes (including the inflation tax). Later on, the model allows for government borrowing, so that the government can run budget deficits instead of levying taxes.

I derive the effects on interest rates, output, and other variables from permanent or temporary changes in government purchases. The results depend on the type of tax finance, for example, on whether the taxes apply to labor income or capital income or are lump sum.

I introduce public debt and work out the conditions for the Ricardian equivalence theorem, that is, conditions where taxes and budget deficits have the same effects on the economy. For a given path of government expenditures (aside from interest payments), the Ricardian result follows from two basic considerations. First, the government's budget constraint in each period implies that budget deficits alter the timing of tax collections but not the total present value of taxes. This result amounts to the absence of a free lunch: the government must pay for its expenditures (in a present-value sense) either now or later, but not never. Second, in determining their path of consumption, labor supply, and so on, households care about the present value of taxes but not their timing. The two points together deliver Ricardian equivalence. Since changes in consumer demand and so on are the route by which budget deficits would affect other variables, such as interest rates and output, the conclusion from this model is that shifts between taxes and deficits do not matter for the economy. Or, equivalently, a deficit-financed tax cut leads to an increase in private saving that exactly offsets the decline in public saving and thereby leaves national saving intact.

The analysis considers the main theoretical objections that have been raised against Ricardian equivalence: finite lifetimes, imperfect private loan markets, uncertainty about future taxes, and substitution effects from changes in the timing of non-lump-sum taxes. In each case precise Ricardian equivalence may fail, but the departures are not necessarily in the direction suggested by standard approaches to fiscal policy. In particular, budget deficits need not reduce desired national saving, or raise real interest rates, or lead to a deficit on the current account.

I also explore the idea that substitution effects from the timing of taxes—say, income taxes—provide a useful positive theory of fiscal policy (the tax-smoothing view of budget deficits). Then the final section summarizes empirical evidence about the effects of budget deficits on interest rates and consumption.

As Ken Rogoff says in Chapter 6, one of the most exciting recent developments in macroeconomics is the application of game theory to analyses of government policy. This literature began with studies that showed that discretionary policies—where the government makes no binding commitments about its future choices—could lead to outcomes that were inferior to those attainable under enforced rules. For example, in the context of monetary policy, discretionary behavior tends to generate excessive inflation, which reflects the government's incentive to inflate at a faster rate than people expect. Yet, under rational expectations, this objective is unattainable and the policymaker ends up merely generating high actual and anticipated inflation. Hence the costs of high inflation arise without the possible benefits from high unexpected inflation. Following Kydland and Prescott, this result is sometimes described as the time-consistent but nonoptimal outcome, whereas the preferred low-inflation behavior is said to be time inconsistent. (Time-inconsistent behavior occurs when the government is predictably motivated to deviate from the path; hence the path cannot be an equilibrium.)

Rogoff investigates the extent to which reputational forces can substitute for formal rules as a mechanism for attaining the preferred outcomes. On the plus side, reputation may work well, because most real-world situations involve repeated interactions between the policymaker and private agents, instead of just a single period of play. Moreover, formal rules or contracts may be inferior to reputation, which can be "flexible" in the sense of avoiding the enumeration of all possible contingencies.

On the other hand, if reputational equilibria exist, they typically come in multiples. In some circumstances the multiplicity of equilibrium can be indexed by the lengths of "punishments" for policymakers who misbehave, and in others, by the severity of these punishments. In some contexts the punishments are merely (credible) threats, which do not arise in equilibrium. In others—for example, where the policymaker has private economic information that agents cannot verify directly—the punishments materialize from time to time as periods where expectations revert (via a trigger-strategy mechanism) to the discretionary level. The richness of the possible solutions is embarrassing, because a theory of how the economy coordinates on one of the possible equilibria is presently lacking. The one with the best operating characteristics is most attractive, but the coordination on this outcome cannot be assured.

In other cases a unique equilibrium exists but the properties of the solution are sensitive to assumptions about information. As one example, Rogoff assumes that the public is uncertain about the policymaker's objectives or about the costs that the policymaker attaches to breaking commitments. In this case the equilibrium may be of the pooling variety, where the "bad" type of policymaker masquerades for a while as the "good" type. But, depending on parameter values, the equilibrium may instead be separating, because the good type is motivated initially to take drastic actions that the bad type would be unwilling to imitate. In other words, the good type is willing to adopt costly policies that immediately signal his type.

Although many loose ends remain, the strategic models have already generated meaningful insights into the formation of government policy. In particular, since the policymaker's motivations and actions are parts of the model, it becomes possible to construct positive theories of policy, which can be tested empirically. (It is unclear how to test a purely normative model of government policy.) As Rogoff says, "It may be constructive to treat the government as a black box in studying certain phenomena, but it is hardly adequate as a framework for studying macroeconomic policy design."

V. V. Chari, Pat Kehoe, and Ed Prescott, in Chapter 7, deal also with models that involve strategic interactions between a government policymaker and an array of private agents. Their main objective is to provide perspectives on the idea of time consistency rather than to survey the literature on this topic.

Chapter 7 begins with the characterization of policy as a rule that specifies actions as a function of the state of the economy. The evaluation of alternative policies requires, first, an economic model specifying how individuals respond to different policies; second, a description of how policy rules are chosen; and third, a specification of the "technology of commitment" for the policymaker. It is this last element that is central to issues of time consistency.

Commitment equilibria are those that arise when the policymaker can bind himself to a particular rule at the beginning of time. Then the policy choice problem is to maximize the social-welfare function (or some other objective), given that individuals respond optimally to these policies. In the absence of such a commitment technology, the policy rules must be sequentially rational. That is, the policy rules maximize a specified objective at each date, given that private agents behave optimally. Moreover, private agents understand that policies satisfy this sequential rationality and make forecasts accordingly. When the commitment and sequentially rational equilibria differ, a time-consistency problem exists.

Within the class of models studied, the authors show that a time-consistency problem can arise only if there is some type of conflict among private agents or between the private sector and the government. One class of examples features competitive private agents and a government that seeks to maximize the utility of the representative person. In this setting external effects are one source of conflict that can generate a time-consistency problem. For example, the government may have to finance public expenditures with distorting taxation. If capital can be taxed, the government has an incentive to implement capital levies, which are non-distorting once investments have been made. But the expectation of these levies deters people from investing in the first place. Hence the outcomes tend to be inferior to those generated with an effective commitment technology, where the government provides a binding promise not to effect capital levies later on. Similar results apply for public debt, because the government has an incentive to default, ex post.

Chari, Kehoe, and Prescott conclude that a society cannot choose between commitment and time-consistent equilibria, because commitment technologies are like production functions and are not objects of choice. Others have concluded that societies can invest in institutions, including legal systems, that do alter the technology of commitment. The resolution of these divergent viewpoints has a lot to do with the meaning of policy choice in an economy.

In the final chapter, Neil Wallace develops some prototypical general equilibrium models in which the demand for money, and hence the value of money, are derived from (more or less) basic principles. The setting is one where other paper assets with the same risk characteristics as money, such as government bonds, dominate money in terms of rate of return. Hence the existence of a demand for money depends on some form of nonpecuniary monetary service. Wallace models these services in three ways: money in the utility function, cash-in-advance constraints, or legal restrictions. The results for open-market policies are basically similar in all three approaches, although some of the conclusions depend on whether consumer behavior comes from an infinite-life model or an overlapping-generations framework. Generally, changes in monetary behavior have fiscal implications, which correspond to the usual inflation tax. Therefore, the results also depend on what type of fiscal adjustments accompany the monetary changes.

Wallace observes that the models fail to capture adequately the notion that exchange is difficult and that money arises somehow to help with this problem. Moreover, the assumption throughout is that the government/ central bank has a monopoly in the issue of paper money. A rationale for this last assumption may, in fact, come from a more satisfactory modeling of the exchange process. In any event, Wallace finds that open-market operations are typically nonneutral in his models. Therefore, he objects to the common practice of treating these types of operations as approximately neutral.

After its favorable reception in the early 1970s, the new classical approach expanded to cover a variety of aspects of macroeconomics in the 1980s. This book summarizes the major developments of this second generation of the new classical macroeconomics. It is my hope that the essays contained here will serve as expositions of these developments for students and as building blocks for further research efforts.

Notes

1. Friedman and Schwartz (1963), in their monetary history of the United States, were well aware of this possibility. But they thought they had evidence that the relation between money and income or prices was similar under different regimes of money supply. Therefore, they argued that their approach isolated mainly the direction of effect from money to the economy, rather than the reverse. But it is unclear whether this conclusion survives a detailed examination of the various episodes that make up the evidence. For example, in the 1929–1933 Depression, the decline in broad monetary aggregates reflects the endogenous collapse of financial intermediation. (The monetary base actually rose during this period.) While this breakdown in the credit process would itself have important real consequences, as argued by Bernanke (1983), such effects are consistent with purely real models. That is, an interruption in the credit process is different from a purely nominal disturbance (such as a decline in the quantity of base money generated by an open-market operation). The increase in the Federal Reserve's reserve requirements in 1936–37 looks more like an exogenous act of policy, which led to a decline in broad monetary aggregates. The reserve requirement is a tax on financial intermediation, however, and would again have real effects in purely real models. For further discussion of this type of evidence, see Barro (1987, chaps. 15 and 16).

References

Attfield, C. L. F., and N. W. Duck. 1983. The Influence of Unanticipated Money Growth on Real Output: Some Cross-Country Estimates. *Journal of Money, Credit, and Banking* 15 (November): 442–454.

Barro, R. J. 1976. Rational Expectations and the Role of Monetary Policy. *Journal of Monetary Economics* 2 (January): 1–32.

—— 1981a. The Equilibrium Approach to Business Cycles. *In* R. J. Barro, *Money, Expectations, and Business Cycles.* New York: Academic Press.

—— 1981b. Unanticipated Money and Economic Activity in the United States. *In* R. J. Barro, *Money, Expectations, and Business Cycles.* New York: Academic Press.

—— 1987. *Macroeconomics,* 2nd ed. New York: John Wiley & Sons.

—— 1989. Interest-Rate Targeting. *Journal of Monetary Economics* 23 (January).

Barro, R. J., and R. G. King. 1984. Time-Separable Preferences and Intertemporal-Substitution Models of Business Cycles. *Quarterly Journal of Economics* 99 (October): 817–839.

Bernanke, B. S. 1983. Non-Monetary Effects of the Financial Collapse in the Propagation of the Great Depression. *American Economic Review* 73 (June): 257–276.

Fair, R. C. 1979. An Analysis of the Accuracy of Four Macroeconometric Models. *Journal of Political Economy* 87 (August): 701–718.

Friedman, M., and A. J. Schwartz. 1963. *A Monetary History of the United States, 1867–1960.* Princeton: Princeton University Press.

Geary, P. T., and J. Kennan. 1982. The Employment-Real Wage Relationship: An International Study. *Journal of Political Economy* 90 (August): 854–871.

Grossman, H. I. 1973. Aggregate Demand, Job Search, and Employment. *Journal of Political Economy* 81 (November/December): 1353–69.

Hayek, F. A. 1945. The Use of Knowledge in Society. *American Economic Review* 35 (September): 519–530.

King, R. G. 1982a. Monetary Policy and the Information Content of Prices. *Journal of Political Economy* 90 (April): 247–279.

—— 1982b. Investment, Imperfect Information, and Equilibrium Business Cycle Theory. Unpublished paper, University of Rochester.

King, R. G., and C. I. Plosser. 1984. Money, Credit, and Prices in a Real Business Cycle. *American Economic Review* 74 (June): 363–380.

Kormendi, R. C., and P. G. Meguire. 1984. Cross-Regime Evidence of Macroeconomic Rationality. *Journal of Political Economy* 92 (October): 875–908.

Lucas, R. E. 1972. Expectations and the Neutrality of Money. *Journal of Economic Theory* 4 (April): 103–124.

—— 1973. Some International Evidence on Output–Inflation Tradeoffs. *American Economic Review* 63 (June): 326–334.

Sargent, T. J. 1973. Rational Expectations, the Real Rate of Interest, and the Natural Rate of Unemployment. *Brookings Papers on Economic Activity* 1973, no. 2, 429–472.

—— 1976. A Classical Macroeconometric Model for the United States. *Journal of Political Economy* 84 (April): 207–237.

Sargent, T. J., and N. Wallace. 1975. Rational Expectations, the Optimal Monetary Instrument, and the Optimal Money Supply Rule. *Journal of Political Economy* 83 (April): 241–254.

Weiss, L. 1980. The Role for Active Monetary Policy in a Rational Expectations Model. *Journal of Political Economy* 88 (April): 221–233.

1 Real Business Cycle Models

Bennett T. McCallum

One of the most striking developments in macroeconomics during the early 1980s was the emergence of a substantial body of literature devoted to the "real business cycle" approach to the analysis of macroeconomic fluctuations. Particularly prominent papers have been contributed by Kydland and Prescott (1982), Long and Plosser (1983), and King and Plosser (1984), whereas many others of interest have been written[1] and a number of critical or skeptical pieces have begun to appear.[2] This literature's implied point of view is an outgrowth of the equilibrium strategy for business cycle analysis that was initiated by Lucas (1972, 1973, 1975) and extended by Barro (1976, 1981), but differs from that of the earlier work in two critical respects. First, the real business cycle (RBC) models place much more emphasis than did the previous equilibrium-approach literature on mechanisms involving cycle *propagation*, that is, the spreading over time of the effects of shocks. Second, as the name implies, RBC models emphasize the extent to which shocks that initiate cycles are real—as opposed to "monetary"—in origin. In particular, the primary driving force is taken to be shocks to technology,[3] rather than the monetary and fiscal policy disturbances that are emphasized in the earlier equilibrium-approach writings.

It will be noted that these two features of the RBC approach are quite different from each other in terms of their relationship to alternative business cycle theories. Specifically, the RBC propagation analysis is entirely compatible with the Lucas-Barro monetary-misperceptions variant of the equilibrium approach and could logically be viewed as an attempt to elaborate and improve upon models of the Lucas-Barro type. Indeed, the point can be taken further by noting that the propagation phenomena stressed by RBC analysis could be relevant and important even in nonequilibrium[4] models that feature nominal wage and/or price stickiness.

With regard to initiating shocks, by contrast, the RBC viewpoint reflects much more of a departure from other theories. In this regard, two positions can usefully be identified. The weaker of the two is that technology shocks are quantitatively more important than monetary disturbances as initiators of business cycle movements, while the stronger is that monetary disturbances are of negligible consequence. The former position is compatible with monetary-misperception variants of equilibrium theory, as these have not involved denials of the role of supply shocks. The stronger RBC position, however—the hypothesis that monetary disturbances are an insignificant source of cyclical fluctuations—is clearly inconsistent with most alternative theories. In this form, the RBC approach presents a distinct challenge to mainstream macroeconomic analysis.[5]

In the discussion that follows, most of the emphasis will be implicitly given to the weaker version of the RBC hypothesis, as it is more clearly representative of the position taken in print by RBC proponents. The strong version will be accorded some attention, however, for two reasons. The more basic of these is that while the main topic of the present survey is RBC theory itself, a secondary topic is the contrast provided by RBC models with theories that rely upon monetary disturbances. Thus the sharp distinction provided by the strong RBC hypothesis is expositionally natural and convenient. But, in addition, it is this strong hypothesis that provides the RBC approach with a truly distinctive identity. As monetary-misperception variants of equilibrium theory do not deny the existence of supply shocks or propagation mechanisms, it is difficult to see how the RBC approach could be distinguished from the more general category of equilibrium analysis without reliance on the strong hypothesis. It is evidently the latter that constitutes the approach's distinguishing characteristic.

The present chapter is organized in the following way. In Section 1.1 the main features of the RBC approach are introduced by means of a simple prototype model. Although this discussion touches upon certain qualitative properties of the model and their relation to actual U.S. data, the main quantitative comparison between theory and evidence appears in Section 1.2. There, more elaborate versions of the model are recognized and a fairly detailed review of evidence of the type emphasized by Kydland and Prescott (1982, 1986) is provided. Then in Section 1.3 other types of evidence and several matters of controversy are reviewed. Finally, some conclusions are tentatively put forth in Section 1.4.

1.1. The Basic RBC Model

The object in this section is to describe a model that provides a simple example of the type featured in the RBC literature. In this demonstration, the intention is to outline the workings of this model in an intuitive manner, not to develop mathematical techniques or provide formal proofs of the relevant propositions. The discussion will accordingly be less than rigorous. A few references will be included, however, to direct readers to sources that contain formal proofs and more complete descriptions of the relevant mathematical concepts and techniques.[6]

Consider an economy composed of a large number of similar, infinite-lived households, each of which acts at time t to maximize

(1.1)
$$E_t\left[\sum_{j=0}^{\infty} \beta^j u\left(c_{t+j}, l_{t+j}\right)\right].$$

Here c_t and l_t denote the household's consumption and leisure during period t, while β is a discount factor $(0 < \beta < 1)$ that reflects a preference for current over future consumption–leisure bundles. Application of the operator $E_t(\cdot)$ yields the mathematical expectation, conditional upon complete information pertaining to period t and earlier, of the indicated argument. Leisure is time not devoted to labor, so an appropriate choice of units implies that $l_t = 1 - n_t$, where n_t is the household's labor supplied during t. The function u is assumed to be increasing in both arguments, differentiable, and "well-behaved"; thus for $i = 1, 2$, we have $u_i > 0$, $u_{ii} < 0$, $u_i(0) = \infty$, $u_i(\infty) = 0$.

Each of the postulated households has access to a production function of the form

(1.2) $y_t = z_t f(n_t^d, k_t^d),$

where y_t is output of the economy's single good during t, with n_t^d and k_t^d denoting labor and capital inputs used during t by the household. The variable z_t is the realization in period t of a random variable that reflects the state of technology. The process generating z_t is assumed to be of the stationary Markov class—the distribution of z_t depends on z_{t-1} but is otherwise constant over time. The function f is taken to be homogeneous of degree one and well-behaved with positive but diminishing marginal products. The household's output can be consumed or stored, with stored output adding to the household's stock of capital in the following period.

During each period, the fraction δ of the capital in existence disappears via depreciation.

Finally, the economy under discussion is assumed to possess competitive markets for labor and capital services—markets on which the wage and rental rates are w_t and q_t, respectively.[7] Thus the budget constraint faced by the typical household in period t is[8]

$$(1.3) \qquad c_t + k_{t+1} = z_t f(n_t^d, k_t^d) + (1 - \delta)k_t - w_t(n_t^d - n_t) - q_t(k_t^d - k_t).$$

At t, consequently, the household acts to maximize (1.1) subject to a sequence of constraints of the form (1.3). The u and f functions have been specified so that corner solutions will be avoided, so the following first-order conditions are necessary for a maximum:[9]

$$(1.4a) \qquad E_t u_1(c_{t+j}, 1 - n_{t+j}) - E_t \lambda_{t+j} = 0,$$

$$(1.4b) \qquad E_t u_2(c_{t+j}, 1 - n_{t+j}) - E_t \lambda_{t+j} \, w_{t+j} = 0,$$

$$(1.4c) \qquad E_t z_{t+j} f_1(n_{t+j}^d, k_{t+j}^d) - E_t w_{t+j} = 0,$$

$$(1.4d) \qquad E_t z_{t+j} f_2(n_{t+j}^d, k_{t+j}^d) - E_t q_{t+j} = 0,$$

$$(1.4e) \qquad -E_t \lambda_{t+j} + E_t \beta \lambda_{t+j+1} [z_{t+j+1} f_2(n_{t+j+1}^d, k_{t+j+1}^d) + 1 - \delta] = 0.$$

Here λ_{t+j} is the shadow price in utility terms of a unit of the economy's good in period $t + j$—a Lagrange multiplier, if one chooses to think of the maximization in those terms. In addition to conditions (1.4), there is also a transversality condition pertaining to the long-range aspect of the household's plans;[10] it may be written as

$$(1.5) \qquad \lim_{j \to \infty} E_t \beta^{j-1} \, \lambda_{t+j} k_{t+j+1} = 0.$$

Together, conditions (1.3), (1.4), and (1.5) are necessary and sufficient for an optimum. Thus they define the typical household's choice at t of c_t, n_t, n_t^d, k_t^d, and k_{t+1} in response to current values of w_t and q_t, its expectations about the future, and its accumulated stock of capital, k_t.

Now consider the matter of market equilibrium. For such a state to prevail, it must be the case that $\Sigma n_t = \Sigma n_t^d$ and $\Sigma k_t = \Sigma k_t^d$, where the sums are taken over all households. But since these households are all alike and all experience the same value for the shock z_t, those equalities imply that $n_t = n_t^d$ and $k_t = k_t^d$. Furthermore, it is assumed that expectations are rational, an assumption that means in this case that the conditional mathematical expectations in Equations (1.4) are based on probability distributions that coincide with those implied by the economy's structure (as represented by the model). Consequently, market equilibrium can be characterized by the following set of equalities, which hold for periods $t = 1, 2, \ldots$:

(1.6) $\qquad c_t + k_{t+1} = z_t f(n_t, k_t) + (1 - \delta)k_t,$

(1.7) $\qquad u_1(c_t, 1 - n_t) - \lambda_t = 0,$

(1.8) $\qquad u_2(c_t, 1 - n_t) = \lambda_t z_t f_1(n_t, k_t),$

(1.9) $\qquad \lambda_t = E_t \beta \lambda_{t+1} [z_{t+1} f_2(n_{t+1}, k_{t+1}) + 1 - \delta].$

Given an initial value for k_1, these four equations define time paths of the economy's per-household values of c_t, k_t, n_t, and λ_t. There will be a multiplicity of such paths, but only one will satisfy the transversality condition (1.5) that is necessary for household optimality.[11]

Before continuing, it is useful to note that precisely the same set of relations would have been obtained if we had simply treated each household as an isolated "Robinson Crusoe" unit for which the distinctions between n_t and n_t^d and between k_t and k_t^d are not applicable. This observation illustrates the point that Crusoe-style analysis can in certain cases be interpreted as pertaining to the behavior of quantity variables for competitive market economies. But for this type of equivalence to hold, all households must be alike and there must be no externalities. Furthermore, if there exists a government sector, then the model must be elaborated so as to recognize its existence, so Crusoe-style analysis is not generally available.[12]

Now consider solutions to the system of Equations (1.6)–(1.9). Inspection of these, plus reflection upon the nature of the economy at hand, leads to the conclusion that the state of the system at time t is fully defined by the current values of k_t and z_t.[13] Consequently, solutions to (1.6)–(1.9) will be of the form

(1.10) $\qquad k_{t+1} = k(k_t, z_t),$

(1.11) $\qquad c_t = c(k_t, z_t),$

(1.12) $\qquad n_t = n(k_t, z_t),$

(1.13) $\qquad \lambda_t = \lambda(k_t, z_t),$

where k, c, n, and λ are continuous functions. Note that this conclusion holds not only for serially uncorrelated technology shocks but also whenever these shocks are generated by a stationary Markov process. This conclusion is possible in the latter case because z_t provides all relevant conditioning information for the probability distribution of values occurring at time $t + 1$.

It should be useful to note parenthetically that government purchases—denoted g_t on a per-household basis—could be incorporated in the structure under discussion by adding to the system an equation reflecting the government's budget constraint and modifying the household budget constraint to reflect taxes. (Effects of g_t on production or utility functions, if any, would also be recognized.) If the taxes were of the lump-sum variety then Equations (1.4) would remain as shown, but these equations would have to be altered if taxes were levied on some productive activity. In either case, if government purchases conformed to a policy rule relating g_t to g_{t-1}, k_t, and z_t, then solution expressions like (1.10)–(1.13) would apply, but with g_t included as a third argument.

Equations (1.10)–(1.13) are simple in appearance, but this simplicity is perhaps deceptive in the following sense: there are very few functional forms for u and f that will permit derivation of explicit closed-form solutions for k_{t+1}, c_t, and n_t. There is one reasonably attractive combination that will do so, however, which consequently has been featured in several papers.[14] That combination involves a log-linear specification for u and a Cobb-Douglas form for f, as follows:

(1.14) $\quad u(c_t, 1 - n_t) = \theta \log c_t + (1 - \theta) \log (1 - n_t)$,

(1.15) $\quad z_t f(n_t, k_t) = z_t n_t^\alpha k_t^{1-\alpha}$.

In addition, this special case requires complete depreciation of capital within a single period, that is, requires that $\delta = 1$.[15]

To lend concreteness to the discussion, let us now consider the example provided by this special case. With the functional forms in (1.14) and (1.15) and with $\delta = 1$, the system of equations (1.6)–(1.9) becomes the following:

(1.6′) $\quad c_t + k_{t+1} = z_t\, n_t^\alpha\, k_t^{1-\alpha}$,

(1.7′) $\quad \theta/c_t = \lambda_t$,

(1.8′) $\quad (1 - \theta)/(1 - n_t) = \alpha\lambda_t z_t n_t^{\alpha-1} k_t^{1-\alpha}$,

(1.9′) $\quad \lambda_t = (1 - \alpha)\, \beta E_t \lambda_{t+1}[z_{t+1} n_{t+1}^\alpha k_{t+1}^{-\alpha}]$.

To obtain solution equations analogous to (1.10)–(1.13) for this special system, we begin by noting that with a utility function of the form (1.14) and complete depreciation, the income and substitution effects of a wage rate change will just offset each other, leaving the leisure choice unaffected (King, Plosser, and Rebelo, 1987). Consequently, it is reasonable to conjecture that n_t will be a constant in the solution, that is, that $n_t = n$. Then the manner in which z_t and k_t enter the production function leads to the further conjecture that c_t and k_{t+1} will be proportional to the product $z_t k_t^{1-\alpha}$. Thus our task can be reduced to the problem of evaluating π_{10} and π_{20} in the two expressions

(1.16) $c_t = \pi_{10} z_t k_t^{1-\alpha}$,

(1.17) $k_{t+1} = \pi_{20} z_t k_t^{1-\alpha}$.

To do so, we first use (1.7′) to eliminate λ_t and λ_{t+1} from (1.9′) and then substitute in (1.16) and (1.17) as follows:

(1.18) $$\frac{\theta}{\pi_{10} z_t k_t^{1-\alpha}} = (1-\alpha)\,\beta E_t \left[\frac{\theta z_{t+1}\, n^\alpha k_{t+1}^{-\alpha}}{\pi_{10} z_{t+1} k_{t+1}^{1-\alpha}}\right] = \frac{(1-\alpha)\,\beta\,\theta\,n^\alpha}{\pi_{10}(\pi_{20} z_t k_t^{1-\alpha})}$$

Then $\theta/\pi_{10}\, z_t k_t^{1-\alpha}$ cancels out in the latter, yielding $\pi_{20} = (1-\alpha)\beta n^\alpha$.

Next, substitution of (1.16) and (1.17) into (1.6′) and cancellation of $z_t k_t^{1-\alpha}$ gives $\pi_{10} + \pi_{20} = n^\alpha$ from which, with the expression for π_{20} obtained above, we find that $\pi_{10} = [1-(1-\alpha)\beta]n^\alpha$. Finally, substitution of these two expressions into a relation, obtained by eliminating λ_t between (1.7′) and (1.8′), results in the following value for n:

(1.19) $$n = \frac{\alpha\theta}{\alpha\theta + (1-\theta)[1 - \beta(1-\alpha)]}.$$

Thus our conjecture regarding n_t is verified, and it is concluded that, in the special example at hand, consumption and capital per household fluctuate over time according to[16]

(1.20) $c_t = [1-(1-\alpha)\beta]n^\alpha z_t k_t^{1-\alpha}$,

(1.21) $k_{t+1} = (1-\alpha)\beta n^\alpha z_t k_t^{1-\alpha}$.

Now, from (1.21), we can immediately observe that the logarithm of k_t obeys a stochastic process of the form

(1.22) $\log k_{t+1} = \phi_0 + (1-\alpha)\log k_t + \log z_t$.

Since $|1 - \alpha| < 1$, moreover, the process for k_t is dynamically stable. Furthermore, it features positive serial correlation: if $\log k_t$ is above normal, then so too will be the expected value of $\log k_{t+1}$, assuming that the process for $\log z_t$ is serially uncorrelated. If, instead, the z_t process is of the first-order autoregressive [that is, AR(1)] form

(1.23) $\log z_t = \rho \log z_{t-1} + \varepsilon_t,$

with ε_t white noise, then $\log k_t$ will be second-order autoregressive [AR(2)]:

(1.24) $\log k_{t+1} = \phi_0(1 - \rho) + (1 - \alpha + \rho) \log k_t - (1 - \alpha)\rho \log k_{t-1} + \varepsilon_t.$

Furthermore, in this case the second-order autoregressive structure carries over to other crucial quantity variables including $\log c_t$ and $\log y_t$. To illustrate that fact, let us express (1.20) as $\log c_t = \phi_1 + (1 - \alpha)\log k_t + \log z_t$. But from (1.22), $\log k_t = [1-(1 - \alpha)L]^{-1} [\phi_0 + \log z_{t-1}]$, where L is the log operator, so substitution and rearrangement give

(1.25) $[1-(1 - \alpha)L] \log c_t =$
$(1 - \alpha)\phi_0 + \alpha\phi_1 + [1-(1 - \alpha)L] \log z_t + (1 - \alpha) \log z_{t-1},$

which may be simplified, using $\log z_t = (1 - \rho L)^{-1}\varepsilon_t$, to yield

(1.26) $\log c_t = (1 - \alpha + \rho)\log c_{t-1} - (1 - \alpha)\rho\log c_{t-2}$
$+ \alpha(1 - \rho)\phi_1 + (1 - \alpha)(1 - \rho)\phi_0 + \varepsilon_t.$

Thus the simple special-case example of the prototype RBC model suggests that, with AR(1) technology shocks, important quantity variables will have the time series properties of second-order AR processes. This conclusion is of interest since *detrended*[17] quarterly U.S. data series for the logs of various aggregate quantities are, in fact, reasonably well described by AR(2) models.[18]

Another interesting property of the special-case model summarized by (1.20) and (1.21) is that the average product of labor is positively correlated with the level of total output. That property is, of course, an immediate implication of the constant-employment feature of the model. But it is a significant property, nevertheless, because the average product of labor is clearly procyclical in the actual U.S. quarterly data. And some of the leading orthodox theories suggest that the marginal product of labor—and thus the average product, if the production function is approximately Cobb-Douglas in form—will be countercyclical.[19]

Nevertheless, even at the qualitative level, there are some prominent ways in which the special-case model fails to match important aspects of the actual U.S. time series. One of these is the constant-employment feature noted above, and another is the model's implication that fluctuations in consumption and investment are of equal severity.[20] Both of these qualitative flaws can be overcome, however, by postulating that capital depreciation is incomplete within the period. With this change, the possibility of an explicit solution is lost, so the claim cannot be verified analytically.[21] But simulation results reported by Gary Hansen (1985, table 1) correspond to the case under discussion, and these involve employment variability and investment fluctuations that are several times as severe (in terms of percentage standard deviations from trend) as those of consumption. So even with the special assumptions (1.14) and (1.15) regarding utility and production functions, the prototype RBC model provides a reasonable match to important features of actual business cycle data. It is time, consequently, to turn to quantitative aspects of the match.

1.2. Quantitative Aspects of RBC Models

Perhaps the strongest single stimulus to analysis with RBC models was provided by the innovative "Time to Build" paper of Kydland and Prescott (1982), which first demonstrated the possibility of obtaining a good quantitative match between RBC model implications and actual business cycle fluctuations. The model developed and simulated by Kydland and Prescott is basically of the type described in the previous section but includes several additional features that were intended to improve its performance, that is, its agreement with cyclical characteristics of the postwar U.S. data. Four such features are

1. Leisure "services" in each period (that is, quarter) are represented by a distributed lag of current and past leisure hours.
2. Investment projects begun in period t require additional expenditures in periods $t + 1$, $t + 2$, and $t + 3$ before becoming productive in period $t + 4$.
3. Producers hold inventories of finished goods that serve as an additional factor of production.
4. The technology shock z_t is composed of transitory and highly persistent components that cannot be directly distinguished by producers or consumers.

Needless to say, with these features and incomplete depreciation, the Kydland-Prescott model does not have an analytical solution. But an approximation can be obtained, parameter values assigned, and simulations conducted. Kydland and Prescott's approach was to follow that strategy, with the average results of a number of stochastic simulations serving to characterize the model's cyclical properties. And the same kind of procedure can be applied to the basic model (with $\delta < 1$) of the previous section, or other structures of the same general type.

To see how well the basic and Kydland-Prescott structures mimic actual U.S. fluctuations, we begin by examining the figures presented in Table 1.1. Here the first column reports, for several important quantity variables, the magnitude of cyclical fluctuations in the actual quarterly U.S. data, 1955.3–1984.1. These magnitudes are standard deviations of the quarterly observations measured relative to trend values, with the departures from trend expressed in percentage form. The trend values themselves are generated by smoothing the raw series in accordance with a procedure developed by Hodrick and Prescott (1980).[22] From this first column it is apparent that actual consumption fluctuates less, and investment much more, than total output (in percentage terms, that is). Also, the extent of fluctuations in total man-hours employed in production (designated "hours") is almost as great as that of total output.

In the second column comparable figures are reported for a version of the basic model that has been specified and simulated by Hansen (1985).[23] Here the standard deviations actually reported by Hansen have all been scaled up, multiplied by the factor 1.31, so that the reported standard deviation for output is the same as in the U.S. data.[24] Thus the values in Table 1.1 are designed to reflect only the *relative* extent of fluctuations of other variables in comparison with output. The magnitude of output fluctuations is governed, for each model, by the variance of the technology shock z_t that is *assumed* and used in the simulations; independent evidence concerning the plausibility of these shock-variance magnitudes will be considered below.

From the data in the second column it is clear that Hansen's version of the basic model implies fluctuations that have some important characteristics in common with the actual U.S. data. In particular, consumption varies less and investment more than output. The *relative* severity of consumption fluctuations is somewhat less in the model economy, however; and the same is true but to a greater extent for the hours (employment) variable.

Table 1.1 Standard deviations of percentage departures from trend

Variable	U.S. economy[a]	Basic model[b]	Kydland–Prescott model[c]	Hansen model[b]
Output	1.76	1.76[d]	1.76[d]	1.76[d]
Consumption	1.29[e]	0.55	0.44	0.51
Investment	8.60[f]	5.53	5.40	5.71
Capital stock	0.63	0.47	0.46	0.47
Hours	1.66	0.91	1.21	1.35
Productivity	1.18	0.89	0.70	0.50

a. Quarterly data, 1955.3–1984.1, seasonally adjusted, from Hansen (1985).

b. Data from Hansen (1985).

c. Data from Prescott (1986).

d. Shock variance set to provide match of output variation with actual data.

e. This figure pertains to GNP-account consumption expenditures, which includes expenditures on durable goods. For expenditure on nondurable goods and services, the figures are about 1.2 and 0.6, respectively, so the relevant number for comparison is about 0.9.

f. For fixed investment, the figure is approximately 5.3.

Also important are the statistics given in Table 1.2, which pertain to contemporaneous correlations of the other variables—again measured as percentage deviations from trend—with output. Here it will be seen that the match with actual data provided by the basic model is rather good, although the hours and productivity (that is, output per hour) variables are more highly correlated with output in the model than in actuality, and to a substantial extent.

Analogous figures for the RBC model of Kydland and Prescott, which includes the four additional features mentioned above, are reported in the third columns of Tables 1.1 and 1.2. It will be seen from these that the extent of hours variability is significantly increased by the additional features, though not enough to make the match entirely satisfactory. In terms of other variables, the extra features do not seem to add much in comparison with the basic model.[25]

Results are given in the fourth column of Tables 1.1 and 1.2 for a variant model that was developed by Hansen (1985)[26] and is like the basic model except that each worker is constrained to work "full time" or not at all. In particular, Hansen's indivisible-labor setup departs from the basic model: "The new commodity being introduced is a contract between the firm and a household that commits the household to work h_0 hours [full time] with probability α_t. The contract itself is being traded, so the household gets

Table 1.2 Contemporaneous correlations with output (departures from trend)

Variable	U.S. economy[a]	Basic model[b]	Kydland–Prescott model[c]	Hansen model[b]
Consumption	0.85	0.89	0.85	0.87
Investment	0.92	0.99	0.88	0.99
Capital stock	0.04	0.06	0.02	0.05
Hours	0.76	0.98	0.95	0.98
Productivity	0.42	0.98	0.86	0.87

a. Quarterly data, 1955.3–1984.1, seasonally adjusted, from Hansen (1985).
b. Data from Hansen (1985).
c. Data from Prescott (1985).

paid whether it works or not. Therefore, the firm is providing complete unemployment insurance to the workers. Since all households are identical, all will choose the same . . . α_t. However, although households are ex ante identical, they will differ ex post depending on the outcome of the lottery: a fraction α_t of the continuum of households will work and the rest will not'' (Hansen, 1985, p. 316).

It is apparent from Table 1.1 that this model generates considerably more variability in man-hours employment, relative to output, than the basic model (but at the cost of a poorer match for productivity). Something that is not apparent from the table is that the assumed variance of z_t, needed to generate output variability equal to that of the U.S. economy, is smaller than that of the basic model. Specifically, the standard deviation of z_t required for the column-four values is only 0.767 times as great as that for column two.[27]

Kydland (1984) and Kydland and Prescott (1986) have explored other specificational modifications that are designed to improve the match between model and actuality. Kydland (1984) postulates two types of labor, of differing effectiveness in production, and finds that this modification increases the variability of hours relative to output. Kydland and Prescott (1986) incorporates a variable rate of capital utilization and shows that a smaller variance for z_t is needed, with this elaboration, to yield output variability that matches actuality. In each of these two cases the magnitude of the improvement is about 20%, and in each case the overall pattern of correlations is not substantially altered.

In all of these numerical investigations, it should be emphasized, the models' parameter values are *not* obtained in a manner that provides the

best fit to the quarterly time series data. Instead, values for parameters—
analogous to those designated α, β, δ, θ, and ρ in Section 1.1—are assigned so as to agree with panel studies of individual households or with
stylized facts relating to magnitudes such as labor's share of national
income (suggesting $\alpha = 0.64$) and the fraction of time spent in market
employment ($\theta = 0.33$).[28] This procedure guarantees that certain properties of the model will be "sensible," in the judgment of the model builders, a situation that might not obtain if the parameters were estimated in a
more orthodox manner. In this regard it is important to note that
Kydland-Prescott and Hansen choose the value 0.95 for the counterpart
of the parameter ρ. In the context of their model, the high implied degree
of serial correlation for the technology shock tends to impart a high degree of serial correlation to endogenous variables such as employment
and output.[29]

One of the main issues considered in the literature is whether the required magnitude of technology shocks is plausible, that is, whether the
variance of z_t needed to generate fluctuations of the amplitude reported in
Table 1.1 could plausibly apply to actual aggregate technology shocks.[30]
This issue is addressed by Prescott (1986), who initially estimates the
variance of ε_t (not z_t) as the sample variance of the residuals from an
aggregate Cobb-Douglas production function, fitted in first-differenced
form.[31] Prescott then goes on to revise downward this straightforward
estimate by attempting to take account of measurement error in the labor
input series. His final estimate of the standard deviation is 0.00763, which
can be compared with the values needed in different models to generate
output fluctuations that match (as shown in Table 1.1) those of the U.S.
economy. The value needed with the basic model is 0.0093, according to
Hansen's (1985) results,[32] whereas the figure with his indivisible-labor
setup is only 0.00712. In the Kydland-Prescott model there are two technology shocks, as mentioned earlier. But the contribution of the purely
transitory shock is very small, so we can focus on the highly persistent
shock. Its standard deviation is reported in Kydland-Prescott (1986) as
0.0091. Given the relationship $z_t = 0.95z_{t-1} + \varepsilon_t$, this last figure implies a
standard deviation for z_t of the value 0.0291.

These numerical results may be viewed as giving some support to the
idea that technology shocks are in fact large enough to give rise to business cycle fluctuations of the magnitude experienced by the postwar U.S.
economy. There are reasons, however, for skepticism. The first of these
involves the type of procedure used by Prescott to estimate the shock

variance. His procedure, to some extent based on that of Solow (1957), relies crucially on the assumption that current capital and labor are the only relevant inputs. If, however, there are in fact adjustment costs, so that previous levels of (say) labor usage are relevant for current output, then the Solow-Prescott procedure will be likely to overestimate the shock variance.[33] In this regard it is worthy of note that the literature on technical progress that followed Solow's 1957 contribution indicated that the magnitude of technical change would be strongly overstated by the Solow procedure unless steps were taken to correct for certain neglected effects. Jorgenson and Griliches (1967), for example, summarize their findings for the U.S. economy over the interval 1945 to 1965 as follows: "The rate of growth of [total factor] input initially explains 52.4 percent of the rate of growth of output. After elimination of aggregation errors and correction for changes in rates of utilization of labor and capital stock the rate of growth of input explains 96.7 percent of the rate of growth of output; change in total factor productivity explains the rest" (p. 272). Thus, in this example, the Jorgenson-Griliches adjustments reduce the average contribution to growth provided by the residual to only 7% of the initial Solow-type estimate.[34] Finally, it should be noted without prejudice that Prescott's procedure is actually not the same as Solow's. Specifically, Prescott's procedure uses the same labor-share parameter for each period, whereas Solow's treats the labor share as a variable. Thus Prescott's procedure is likely to fit the observations less closely and leave more variation to be accounted for by the residual, thereby yielding— perhaps appropriately—a larger estimate of its variance.

A second problem is related to the *nature* of the unobserved random components that the RBC literature refers to as "technology shocks." If this term is taken literally to refer to shifts in the state-of-knowledge technological relationship between inputs and outputs, then it seems highly unlikely that there could exist any substantial *aggregate* variability. Here the point is that highly distinctive technologies involving entirely different types of machines (and other sorts of capital) are used in different industries—and for different products within any single industry. Accordingly, any specific technological discovery can impact on the production function for only a few products. According to this perspective, RBC models should be formulated so as to recognize that there are many different productive sectors whose technology shocks should presumably be nearly independent. Averaging across industries, then, the economy-wide technology shock would have a variance that is small in relation to the variance for each industry, much as the mean of a random sample of size n has a variance that is only $1/n$ times the variance of each observation.[35]

There is one prominent type of "supply side" disturbance that has effects across a very wide category of industries, namely, a change in the real price that must be paid for imported raw materials—especially, energy. The oil-price shocks of 1974, 1979, and 1986 clearly have had significant impact on the U.S. economy at the aggregate level (Hamilton, 1983). And since the Kydland-Prescott and Hansen models have no foreign sector, such effects are treated by their analyses as "residuals"—shifts in the production function.[36] Such a treatment is, however, avoidable since these price changes may be observed and are documented in basic aggregate data sources. It is also analytically undesirable: to lump input price changes together with production-function shifts is to blur an important distinction. Presumably future RBC studies will explicitly model these terms-of-trade effects and thereby reduce their reliance on unobserved technology shocks.

A good bit of relevant research has been prompted by the contribution of Lilien (1982), who suggested that unusually large shifts in the sectoral composition of output would necessitate unusually large employment reallocations which, being costly, tend to reduce aggregate employment and output. While Lilien emphasized relative demand shifts as a source of sectoral imbalance, sector-specific technology shocks would likewise call for reallocations. Some evidence in support of the sectoral shift hypothesis is presented by Lilien (1982), who shows that a measure of the dispersion of employment growth across two-digit industries has considerable explanatory power for the aggregate unemployment rate. A pair of subsequent studies—succinctly described by Barro (1986)—are, however, largely unsupportive of Lilien's hypothesis. In particular, Abraham and Katz (1986) find evidence to be inconsistent with the implication that job-vacancy rates should be positively related to the employment-growth dispersion measure, while Loungani (1986, p. 536) finds that "once the dispersion in employment growth due to oil shocks is accounted for, the residual dispersion has no explanatory power for unemployment." More recently, Davis (1987) has challenged the Abraham-Katz conclusion—on the basis of the stock-flow distinction as applied to vacancies—and has developed a reallocation *timing* hypothesis that stresses cyclical variations in the cost of unemployment that accompanies sectoral reallocations. In addition, Davis (1987) presents various bits of evidence in support of the idea that sectoral shifts and reallocation timing are important determinants of aggregate unemployment; useful observations and caveats are provided by Oi (1987). Conclusions regarding the significance of this line of research for RBC models would seem to be as yet premature.

While considerable attention has been devoted in the literature to questions regarding (a) technology shocks and (b) the variability of hours relative to output, other important aspects of the Kydland-Prescott results have been neglected. One example is provided by the excessively strong correlation between productivity and output that is implied by the models. A related problem—noted by Kydland and Prescott (1982, p. 1366)—that is potentially crucial concerns productivity–output correlations at various lags and leads. In this regard, Table 1.3 compares a few of these autocorrelations for the Kydland-Prescott model with those that pertain to the U.S. data. Evidently, the pattern implied by the model is markedly different from that existing in actuality, productivity being positively correlated with past output in the model but negatively correlated in reality. As the actual pattern is rather like that which would exist if the bivariate relationship were dominated by exogenous (demand-induced?) output movements and "labor hoarding,"[37] this discrepancy would seem to warrant particular attention by RBC proponents and critics.

Another significant topic that has been neglected in the main RBC literature is the cyclical behavior of relative *price* variables, including the real wage and the real interest rate. Their models' implications for the latter have been reported by Kydland and Prescott (1982, 1986), but not the counterpart statistics for the U.S. data. One reason for this omission, presumably, is that the ex-ante real rate is the relevant variable but only ex-post values are directly observable. Attempts to estimate ex-ante real

Table 1.3   Correlation of output in period t with labor productivity in period indicated (departures from trend)

Period	U.S. data	Kydland–Prescott model
$t - 2$	0.60	0.37
$t - 1$	0.51	0.68
t	0.34	0.90
$t + 1$	-0.04	0.59
$t + 2$	-0.28	0.44

Source: Kydland and Prescott (1986).

rates have been made, however, by Hamilton (1985) and Mishkin (1981). The impression that one gets from examination of their charts is that the ex-ante real rate is not nearly as strongly procyclical as the Kydland-Prescott model implies.[38] But numerical analysis is needed to be confident on this point.

In the case of the real wage, Kydland and Prescott report neither actual nor model-implied results. But with a production function that is basically Cobb-Douglas in specification, the marginal product of labor will fluctuate closely with the average product of labor—which is the "productivity" variable that appears in Tables 1.1 through 1.3. Many investigators, including Bils (1985) and Geary and Kennan (1982, 1984), have found the real wage to be positively correlated with output. But the magnitude of the contemporaneous correlation in these studies is quite small,[39] a far cry from the 0.86–0.98 values implied by the Kydland-Prescott and Hansen models.

Let us now turn to relevant evidence obtained by other empirical methods. Incomplete models with specifications that are compatible with the RBC approach have been studied by means of econometric techniques that are quite different from those utilized by Kydland-Prescott and Hansen. Most notably, there are a number of papers that estimate, using aggregate time series observations, household optimality conditions analogous to Equations (1.6)–(1.9) above—but with the typical household viewed as facing market-determined wage and interest rates rather than operating its own production facility. Leading examples in this genre are provided by Lars Hansen and Singleton (1982), Eichenbaum, Hansen, and Singleton (1986), and Mankiw, Rotemberg, and Summers (1985).

Because these studies are designed to utilize models in which the production sector is left unspecified, it is not possible to obtain implications concerning fluctuations of the type that are emphasized by Kydland and Prescott. There are certain results obtained that have some relevance, however, for the RBC type of model. In particular, the models' assumptions (including rational expectations) imply that certain variables should be orthogonal to composite "disturbances" that are involved in the instrumental-variable (or "method of moments") estimation procedure. This orthogonality in turn implies that certain test statistics developed by Hansen (1982) have, under the hypothesis that the model is well-specified, asymptotic chi-square distributions with known degrees of freedom. Computed values that are improbable under this hypothesis therefore constitute formal evidence against the model at hand. In the recent study by Eichenbaum, Hansen, and Singleton (1986), five of the six such statistics computed for a model composed of equations similar to (1.6)–(1.9)[40] call for rejection at significance levels below 0.01.[41] In addition, Eichenbaum, Hansen, and Singleton report that "estimated values of key parameters differ significantly from the values assumed in several studies," that is, those of Kydland and Prescott. It is not clear, however, that these results are unfavorable for RBC models in general, even though they do not support the Kydland-Prescott specification in particular.

Finally, mention should be made of an ambitious study conducted by Altug (1985), who has obtained maximum likelihood estimates of a model that is fairly close in specification to that of Kydland and Prescott (1982). No single test statistic for the Kydland-Prescott parameter values is reported by Altug, but the impression obtained from her various tables and charts is that agreement with the data is not very good. Also, Altug's estimated version of the model has properties that fail to match actuality in several respects. For example, spectra of individual series implied by the model have shapes that are quite different from the unrestricted estimates of these spectra.

It can be argued that the value of formal econometric test results is small in the present context, that is, in indicating whether models like that of Kydland and Prescott (1982) do a good job of matching the actual data. *Any* model that is both manageable and theoretically coherent will necessarily be too simple to closely match the data in all respects; so with the number of quarterly observations available, such models will inevitably be rejected at low significance levels in formal tests against generalized alternatives. There is considerable merit to this argument, in my opinion, as a general matter. It is unclear, however, that the particular models mentioned in Tables 1.1 through 1.3 provide good data matches according to the builders' own criteria. To some extent, these weaknesses may be due to the current models' simplicity rather than to any basic flaw in the RBC strategy. Future work on the topic should be designed with that consideration in mind.

1.3. Additional Issues

There are numerous additional matters of controversy—both substantive and methodological—pertaining to RBC analysis that could be discussed. A few of the more important ones will be taken up in this section.

The first of these topics concerns the issue of social optimality. In the models of Kydland and Prescott (1982, 1986) and Hansen (1985), there are by construction no externalities, taxes, government consumption, or monetary variables. Furthermore, all households are alike and each is effectively infinite-lived. Consequently, competitive equilibria in these particular models have the property of Pareto optimality.[42] One message that should be taken from that fact is that the mere existence of cyclical fluctuations is *not* sufficient for a conclusion that interventionist government policy is warranted. These models provide no basis, on the other hand, for concluding that the solutions generated by actual economies are Pareto optimal. To overturn that notion it should be sufficient to recall that in the U.S. economy, to take one example, about 20% of total output is absorbed by government purchases. Therefore, unless government services are precisely chosen to reflect individuals' preferences, some departure from Pareto optimality will result. In addition, taxes used to finance these purchases are likely to have distorting allocational effects. Because the RBC models in question do not recognize the existence of government activities, they simply have nothing to say on this matter.

Another particularly prominent omission pertains to money. It is not true, as Eichenbaum and Singleton (1986) have pointed out, that the models must be interpreted as implying the literal absence of money. Indeed, it is doubtful that RBC proponents intend to advance the proposition that no less output would be produced in the United States (with the existing capital stock) if there were no medium of exchange—that is, if all transactions had to be carried out by crude or sophisticated barter. But the models do imply that, to a good approximation, policy-induced fluctuations in monetary variables have no effect on the real variables listed in Table 1.1—at least for fluctuations of the magnitude experienced since World War II. Of course, RBC proponents do not deny that there exist correlations between monetary and real variables, but they claim that these reflect responses by the monetary system to fluctuations induced by technology shocks—"reverse causation," in the words of King and Plosser (1984).

It is somewhat ironic that the reverse-causation viewpoint should be featured in a body of analysis that is a direct outgrowth of the monetary-misperception class of equilibrium business cycle models. For the problem that Lucas set out to solve, in his papers (1972, 1973) that created this class, was to construct a competitive equilibrium model that incorporates a Phillips-type money-to-income relationship even though the modeled economy is populated with rational agents—that is, agents devoid of money illusion and expectational irrationality. In his words, Lucas's *JET* paper was designed to provide a model "of an economy in which equilibrium prices and quantities exhibit what may be the central feature of the modern business cycle: a systematic relation between the rate of change in nominal prices and the level of real output" (Lucas, 1972, p. 103).[43]

It is important, then, to reflect on the process by which the equilibrium business cycle program was transformed into one in which monetary impulses play no significant role. In that regard, there are both theoretical and empirical findings that have been important. Little needs to be said here about the former, for the basic objection to monetary misperception models has become widely understood.[44] Some space must be devoted, however, to the empirical findings.

Chronologically, the first major empirical development was provided by Sims's (1980, 1982) demonstration that money stock innovations, in small VAR systems, have little explanatory power for output fluctuations when a nominal interest rate variable is included in the system.[45] The interpretation offered by Sims is that money stock innovations represent surprise policy actions by the monetary authority—that is, the Fed—so the finding is indicative of the unimportance of monetary policy actions. But this interpretation is open to objection. Suppose that the monetary authority implements its actions by manipulating, on a quarter-to-quarter or month-to-month basis, the nominal interest rate. Then interest rate innovations would reflect monetary policy surprises, with money stock innovations representing linear combinations of disturbances afflicting money demand, saving-investment, and production relations as well as policy behavior. In this case, interest rate innovations would measure monetary policy surprises better than would money stock innovations. And in fact, U.S. monetary policy has been implemented throughout the postwar period by means of interest rate instruments, even during the period 1979–1982.[46] So the finding that money stock innovations provide little explanatory power for output or employment movements simply does not imply that monetary *policy* has been unimportant.[47] On the contrary, the considerable explanatory power provided by interest rate innovations in Sims's studies suggests just the opposite.

For analogous reasons, moreover, it is incorrect to presume that movements in the monetary base are accurate reflections of U.S. monetary policy behavior. While the Fed *could* use the base as its operating instrument if it chose to do so, in fact it never has. Consequently, empirical analyses that treat the base as the Fed's instrument involve a serious misspecification that must be accounted for in interpreting their findings.

These particular difficulties concerning the monetary authority's operating procedures can in principle be partially circumvented by noting that, in a system that includes all variables of macroeconomic importance to agents, *output, employment, and other real variables will be block exogenous to all nominal variables*—prices and interest rates, for example, as well as monetary aggregates. It would then appear that this property of RBC models could be used as the basis of a statistical test; if the RBC hypothesis were true, then output, employment, and so on should not be Granger-caused by any nominal variable or variables.[48] Unfortunately, further analysis indicates that *in practice* the presence of Granger causality from nominal to real variables is neither necessary nor sufficient for rejection of the RBC hypothesis. It is not necessary because a Lucas-style monetary misperceptions model, in which monetary policy actions affect output but only if they are unanticipated, will not imply Granger causality from nominal to real variables.[49] Conversely, a finding of such causality is not sufficient for RBC rejection if variables that are important to private agents are not observed by the econometrician. In such cases, as Litterman and Weiss (1985), King (1986), and Eichenbaum and Singleton (1986) have shown, monetary variables may move in response to real shocks in a manner that has predictive content for real variables even though the latter would be block exogenous in a wider system that included the (practically unobserved) variables.

Furthermore, it is unclear whether or not significant nominal-to-real Granger causality prevails in the available data. Some studies report test statistics that imply strong rejections of noncausality null hypotheses (see, for example, Geary and Kennan, 1984, table 2, or Litterman and Weiss, 1985, table VII, line 18). But Eichenbaum and Singleton (1986) have documented a marked tendency for nominal-to-real causality to become insignificant when the data series are rendered stationary, prior to analysis, by means of first-differencing rather than by removal of deterministic trend components. Despite much recent research, it is not entirely clear what conclusion should be drawn regarding the presence of causality when results differ in this fashion.[50]

The subject of first-differencing leads naturally to a relevant argument put forth by Nelson and Plosser (1982) that has recently attracted considerable attention. This argument begins with the presumption that monetary impulses can have no effects on the trend component of output (or employment) and continues with the claim that, in fact, output fluctuations are dominated by trend (as opposed to cyclical) movements. The argument's conclusion, then, is that output movements must be primarily induced by real rather than monetary impulses—a notion that is clearly pertinent for the RBC hypothesis.

The Nelson-Plosser argument is related to the first-differencing of data, because its contention that output fluctuations are trend-dominated relies critically upon the analysis of output (and other) measures that have been first-differenced to remove the nonstationary trend component. For most aggregate U.S. data series, the variability that is left to be studied, or classified as "cyclical," is much smaller after differencing than after removal of deterministic trends.

With regard to the Nelson-Plosser line of argument, McCallum (1986) has objected that the empirical evidence does not warrant the conclusion that first-differencing is appropriate (and deterministic trend removal inappropriate) as a method for rendering the series stationary. Such would be the case if the series in question were generated by ARMA processes in which the AR polynomial possesses a root precisely equal to 1.0. That is, if the process for the variable y_t is expressed as

$$(1.27) \qquad y_t = \frac{\theta(L)}{\psi(L)} \, \varepsilon_t = \frac{\theta_0 + \theta_1 L + \ldots + \theta_q L^q}{\psi_0 + \psi_1 L + \ldots + \psi_p L^p} \, \varepsilon_t,$$

with ε_t the white-noise innovation, then differencing would be required if the solutions to the equation $\psi_0 + \psi_1 z + \psi_2 z^2 + \ldots + \psi_p z^p = 0$ include one root that equals 1.0 precisely. The Nelson-Plosser evidence only shows, however, that the hypothesis that such a root exists cannot be rejected at conventional significance levels. But such test results are entirely consistent with the possibility that the root in question is close to but not precisely equal to unity; power against alternative hypotheses that the true value is 0.98 or 0.96 (for example) is extremely low. Thus the variables' ARMA processes may easily be of a form such that deterministic detrending would be entirely appropriate.

The foregoing objection to the Nelson-Plosser position constitutes a claim not that output (employment, and so on) series can be firmly shown to be trend-stationary but rather that the Nelson-Plosser tests are incapable of establishing their contention, that is, that the data series are such that differencing is necessary to induce stationarity. But without that contention, the Nelson-Plosser evidence does not provide support for the RBC hypothesis.[51]

The final matter to be taken up in this section concerns the connection between business cycles and economic growth. Traditionally, of course, macroeconomic analysis has typically proceeded under the maintained assumption that these two types of phenomena can without serious loss be studied separately—that the latter basically involves capital accumulation and technical progress whereas the former concerns the extent to which existing capital and labor are utilized. More recently, however, support has grown for the idea that if technology shocks are the principal driving force behind cyclical movements, as the RBC models presume, then the two types of phenomena may be simply different manifestations of the same basic process.

Partly for that reason, perhaps, Prescott (1986, pp. 12–13) has emphasized the desirability of simultaneously accounting for both growth and cycles. In practice, however, the Kydland and Prescott (1982, 1986) studies have not provided an integration at either the theoretical or the empirical level. Thus their theoretical specification pertains to an economy in which there is no growth, either in total or per-capita terms.[52] And the Kydland-Prescott empirical procedure involves detrending of the data series prior to analysis, so the economy's growth is abstracted from before the study of cycles is begun. This latter aspect of the Kydland-Prescott procedure has been criticized by Singleton (1986), who emphasizes that maximizing behavior implies certain restrictions relating to the trend or growth components of *different* variables. When such restrictions are ignored, parameter estimation will be inefficient and some opportunities for model testing will go unexploited.

It is possible, depending on the extent to which technical progress can be appropriately viewed as exogenous, that the current emphasis on integration of growth and cycle analysis may be misplaced or excessive. The point is this: if technical progress were exogenous, then even if RBC views were correct there would be little necessary relation between the magnitude of growth and the extent of cycles, because they depend upon two different aspects of the technical-progress process. Specifically, if the stochastic process for z_t is $\log z_t = \gamma_0 + \gamma_1 t + \gamma_2 \log z_{t-1} + \varepsilon_t$, with $|\gamma_2| < 1$, then growth will depend upon γ_1 and cyclical properties will be related to the independent parameter σ_ε^2.[53] If $\gamma_1 = 0$, the system would be one that features cycles but no growth.[54] In this case the Kydland-Prescott practice—as opposed to rhetoric—would be largely appropriate.

On the other hand, it may be that growth results not from exogenous technical progress but from *endogenous* forces. Quite recently, King and

Rebelo (1986) have—following some leads provided by Romer (1986)—begun an investigation of the idea that growth may be the consequence of human-capital accumulation with the latter determined endogenously. In the particular example described by King, Plosser, and Rebelo (1987), the economy's rate of steady growth per capita depends upon the ratio of human to physical capital and the fraction of resources that are devoted to human capital formation and maintenance, all of which are determined endogenously. There is in this model no parameter, analogous to γ_1 in the previous paragraph, for which a special value would imply zero growth without affecting cyclical properties. The link between growth and cycles is, therefore, more intimate.

Some versions of the endogenous growth model have been formulated in a manner that could lead readers to believe that steady-state growth, as opposed to growth at ever-increasing or ever-decreasing rates, is possible only with a production function for human capital that is excessively special. King, Plosser, and Rebelo (1987) showed, however, that the situation is essentially the same as in the standard competitive growth model: steady growth requires constant returns to scale in production, labor-argumenting technical change, and utility functions of a certain class. Thus criticism on this basis is unwarranted; these requirements for steady growth apply quite generally.

The discussion in King, Plosser, and Rebelo (1987) suggests that the endogenous growth approach can account for the presence of autoregressive unit roots in the univariate time series processes for capital stock and other real variables. But while their analysis is promising in this regard, it apparently implies roots *precisely* equal to unity only when production functions are homogeneous of degree precisely one. While many analysts would accept constant returns as a good approximation, the implication for autoregressive roots is only that values close to unity will be found.

1.4. Concluding Remarks

As an identifiable topic of study, RBC analysis is only a few years old. Accordingly, it is perhaps too early for any reliable conclusions to be drawn. But the arguments presented above can be summarized and a few judgments attempted, even though the latter should be regarded as highly preliminary and more of the nature of predictions than settled opinions.

Basically, we have seen in our discussion that a model of a competitive market economy, in which an aggregate technology shock affects the quantity of output producible from capital and labor inputs, will experience fluctuations in per-capita quantities of consumption, investment, and total product. Under most functional specifications for preferences and technology, the quantity of labor employed will also fluctuate and investment variability will exceed that of consumption. If the technology shock process is strongly autoregressive—close to a random walk—so too will be the model's quantity variables; and the contemporaneous correlations among these variables will in several ways be notably similar to those that appear in detrended postwar quarterly data for the U.S. economy. Furthermore, if the technology shock has a standard deviation of about 3% of its mean value—about 1% for the surprise component of this shock—then the magnitude of the model's output fluctuations will match those of quarterly postwar real GNP, with a fairly good variability match for other key variables as well.

Of course there are ways in which the model's stochastic properties do not closely match actual data. For example, the correlations with output of hours worked and productivity are much higher in the model than in reality, and the correlation of productivity with lagged output provides a serious mismatch. It is possible that such discrepancies are simply due to the model's simplicity, however, rather than to any fundamental flaw in the RBC approach. Until studies have been conducted that convincingly distinguish between sources of fluctuations, it will be possible for responsible researchers to maintain sharply differing beliefs in this regard. An important gap in the RBC analysis has been a clear and convincing story concerning the nature of the postulated aggregate shock variable. If the latter were actually a proxy for observable variables that have been omitted from the models—fiscal policy and/or import prices, for example— then the interpretation and conclusions of the work would be quite different from those obtained if the shocks were of a strictly technological nature.

As for the notion that monetary policy irregularity has been an unimportant source of output fluctuations, at least during the postwar era, it is too early to reach any firm conclusion. RBC proponents have pointed to empirical findings that are suggestive of that hypothesis, but there are significant problems with the evidence that has been developed to date.

It would seem to be virtually indisputable that the RBC literature has provided a substantial number of innovative and constructive technical developments that will be of lasting benefit in macroeconomic analysis. In particular, the example of Kydland and Prescott (1982) has suggested one route toward the goal of a dynamic equilibrium model with optimizing agents that can be used for quantitative macroeconomic analysis. The type of model employed does not, it should be emphasized, require a belief that the workings of the economy are socially optimal. In addition, the literature has spurred interest in several purely methodological topics, including alternative methods for the investigation of the dynamic properties of nonlinear general equilibrium models and for the detrending of time series data. Also, issues concerning the practical reliability of Granger-causality tests have been highlighted by controversies initiated by RBC analysis.

From a substantive perspective, the RBC studies have provided a healthy reminder that a sizable portion of the output and employment variability that is observed in actual economies is probably the consequence of various unavoidable shocks, that is, disturbances not generated by erratic monetary or fiscal policy makers. Thus it is unlikely that many scholars today would subscribe to the proposition that all or most of the postwar fluctuation in U.S. output has been attributable to actions of the Federal Open Market Committee. Whether a substantial fraction can be so attributed remains a topic of interest and importance.

Acknowledgments

I am indebted to Martin Eichenbaum, Marvin Goodfriend, Robert King, Finn Kydland, Allan Meltzer, and Kenneth Singleton for helpful discussions. In addition, I have benefited from a generous quantity of criticism furnished by the Rochester RBC Group of Ten and the following individuals: Robert Barro, William Brock, Larry Christiano, John Kennan, and Edward Prescott. Partial financial support was provided by the National Science Foundation.

Notes

1. An incomplete list of other notable items includes Black (1982), Kydland and Prescott (1980, 1986), Kydland (1984), King (1986), King, Plosser, and Rebelo (1987), King, Plosser, Stock, and Watson (1987), Hansen (1985), and Prescott (1986).

2. To date, these include critical pieces by Fischer (1987), McCallum (1986), and Summers (1986) and sympathetic but skeptical discussions by Barro (1986), Eichenbaum and Singleton (1986), Dotsey and King (1987), Lucas (1987), and Mankiw (1986). A guide to the Prescott-Summers exchange is provided by Manuelli (1986) and expository articles have been prepared by Rush (1987) and Walsh (1986).

3. Clearly, real shocks could in principle pertain as well to individuals' preferences, but in fact the literature has emphasized technology disturbances.

4. Here the term *equilibrium* is being used as a shorthand substitute for the more precise term *flexible-price equilibrium*. McCallum (1982) suggests that there is no inherent reason why equilibrium models could not accommodate sluggish price adjustments.

5. That such a challenge is intended by some of the leaders of RBC analysis is suggested by King and Plosser's (1984, p. 363) statement that "there are good reasons for dissatisfaction with existing macroeconomic theories" in conjunction with a reference to "alternative hypotheses."

6. A basic reference in this regard is Brock and Mirman (1972), which provides formal analysis of a social planner's problem in the context of a related stochastic growth model. Brock (1972) indicated how the mathematics could be reinterpreted to constitute a descriptive model of a competitive economy with a large number of similar households. The only significant differences between the reinterpreted Brock-Mirman model and the one with which we begin is the nonrecognition of leisure in the former—a difference that is of very little importance on the design of proofs—and the former's assumption of serially independent technology shocks. This latter limitation was removed by Donaldson and Mehra (1983).

7. Alternatively, we could proceed under the assumption that there is a market for one-period bonds instead of one for capital services. Suppose that a bond purchased in t for $1/(1 + r_t)$ is a claim to one unit of output in $t + 1$. Then the household's net expenditure on bonds during t could be denoted $(1 + r_t)^{-1}b_{t+1} - b_t$, with b_{t+1} the number of bonds purchased in t. The price $(1 + r_t)^{-1}$ would be determined by the market-clearing condition, implied by the similarity of all households, that $b_{t+1} = 0$. Equilibrium values of c_t, n_t, and k_{t+1} would be precisely the same as those attained with the market structure implied by Equation (1.3).

8. Obviously, the equality in (1.3) should properly be written as the inequality "≤." But our assumptions are such that the equality will in fact hold. This type of notational shortcut is used extensively in what follows.

9. If the variable-leisure aspect of this model is neglected, then proofs can be found in Brock (1982) and Donaldson and Mehra (1983).

10. Since λ_{t+j} is the utility value of a unit of capital acquired in period $t + j$, $\beta^{j-1}\lambda_{t+j}k_{t+j+1}$ is the present value in t of capital held by the household at the end of period $t + j$. Condition (1.5) serves to rule out the possibility that the household would forever accumulate capital at an excessive rate, something that is not precluded by any of conditions (1.4).

11. On this, see Brock (1982).

12. Some readers have objected to the way in which the optimization analysis is here described, suggesting that instead it be expressed in terms of the identity between Pareto-optimality and competitive equilibrium that has been used in several of the key RBC papers. I have quite deliberately chosen not to pro-

ceed in that manner to avoid portraying RBC analysis in an overly restrictive manner. An approach that is applicable only to economies known to be Pareto optimal would have quite limited usefulness, but such is in fact not the case for RBC analysis. The latter point is recognized by King, Plosser, and Rebelo (1987).

13. For a more complete discussion, see Lucas (1987). Strictly speaking, our statement presumes that interest is limited to *minimal* sets of state variables, a limitation that rules out "bubbles." But since any bubble path would in the present model be inconsistent with the transversality condition (1.5), this limitation is not significant.

14. These include Long and Plosser (1983).

15. Very recently Hercowitz and Sampson (1986) have developed a different special case that does not require complete depreciation yet results in explicit log-linear solutions that feature variable employment. These attractive features are obtained at the price of adopting unfamiliar specifications for utility and depreciation functions. Specifically, the within-period utility function is $u(c_t, 1 - n_t) = \log(c_t - an_t^\gamma)$ with $a > 0$ and $\gamma > 1$, a form that makes the marginal rate of substitution between consumption and leisure independent of c_t. Ignoring complications involving human capital that are stressed by Hercowitz and Sampson, let technology continue to be $y_t = z_t\, n_t^\alpha\, k_t^{1-\alpha}$ as in (1.15) and maintain the usual concept of gross investment, $i_t = y_t - c_t$. Regarding depreciation, however, assume that $k_{t+1} = k_t^{1-\delta} i_t^\phi$, where $\phi > 0$ and $1 > \delta > 0$. One can think of this log-linear expression as departing from the usual linear form for adjustment-cost reasons as in Lucas and Prescott (1971), or alternatively as an approximation adopted for analytical convenience. In any event, with this specification the model yields solutions of the form $c_t = \phi_{11} z_t^{\phi 12} k_t^{\phi 13}$, $n_t = \phi_{21} z_t^{\phi 22} k_t^{\phi 23}$, $k_{t+1} = \phi_{31}\, z_t^{\phi 32} k_t^{\phi 33}$.

16. The shadow price λ_t obviously obeys $\lambda_t = \theta[1 - (1-\alpha)\beta]^{-1}\, n^{-\alpha} z_t^{-1}\, k_t^{\alpha-1}$.

17. Whether it is appropriate to use detrended data is an important issue that will be briefly discussed in Section 1.3.

18. For output, this is well known. For consumption the relation is $\log c_t = 0.06 + 1.21 \log c_{t-1} - 0.24 \log c_{t-1} + 0.00024t$, $\sigma = 0.007$, $DW = 2.08$.

19. In these models, positive demand shocks result in high output because they induce high employment in response to low real wages.

20. To obtain this implication, note that with $\delta = 1$ investment during period t is identically the same as k_{t+1}. Then recall that the stochastic processes for k_t and c_t have the same autoregressive components and the same forcing variable, ε_t.

21. More precisely, the claim cannot be verified without resort to some sort of approximation procedure. Using one, King, Plosser, and Rebelo (1987) are able to show that, in a version with no labor-leisure decision, consumption variability is greater than for investment.

22. The smoothing procedure for measuring the trend component of the various series is somewhat unorthodox. If x_t is the variable to be smoothed and s_t

the smoothed value for period t, the method entails minimizing the sum of $T^{-1} \sum_{t=1}^{T} (x_t - s_t)^2$ and $\mu T^{-1} \sum_{t=2}^{T} [(s_{t+1} - s_t) - (s_t - s_{t-1})]^2$, where μ is a weighting factor that is chosen to provide the desired degree of smoothness. Use of this particular method of detrending the data has not attracted much discussion or criticism to date, but inspection of material in King, Plosser, and Rebelo (1987) suggests that cross-variable correlations may be sensitive to the method. Some issues concerning detrending (by any method) will be briefly considered in Section 1.3.

23. The parameter values utilized by Hansen are $\theta = 0.33$, $\alpha = 0.64$, $\beta = 0.99$, and $\delta = 0.025$. Also, the counterpart of ρ is taken to be 0.95. It is necessary to refer to "the counterpart of ρ" rather than to ρ itself because Hansen's specification (like that of Kydland and Prescott) is of the form $z_t = 0.95 z_{t-1} + \zeta_t$, with ζ_t log-normal, rather than $\log z_t = \rho \log z_{t-1} + \varepsilon_t$.

24. Since the model is not linear in logs of the variables, this scaling is not strictly legitimate; an increase in the variance of the technology shock would change the relative standard deviations to a small extent. It is my belief that such an effect would be negligible in the case at hand.

25. It is possible that serial correlation properties are enhanced, however. Statistics relating to this dimension of performance are not reported by Hansen (1985).

26. As Hansen (1985) emphasized, his specification is based on theoretical analysis originally developed by Rogerson (1985).

27. Again, this magnitude is (because of ignored nonlinearities) only approximate. The correct statement is that in Hansen's simulations the basic model has output variability only $0.134/0.176 = 0.767$ times as large as that for the indivisible labor model when the same z_t variance is used for both.

28. As previously mentioned, other typical values are $\beta = 0.99$ and $\delta = 0.025$ (quarterly data). There is room for dispute regarding some of these magnitudes. Significantly, Summers (1986) has questioned the Kydland-Prescott-Hansen choices for β, which implies a steady-state real rate of return of 4% per year, and for θ, which implies that about a third of the typical household's time is spent in employment. Summers notes that the actual figure for θ is closer to one-sixth, a magnitude that is borne out by estimates obtained by Eichenbaum, Hansen, and Singleton (1986).

29. A sensitivity of this type has been mentioned by Christiano (1987a, p. 341). Some related facts are brought out by King, Plosser, and Rebelo (1987).

30. The issue has been raised by Barro (1986), Lucas (1987), and Summers (1986), among others.

31. Thus this estimate pretends that $\rho = 1$. Although this is inconsistent with the 0.95 value used by Kydland and Prescott (1982, 1986), the resulting effect is probably small in the present context (that is, obtaining an estimate of the variance of ε_t). Prescott's procedure involves a weighted man-hours series and imposes the restriction that $\alpha = 0.75$.

32. Actually, this number is here inferred, in the manner described in note 27, from Hansen's reported level of output fluctuations.

33. By failing to take account of quarter-to-quarter dynamics, the procedure throws into the residual fluctuations that which would properly be attributed to this source of dynamics (if the adjustment-cost hypothesis were true). This problem, it might be said, concerns misspecification of the (dynamic) production–employment relation, not measurement error. The omission of relevant lagged variables is only likely (rather than certain) to lead to overestimation of the shock variance, because the procedure uses factor shares as parameters rather than estimating the latter in a regression designed to yield Δz_t residuals.

34. This calculation, it should be said, pertains to the *mean* level of productivity change, not its variance.

35. Long and Plosser (1983) have presented an interesting discussion of a multi-sector RBC framework. From their Figure 3, it would appear that the magnitude of aggregate fluctuations is smaller than that for individual sectors, but numerical statistics relating to this particular point are not included. The discrepancy between sectoral and aggregate magnitudes would be heightened, of course, by recognition of more sectors; the Long and Plosser example has only six.

36. An increase in the price of imported materials will lead to a decline in their quantity utilized, relative to the quantities of domestic factors. That will reduce the quantity of output for any given usage of domestic factors, that is, will shift downward the production schedule relating output to domestic factors alone.

37. Labor hoarding is mentioned by Summers (1986). What I understand by the term is that costs of hiring and firing lead firms to adjust their workforce much more slowly than if no such costs existed. To see that the lag correlation pattern could easily be as claimed, consider an example in which $y_t = by_{t-1} + e_t$ and $n_t = ay_t + (1 - a)y_{t-1}$, where y_t and n_t denote logs of output and hours so that the log of productivity is $x_t = y_t - n_t$. Then it is easy to show that $Ey_t x_{t+1} < 0$ while $Ey_t x_{t-1} > 0$ and $Ey_t x_t > 0$. An interesting recent attempt to discriminate between the supply-shock and labor-hoarding hypotheses has been made by Shapiro (1987), whose results are supportive of the former. Some apparent inconsistencies with other wage-productivity studies may be due to Shapiro's use of annual data.

38. The Kydland-Prescott correlations with output analogous to those of Table 1.3 are as follows: 0.46, 0.68, 0.84, 0.56, 0.42.

39. The U.S. correlation in Geary and Kennan (1984), for example, is 0.20.

40. The model is *less* restrictive than (1.6)–(1.9) as it permits current utility to be affected by a distributed lag of leisure hours.

41. Eichenbaum, Hansen, and Singleton (1986) develop evidence suggesting that the model's rejection stems primarily from a failure to satisfy the intratemporal, as opposed to intertemporal, optimality conditions.

42. In fact, the competitive equilibria are computed in these papers by solving Pareto optimality problems for a fictitious social planner.
43. From its context, it is clear that Lucas presumed the causal relation to be from money to income.
44. The point is that in actual developed economies data is available on monetary aggregates too promptly to be consistent with the assumption—critical in the Lucas-Barro models—that individuals are ignorant of contemporaneous monetary magnitudes. A key item in the literature is King's (1981) demonstration that this problem is not circumvented by measurement error on the "true" aggregate.
45. This statement pertains to the postwar U.S. data, quarterly and monthly.
46. Relevant discussion of the 1979–1982 episode appears in McCallum (1985).
47. For an elaboration on this argument, see McCallum (1986) and references cited therein.
48. Block exogeneity of x_t of course implies that x_t is not Granger-caused by any variable not included in the vector x.
49. See Sargent (1976) and the comments on this paper that appeared in the April 1979 issue of the *Journal of Political Economy*.
50. Christiano (1987b) has provided some simulation results that suggest (but do not establish) that the results with undifferenced data are more reliable in this particular context. On the other hand, it might be noted that only a small fraction of the predictive power for output movements can be attributed to nominal variables even in those studies that feature strong rejections of the no-causality hypothesis; most of the explanatory power lies in past movements of output itself. But this type of finding appears so frequently in Granger-causality studies of other, entirely unrelated, issues that one is led to suspect that the basic procedure is seriously flawed in some respect—possibly involving measurement error—that has thus far eluded formal analysis.
51. Some support for the foregoing argument is provided by interesting recent studies by Cochrane (1986), Watson (1986), and Evans (1986). A contrary position is taken in a notable paper by Campbell and Mankiw (1986).
52. Exogenous technical progress can be added to the model, of course, but that step does not constitute much of an integration.
53. This fact is not invalidated by the dependence of both growth and cycle magnitudes on γ_2.
54. If the log z_t process were a random walk with drift, the definition of "cycles" would become problematical. But it would remain reasonable to say that zero drift implies zero growth while leaving scope for cycles.

References

Abraham, K. G., and L. F. Katz. 1986. Cyclical Unemployment: Sectoral Shifts or Aggregate Disturbances? *Journal of Political Economy* 94 (November): 507–522.

Altug, S. G. 1985. Essays in the Equilibrium Approach to Aggregate Fluctuations and Asset Pricing. Unpublished doctoral dissertation, Carnegie Mellon University.

Barro, R. J. 1976. Rational Expectations and the Role of Monetary Policy. *Journal of Monetary Economics* 2 (January): 1–32.

——— 1981. The Equilibrium Approach to Business Cycles. *In Money, Expectations, and Business Cycles.* New York: Academic Press.

——— 1986. Comments. *NBER Macroeconomics Annual 1986.* Cambridge, Massachusetts: MIT Press.

Bils, M. J. 1985. Real Wages over the Business Cycle: Evidence from Panel Data. *Journal of Political Economy* 93 (August): 666–689.

Black, F. 1982. General Equilibrium and Business Cycles. Working paper 950, National Bureau of Economic Research.

Brock, W. A. 1974. Comments. *In* M. D. Intriligator and D. A. Kendrick (eds.), *Frontiers of Quantitative Economics,* Vol. II. Amsterdam: North-Holland.

——— 1982. Asset Prices in a Production Economy. *In* J. J. McCall (ed.), *The Economics of Information and Uncertainty.* Chicago: The University of Chicago Press.

Brock, W. A., and L. J. Mirman. 1972. Optimal Economic Growth and Uncertainty: The Discounted Case. *Journal of Economic Theory* 4: 479–515.

Campbell, J. Y., and N. G. Mankiw. 1986. Are Output Fluctuations Transitory? Working paper 1916, National Bureau of Economic Research.

Christiano, L. J. 1987a. Is Consumption Insufficiently Sensitive to Innovations in Income? *American Economic Review* 77 (May): 337–341.

——— 1987b. Money Does Granger-Cause Output in the Bivariate Output-Money Relation, Working paper, Federal Reserve Bank of Minneapolis.

Cochrane, J. H. 1986. How Big Is the Random Walk in GNP? Working paper, University of Chicago.

Davis, S. J. 1987. Fluctuations in the Pace of Labor Reallocation. *Carnegie-Rochester Conference Series on Public Policy* 27: 335–402.

Donaldson, J. B., and R. Mehra. 1983. Stochastic Growth with Correlated Production Shocks. *Journal of Economic Theory* 29: 282–312.

Dotsey, M., and R. G. King. 1987. Business Cycles. *The New Palgrave: A Dictionary of Economics.* New York: Stockton Press.

Eichenbaum, M. S., L. P. Hansen, and K. J. Singleton. 1981. A Time Series Analysis of Representative Agent Models of Consumption and Leisure Choice Under Uncertainty. Working paper 1981, National Bureau of Economic Research.

Eichenbaum, M., and K. J. Singleton. 1986. Do Equilibrium Real Business Cycle Theories Explain Postwar U.S. Business Cycles? *NBER Macroeconomics Annual 1986.* Cambridge, Massachusetts: MIT Press.

Evans, G. W. 1986. Output and Unemployment Dynamics in the United States: 1950–1985. Working paper, Stanford University.

Fischer, S. 1987. New Classical Macroeconomics. *The New Palgrave: A Dictionary of Economics.* New York: Stockton Press.

Geary, P. T., and J. Kennan. 1982. The Employment-Real Wage Relationship: An International Study. *Journal of Political Economy* 90 (August): 854–871.

———— 1984. Intertemporal Substitution and the Phillips Curve: International Evidence. Working paper 84–35. University of Iowa.

Hansen, G. D. 1985. Indivisible Labor and the Business Cycle. *Journal of Monetary Economics* 16 (November): 309–327.

Hansen, L. P. 1982. Large Sample Properties of Generalized Method of Moments Estimators. *Econometrica* 50 (July): 1029–54.

Hansen, L. P., and K. J. Singleton. 1982. Generalized Instrumental Variables Estimation of Nonlinear Rational Expectations Models. *Econometrica* 50 (September): 1269–86.

Hamilton, J. D. 1983. Oil and the Macroeconomy since World War II. *Journal of Political Economy* 91 (April): 228–248.

———— 1985. Uncovering Financial Market Expectations of Inflation. *Journal of Political Economy* 93 (December): 1224–41.

Hercowitz, Z., and M. Sampson. 1986. Growth and Employment Fluctuations. Working paper.

Hodrick, R. J., and E. C. Prescott. 1980. Post-War U.S. Business Cycles: An Empirical Investigation. Working paper, Carnegie Mellon University.

Jorgenson, D. W., and Z. Griliches. 1967. The Explanation of Productivity Change. *Review of Economic Studies* 34 (April): 249–283.

King, R. G. 1981. Monetary Information and Monetary Neutrality. *Journal of Monetary Economics* 7 (March): 195–206.

———— 1986. Money and Business Cycles: Comments on Bernanke and Related Literature. *Carnegie-Rochester Conference Series on Public Policy* 25: 101–116.

King, R. G., and C. I. Plosser. 1984. Money, Credit, and Prices in a Real Business Cycle. *American Economic Review* 74 (June): 363–380.

King, R. G., C. I. Plosser, and S. T. Rebelo. 1987. Production, Growth, and Business Cycles. Working paper, University of Rochester.

King, R., C. Plosser, J. Stock, and M. Watson, 1987. Stochastic Trends and Economic Fluctuations. Working paper 2229, National Bureau of Economic Research.

King, R. G., and S. T. Rebelo. 1986. Business Cycles with Endogenous Growth. Working paper, University of Rochester.

Kydland, F. E. 1984. Labor Force Heterogeneity and the Business Cycle. *Carnegie-Rochester Conference Series on Public Policy* 21 (Autumn): 173–208.

Kydland, F. E., and E. C. Prescott. 1980. A Competitive Theory of Fluctuations and the Feasibility and Desirability of Stabilization Policy. *In* S. Fischer (ed.), *Rational Expectations and Economic Policy*. Chicago: The University of Chicago Press.

———— 1982. Time to Build and Aggregate Fluctuations. *Econometrica* 50 (November): 1345–70.

———— 1986. The Workweek of Capital and Its Cyclical Implications. Working paper, Federal Reserve Bank of Minneapolis.

Lilien, D. M. 1982. Sectoral Shifts and Cyclical Unemployment. *Journal of Political Economy* 90 (August): 777–793.

Litterman, R. B., and L. Weiss. 1985. Money, Real Interest Rates, and Output: A Reinterpretation of Postwar U.S. Data. *Econometrica* 53 (January): 129–156.

Long, J. B., and C. I. Plosser. 1983. Real Business Cycles. *Journal of Political Economy* 91 (February): 39–69.

Loungani, P. 1986. Oil Price Shocks and the Dispersion Hypothesis. *Review of Economics and Statistics* 68 (August): 536–539.

Lucas, R. E., Jr. 1972. Expectations and the Neutrality of Money. *Journal of Economic Theory* 4 (April): 103–124.

———— 1973. Some International Evidence on Output–Inflation Tradeoffs. *American Economic Review* 63 (June): 326–334.

———— 1975. An Equilibrium Model of the Business Cycle. *Journal of Political Economy* 83 (December): 1113–44.

———— 1987. *Models of Business Cycles*. Oxford: Basil Blackwell.

Lucas, R. E., Jr., and E. C. Prescott. 1971. Investment under Uncertainty. *Econometrica* 39 (September): 659–682.

Mankiw, N. G. 1986. Comments. *NBER Macroeconomics Annual 1986*. Cambridge, Massachusetts: MIT Press.

Mankiw, N. G., J. J. Rotemberg, and L. H. Summers. 1985. Intertemporal Substitution in Macroeconomics. *Quarterly Journal of Economics* 100 (February): 225–251.

Manuelli, R. E. 1986. Modern Business Cycle Analysis: A Guide to the Prescott-Summers Debate. Federal Reserve Bank of Minneapolis *Quarterly Review* 10 (Fall): 3–8.

McCallum, B. T. 1982. Macroeconomics after a Decade of Rational Expectations: Some Critical Issues. Federal Reserve Bank of Richmond *Economic Review* 68: 3–12.

———— 1985. On Consequences and Criticisms of Monetary Targeting. *Journal of Money, Credit, and Banking* 17 (November, Part 2): 570–597.

———— 1986. On 'Real' and 'Sticky Price' Theories of the Business Cycle. *Journal of Money, Credit, and Banking* 18 (November): 397–414.

Mishkin, F. S. 1981. The Real Interest Rate: An Empirical Investigation. *Carnegie-Rochester Conference Series on Public Policy* 15 (Autumn): 151–200.

Nelson, C. R., and C. I. Plosser. 1982. Trends and Random Walks in Macroeconomic Time Series. *Journal of Monetary Economics* 10 (September): 139–162.

Oi, W. Y. 1987. Comment on the Relation between Unemployment and Sectoral Shifts. *Carnegie-Rochester Conference Series on Public Policy* 27 (Autumn): 403–420.

Prescott, E. C. 1986. Theory Ahead of Business Cycle Measurement. *Carnegie-Rochester Conference Series on Public Policy* 25 (Autumn): 11–44.

Rogerson, R. D. 1985. Indivisible Labor, Lotteries, and Equilibrium. Working paper, University of Rochester.

Romer, P. M. 1986. Increasing Returns and Long-Run Growth. *Journal of Political Economy* 94 (October): 1002–37.

Rush, M. 1987. Real Business Cycles. Federal Reserve Bank of Kansas City *Economic Review* 72 (February): 20–32.

Sargent, T. J. 1976. The Observational Equivalence of Natural and Unnatural Rate Theories of Macroeconomics. *Journal of Political Economy* 84 (August): 631–640.

Shapiro, M. D. 1987. Are Cyclical Fluctuations in Productivity Due More to Supply Shocks or Demand Shocks? Working paper 2147. National Bureau of Economic Research.

Sims, C. A. 1980. Comparison of Interwar and Postwar Business Cycles: Monetarism Reconsidered. *American Economic Review* 70 (May): 250–257.

—— 1982. Policy Analysis with Econometric Models. *Brookings Papers on Economic Activity,* No. 1: 107–152.

Singleton, K. J. 1986. Econometric Issues in the Analysis of Equilibrium Business Cycle Models. Working paper, Carnegie Mellon University.

Solow, R. M. 1957. Technical Change and the Aggregate Production Function. *Review of Economics and Statistics* 39 (May): 312–320.

Summers, L. H. 1986. Some Skeptical Observations on Real Business Cycle Theory. Federal Reserve Bank of Minneapolis *Quarterly Review* 10 (Fall): 23–27.

Walsh, C. E. 1986. New Views of the Business Cycle: Has the Past Emphasis on Money Been Misplaced? Federal Reserve Bank of Philadelphia *Business Review* (January-February): 3–13.

Watson, M. W. 1986. Univariate Detrending Methods with Stochastic Trends. *Journal of Monetary Economics* 18 (July): 49–75.

2 Capital Accumulation in the Theory of Long-Run Growth

Paul M. Romer

After more than a decade of quiescence, growth theory may once again be entering a period of ferment. By the end of the 1960s there was a general consensus about the basic elements of growth theory, and this theory formed the basis for a great deal of empirical work in growth accounting. This agreeable state of affairs was achieved only by narrowing the range of the questions that growth theory was expected to address. From the point of view of classical economists, the two most interesting questions about growth were dropped from consideration. How can one reconcile extraordinary, continuing increases in average per capita income with the notion of diminishing returns? What determines the rate of growth of the population? Attention is once again turning to these issues.

During the 1960s the consensus view on these bothersome questions came to be that each should be assigned an exogenous, exponential trend term. Then the economic analysis of the other features of an economy could proceed. From a practical point of view, this finesse of the problems of endogenous per capita income growth and endogenous population growth was useful. Important theoretical progress in the understanding of dynamic models was made precisely because the most difficult questions about growth were set aside. But because it ignored the fundamental questions and concentrated on abstraction and formalism, growth theory came increasingly to be viewed as a sterile exercise. From the point of view of policy advice, growth theory had little to offer. In models with exogenous technological change and exogenous population growth, it never really mattered what the government did. Partly in reaction, development branched off as a separate endeavor, designed to offer the direct policy advice that growth theory could not.

The irony underlying the disrepute that growth theory fell into is that many economists missed the self-referential nature of the theory. Economics, like any science, has a two-sector technology. The final output good of economics, produced in one sector, is correct answers to questions that noneconomists care about. A separate investment sector produces the intellectual capital that is the key input into the final output sector. Development for the most part took 1960s vintage intellectual capital and has been producing policy advice with it ever since. In contrast, growth theory gave up any pretense of having anything to say about questions that a policymaker might care about and concentrated on intellectual capital accumulation.

This capital accumulation now shows signs of a significant payoff. One of the major themes of this chapter is that the substantive contribution of growth theory has so far been quite small but the methodological impact has been far-reaching and fundamental. The methodological advances have had their greatest impact in macroeconomics, where they can truly be said to have revolutionized accepted practice. To cite just one example from the other chapters in this volume—in the years between 1970 and 1980, the discussion of the theory of aggregate consumption moved from a point where it would have been impolite to mention Euler equations to a point where it was impossible to carry on a discussion without them. By itself, this methodological impact has long justified attention to developments in this area; but now may be an especially good time to tune into growth theory. The second theme developed here is that the tools have evolved to the point where growth theory is on the verge of having something interesting to say about growth.

Of all the policy questions concerning growth, the most fundamental is whether there are any policies that an omniscient, omnipotent, benevolent social planner could implement to raise the welfare of all the individuals in an economy. An affirmative answer to this question is of course a necessary condition (but not a sufficient condition) for justifying interventions by actual governments. In formal terms, the question is whether or not equilibria are Pareto optimal. To treat this question seriously, economists must have available models with Pareto optimal equilibria and models with Pareto suboptimal equilibria. Given a range of models, the answer to this question reduces to a choice of the type of model that best describes the data.

Until recently, virtually all explicit models of growth had Pareto optimal equilibria. [Overlapping-generations models, as used for example in Diamond (1965), are an exception, but one of questionable relevance for growth theory. The conclusion of these models is that an equilibrium may be suboptimal because the capital stock is too high.] In the last few years, the most important technical advance in the analysis of dynamic models is a recognition that it is almost as easy to characterize dynamic equilibrium models with a wide variety of distortions as it is to characterize the more familiar models with all of the requisites for perfect competition. Virtually all of the analysis of dynamic models is based on the analysis of a maximization problem, but the problem need not be a first best social planning problem.

Since this observation is fundamental to the expanded range of recent growth models, much of this chapter is devoted to a detailed discussion of the relationship between maximization problems and equilibria. In part, this discussion is intended as a self-contained introduction to the tools used in the study of dynamic models. Methods are described in the context of earlier work on growth theory in cases where this is convenient, but what is offered here is a synthesis, not a survey.[1] It takes advantage of hindsight and interprets the methods in the context of a unifying result from the mathematical theory of convex analysis, the abstract Kuhn-Tucker theorem.

The plan of the chapter is as follows. Section 2.1 sets the stage with a description of some of the basic data about economic growth. The data naturally suggest specific questions that a theory of growth should be able to address. Does international trade affect growth? What explains the negative correlation between income growth and population growth? What explains the dispersion in growth rates observed across countries? Are less-developed countries systematically catching up with developed countries? Why is there continuing pressure for migration from low-income countries to high-income countries? Is growth slowing down? Section 2.2, the bulk of the chapter, describes the tools that can be used to study questions of this kind. It covers a subset of the standard methods for solving dynamic maximization problems, with emphasis on the methods that translate most easily to models with distortions. Section 2.3 concludes with a discussion of recent models that use the methods outlined in Section 2.2 and that address one or more of the specific questions suggested by the data.

2.1. Data

In an influential article on growth written in 1961, Nicholas Kaldor stated his view that a theorist ought to start with a summary of the facts that are relevant to the problem of interest. This summary should be "stylized," he claimed, concentrating on broad tendencies. One could then construct hypotheses to explain these stylized facts. In the formative stages of a body of theory, this kind of informal treatment of the data can be quite useful, for without stylized facts to aim at, theorists would be shooting in the dark. When Kaldor wrote, the basic elements of a theory of growth seemed to be up for grabs in a developing debate between Cambridge, England and Cambridge, Massachusetts, and the facts he set out became the target for economists on both sides.

If, as is claimed in the introduction, growth is entering a similar phase—namely, one in which the basic questions about growth are being re-examined—it may be useful to review and update Kaldor's list of facts. To do this in a way that does not bias the outcome, it is important to make sure not only that the facts have some connection with measured data but also that the list be as inclusive as possible. Different theories can often explain different subsets of the facts. For example, depending on the set of countries one looks at, one can conclude either that per capita income across countries is converging rapidly or that no tendency toward convergence is present. (This point is discussed in greater detail below.) Another example: Solow (1970) observes that his model of growth can explain five of the six stylized facts described by Kaldor, but he acknowledges that the sixth—the wide dispersion in growth rates across countries—is something of a problem for his model. Subsequent advocates of the neoclassical model have sometimes been less forthcoming, listing only five facts that a model of growth should explain.

Here are Kaldor's six stylized facts:

1. Output per worker shows continuing growth "with no tendency for a *falling* rate of growth of productivity" (emphasis in the original).
2. Capital per worker shows continuing growth.
3. The rate of return on capital is steady.
4. The capital–output ratio is steady.
5. Labor and capital receive constant shares of total income.
6. There are wide differences in the rate of growth of productivity across countries.

It is readily seen that these statements are not all independent. Let Y, K, and L represent total output, capital, and labor, respectively. Let r denote the return on capital. If Y/L is growing and Y/K is constant, K/L must also be growing. Thus, fact 2 follows from facts 1 and 4. If Y/K is constant and rK/Y is constant, then r must also be constant. Thus, 4 and 5 imply 3. With no loss in generality, one can concentrate on 1, 4, 5, and 6. On the basis of the kind of data exhibited below, 1, 4, and 6 may still be reasonable stylized characterizations of the data. On the other hand, there is some evidence of a long-run trend in factor shares.

There are five other prominent features of the data:

7. In cross section, the mean growth rate shows no variation with the level of per capita income.
8. Growth in the volume of trade is positively correlated with growth in output.
9. Population growth rates are negatively correlated with the level of income.
10. The rate of growth of factor inputs is not large enough to explain the rate of growth of output; that is, growth accounting always finds a residual.
11. Both skilled and unskilled workers tend to migrate toward high-income countries.

Observation 7 can be discerned from the wider array of data that are now available. Observation 8 has been noted in discussions of export-led development and 9 has been the focus of considerable study among demographers. However, since formal theories of growth have until recently been silent on the determinants of population growth and of international trade, they have not been considered relevant parts of the target that growth theories should aim at. Observation 10 describes the widely noted conclusion from the work on growth accounting. Observation 11, concerning migration, may not appear to have any direct bearing on theories of income growth; however, recent theoretical work by Robert Lucas suggests that this may be a crucial piece of evidence in distinguishing between theories of growth based on constant returns to scale and those based on increasing returns.

Tables 2.1 and 2.2 bear on Kaldor's first observation. Viewed from a long-run perspective, there is no question that cumulative growth in output per worker has been truly remarkable and that the rate of growth increased over a long period of time. Table 2.1, taken from Maddison (1982), identifies the country with the highest level of output per hour worked during different historical epochs and estimates the rate of productivity growth for that country. The trend is clear, but the magnitudes may need some amplification. The natural logarithm of 2 is 0.69, so it follows that the observed productivity growth rate of 2.3% per year for the United States leads to a doubling of output per worker every 30 years.

Table 2.1 Productivity growth rates for leading countries

Leading country	Interval	Average annual growth rate of GDP per man-hour (%)
Netherlands	1700–1785	−0.07
United Kingdom	1785–1820	0.5
United Kingdom	1820–1890	1.4
United States	1890–1970	2.3

Source: Maddison (1982).

Table 2.2 Increases in output per man-hour

Country	Symbol[a]	Output per man-hour 1870	Output per man-hour 1979	Ratio
Australia	A	1.30	6.5	5
Austria	T	0.43	5.9	14
Belgium	B	0.74	7.3	10
Canada	C	0.64	7.0	11
Denmark	D	0.44	5.3	12
Finland	L	0.29	5.3	18
France	F	0.42	7.1	17
Germany	G	0.43	6.9	16
Italy	I	0.44	5.8	13
Japan	J	0.17	4.4	26
Netherlands	N	0.74	7.5	10
Norway	W	0.40	6.7	17
Sweden	S	0.31	6.7	22
Switzerland	Z	0.55	5.1	9
United Kingdom	K	0.80	5.5	7
United States	E	0.70	8.3	12

Source: Maddison (1982).
a. Country symbols are used in Figures 2.3 and 2.7.

Table 2.2 shows that growth rates of this magnitude are not unique to the United States. It lists the factor by which output per hour worked increased over the period 1870 to 1979 for 16 developed countries. These magnitudes speak for themselves. (Table 2.2 also introduces symbols used to identify different countries in subsequent figures.)

Figures 2.1 and 2.2 show the behavior of labor productivity in the United States in more detail and address the perception that growth rates are falling rather than increasing. Figure 2.1 shows the annual rate of change of output per man-hour for the private business sector in the postwar era. Careful examination reveals a lower average rate of labor productivity growth in the period since 1969. This reduction in the rate of productivity growth has been the source of much concern and attention and is indicative of the kind of evidence that has led to concern that growth rates are slowing. Because these data are sensitive to business cycle variation that does not seem to impinge uniformly on the two halves of the sample, it is not clear that one should draw strong inferences about secular trends from them yet.

The data plotted in Figure 2.2 show the long-run behavior of labor productivity.[2] For comparison, the figure also shows the behavior of per capita income. Year-to-year variation is smoothed by taking 20-year averages. The period 1919 to 1939 shows relatively strong growth in output per

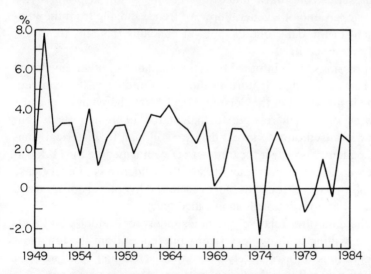

Figure 2.1 Postwar productivity growth. Data are from the Bureau of Labor Statistics figures published in the *Monthly Labor Review*.

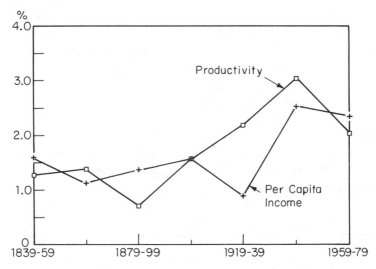

Figure 2.2   Long-run income and productivity growth.[2]

hour worked that masks a fall in employment and hours worked during the Depression. Similarly, the fall in productivity growth at the end of the sample masks a sizable increase in the fraction of the population at work. Using either series, one must judge the recent decline in productivity against the background of a general upward trend. Judging from the variability evident in the data, one cannot yet conclude that this trend has permanently reversed itself.

These impressions are reinforced by an examination of other developed countries. The outstanding feature in the long-run data is the unprecedented surge in growth after the Second World War. There has been some recent slowing of growth relative to that of the 1950s and 1960s, but growth has decreased only to levels that are still high by historical standards. Consequently, in a test for trend in per capita income for 11 developed countries described in Romer (1986), the evidence is in every case supportive of a positive trend; in most cases, the hypothesis of no trend can be rejected at conventional significance levels.

Overall, the data offer relatively strong support for Kaldor's first fact. Unless one is willing to draw very strong inferences from the few most recent observations on a relatively noisy time series and conclude that they represent a break with historical patterns, there is no reason for a theory of growth to aim for falling growth rates and stagnation.

Figure 2.3 bears on the constancy of the capital output ratio. Using data from Maddison (1982), it reports the growth rate of capital per hour worked and of output per hour worked for three time intervals and seven countries. Each country is represented by a letter listed in Table 2.2. The numbers refer to different periods: 1 is the period 1870 to 1913; 2 is the period 1913 to 1950; 3 refers to the period 1950 to 1979. (Like the other data reported here, this sample includes all the countries and time periods for which data are reported in the specified source. Maddison's study covers 16 countries, but these seven, for the specified intervals, are the only ones for which capital stock data are reported.) For the capital–output ratio to be constant, capital and output must grow at the same rate, so a scatter plot of the growth rates should line up on the 45-degree line. Subtracting a constant from each pair—the growth rate of hours worked—should leave each pair on the 45-degree line. In Figure 2.3 they cluster around this line to a surprising extent.

Further evidence on this result can be offered. Let i denote the fraction of total income devoted to investment and let δ denote the depreciation rate on capital. Then the equation for the evolution of the capital stock is $\dot{K} = iY - \delta K$. Let g denote the rate of growth of output, $g = \dot{Y}/Y$. If g, i,

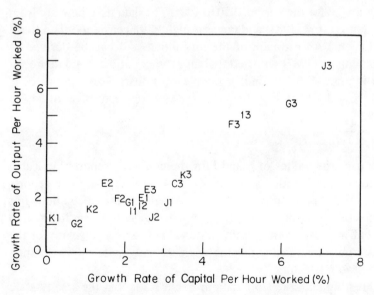

Figure 2.3 Output and capital per hour worked. Data from Maddison (1982).

Table 2.3 Investment, GDP growth, and the capital–output ratio

Country	Investment share (%)	GDP growth (%)	Capital–output ratio Depreciation rate $\delta = 0.03$	$\delta = 0.04$
Japan	31	7.4	3.0	2.8
Germany	28	4.7	3.7	3.3
Canada	28	4.2	3.9	3.4
Italy	26	4.4	3.6	3.1
France	25	4.2	3.5	3.1
United States	24	3.0	3.9	3.4
United Kingdom	17	2.1	3.4	2.8

Source: Summers and Heston (1984).

and δ are constant, then the capital–output ratio will converge to the value

$$\frac{K}{Y} = \frac{i}{\delta + g},$$

with dynamics that behave like $e^{-(g+\delta)t}$. Table 2.3 reports average values for i and g using data from national income accounts for the seven countries in Figure 2.3 for the period 1950 to 1981. The data used here are from Summers and Heston (1984) and cover a slightly longer period than those from Maddison.[3] An estimate of the magnitude of δ can be derived as follows: Maddison (1987) reported that an average ratio of total depreciation D to income Y for a similar sample of industrialized countries is between 11% and 12%. Using this value for D/Y, one can solve for δ from

$$\delta = \frac{D}{Y}\frac{Y}{K} = \frac{D}{Y}\frac{g + \delta}{i}.$$

When one uses the values of g and i for the countries reported in Table 2.3, this calculation yields values of 3% or 4% for δ. The table reports estimates of the capital output ratio on the basis of this calculation. For these values of δ and for a value for g of 3% or 4%, the time for K/Y to converge halfway toward its steady-state value is about 10 years; for the 31-year interval covered by the table, this steady-state approximation may not be too misleading.

   The interesting feature of the data in Table 2.3 is that the steady-state capital-output ratios are relatively similar. There is a relatively large amount of variation in the investment share *i* and the growth rate *g*, but there is no systematic variation in the estimated value of *K/Y* across countries. Note that this result is stronger than the finding from Figure 2.3 that *K* and *Y* increase in roughly equal proportions in a given country and time period. Equiproportionate increases in *Y* and *K* could arise in a world where output varies exogenously and the investment rate stays constant, but Table 2.3 shows that the investment share varies closely with the growth rate. The question suggested by these data is, Why do the share of investment and the rate of growth of output move together in such a way that the implied capital–output ratio shows little systematic variation?

These statements must be qualified to some extent because the findings are weaker if one significantly increases the sample of countries considered. The conventional wisdom is that the data for developing countries do not show a strong correlation between growth and the share of output devoted to investment. Figure 2.4 shows why. It uses data from Summers and Heston (1984) and is a plot of the average investment share and the average rate of growth of output for all 115 of the economies that they label (somewhat loosely) as market economies. For 50 of these countries—those denoted in the figure with an "x"—data are available only

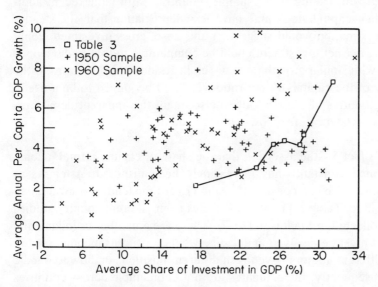

Figure 2.4   Investment share and GNP growth. Data from Summers and Heston (1984).

for the 20-year interval 1960 to 1981. For the other 65 countries, data
cover the interval 1950 to 1981. Seven of these countries, the ones from
Figure 2.3 and Table 2.3, are denoted with squares and are plotted from
right to left in the order in which they appear in Table 2.3. For clarity they
are connected by a line. The remaining 58 countries with data for the
period 1950 to 1981 are denoted with plus signs. The growth rate is the
average annual (continuously compounded) growth rate of gross domestic
product, valued at international prices. The investment measure includes
investment by both the private and government sectors.

Judging solely from the countries denoted with a plus sign, one finds no
strong evidence of a positive association between investment and growth.
With the addition of the countries denoted by an x, for which data are
available only since 1960, a positive association is once again apparent,
but it is not as tight as the relation observed among the seven developed
countries connected by the line. Moreover, both the x countries and the +
countries tend to lie systematically to the left of the locus for the developed countries. This pattern suggests either that the process of growth for
the developing countries differs fundamentally from that for the developed countries, or that investment tends to be systematically underesti-
mated in the less developed countries, or that the steady-state assumption
used here is misleading. For example, countries with large recent addi-
tions to their capital stock may have less depreciation than the steady-
state approximation would suggest. In this case, gross investment could
be smaller, but net investment could be comparable to that in developed
countries with similar growth rates. Overall, Kaldor's observation 4—the
constancy of the capital–output ratio—can still be judged to be a useful
target for theories of growth, but so also might the apparent departures
from this tendency for low-income countries suggested by Figure 2.4.

Kaldor's fact 5—the assertion that the share of capital in total income
has remained constant—has increasingly been disputed. Attempts to
measure this share in a consistent fashion over time tend to show a fall in
capital's share. Table 2.4 reports estimates from different country studies
that are collected in Maddison (1987). There are a number of judgmental
issues that must be resolved in deciding what constitutes income to capital, and different authors have taken different positions on how to handle
them. Consequently, the estimates are not comparable across countries
and authors. Looking only within countries, the trend is for the share of
capital to decline from about 0.4 to 0.3. Of course, realistic standard

Table 2.4 Estimates of the share of capital in total income[a]

Country	Interval	Share of capital (%)	Reference
Japan	1913–1938	40	Ohkawa and Rosovsky (1973)
	1954–1964	31	
United Kingdom	1856–1873	41	Matthews, Feinstein, and
	1873–1913	43	Odling-Smee (1982)
	1913–1951	33	
	1951–1973	27	
United States	1899–1919	35	Kendrick (1961)
	1919–1953	25	
	1929–1953	29	Kendrick (1973)

a. Results collected in Maddison (1987).

errors for these estimates might be on the same order of magnitude as this decline. The kind of problem that adds to the uncertainty is a systematic and sizable reduction over time in the fraction of self-employed workers and sole proprietorships, for whom it is particularly difficult to distinguish returns to capital from returns to labor. Another source of uncertainty is the somewhat arbitrary methods for imputing income on capital like housing that is outside of the corporate sector. Given this uncertainty, Maddison argued that for some purposes it may not be too serious a distortion of the data to use identical shares for different countries and to assume that the weights are constant over time. Nonetheless, after acknowledging the uncertainty involved, one must give some credence to the assertion that capital's share is falling.

Kaldor's fact 6—that growth rates differ substantially across countries—and the added fact 7—that the growth rates do not vary systematically with the level of income—are both clearly evident from Figure 2.5. This figure is a plot of the data for all 115 market economies from Summers and Heston. The horizontal axis measures the ratio of per capita income in a country relative to that in the United States, with income in both countries measured in 1960. One of the major contributions made by Summers, Heston, and Kravis was to correct official exchange rates for departures from purchasing power parity so that this kind of comparison of levels is meaningful. The vertical axis measures the growth rate of per capita income for each country in the subsequent interval 1960 to 1981.

The main result here is that the growth rate shows no systematic varia-

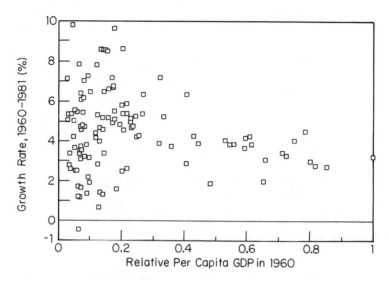

Figure 2.5   Growth vs. rank for per capita GDP, 1960 sample. Data from
Summers and Heston (1984).

tion with the level of income. For countries with any initial level of income, the average growth rate is 3% to 4%. The variance does seem to
vary systematically, falling rapidly with per capita income, but this may at
least partially reflect the fact that the low-income countries are much
more heavily sampled than the high-income countries. In a sample drawn
from any distribution, the difference between the minimum and the maximum values will be monotonically increasing in the sample size.

It is perhaps worth emphasizing that the range of growth rates of over
10% is quite large. Over the span of a mere 21 years, the ratio of per capita
income in the fastest growing country to that in the slowest growing
country more than tripled. If even one-tenth of this variation in growth
rates is due to forces that government policy can influence, the potential
long-term gains from better policy are sizable.

The absence of any negative slope in this scatter plot is evidence
against the assertion that low-income countries tend to grow more rapidly
than high income countries and that convergence in per capita income is
taking place.[4] One can of course select a set of countries where convergence has taken place. Figure 2.6 is based on data for the interval 1950 to
1981, the period when substantial convergence is typically alleged to have
taken place. Overall, for this smaller sample of 65 countries with data

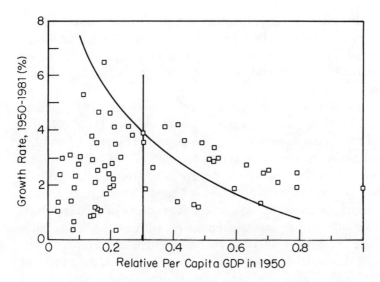

Figure 2.6   Growth vs. rank for per capita GDP, 1950 sample. Data from
Summers and Heston (1984).

extending back to 1950, one finds the same pattern as for the larger sample
in Figure 2.5—a triangular shape that is roughly symmetric about a horizontal line. This figure also has two lines that intersect at the point corresponding to Italy. These lines allow one to make income comparisons at
the beginning and at the end of the period. The vertical line divides the
sample into countries on the right, which had a higher per capita income
than Italy in 1950, and those on the left, which had a lower per capita
income. The downward sloping line divides the countries on the basis of
income comparisons at the end of the period. Countries that lie above this
line had per capita income in 1981 that was higher than that in Italy in
1981. It is downward sloping because there are two ways to end up richer
than Italy. If a country starts out poorer, it must grow more rapidly. If it
starts out richer, it can grow more slowly.

   Although a selection criterion based on levels of per capita income at
the end of the period seems suspect for purposes of testing for a downward slope, it is implicitly what one uses when one specifies a sample of
countries that are now thought of as being industrialized. The list of
countries that lie above the downward sloping line corresponds almost
exactly with the list of countries that Maddison (1982) studied and that
Baumol (1986) subsequently used in his analysis of convergence. The only

difference is that New Zealand, Luxembourg, and Iceland have levels of income as high as those of Italy in 1981 but are omitted from Maddison's study, presumably because they are so small. If one had picked developed countries in 1950, Japan would not have made the list and Argentina would have.

Ex post, it is always possible to tell stories about why Japan should have been included and why Argentina should not have been included, but this seems like a risky methodology. Judging from Figures 2.5 and 2.6, one finds no obvious reason for treating some countries as being so different from the others that they must be excluded from the analysis of questions like convergence. Even if one did conclude that some truncation of the sample is called for—for example, because of concern about data reliability—the way to truncate the sample without biasing the inferences is to use the initial level of income rather than the terminal level. Regardless of the initial level of income chosen (that is, regardless of where one chooses to draw a vertical line), the remaining points will not have an obvious negative slope.[5]

Fact 8—the correlation between growth and trade for developed countries—is summarized by the three panels of Figure 2.7. Over time and across countries, income growth and trade growth are positively correlated, with trade growth varying more than income growth. The data are drawn from Maddison (1982). Each panel represents a different time period. The variation across countries in a particular period suggests the kind of concern that is voiced in current trade disputes, that somehow increases in trade by some countries may increase their rate of growth at the expense of growth in other countries. In contrast, the variation over time suggests that in terms of growth rates, trade may not be a zero sum game. The rate of growth in all countries may be positively related to the rate of growth of world trade.

Fact 9 refers to a negative correlation between per capita income and population growth. Data from Summers and Heston for the years 1960 to 1981 is presented in Figure 2.8, which shows a scatter plot of this relationship. A better test for the influence of per capita income on individual decisions would look at fertility rates, which correct for the age structure of the population and subtract out the effects of mortality and migration, but the gross correlation shown in the figure will almost surely survive any such refinement.

This cross-sectional variation has a time series counterpart that is re-

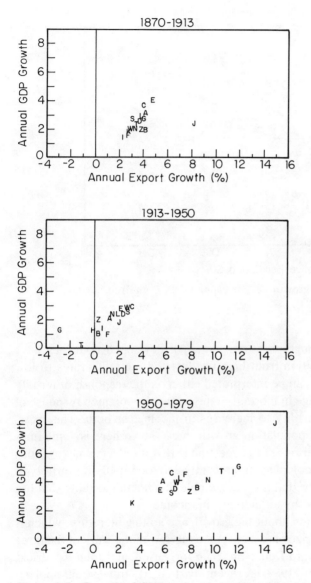

Figure 2.7 Growth of GDP and exports. Data from Maddison (1982).

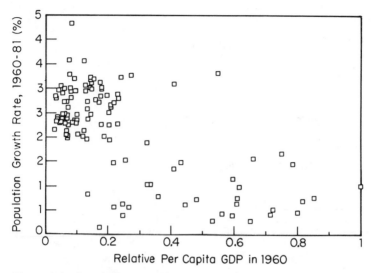

Figure 2.8 Population growth vs. per capita GDP. Data from Summers and Heston (1984).

ferred to as the demographic transition. All developed countries have gone through a transition from high fertility and mortality rates to low rates. This transition can be interpreted either as the response of fertility to an exogenous change in mortality rates, or as the common response of both mortality and fertility to increases in income, or both. The cross-sectional variation in population growth rates shown here is sometimes interpreted in these terms. The suggestion is that it reflects an exogenous fall in mortality that took place too recently and too rapidly for fertility to have yet responded, or that it is an example of a fall in mortality that has not been accompanied by an increase in income.

Fact 10 is an assertion about the growth accounting literature, which is far too vast to summarize here. A useful overview of the work of the three key participants, Edward Dennison, Dale Jorgenson, and John Kendrick, is given in Norsworthy (1984). A recent, particularly transparent application of the methodology is given in Maddison (1987). The basic reason for the persistent finding of a residual in growth accounting can be seen from Figure 2.3. Let $Y = F(K,L)$ denote the output from a constant returns to scale production function of aggregate capital and aggregate hours worked. Let $y = Y/L$ and $k = K/L$ denote output per hour worked and capital per hour worked. Then differentiating with respect to time and using the assumption of competitive markets so that $r = f'(k)$ gives

$$\frac{\dot{y}}{y} = \frac{rK}{Y} \frac{\dot{k}}{k}.$$

For values of capital's share rK/Y on the order of 0.3 or even 0.4, there is no way to match the data in Figure 2.3. Fitting a regression line of $\dot{y}/y$ on $\dot{k}/k$ to this data gives a coefficient on $\dot{k}/k$ that is very close to one. For a country like Japan with capital and output growth rates of over 7%, a share parameter of even 0.4 will imply unexplained growth of over 4% per year for nearly 30 years.

This analysis also casts doubt on simple arguments that capital deepening in the neoclassical model explains why low-capital countries like Japan and Germany grew faster and caught up with the leaders. This explanation is typically identified as one of the great successes of the model, but the numbers do not fit the story. If the growth of capital per worker was 4 percentage points higher in Germany than in the United States, the model would predict a growth rate that is higher by 0.3 or 0.4 times 4 percentage points, or less than 2 percentage points. In fact, the growth rate is higher by the same 4 percentage points. The difference between these two numbers is of course the same residual identified above for Japan. One can argue about what accounts for this difference. A die-hard neoclassicist could claim that the exogenous rate of technological change was higher in countries like Germany and Japan, but this position reduces the neoclassical model from a theory to a description of the data. Countries that grow fast are countries with fast exogenous growth in the technology. Whatever it is, something other than neoclassical physical capital accumulation was taking place.

One possible other factor is accumulation of skills and education, that is, of human capital as well as physical capital. To the extent that this kind of accumulation takes place, the correct measure of labor input is not man-hours, but man-hours adjusted for quality change due to better education or on-the-job experience. One can use the cross-sectional variation in wages, education, and experience in a country together with time series estimates of average experience and education in the labor force to construct an estimate of growth in quality-adjusted labor input. There is considerable latitude in how one goes about the details of this construction, with a corresponding variation in the resulting estimate of the unexplained residual. The consensus view seems to be that in long-run data for the United States, there is still a sizable component of growth, on the order of 1% or more, that is not explained by growth in capital or quality-adjusted labor input. Unless fast-growing countries in Figure 2.4 like Japan, Germany, France, and Italy had substantially more rapid growth in the level of education and experience than that observed in the United States, they will have even larger residuals.

Evidence on fact 11 concerning migration flows is heavily influenced by the constraints imposed on these flows. Historical evidence suggests that the unconstrained flows into industrialized countries could be quite large. Greenwood and McDowell (1986) report that during the late 1960s and early 1970s, quotas on immigration into the United States favored migration of skilled workers and professionals. Attention then turned most naturally to consideration of the brain drain. More recently, a policy shift in favor of applicants with refugee status or relatives in the United States combined with legislative debates about illegal immigration have focused attention on unskilled migrants. Potential flows from either source are apparently large.

2.2. The Kuhn-Tucker Theorem and Dynamic Equilibrium Theory

Growth is a general equilibrium process. All markets and all participants in an economy influence growth and are influenced by it. A growth theorist must therefore construct a dynamic general equilibrium model, starting with a specification of preferences and the technology and specifying an equilibrium concept. To be able to say anything about the properties of the model beyond an assurance that some equilibrium exists, the theorist must be able to explicitly solve the model or at least give a qualitative description of the solution.

Either explicitly or implicitly, the central tool used in the characterization of dynamic competitive equilibrium models is the Kuhn-Tucker theorem. It offers a general procedure for reducing the problem of calculating a competitive equilibrium to the problem of solving a maximization problem. All of the theory of growth can be understood in terms of the application of this theorem to models with tractable functional forms for preferences and the technology. To develop these claims, it is best to start with a simple Irving Fisher-type economy that has a finite number of choice variables and is assumed to have perfect markets. Next, this procedure for studying perfect markets equilibria is extended to the kind of infinite dimensional space that arises in infinite horizon maximization problems, covering the cases of both discrete time and continuous time. Section 2.2.4 concludes by showing how these techniques can be extended to equilibria that do not satisfy all of the assumptions necessary for perfec competition.

2.2.1. The Kuhn-Tucker Theorem in $\mathbb{R}^n$

Recall that a function $f:\mathbb{R}^n \to \mathbb{R}$ is concave if the cord connecting any two points on the graph of f lies on or below the graph of f. Concave functions are central to the theory of maximization because they allow a complete characterization of solutions to maximization problems. For example, if the function $f:\mathbb{R} \to \mathbb{R}$ is differentiable, a point $x \in \mathbb{R}$ solves the problem of maximizing $f(x)$ over all of $\mathbb{R}$ if and only if $f'(x) = 0$. That is, $f'(x) = 0$ is a necessary and a sufficient condition for x to be a solution. This maximization problem is unconstrained in the sense that x can be drawn from anywhere in $\mathbb{R}$. The Kuhn-Tucker theorem (1951) generalizes this complete characterization to concave maximization problems with constraints on the feasible choices of x. To be a concave problem, the objective function must be concave and the constraint set must be convex.

Consider a generic constrained maximization problem P:

P   max $f_0(x)$
      s.t. $x \in \Omega; f_1(x) \geq 0, f_2(x) \geq 0, \ldots, f_m(x) \geq 0.$

To make this a concave problem, assume that $f_0, f_1, \ldots, f_m$ are differentiable, concave, real-valued functions defined on a convex domain $\Omega \subset \mathbb{R}^n$. One further assumption is crucial in what follows, and it is convenient to give it a name. I shall say that problem P satisfies the *Slater condition* if there is a point $\bar{x}$ in the interior of Ω such that $f_i(\bar{x}) > 0$ for all $i = 1, \ldots, m$. This is an example of an interiority condition. It says that there is at least one point in the interior of the set of feasible points.

Associated with the problem P, I can define a function $\mathcal{L}:\Omega \times \mathbb{R}^m_+ \to \mathbb{R}$ by the rule

$$\mathcal{L}(x,\lambda) = f_0(x) + \sum_{i=1}^m \lambda_i f_i(x).$$

This function is typically called a Lagrangian. In the description of $\mathcal{L}$, $\mathbb{R}^m_+$ denotes the nonnegative orthant in $\mathbb{R}^m$, so $\mathcal{L}(x,\lambda)$ is not defined for a vector λ that has a negative component. Components equal to zero are allowed. The key property of this function is that it is concave–convex. When λ is held fixed, the function $\mathcal{L}_\lambda(x)$ that sends x to $\mathcal{L}(x,\lambda)$ is a concave function. When x is fixed, the function $\mathcal{L}_x(\lambda)$ that sends λ to $\mathcal{L}(x,\lambda)$ is a convex function.[6] (Recall that a function g is convex if $-g$ is concave.) A concave–convex function is sometimes referred to as a saddle function. A point $(\hat{x},\hat{\lambda})$ is said to be a saddle point (or maxi–min point) of $\mathcal{L}$ if the following inequality holds:

$$\mathcal{L}(x,\hat{\lambda}) \leq \mathcal{L}(\hat{x},\hat{\lambda}) \leq \mathcal{L}(\hat{x},\lambda).$$

This expression says that for fixed $\hat{\lambda}$, $\hat{x}$ maximizes $\mathcal{L}_{\hat{\lambda}}(x)$ and that for fixed $\hat{x}$, $\hat{\lambda}$ minimizes $\mathcal{L}_{\hat{x}}(\lambda)$.

For this kind of problem, one can list three simple conditions that are equivalent to the statement that a point $(\hat{x},\hat{\lambda})$ is a saddle point of $\mathcal{L}$ with $\hat{x}$ in the interior of Ω:[7]

(C1) $Df_0(\hat{x}) + \sum_{i=1}^{m} \lambda_i \, Df_i(\hat{x}) = 0;$

(C2) $f_i(\hat{x}) \geq 0, \quad \hat{\lambda}_i \geq 0 \qquad i = 1, \ldots , m;$

(C3) $\sum_{i=1}^{m} \hat{\lambda}_i f_i(\hat{x}) = 0.$

If $\hat{x}$ were actually on the boundary of Ω, the derivative condition in condition C1 might not hold and would need to be replaced by a slight generalization. In practice, this is not a problem. If Ω imposed binding constraints on the choice of x, it would be better to make this constraint explicit by describing it in terms of an additional constraint function $f_{m+1}(x) \geq 0$ and giving it its own multiplier. The whole point of the Kuhn-Tucker theorem is to get all of the binding constraints attached to a multiplier in the Lagrangian so that one can take derivatives as in C1.

Condition C1 implies that $\hat{x}$ maximizes $\mathcal{L}_{\hat{\lambda}}(\cdot)$. Condition C2 ensures that $\hat{x}$ satisfies the constraints and that $\hat{\lambda}$ is nonnegative. Condition C3 implies that $\hat{\lambda}$ minimizes $\mathcal{L}_{\hat{x}}(\cdot)$; since λ_i and $f_i(x)$ must be nonnegative, the smallest value the summation involving λ can take on is 0. Condition C3 makes sure that this minimum is achieved. Given the nonnegativity restrictions from C2, condition C3 can also be written as:

(C3') $\hat{\lambda}_i f_i(\hat{x}) = 0 \qquad \text{for} \quad i = 1, \ldots , m.$

Stated in this form, these conditions are sometimes referred to as complementary slackness conditions.

These conditions are what one actually uses to solve problems like P; but for the purposes of economic theory, it is useful to work directly with the notion of a saddle point. The essence of the Kuhn-Tucker theorem is that saddle points of $\mathscr{L}$ are equivalent to solutions to P.

THEOREM (Kuhn-Tucker). Assume that $f_0, f_1, \ldots, f_m$ are concave, continuous functions from $\Omega \subset \mathbb{R}^n$ into $\mathbb{R}$.[8] Let the problem P and the function $\mathscr{L}:\Omega \times \mathbb{R}_+^m \to \mathbb{R}$ be defined as above.

   (i) *Sufficient conditions for an optimum:* If $(\hat{x},\hat{\lambda}) \in \Omega \times \mathbb{R}_+^m$ is a saddle point of $\mathscr{L}$, then $\hat{x}$ is a solution to P.

   (ii) *Necessary conditions for an optimum:* Assume that the Slater condition holds. Then if $\hat{x} \in \Omega$ is a solution to P, there exists a value $\hat{\lambda} \in \mathbb{R}_+^m$ *such that* $(\hat{x},\hat{\lambda})$ *is a saddle point of* $\mathscr{L}$.

The theorem stated here is a special case of a result that can be generalized. For a proof that uses a slightly weaker version of the Slater condition, see Theorems 28.2 and 28.3 in Rockafellar (1970).

The components of $\hat{\lambda}$ are referred to as Lagrangian multipliers, or more suggestively as shadow prices for the constraints. The notion of price is quite appropriate here, for the difference between the maximization problem P and the problem of maximizing $\mathscr{L}_\lambda(x)$ over x is precisely the difference between the problem faced by a social planner and that faced by a competitive, price taking agent. In the problem P and in a social planning problem, the maximization problem must take explicit account of the resource constraints on the choice variables. In contrast, at the market prices, a competitive agent is assumed to act as if it were possible to purchase an unlimited quantity of all goods. Similarly, at the prices λ, someone solving the problem P is free to behave as if the constraints f_1 to f_m could be violated in the process of maximizing $\mathscr{L}_\lambda(x)$ over x. In each case, the prices convert a constrained maximization problem into an unconstrained problem, with prices that are determined separately. This similarity is indicative of a much deeper connection between saddle points for Lagrangians and equilibria for competitive systems. Formally, they are equivalent. Here, it is sufficient to show this equivalence in a simple example that forms the basis for all of the growth models that follow. The arguments in the general case are essentially the same.

Consider a two-period economy with a representative consumer. For ease of comparison with the dynamic models that follow, let $U:\mathbb{R}^2_{++} \to \mathbb{R}$ take on the additively separable discounted form, $U(c_1, c_2) = u(c_1) + \beta u(c_2)$. The function u is assumed to be concave.[9] Let $e > 0$ denote the period 1 endowment in this economy and let $f:\mathbb{R}_+ \to \mathbb{R}$ be a concave production function for converting forgone consumption in period 1 into consumption in period 2. Define an aggregate maximization problem for this economy (labeled P1 because it is the first in a series of similar problems) as follows:

P1 $\max u(c_1) + \beta u(c_2)$

$\quad$ s.t. $\quad e - c_1 - k \geq 0, \quad f(k) - c_2 \geq 0, \quad c_1, c_2 > 0, \quad k \geq 0.$

This can be put in the form of the generic problem P by letting the choice vector x be a triple $(x_1, x_2, x_3) = (c_1, c_2, k)$, letting Ω be the domain $\mathbb{R}^2_{++} \times \mathbb{R}_+$ in $\mathbb{R}^3$, letting $f_0(x) = u(x_1) + \beta u(x_2)$, letting $f_1(x) = e - x_1 - x_3$, and letting $f_2(x) = f(x_3) - x_2$. In conformity with the numbering scheme for problems, let $\mathcal{L}1:\Omega \times \mathbb{R}^n \to \mathbb{R}$ denote the Lagrangian associated with P1:

$$\mathcal{L}1(x,\lambda) = u(x_1) + \beta u(x_2) + \lambda_1(e - x_1 - x_3) + \lambda_2[f(x_3) - x_2].$$

Associated with the aggregate maximization problem P1 are the problems for a price taking consumer and a price taking firm. Let $PF(p)$ denote the firm's problem for this economy when faced with given prices $p \in \mathbb{R}^2_+$, and let $\Pi(p)$ denote the profits it earns:

PF(p) $\Pi(p) = \max_{k \in \mathbb{R}_+} p_2 f(k) - p_1 k.$

Let $PC(p,\pi)$ denote the problem of the price taking consumer who also takes as given the profits π received from ownership of the firm:

PC(p,π) $\max_{c \in \mathbb{R}^2_+} u(c_1) + \beta u(c_2)$

s.t. $\pi + p_1(e - c_1) - p_2 c_2 \geq 0.$

I shall say that a pair $(\hat{x},\hat{p})$ is a competitive equilibrium if $\hat{x}_3$ solves $PF(\hat{p})$, if $(\hat{x}_1,\hat{x}_2)$ solves PC $(\hat{p},\pi)$ when $\pi = \Pi(\hat{p})$, and if supply is greater than demand: $e \geq \hat{x}_1 + \hat{x}_3, f(\hat{x}_3) \geq \hat{x}_2.$

This is an example of an equilibrium with all trading in the initial period. The problems of the consumer and firm are described as if they meet and arrange all trades at time 1. This formulation is chosen only for the convenience of the theorist. There is an equivalent formulation of the equilibrium in terms of the spot prices and securities returns that people use on an everyday basis. For example, the interest rate in this two-period example will simply be the ratio of the prices for the dated goods, $r = p_1/p_2$. Throughout this chapter, all of the equilibria will be described as if all trading took place at time zero, with the understanding that they can be converted into equilibria with spot prices and a large enough set of security returns.

The next proposition shows that if the Slater condition holds (which is equivalent here to assuming that f is productive and e is greater than zero), then saddle points of $\mathcal{L}1$ are equivalent to competitive equilibria. As always, competitive prices are determined only up to a nonnegative scale factor.

PROPOSITION 2.1. Assume that u and f are continuous, strictly increasing, concave functions. Suppose that $e > 0$ and that $f(0) = (0)$. If $(\hat{x},\hat{p})$ is a competitive equilibrium, then $(\hat{x},\hat{\gamma}\hat{p})$ is a saddle point of the Lagrangian $\mathcal{L}1$ for some nonnegative scale parameter $\hat{\gamma}$. Conversely, if $(\hat{x},\hat{p})$ is a saddle point of $\mathcal{L}1$, then $(\hat{x},\hat{p})$ is a competitive equilibrium.

The essence of the proof of this proposition is to apply the Kuhn-Tucker theorem to all three of the problems P1, PC, and PF. The necessary conditions for the maximization problem P1 imply the sufficient conditions for the maximization problems PC and PF, and vice versa. The details, which amount to keeping track of notation, are given in the appendix.

For concreteness, the statement and proof are given in the context of a particular economy, but they can both be extended immediately to a more general setting. Under the mild assumption that preferences can be represented by concave utility functions, this proof can be generalized to apply in any economy where the equilibrium is Pareto optimal. If there is more than one agent, the objective becomes a weighted sum of the individual utility functions, and the problem is transformed into one of calculating one of many possible Pareto optima.

In light of the equivalence between saddle points and competitive equilibria, one can reinterpret the Kuhn-Tucker theorem. The sufficient conditions from the theorem embody the First Welfare Theorem: competitive equilibria are Pareto optimal. The necessary conditions embody the Second Welfare Theorem: for any Pareto optimal quantities, there exist prices that decentralize these quantities as a competitive equilibrium.

2.2.2 Discrete-Time Extensions of the Kuhn-Tucker Theorem

In a dynamic application of this kind of procedure, the possibility of an infinite time horizon seems to remove a crucial upper end point. Depending on whether time is discrete or continuous, the links between periods that arise from possibilities for intertemporal substitution show up in the first-order conditions as difference equations or as differential equations. In a finite horizon model, the upper end point plays a special role in establishing boundary conditions for these equations.

To see how these issues arise in a simple setting, consider a multiperiod extension of the growth model described in problem P1 but assume that the equilibrium quantities are exogenously specified so that no assumptions about the form of preferences are needed. Let the technology be like that in the two-period model, but extended over more periods. The notation can be simplified by letting the initial endowment k_0 be given in terms of the capital stock so that the initial amount of resources available for use is $f(k_0)$. Then consumption in all periods $t \geq 0$ is related to the capital stock by

$$f(k_t) - c_t - k_{t+1} \geq 0.$$

The evolution of k_t is also limited by the restriction that it must be nonnegative for all t. Even though this constraint is often neglected, it will become clear that this restriction has important economic content.

Consider first a finite horizon problem in which t runs from 0 to T. Let the values for consumption in periods 1 to T take on exogenously specified values $\bar{c}_1, \bar{c}_2, \ldots, \bar{c}_T$ and consider the problem of maximizing consumption in time 0 subject to these constraints:

P2
$$\max c_0$$
$$\begin{aligned}
\text{s.t.} \quad & f(k_t) - c_t - k_{t+1} \geq 0 && \text{for} \quad t = 0, 1, \ldots, T \\
& k_t \geq 0 && \text{for} \quad t = 1, \ldots, T + 1 \\
& c_t \geq \bar{c}_t && \text{for} \quad t = 1, \ldots, T. \\
& k_0 = \bar{k}.
\end{aligned}$$

Solving this problem for the quantities is not of much interest. Its usefulness will lie in what it can tell us about prices. Since the problem fits into the form of the generic problem P, its Lagrangian can be copied from the Lagrangian for P. Using boldface letters to denote sequences, let $\mathbf{c} = \{c_t\}_{t=0}^{T}$ and $\mathbf{k} = \{k_t\}_{t=1}^{T+1}$ denote the vectors of quantities that must be chosen. In a T period problem, the constraint on c_T involves k_{T+1}, which must also be specified. This constraint is where the nonnegativity condition on capital becomes relevant. Let $\lambda = \{\lambda_t\}_{t=0}^T$ denote the vector of multipliers on the constraints linking periods, let $\gamma = \{\gamma_t\}_{t=1}^{T+1}$ and $\omega = \{\omega_t\}_{t=1}^T$ denote the multipliers on the nonnegativity constraints. Then $\mathscr{L}2$ takes the form

$$\mathscr{L}2(\mathbf{c},\mathbf{k},\boldsymbol{\lambda},\boldsymbol{\gamma},\boldsymbol{\omega}) = c_0 + \lambda_0[f(k_0) - c_0 - k_1]$$

$$+ \sum_{t=1}^{T} \{\lambda_t[f(k_t) - c_t - k_{t+1}] + \gamma_t k_t$$

$$+ \omega_t(c_t - \bar{c}_t)\} + \gamma_{T+1}k_{T+1}.$$

The first-order conditions for this problem are straightforward. First, hold the shadow prices fixed and maximize $\mathscr{L}2$ over the quantities c and k. Differentiating with respect to c_0 gives $\lambda_0 = 1$, and with respect to c_t, $\omega_t = \lambda_t$. Differentiating with respect to k_t for $t \in \{1, 2, \ldots, T\}$ gives

(2.1) $\qquad \lambda_{t-1} = f'(k_t)\lambda_t + \gamma_t.$

The derivative with respect to k_{T+1} gives

$$\lambda_T = \gamma_{T+1}.$$

Consider next the complementary slackness conditions for minimizing $\mathscr{L}$ with respect to $\boldsymbol{\lambda}$, $\boldsymbol{\gamma}$, and $\boldsymbol{\omega}$. If I assume that $f(0) = 0$ and that $\bar{c}_t > 0$ for all t, then k_t must be positive for all $t = 1, \ldots, T$. Then the complementary slackness condition implies that $\gamma_t = 0$ over the same range. If I assume that $f'(k)$ is positive for all k, then the initial condition $\lambda_0 = 1$ together with the difference equation for λ implies that λ_t is positive for all t. Then the complementary slackness condition associated with λ_t implies that k_{t+1} must equal output minus consumption,

(2.2) $\qquad k_{t+1} = f(k_t) - c_t.$

Since λ_t equals ω_t, it follows that c_t must equal $\bar{c}_t$. Finally, the equality $\gamma_{T+1} = \lambda_T$ together with the complementary slackness condition $\gamma_{T+1}k_{T+1} = 0$ implies

$$\lambda_T k_{T+1} = 0.$$

The equations for λ and k are the only ones of any economic interest. The shadow prices γ and ω are superfluous. Equations (2.1) and (2.2) form a pair of coupled, first-order difference equations. Generally, this kind of equation system requires two boundary conditions to pin down all of the values. They are the given initial value for k_0 and the terminal condition $\lambda_T k_{T+1} = 0$. The first is an example of an initial condition. For obscure reasons, the second is called a transversality condition. In this problem, one additional condition is needed to pin down c_0. This is given by the condition $\hat{\lambda}_0 = 1$. Taken together, these conditions and the difference equations are just sufficient to determine the values for λ_t and k_t for all t.

In this particular problem, it is intuitively obvious that the condition $\lambda_T k_{T+1} = 0$ is satisfied by setting $k_{T+1} = 0$. There is no reason to leave anything after everyone is gone. In more general problems—for example, a problem where it is costly to convert capital goods back into consumption goods—the case $\lambda_T = 0$ and $k_{T+1} > 0$ can also arise. The intuition for the zero price is clear. If capital is going to be abandoned anyway, having more of it is of no value.

This kind of analysis does not offer a very interesting theory of quantity determination, but conditional on the quantities, it determines the equilibrium prices $\hat{\lambda}_t$. By converting the prices here, which have the interpretation of time-0 prices, into the kind of prices used by individuals in spot markets, it is straightforward to show that the gross rate of return on one-period bonds sold in period t is

$$R_t = \frac{\hat{\lambda}_t}{\hat{\lambda}_{t+1}} = f'(k_{t+1}).$$

This kind of problem has a natural extension to an infinite horizon. The difficulty that the infinite horizon poses is that the absence of an upper bound for time at first seems to remove the boundary condition $\hat{\lambda}_T \hat{k}_{T+1} = 0$. Because of the links between periods implicit in the difference equations, the loss of one of the boundary conditions would mean that none of the quantities and prices are determined. This indeterminacy, sometimes referred to as the Hahn problem, is only apparent. It arises only if one does not take account of the nonnegativity condition on k. In the complete markets equilibrium concept used here, there is a second boundary condition and all prices and quantities are determined.

One can see this by letting P3 denote the extension of the problem P2 when the upper bound T is removed, so t runs from 0 to ∞. It takes some sophisticated mathematics to be precise about what the definition of a Lagrangian is in an infinite dimensional space and to prove a version of the Kuhn-Tucker theorem that applies in this context, but the result is intuitively appealing.[10] Subject to an interiority or Slater condition, the

Kuhn-Tucker theorem still says that solutions to maximization problems are equivalent to saddle points of a Lagrangian. In this case, the Lagrangian takes the form

$$\mathcal{L}3(c,k,\lambda,\gamma,\omega) = c_0 + \lambda_0[f(k_0) - c_0 - k_1]$$

$$+ \sum_{t=1}^{\infty} \{\lambda_t[f(k_t) - c_t - k_{t+1}]$$

$$+ \gamma_t k_t + \omega_t(c_t - \bar{c}_t)\}.$$

The difference equations for k and λ from this Lagrangian are exactly those from the finite horizon problem. The initial condition is still given by k_0.

Provided $f(0) = 0$ and $\bar{c}_t > 0$ for all t, it follows that k_t must be strictly positive for all t. This observation makes it appear that the nonnegativity constraint on k_t is never binding and can be dropped from consideration, but this is not quite right. It is true that $\gamma_t = 0$ for all t. For any finite T, the nonnegativity constraints on k_t could be dropped for all t between 1 and T, but this does not mean that the entire infinite sequence of constraints can be dropped. One can see why by supposing that $f(k)$ takes the form $f(k) = rk$ for some constant r and for values of k that can be either positive or negative. This technology is like having a bank that offers deposits and loans at the rate r. In this case, if all the nonnegativity constraints are dropped, the initial value of c_0 can be made arbitrarily large by letting k_t take on negative values that diverge to $-\infty$.

In a sense, the nonnegativity constraint is binding at infinity. Corresponding to this constraint, there is a complementary slackness condition at infinity:

$$\lim_{t\to\infty} \hat{\lambda}_t \hat{k}_{t+1} = 0.$$

This is the transversality condition at infinity that serves as the second boundary condition for this problem. Intuitively it is just the limit of the transversality condition $\hat{\lambda}_T \hat{k}_{T+1} = 0$ for the finite horizon problem. It can be shown that this is a part of the Kuhn-Tucker necessary and sufficient conditions in the same sense that $\hat{\lambda}_T \hat{k}_{T+1} = 0$ is a part of these conditions in the finite horizon problem. In a problem satisfying the Slater condition, this condition holds for any saddle point $(\hat{k}, \hat{\lambda})$;[11] if a pair satisfies this condition plus the difference equations for k and λ, then it is a saddle point of $\mathcal{L}3$.

Subject to the assumptions noted along the way [for example, that $f'(k) > 0$ and that the Slater condition holds], this result shows that for the specified technology and sequence of quantities for aggregate consumption starting at date 0, there exist prices that support an efficient allocation as a complete markets competitive equilibrium. By construction, the allocation is efficient in the sense of maximizing time-zero consumption, taking as given the consumption in all subsequent periods. As noted above, there are overlapping-generations models like that used in Diamond (1965) with the property that equilibria are not efficient. These equilibria cannot be calculated using the method described here, and in these models, the analogue of the transversality condition at infinity can fail to hold.

The best-known example of a theory of growth with exogenously specified quantities is the model identified with Solow and Swan (Solow, 1956; Swan, 1956). In the simplest form with constant population, these models, both posed in continuous time, assume that capital per capita k evolves according to the equation

$$\dot{k}(t) = sf(k(t)) - \delta k(t),$$

where s is the saving rate, δ is an exponential depreciation rate, and $f(k)$ denotes output per worker $f(k) = F(k, 1)$ before allowance is made for depreciation. The function $F(\cdot)$ is assumed to exhibit constant returns to scale. Consumption is the residual,

$$c(t) = (1 - s)f(k(t)).$$

Under standard assumptions on f and F, the differential equation for k has a stable steady state. As is now quite familiar, exogenous population growth can be added to the model to generate growth in total income with constant per capita income. Exogenous technological change can be added to generate growth in per capita income.

Given this description of the evolution for the quantities, prices follow by exactly the kind of analysis given for the discrete model above. In particular, one can give a rigorous explanation for why $f'(k(t))$ is the instantaneous interest rate at time t. The analysis is incomplete in the sense that preferences are not fully specified; but conditional on the specification of the quantities, it is a perfectly reasonable general equilibrium model, one that can be readily taken to the data.

One of the key contributions of the Solow-Swan analysis was the renewed impetus it gave to the use of simple aggregate models along the lines suggested by Ramsey (1928). Once Ramsey's technology was recognized as a powerful tool, it was natural that his preferences should be adopted as well. The key hurdle here seems to have been the idea of discounting. Ramsey denounces discounting as "ethically indefensible" on the first page of his article, then proceeds to use discounting in the most interesting parts of his analysis. Samuelson and Solow (1956) reproduced and extended Ramsey's analysis, but they abided by his admonition not to discount, and their analysis of optimal growth has not been given much recognition. Koopmans (1965) and Cass (1965) are generally recognized as the key contributions in the process of legitimizing discounting and taking the analysis out of the realm of tricks and special cases needed to work with the undiscounted model.

Implicit in Ramsey's ambivalence about discounting is a sense that the objective function in such a problem should reflect preferences other than those of the individuals in the economy. What can be called his positive analysis allows for discounting, and he speaks in this case of an infinite-lived family; but he clearly had in mind a separate welfare analysis that did not respect the preferences of such families. Even after discounting was a firmly established practice, many papers in the 1960s seemed to retain the view that the objective function had only a normative basis. Macroeconomic applications of these tools were crucial in moving the profession away from this normative interpretation of Ramsey models and establishing these models as positive models of equilibria.[12]

The mathematical treatment of a model with discounted Ramsey preferences is another application of the Kuhn-Tucker theorem. One can see this in the discrete-time case by adding discounted Ramsey preferences to the technology from problem P3. Then the aggregate maximization problem for this economy is

P4
$$\max \sum_{t=0}^{\infty} \beta^t U(c_t)$$
$$\text{s.t.} \quad f(k_t) - k_{t+1} - c_t \geq 0, \qquad t = 0, 1, 2, \ldots$$
$$k_t \geq 0, \qquad t = 1, 2, \ldots$$

The Lagrangian for this problem is exactly what one would expect:[13]

$$\mathscr{L}4(\mathbf{k},\mathbf{c},\boldsymbol{\lambda},\boldsymbol{\gamma}) = \sum_{t=0}^{\infty} \beta^t u(c_t) + \lambda_t[f(k_t) - k_{t+1} - c_t] + \gamma_t k_t.$$

For sensible specifications of $u(\cdot)$ and $f(\cdot)$, the nonnegativity constraint on k_t is not binding for any finite t. In this case the multipliers γ_t are equal to zero for all t and can therefore be ignored, provided one keeps in mind that the nonnegativity constraint is still binding at infinity. This constraint gives the transversality condition at infinity. For fixed shadow prices $\boldsymbol{\lambda}$, maximizing $\mathcal{L}$ with respect to $\mathbf{c}$ gives c_t as a function of λ_t and t, $c(\lambda_t, t) = u'^{-1}(\lambda_t/\beta^t)$. If $u(\cdot)$ is increasing, λ_t must be positive. Then the complementary slackness condition $\lambda_t[f(k_t) - k_{t+1} - c_t] = 0$ gives k_{t+1} in terms of λ_t and k_t. Differentiation of $\mathcal{L}$ with respect to k_t gives an equation linking shadow prices in adjacent periods that is the same as that derived in problems P2 and P3. Taken together, these two equations, one for k and one for λ, form a coupled system of first-order difference equations in two variables:

(2.3) $\lambda_t = \lambda_{t-1}/f'(k_t),$

(2.4) $k_t = f(k_{t-1}) - c(\lambda_{t-1}, t - 1).$

By comparison, this system shows why the Solow model with fixed savings is easier. In that model, these equations have a triangular structure. The second equation does not depend on the first, because c is exogenously specified in terms of k. It can be solved independently. An analogous case arises here if $f(k)$ is linear so that $f'(k)$ is constant. Then the path for λ can be found without solving for the path for k. The boundary conditions for these equations are the initial value for k_0 and the transversality condition at infinity,

(2.5) $\lim_{t \to \infty} \lambda_t k_{t+1} = 0.$

Terminology in this area is not well established. Equations (2.3) and (2.4) are referred to variously as Lagrangian or Hamiltonian equations. In current usage, the term Euler equations is applied most often to a transformed version of these equations. Solving Equation (2.4) for λ_t in terms of k_t and k_{t-1}, then substituting the result into Equation (2.3) yields a second-order difference equation in k_t,

(2.6) $\beta U'(f(k_t) - k_{t+1})f'(k_t) = U'(f(k_{t-1}) - k_t).$

The Euler equation (2.6) can be derived directly by assuming that the evolution equation for k_t holds with equality and then substituting it into the objective function. This equation then follows by differentiation with respect to k_t. Treating the problem this way makes it seem as if all constraints can be transformed away so that the problem becomes an unconstrained maximization problem; no constraints or multipliers are in evidence. For finite horizon problems with fixed initial and terminal values for k—the kind of problem typically studied by physical scientists—this transformation into an unconstrained problem is possible. Hence, many treatments of dynamic maximization problems describe the methods for solution in terms of the techniques from calculus for unconstrained maximization; just set all the derivatives in sight equal to zero. However, for infinite horizon problems, substitution cannot remove the binding nonnegativity constraint on capital at infinity. To fully understand the transversality condition at infinity associated with this constraint, it is essential to have available the full machinery of the Kuhn-Tucker theorem for constrained problems. Viewed from the perspective of constrained maximization problems, it is an obvious generalization of a complementary slackness condition.

Actually proving that the transversality condition (2.5) is a necessary condition for the problem P4 requires checking the assumptions for the Kuhn-Tucker theorem. In particular, it requires checking that the infinite dimensional version of the Slater interiority condition holds. In models with no discounting, this condition can fail, and such models can be used to construct counterexamples to the transversality condition at infinity. In most applications with discounting, the condition will hold. For example, if the utility function $u(\cdot)$ is bounded from below or goes to $-\infty$ no faster than c raised to a negative power, and if $\lim_{t\to\infty}\beta^t k_{t+1} = 0$ along any feasible path for capital, it will hold.[14]

2.2.3. Continuous-Time Extensions of the Kuhn-Tucker Theorem

The extension of the infinite horizon model to continuous time is comparable to the extension of a model with discrete uncertainty to one with continuous random variables. Essentially, sums are replaced by integrals and difference equations become differential equations. Without covering the formal details, it is straightforward to give a heuristic derivation of the continuous-time Lagrangian or Hamiltonian equations.

Write the continuous-time maximization problem as

P5 $\qquad \max \int_0^\infty U(c(t))e^{-\rho t}\, dt$

$\qquad$ s.t. $\quad \dot{k}(t) = f(k(t)) - c(t) \qquad$ for all $t \geq 0$

$\qquad\qquad k(t) \geq 0 \qquad$ for all $t \geq 0$.

Note that there is some freedom in the definition of the production function f. As written here it appears that there is no depreciation, but it is a simple matter to define $g(k)$ as output before depreciation and then to let $f(k) = g(k) - \delta k$ represent output net of depreciation.

Letting boldface letters **c**, **k**, **λ**, and **γ** stand this time for functions defined on $[0, \infty)$, and using $c(t)$, $k(t)$, $\lambda(t)$, and $\gamma(t)$ or c, k, λ, and γ for their values at a point in time, the Lagrangian $\mathscr{L}5$ takes the form

$$\mathscr{L}5(\mathbf{c},\mathbf{k},\boldsymbol{\lambda},\boldsymbol{\gamma})$$
$$= \int_0^\infty \{U(c(t))e^{-\rho t} + \lambda(t)[f(k(t)) - c(t) - \dot{k}(t)] + \gamma(t)k(t)\} \, dt.$$

As in the discrete-time problem, $\gamma(t)$ will be zero for all finite t in any reasonable model; so the term $\gamma(t)k(t)$ will henceforth be ignored. For fixed shadow prices $\boldsymbol{\lambda}$, the operation of maximizing $\mathscr{L}5$ with respect to c can be passed through the integral, and the maximization can be done point by point for each fixed t. It is then useful to define the terms inside the integral other than $\lambda(t)\dot{k}(t)$ as a new function $\mathscr{H}: \mathbb{R}^3_+ \to \mathbb{R}$:

$$\mathscr{H}(k,\lambda,t) = \max_c \ U(c)e^{-\rho t} + \lambda(f(k) - c).$$

Thus,

$$\max_{\mathbf{c}} \ \mathscr{L}5(\mathbf{c},\mathbf{k},\boldsymbol{\lambda}) = \int_0^\infty [\mathscr{H}(k(t),\lambda(t),t) - \lambda(t)\dot{k}(t)] \, dt.$$

To complete the calculation of a saddle point of $\mathscr{L}5$, it remains to maximize $\mathscr{L}5$ over **k**. Because $\mathscr{H}$ depends on k and $\dot{k}$, one cannot simply maximize point by point as one could with c. At each point one must trade off the effect of increasing the level k with the effect of increasing its rate of change $\dot{k}$, which, after all, is the only way to increase the level. To do this kind of maximization and make this trade-off explicit, one needs to apply the tools of the calculus of variations. The basic result needed here is the first-order condition for maximizing an integral of the form $\int M(k(t),\dot{k}(t),t) \, dt$ with respect to a path $k(t)$. It is given as a differential equation,[15]

$$D_1 M(k(t),\dot{k}(t),t) - \frac{d}{dt}[D_2 M(k(t),\dot{k}(t),t)] = 0.$$

To apply this result here, define M as follows:

$$M(k,\dot{k},t) = [\mathscr{H}(k,\lambda(t),t) - \lambda(t)\dot{k}].$$

The time dependence in M corresponds to the dependence of $\mathcal{H}$ on $\lambda(t)$ and on the exponential discounting. The partial derivative of M with respect to $\dot{k}$ is simply $-\lambda(t)$. Then the differential equation becomes

(2.7) $\dot{\lambda}(t) = -D_1\mathcal{H}(k(t),\lambda(t),t)$.

To derive the other differential equation, note that the first-order condition for the maximum over c in the definition of $\mathcal{H}$ is

(2.8) $U'(c)e^{-\rho t} = \lambda$,

which is analogous to the expression for c derived for the discrete time model. This expression implicitly defines c as a function of λ and t, which we can denote $\hat{c}(\lambda,t)$. Substituting this into the definition of $\mathcal{H}$, then differentiating with respect to λ and using the first-order condition (2.8) gives

$$D_2\mathcal{H}(k(t),\lambda(t),t) = f(k(t) - c(\lambda(t),t)).$$

If $u(\cdot)$ is strictly increasing, Equation (2.8) implies that $\lambda(t)$ is positive. Then the complementary slackness condition $\lambda(t)[f(k(t)) - c(t) - \dot{k}] = 0$ implies that

(2.9) $\dot{k} = D_2\mathcal{H}(k(t),\lambda(t),t)$.

Equations (2.7) and (2.9) form a coupled system of first-order differential equations. The function $\mathcal{H}$ is called a Hamiltonian, and the equations are called Hamiltonian equations. Like the analogous difference equations for the discrete problem, they require two boundary conditions to completely specify the solution. As in the discrete case, one is given by the constraint on k at time zero, the other by the transversality condition at infinity, $\lim_{t\to\infty} \hat{\lambda}(t)\hat{k}(t) = 0$.

Compared with discrete time, which is conceptually simpler and lends itself more readily to uncertainty, continuous time is to be preferred only for the ease with which nonlinear systems of differential equations can be characterized by geometrical means. In the present form, the equations for k and λ are nonautonomous; that is, they depend explicitly on time. By a change of variable, however, they can be transformed into an autonomous system of equations that have no explicit time dependence and can be studied by drawing pictures.

To accomplish the change of variable, let $\theta(t) = e^{\rho t}\lambda(t)$ and define a new Hamiltonian $\tilde{\mathcal{H}}$:

$$\tilde{\mathcal{H}}(k,\lambda) = \max_c u(c) + \theta(f(k) - c).$$

The variable θ is called a current-value shadow price, in contrast with λ, which is a present-value shadow price. $\tilde{\mathcal{H}}$ is called a current-value Hamiltonian, in contrast with the present-value Hamiltonian $\mathcal{H}$. $\tilde{\mathcal{H}}$ has no explicit time dependence. The equation that justifies the terminology current- and present-value is

$$\mathcal{H}(k(t),\lambda(t),t) = e^{-\rho t}\tilde{\mathcal{H}}(k(t),\theta(t)).$$

$\mathcal{H}$ and λ are like discounted versions of $\tilde{\mathcal{H}}$ and θ.

By the formula for a change of variables and a simple substitution, the Hamiltonian equations can be restated in current-value terms:

$$\dot{\theta}(t) = \rho\theta(t) - D_1\tilde{\mathcal{H}}(k(t),\theta(t)),$$

$$\dot{k}(t) = D_2\tilde{\mathcal{H}}(k(t),\theta(t))$$

This autonomous system can be represented by a picture in a plane. In the language used by physicists, it is known as the phase plane. At each point in the $k - \theta$ plane, imagine an arrow that indicates the direction and speed of a point following these equations. This arrow will have components $\dot{k}$ and $\dot{\theta}$.

To characterize all of the arrows at all of the different points, it is useful to identify two different lines, called isoclines (*iso* for "same," *cline* for "slope"). The first isocline is the locus of points such that $\dot{\theta} = 0$; the second, the locus of points such that $\dot{k} = 0$. If k is on the horizontal axis as shown in Figure 2.9, the $\dot{k} = 0$ isocline denotes those points where trajectories in the plane have a vertical tangent or slope. The $\dot{\theta} = 0$ isocline denotes points where trajectories have a horizontal tangent. Their intersection, if any, is a stationary point.

To illustrate how these can be used, it is useful to describe the kind of analysis that Cass (1965) gives to the problem P5. Suppose that both $f(k)$ and $u(c)$ satisfy Inada conditions, $u'(0) = f'(0) = \infty$, $u'(\infty) = f'(\infty) = 0$. From the first-order condition for maximizing $\tilde{\mathcal{H}}$ with respect to c, it follows that $u'(c) = \theta$, which can be inverted to give $c(\theta)$. From the properties of u, it follows that $c(\theta)$ goes to zero as θ goes to infinity and vice versa. Substituting this into $\dot{k} = f(k) - c(\theta)$ implies that the $\dot{k} = 0$ isocline is a downward sloping curve in the plane that must have both axes as asymptotes. The $\dot{\theta} = 0$ isocline is specified by the unique value of k such that $f'(k) = \rho$. From these properties, it follows that the two curves must intersect at a unique stationary point as shown in Figure 2.9. The arrows indicate possible directions for trajectories in the plane. For exam-

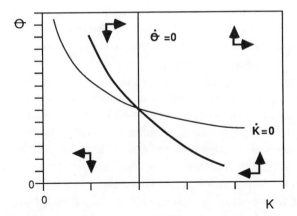

Figure 2.9   Phase plane for the Cass model.

ple, starting from a point on the $\dot{k} = 0$ isocline, an increase in k holding θ constant will cause $\dot{k}$ to become positive. Thus, the horizontal arrows to the right of this locus point in the direction of increasing k, arrows to the left, of decreasing k.

Judging from the pattern of arrows, it is evident that there will be two paths that converge to the stationary point and two that diverge from it. The two convergent paths are sometimes referred to as branches of the stable manifold. They contain the points of economic interest. For any given initial value of k, there is a unique value of θ such that (k,θ) lies on the stable manifold. This point determines the initial value $\theta(0) = \lambda(0)$. Along this trajectory, $k(t)$ and $\theta(t)$ stay bounded, so $e^{-\rho t}k(t)\theta(t) = k(t)\lambda(t)$ will converge to zero. Because the transversality condition at infinity, the Hamiltonian equations, and the initial condition characterize a saddle point of the Lagrangian $\mathcal{L}5$, the stable manifold describes both the optimal quantities and the competitive equilibrium quantities.

It is the functions of time $\mathbf{k}, \boldsymbol{\lambda}:[0,\infty) \to \mathbb{R}$ that form a saddle point of $\mathcal{L}5$, but there is another sense in which the stationary point $(k^*,\theta^*) \in \mathbb{R}^2$ where both $\dot{\theta}$ and $\dot{k}$ are equal to zero is itself a saddle point. The dynamics around this point are described as saddle-point dynamics, because they are suggestive of the dynamics one would observe if one rolled marbles down a saddle-shaped surface. Formally, this can be captured by linearizing the differential equations around the stationary point. A linear differential equation system of two variables has the saddle-point dynamics indicated here if one of its characteristic roots is positive and one is negative, properties that can readily be verified for this system.

Once the general methods have been set forth, this kind of analysis lets one say a surprising amount about the qualitative properties of a fairly complicated dynamic competitive equilibrium. Its evolution is described by a nonlinear system of equations. The solution determines the path for interest rates and profits of the firm. Alternatively, if $f(k)$ is interpreted as output per worker, $f(k) = F(k,1)$ where F exhibits constant returns to scale, the model determines the path of wages rather than the path of profits. Savings and investment decisions by consumers and firms respectively are guided not just by current interest rates but also by expectations about the entire path of future rates. Stated in spot market terms, both investment and savings decisions at each point in time depend on the entire yield curve at that time. Moreover, the entire yield curve changes over time. If one were to contemplate calculating this kind of system by equating some specification of demand and supply curves for savings and investment at each point in time, this would seem to be a hopelessly complicated task. Here it is a matter of a little calculus and algebra and remains so when the model is complicated. For example, it is a simple (and instructive) exercise to work out how the dynamics change when the degree of intertemporal substitution in consumption changes or when firms face adjustment costs so that $\dot{k}$ is a nonlinear function of forgone consumption. Another useful exercise is to contemplate the effect of an announcement at time 0 that there will be an exogenous jump in the capital stock (funded from outside the economy) at a future date T. When this information is revealed, the price $\theta(0)$ can jump, but subsequently, it cannot have a foreseen discontinuity. Using this, one can infer that the yield curve tilts, with yields on near-term maturities increasing and on long-term maturities falling, with the net effect that current investment falls relative to investment before the announcement.

2.2.4. Suboptimal Equilibria

If the approach described in the previous sections were applicable only to equilibria that are full information Pareto optimal, it would be of limited value. In fact, this method, or something very close to it, can be used in cases where the equilibrium is suboptimal because of some violation of the perfect markets assumptions. Even suboptimal equilibria maximize some kind of criterion. If one can add restrictions to the aggregate problem or change the objective in a suitable way, the solution to the modified problem may generate the outcomes observed in equilibrium.

This observation has emerged in the context of several different problems in economics. In contexts where agents have private information, the added restrictions take the form of incentive compatibility constraints. Many applications of this methodology are interested in contracts or mechanisms that are not competitive equilibria with price taking agents, but Prescott and Townsend (1984) showed that the solution to this kind of constrained maximization problem can be decentralized as a price taking equilibrium if one extends the set of goods that are allowed in the model. In a model with differentiated commodities, Hart (1980) observed that an equilibrium might not generate the correct number of different types of goods, but taking the set of goods that are produced as a given constraint, the equilibrium will produce the optimal amount of each good that is produced. In this case, if one knew the set of goods that would be produced in equilibrium, one could calculate equilibrium quantities by writing down the problem of maximizing welfare subject to the given set of goods that can be produced and consumed. In dynamic models, this kind of approach was implicitly used by Arrow (1962) in a model with externalities, and by Brock (1975) in a model with money demand and inflation that acts like a tax on money holdings. Brock (1977) also considered a growth model with pollution externalities. No doubt, other examples of this kind could be cited.

What is important about this observation is that it is operational. It describes a procedure that can actually be implemented to solve for equilibria in a way that is potentially as simple as the phase plane analysis given in the last section, and can ultimately form the basis for empirical work. To make this point, it is useful to start once again with a simple example, one that has some relevance for issues first raised by Alfred Marshall (1961) about increasing returns that were external to individual firms.

Extend the two-period model P1 to allow for an externality associated with the accumulation of capital. Let the total number of identical firms in the economy be N, where N is assumed to be large. Let k_j be the capital held by firm j and let K be the aggregate stock of capital,[16]

$$K = \sum_{j=1}^{N} k_j.$$

To capture the external effect that total capital has on the production possibilities of firm j, write production as $f(k_j, K)$. The rationale for this formulation is based on the public good character of knowledge. Suppose that new physical capital and new knowledge or inventions are produced in fixed proportions so that K is an index not only of the aggregate stock of physical capital but also of the aggregate stock of public knowledge that any firm can copy and take advantage of. Because each firm is only a vanishingly small part of the total economy, it chooses k_j to maximize profits, taking the aggregate stock K as given.

As always, a competitive equilibrium with externalities for this economy can be stated in terms of the problem of a representative consumer and the problem of a representative firm. The problem of the consumer is exactly the same as the problem $PC(p,\pi)$ given previously:

$$PC(p,\pi) \quad \max_{c \in \mathbb{R}^2_+} u(c_1) + \beta u(c_2)$$

$$\text{s.t.} \quad \pi + p_1(e - c_1) - p_2 c_2 \geq 0.$$

The problem of the firm differs. Now $PF(p,K)$ depends parametrically on the aggregate stock K as well as on prices p:

$$PF(p,K) \quad \Pi(p,K) = \max_{k \in \mathbb{R}_+} p_2 f(k,K) - p_1 k.$$

For notational convenience, I shall maintain the assumption that the number of consumers (and workers) is the same as the number of firms. Under this assumption, the market clearing conditions for goods 1 and 2 are $e - c_1 - k \geq 0$, $f(k,K) - c_2 \geq 0$, where e denotes the per capita endowment of period 1 resources. The equilibrium expression for the profits is $\pi = \Pi(p,K)$. To these conditions is added the equilibrium condition $K = \sum_{j=1}^{N} k_j$. Formally, a competitive equilibrium with externalities will be a price quantity pair such that the quantities solve the maximization problems given the prices and the aggregate variable K, and such that all the equilibrium conditions are satisfied.

This notion of an equilibrium has been described, taking the set of firms as given and assuming that the firms earn profits. This constraint simplifies the exposition but is not essential. The production function $f(k,K)$ could represent the output per worker for a firm with an underlying technology $F(K,L,K)$ that exhibits constant returns to scale in the variables K and L, holding K fixed. Then the profits can be reinterpreted as payments to workers, and free entry of firms is allowed. Since the scale and number of firms is indeterminate, it is harmless to assume that the number of firms is equal to the number of workers and that they all produce at the same scale. Under this interpretation, K still signifies the total stock of capital in the economy.

Relying on the intuition described in the beginning of this section, consider an aggregate maximization problem that is restricted in the sense that a given level of aggregate capital (and knowledge) K is imposed. For each assumed level of K, a different problem is defined, so the aggregate problem, like the problems of the consumer and firm, is actually a parametric family of problems:

P6(K) $\max\limits_{c_1,c_2,k} u(c_1) + \beta u(c_2)$

s.t. $e - c_1 - k \geq 0,$ $f(k,K) - c_2 \geq 0.$

Associated with P6(K) there is a Lagrangian $\mathcal{L}6_K$. As before, x denotes the triple $x = (c_1,c_2,k)$; so one can write:

$$\mathcal{L}6_K(x,\lambda) = u(c_1) + \beta u(c_2) + \lambda_1(e - c_1 - k) + \lambda_2(f(k,K) - c_2).$$

As long as f is a concave function of its first argument for each fixed K, this is a concave problem and the Kuhn-Tucker theorem will apply. By exactly the same argument as applied to Proposition 2.1, it will follow that any solution $\hat{x}$ to P6(K) will have associated with it prices $\hat{\lambda}$ such that $(\hat{x},\hat{\lambda})$ is a saddle point of $\mathcal{L}6_K$ and therefore solves the consumer's problem and the firm's problem at prices $\hat{\lambda}$. This solution does not ensure that it is a competitive equilibrium with externalities for this economy, because the equilibrium condition $Nk = K$ may not be satisfied. However, it is a simple matter to pick K so that this condition holds as well.

To see why this is so, consider the conditions C1, C2, C3 that characterize the saddle point of the Lagrangian associated with the problem P6(K).

(C1)   (i) $u'(x_1) = \lambda_1,$
        (ii) $\beta u'(x_2) = \lambda_2,$
        (iii) $\lambda_1 = \lambda_2 D_1 f(x_3,K);$

(C2) $\lambda_i \geq 0,$ $e - c_1 - k \geq 0,$ $f(k,K) - c_2 \geq 0;$

(C3) $\lambda_1(e - c_1 - k) = 0,$ $\lambda_2(f(k,K) - c_2) = 0.$

Assuming that the utility function $u(\cdot)$ is strictly increasing, the multipliers $\hat{\lambda}_i$ will be positive. Then the constraints on the quantities must be binding and can therefore be substituted into (C1,i) to yield

$$\frac{u'(e - k)}{\beta u'(f(k,K))} = D_1 f(k,K).$$

At this point, the equilibrium condition $K = Nk$ can be imposed by a simple substitution. All that remains is to find a value $\hat{k}$ that solves the equation

$$(2.14) \qquad \frac{u'(e - k)}{\beta u'(f(k,Nk))} = D_1 f(k,Nk).$$

Working back from the solution $\hat{k}$, one can easily derive the quantities $\hat{c}_1$, $\hat{c}_2$, and $K = N\hat{k}$, and the prices $\hat{\lambda}_1$ and $\hat{\lambda}_2$.

The fact that this does not give the socially optimal quantities can be clearly seen from Equation (2.14). The social optimum would recognize the true marginal rate of transformation between periods $D_1 f(k,Nk) + ND_2 f(k,Nk)$. In the equilibrium, each firm has no incentive to take account of the second term. It reflects the positive effect that accumulation of its capital and knowledge has on the production possibilities of all other firms.

The general procedure that this illustrates is to start with a statement of a parametric family of restricted aggregate maximization problems. The parameters in this problem may be variables that are endogenously determined in the equilibrium, but for calculating the equilibrium they are treated as fixed when taking first-order conditions. If this problem is concave for fixed values of the parameters, the Kuhn-Tucker theorem will apply. Derive the conditions from the theorem that characterize the quantities and shadow prices, and then substitute in the expression for the parameters of the problem in terms of the endogenous quantities. The order here is essential; one must take derivatives first, then substitute for the parameters. By the arguments of Proposition 1, the quantities and prices that solve the resulting equations will form a suboptimal competitive equilibrium.

The idea of inserting an equilibrium condition into a first-order condition and then solving for quantities is an old trick in static tax analysis. The surprising fact about the analysis is that it works even when f is not a concave function. For example, f could be an increasing returns function $f(k,K) = k^\alpha K^\eta$, with $\alpha + \eta > 1$. All that is required is $\alpha \le 1$. Even more surprising, it is as easy to do in an infinite horizon dynamic model as in a static model.

To see this, consider problem P7, an extension of the Cass model with productive externalities. Suppose that production for each of N firms takes the form $F(K,L,\mathbb{K})$ where F exhibits constant returns to scale in own capital K and labor L, taking the aggregate $\mathbb{K}$ as given. Normalizing by L in the usual way, define output per worker $f(k,K) = F(k,1,K)$ and assume for convenience that the number of firms is equal to the number of workers, which is equal to the number of consumers and is held constant. Let $\mathbf{K}:[0,\infty) \to \mathbb{R}$ denote a path for aggregate capital and knowledge and define the restricted social planning problem as

P7(**K**) $\max \int_0^\infty u(c(t))e^{-\rho t}\, dt$

       s.t. $\dot{k}(t) = f(k(t),K(t)) - c(t)$ for all $t \geq 0$

           $k(t) \geq 0$ for all $t \geq 0$.

The analysis here is exactly like that for the two-period problem. The conditions for the saddle point are the Hamiltonian equations. Using the current-value formulation, one defines

$$\mathcal{H}(k,\theta,K) = \max_c u(c) - \theta(f(k,K) - c).$$

The differential equations are then

$$\dot{\theta}(t) = \rho\theta - D_1\mathcal{H}(k(t),\theta(t),K(t))$$

$$\dot{k}(t) = D_2\mathcal{H}(k(t),\theta(t),K(t)).$$

This system is not yet an autonomous one that can be studied in the phase plane because of the dependence on the exogenously given path $K(t)$. But after the substitution of $Nk(t)$ for $K(t)$, it is autonomous.[17] For specific functional forms, the phase plane can immediately be characterized.

The easiest form of utility to work with is always $u(c) = \ln(c)$, because in this case the maximum over c in the definition of the current-value Hamiltonian yields the first-order condition $1/c = \theta$. Let F have the log-linear form $F(K,L,K) = K^\alpha L^{1-\alpha}K^\eta$, so f becomes $f(k,K) = k^\alpha K^\eta$. Inserting these into the Hamiltonian, differentiating to get the differential equations for k and θ, then substituting $K(t) = Nk(t)$ gives

$$\frac{\dot{\theta}}{\theta} = \rho - \alpha N^\eta k^{\alpha+\eta-1},$$

$$\dot{k} = N^\eta k^{\alpha+\eta} - \frac{1}{\theta}.$$

If $\alpha + \eta$ is less than 1, this system has the same saddle-point dynamics as the Cass model. As before, growth stops when the private marginal productivity of capital is equal to the discount rate; $D_1 f(k,Nk) = \rho$ is the equation of the $\dot{\theta} = 0$ isocline, which is analogous to the equation $f'(k) = \rho$

for the model with no externalities. This result shows that increasing returns of the form $F(K,L,Nk) = K^\alpha L^{1-\alpha}(Nk)^\eta$ are not by themselves enough to sustain persistent growth. In addition, the private marginal product $D_1 f(k,K)$ must not fall too rapidly as k grows. Accordingly, the dynamics change when $\alpha + \eta$ equals 1. When this is true, this economy will exhibit unceasing growth, provided αN^η is greater than ρ. In the phase plane, there is no $\dot\theta = 0$ isocline, hence no stationary point.

In fact, it is possible to explicitly solve the equations for this model and show that growth takes place at a constant rate. Since $-\dot\theta/\theta > 0$ is equal to the constant $g = \alpha N^\eta - \rho$, one can write $\theta(t) = \theta(0)e^{-gt}$. Then the expression for c is $c(t) = \theta(0)^{-1}e^{gt}$, and the equation for k becomes

$$\dot k = N^\eta k - \theta(0)^{-1}e^{gt}.$$

Since this is a linear differential equation, its solution can be found in any textbook. Using the fact that $k(0)$ is given, the solution is

$$k(t) = [\theta(0)(N^\eta - g)]^{-1}e^{gt} + \{k(0) - [\theta(0)(N^\eta - g)]^{-1}\}e^{(N^\eta)t}.$$

The undetermined value $\theta(0)$ in this expression is determined by imposing the transversality condition at infinity, $\lim_{t\to\infty} e^{-\rho t}\theta(t)k(t) = 0$. Since $\theta(t)$ grows like e^{-gt}, $e^{-\rho t}\theta(t)$ times the first term in the expression for k goes to zero for any choice of $\theta(0)$. Since $g - \rho = \alpha N^\eta$, the second term goes to zero only if

$$\theta(0) = [k(0)(N^\eta - g)]^{-1}.$$

It follows that both k and c grow at the rate $g = D_1 f(k,Nk) - \rho = \alpha N^\eta - \rho$.

In the equilibrium represented by this solution, interest rates are constant, $r = D_1 f(k,Nk) = \rho + g$. If one normalizes initial capital so that $K(0) = 1$, exponential growth in K implies production possibilities for individual firms at each point in time of the form $e^{gt}K^\alpha L^{1-\alpha}$. The wage rate grows at the rate g, and labor and capital receive a constant share $1 - \alpha$ of national income. The share of capital could be made to fall and the share of labor made to raise if the part of output due to private choices $K^\alpha L^{1-\alpha}$ were replaced by a constant elasticity production function.

It appears that this economy is observationally equivalent to one with constant exogenous technological change at the rate g, but they respond differently to interventions. It is best thought of as a model of endogenous technological change; and, as such, the rate of technological change will be influenced by any intervention. If a proportional tax τ on output is introduced, this tax will change the incentives to invest, reducing both $k(t)$ and the aggregate path $K(t)$. In the exogenous technological change model, the analog of $K(t)$ is exogenous and hence does not respond to the tax. The combined effect here is to reduce the rate of growth from $\alpha N^\eta - \rho$ to $(1 - \tau)\alpha N^\eta - \rho$. For large enough values of the tax rate, growth can even stop or reverse.

In this informal analysis, no explicit account is taken of the tax revenue—as if it were simply thrown away. The results are the same if one does the more sensible balanced budget tax exercise where the proceeds are rebated to consumers. This analysis requires only an additional parameter in the restricted aggregate maximization problem. Let P8(K,T) denote a problem that depends on an exogenously specified path for aggregate capital $K(t)$ and a path of per capita transfers $T(t)$ received by consumers:

P8(K,T) $\max \int_0^\infty u(c(t) + T(t))\, e^{-\rho t}\, dt$

$\quad$ s.t. $\quad \dot{k}(t) = (1 - \tau)f(k(t),K(t)) - c(t) \qquad$ for all $t \geq 0$

$\qquad\qquad k(t) \geq 0 \qquad$ for all $t \geq 0$.

In addition to the previous equilibrium condition $K(t) = Nk(t)$, this problem requires the balanced budget condition $\tau f(k(t),Nk(t)) = T(t)$. Proceeding as above, define a current-value Hamiltonian and take derivatives to get the differential equations

$$\frac{\dot{\theta}}{\theta} = \rho - \alpha(1 - \tau)k^{\alpha-1}K^\eta(t),$$

$$\dot{k} = (1 - \tau)k^\alpha K^\eta - \frac{1}{\theta} + T(t).$$

After imposing the equilibrium conditions, one finds that, as before, the growth rate is $\alpha(1 - \tau)N^\eta - \rho$.

The difference between exogenous and endogenous technological change is of more than academic interest. For example, one analysis of the tax reform act of 1986 conducted in the context of a model with exogenous technological change suggests that reductions in tax distortions between the household and corporate sectors and between short-lived and long-lived types of capital could lead to efficiency gains on the order of 1% of GNP per year (Jorgenson, 1987). Since growth in this model is exogenous, removing the investment tax credit and increasing the capital gains tax can have no effect on the rate of growth of labor augmenting technological progress, estimated to be on the order of 2% per year. It therefore has no long-run effect on the rate of growth of capital. For comparison, suppose that the rate of growth of the technology is endogenous and that the legislated change in the investment tax credit or the capital gains rate leads to changes in research and development and to venture capital availability that cause a reduction of 0.1% in the rate of growth of technology from 2% per year to 1.9% per year. In an equilibrium where the real interest is 5% and aggregate GNP grows at 3% per year[18] (roughly the figures used by Jorgenson), the present discounted value of future GNP is 1/0.020 = 50 times current GNP. An increase in GNP of 1% in all future periods due to reduced tax distortions would give wealth of 1.01/0.020 = 50.5 times pre-reform GNP, an increase in wealth worth half a year's GNP. But at the pre-reform interest rates, a fall in the growth of output from 3.0% to 2.9% reduces the present value of future GNP to 1.01/0.021 = 48.1 times pre-reform GNP, a loss compared to the pre-tax reform situation of nearly two years' worth of GNP. As one should have suspected, even small growth effects can swamp large increases in levels.

A reduction in the growth rate of 0.1% is quite significant from an economic point of view, but it is quite small compared with the range of variation in output growth rates observed in the data, even among apparently similar industrialized nations. Compare for example the behavior of the United Kingdom with that of Japan, or even of France, in the postwar period (see Table 2.3 and Figure 2.4.) Something causes these differences; and if policy choices account for even a small fraction of the variation, the indirect effects of policy on growth rates may completely dominate the direct effects that one can quantify in an exercise with an exogenous growth model.

One can argue about many of the specifics of this particular model of endogenous technology, but the main objective here is to illustrate the power of the methodology. It gives price paths for interest rates and wages; allows firms and consumers to make their investment and savings decisions at every point either based on expectations about the future or equivalently based on the entire array of securities returns that can be observed; lets the rate of what looks like exogenous technological change actually depend on endogenous investment decisions and assumes that individuals understand how this dependence operates; describes an equilibrium that is not Pareto optimal and therefore is not the solution to a simple Pareto optimization problem; gives an explicit dynamic formulation of one of Marshall's examples of external increasing returns; and permits a balanced budget analysis of taxes with both direct effects on individual choices and indirect effects on the rate of knowledge creation or technological change.

The discussion here has neglected dynamic programming methods and the Bellman equation, in part because a good introduction to those methods is available in Stokey, Lucas, and Prescott (1989). This choice also reflects the view that methods for characterizing suboptimal dynamic equilibria are easier to understand when they are stated in Lagrangian or Hamiltonian form rather than in the form of a functional equation for a policy function. One piece of evidence in support of this belief is the fact that the first complete analysis of suboptimal dynamic equilibria by Brock appeared in 1975, but policy function versions of this model did not appear for more than ten years. (See, for example, Danthine, Donaldson, and Smith, 1987.) Although it is less intuitive, the policy function approach has the advantage that it is better suited to the study of problems with uncertainty than are the variational methods described here. Despite the superficial differences, the basic ideas underlying these methods is the same. The procedure is to derive first-order conditions for individual maximization problems taking aggregate quantities as given, then relate the aggregate quantities from the individual choices. Equilibrium prices follow from the shadow prices from the individual maximization problem or equivalently from the marginal valuations implicit in these problems.

2.3. Recent Models of Growth

The models of growth that have been proposed in the last few years, like all general equilibrium models, can be characterized in terms of the assumptions they make on preferences, the technology, and the equilibrium concept. In all but one case, the equilibrium concept for the models described here is a complete markets competitive equilibrium or a complete markets competitive equilibrium with externalities. The exception, the Marshall-Young-Romer model, uses a notion of monopolistic competition, but its dynamic behavior is identical with that of a model of competitive equilibrium with externalities.

In terms of the technology, all of the models assume the existence of an aggregate production function $F(\cdot)$ that depends on a subset of the following list of inputs: services from physical capital K, labor services L from a person with a minimal level of schooling and training, services from additional human capital H, and measure of the technology or state of the art A. This production function can exhibit increasing returns or constant returns. In all cases except the Marshall-Young-Romer model, $F(\cdot)$ can be thought of as a description of the technology available to a representative firm. In the exceptional case, $F(\cdot)$ is a reduced form that reflects elements of the technology and of the market structure relating final goods producers and intermediate goods producers.

With the exception of the Barro-Becker model, all of the models use standard discounted Ramsey preferences and assume that the population growth rate is exogenously given. Becker and Barro extend the specification to give parents preferences over both consumption per child and the number of children.

2.3.1. The Arrow-Romer Model

The model of endogenous technological change described in the last section is a special case of the model of Romer (1983, 1986). The technology depends on physical capital K, physical labor L, and technology A. The production function $F(K,L,A)$ exhibits constant returns in K and L taken alone and therefore exhibits increasing returns when all three variables are taken together. Equilibrium is possible because K and L are the only factors that receive explicit compensation; A is like a public good. Movements in A are induced by assuming that private investments in capital induce increases in public knowledge A. For simplicity, the movements in A are assumed to take place one for one with movements in K, so the analysis can concentrate on a model with a single-state variable.[19]

Previous attempts at making technological change endogenous were made during the 1960s, but the presence of increasing returns always limited progress in the theory (see, for example, Shell, 1967; Phelps, 1966; von Weizsacker, 1966). The issue of aggregate increasing returns seems unavoidable in any discussion of endogenous technological change if one interprets technology in terms of the variable A: disembodied knowledge about things like mathematics, physics, chemistry, engineering, or manufacturing processes, that is contained in books, designs, blueprints, copyrights, patents, and so on. Knowledge like this can be used repeatedly at essentially zero marginal cost; and in this sense A is quite different from the skills H that are embodied in workers. A clear example of goods A and H that serve the same function is to think of H as the skills of an expert, A as a computer programmed expert system that makes the same decisions.

The expert system is expensive to create but essentially costless to replicate.

If one acknowledges the existence of this kind of input, increasing returns follows directly. One should be able to double output by doubling all tangible inputs and replicating all existing productive activities with no change in the underlying knowledge A. Once one allows A to vary as well, there must be increasing returns to scale. Whether or not it is actually possible to double all factors, this argument shows that it is mathematically impossible for all factors of production to be paid their marginal products. With increasing returns, this would more than exhaust total output. Models constructed during the 1960s resolved this by assuming that A came from the sky, or perhaps from the National Science Foundation, and therefore did not need to be compensated in the market. The suggestion here is that A is a side effect of investment but still does not receive direct compensation. Unlike the exogenous descriptions, this description makes accumulation of A responsive to economic incentives. An alternative that accomplishes the same thing is explored in Section 2.3.5; it supposes that A is compensated out of monopoly profits.

Arrow (1962) used the formulation considered here, assuming that improvements in the aggregate technology are the result of investment in physical capital.[20] He attributes the inspiration to Kaldor (1961). However, Arrow restricts attention to the case where the aggregate elasticity of output with respect to capital and knowledge ($\eta + \alpha$ in the example worked out above) is less than one. As a result, there is still a steady state. Arrow keeps growth going by adding exogenous population growth, but this is not completely satisfactory. Population growth becomes the only driving force in the model and plays a role analogous to exogenous technical change in the Solow model. The growth rate of per capita income increases directly with the growth rate of the population and goes to zero if population growth goes to zero. Neither savings rates nor taxes can influence the growth rate. A permanent increase in the share of output devoted to investment, arising for whatever reason, has no permanent effect on the rate of growth.

Arrow's restriction to steady-state analysis seems to have been made largely for technical reasons. One of the issues is how to make sure that the integral defined over $[0,\infty)$ in the objective function converges. If growth took place at a rate that was too fast, this could diverge. The second issue has to do with the equilibrium theory for the model. Arrow gives heuristic arguments about how the quantities he derives can be supported as a competitive equilibrium, but does so only for steady-state growth paths. Thus, for example, the interest rate he derives is a number rather than a function of time. Brock (1975, 1977) presented analyses of dynamic models with inflation and pollution distortions respectively, and in these papers he applied the equilibrium analysis to the entire path for the economy, not just to the steady state. The equilibrium analysis was heuristic and did not consider increasing returns and endogenous growth. Romer (1983) offered the first general formulation of the equilibrium theory behind this kind of model, with a statement and proof of a result like Proposition 2.1 above for dynamic models.

Romer (1983, 1986) actually went beyond the suggestion given above that the exponents α and η in the aggregate production function $k^\alpha K^\eta$ can sum to 1. Under a modification of the technology for converting consumption goods into investment goods, the analysis in these papers showed how a sum greater than 1 can be accommodated. In this case, explicit solutions are not possible, but the equilibrium can be studied using phase plane analysis. The rate of growth can be monotonically increasing over time rather than decreasing, as it must ultimately be when $\alpha + \eta$ is less than 1, or constant, as is the tendency when the sum is equal to 1. In this sense, the model can capture even the long-run trend behavior of growth rates demonstrated in Tables 2.1 and 2.2. The analysis also shows that when the sum is greater than 1, the resulting increasing marginal productivity of capital can overturn standard convergence results. Capital and investment might flow from countries with low per capita income and capital to more developed countries.

2.3.2. The Uzawa-Lucas Model

Using a different model, Lucas (1988) made a similar, but empirically more relevant point about the effects of increasing returns on flows between countries. Increasing returns can lead to pressure for migration even if there is full mobility of capital between countries.[21] The basic model depends on the variables K and H and builds on an earlier model of Uzawa (1965).[22] This kind of model can be thought of as allowing for physical labor L as well as human capital H, provided these two inputs are good substitutes. In particular, if they are perfect substitutes, H can simply be taken to be the sum of tangible and intangible human capital.

The input H resembles physical capital more closely than it does labor L or the technology A. In contrast to L, it is possible to increase H by investment, just as it is possible to increase K. In contrast to A, if one wants to replicate a productive activity, it is necessary to incur a cost to produce more H (that is, train additional workers). The model is therefore a two-capital good model, and it specifies two different sectors where investment can take place. The key sector for determining the rate of growth is the sector for producing new human capital. The specific technology assumed for the accumulation of H is linear in H, and this assumption simplifies the analysis a great deal. If H_1 is the amount of human capital devoted to the production of consumption goods and H_2 is the amount of human capital devoted to the production of new human capital, then $\dot{H}$ is given by

$$\dot{H} = \delta H_2.$$

Consumption goods and physical capital are produced in the first sector according to a production function $F(K,H_1)$. In the Uzawa formulation, this function exhibits constant returns to scale. Lucas suggests that there are increasing returns to scale, with external effects that are associated with human capital H. By analogy with the previous formulation, output can be written in the form $F(K,H,H)$, where in equilibrium, the aggregate stock of human capital H is given by $H(t) = NH(t)$. The externalities in the Arrow-Romer model arise from an indirect link between production of physical capital K and the technology A, which can be copied and used by all. In contrast, Lucas emphasizes direct interaction effects of human capital, of the kind that would arise from conversations between colleagues and co-workers. In his formulation of the model, Lucas makes the externality depend on the average level of human capital rather than on the total amount as used here; but as long as the population is held constant, these specifications are equivalent.

To write down the aggregate maximization problem for this economy, it is notationally convenient to define a variable, u in Lucas's notation, that is equal to the fraction of total human capital that is devoted to the production of physical goods. Thus, $u(t) = H(t)_1/H(t)$. The relevant parametric maximization problem for calculating equilibria in this model is

P9(**H**) $\max \int_0^\infty u(c(t))e^{-\rho t}dt$

s.t. $\dot{K}(t) = F(K(t),u(t)H(t),H(t)) - c(t),$

$\dot{H}(t) = \delta(1 - u(t))H(t).$

Calculating an equilibrium proceeds just as for the previous models. Taking the path for H(*t*) as given, write down the Hamiltonian for this system, which will depend on the two capital stocks, or state variables K and H, and two multipliers, or co-state variables. The maximum in the definition of the Hamiltonian will be over the choice of the control variables $c(t)$ and $u(t)$. Differentiate to get Hamiltonian equations, then substitute in the equilibrium condition $H(t) = NH(t)$.

This model does generate unbounded growth but does not rely on the aggregate increasing returns to do so. In Uzawa's original formulation of the model with no increasing returns and no external effects, there is also unbounded growth. What makes this possible are the assumptions of constant returns in the investment sector, combined with the assumption that all inputs can be accumulated so that there are no essential fixed factors. The form of constant returns in the human capital sector is particularly simple, $\dot{H} = \delta H_2$. This equation obviously exhibits no diminishing returns, and one accumulation equation of this type is enough to keep things going. If H grows without bound, its effect on the output equation is like the effect of exogenous technological change in the Solow model or exogenous population growth in the Arrow model: it raises the marginal productivity of physical capital over time, inducing physical capital accumulation. The asymptotic dynamics are essentially determined by the linearity of $\dot{H}$ in terms of H. Combined with constant elasticity utility functions, this feature makes the model behave like other models with linear production and constant elasticity utility. If the model starts from the correct ratio of K to H, it will grow at a constant rate forever. Starting from a different ratio of K to H will give transitory dynamics associated with the adjustment of the ratio toward the value consistent with aggregate growth at a constant rate. Growth approaches the constant rate asymptotically.

The Lucas model has all of these features in common with the Uzawa model. But the presence of increasing returns in the production of physical goods changes the implications of the Lucas model for wages. In the Uzawa model, K and H grow at the same rate. There is no deepening of physical capital relative to human capital, so the rental rate on both types of capital is constant. Payments per worker increase because human capital per worker increases; but the quality-adjusted wage, for example, the wage of a high school-educated male with no work force experience, will be constant over time. Once increasing returns are added, this is no longer true. The ratio of K to H will increase over time, with something resembling capital deepening taking place. Quality-adjusted wages will increase over time.

The cross-sectional implication of this model is that wages will be higher in a more developed country even if there is free capital mobility. To see why, consider two countries and suppose that aggregate output takes the form

$$F(K,H,\mathrm{K},\mathrm{H}) = \mathrm{K}^{\eta}\mathrm{H}^{\phi}(K^{\alpha}H^{1-\alpha}).$$

Here, K^{α} and $H^{1-\alpha}$ represent the usual private marginal productivities of nonhuman and human capital; K^{η} and H^{ϕ} represent possible external effects. Lucas focuses on the case of human capital externalities, but the point here is symmetric in the arguments H and K.

Let K_b, H_b, K_s, H_s denote the quantities of inputs in a big country b and a small country s. Equalization of interest rates across the two countries implies that

$$\alpha K_b^{\eta+\alpha-1}H_b^{1-\alpha+\phi} = \alpha K_s^{\eta+\alpha-1}H_s^{1-\alpha+\phi}.$$

In a model with constant returns, that is, where production is homogeneous of degree 1, the interest rate is homogeneous of degree 0; an increase in the scale of both arguments K and H leaves the interest rate unchanged. Since the production function here is homogeneous of degree $1 + \eta + \phi > 1$, the interest rate is homogeneous of degree $\eta + \phi > 0$. It follows that the ratio of K to H cannot be the same in the two countries. If it were, the interest rate would be higher in the big country. Rather, interest rate equalization implies

$$\frac{K_b}{H_b} > \frac{K_s}{H_s}.$$

But from this it follows that wages in the big country will be higher for two reasons. The scale effect increases wages because the wage rate will also be homogeneous of degree $\eta + \phi > 0$. The higher ratio of nonhuman capital to human capital in the big country will raise the wage even more. All that matters for this argument is that increasing returns be present, that is, that one of η or ϕ be bigger than 0, and that $\eta + \alpha$ and $\phi + 1 - \alpha$ be less than 1. It does not matter which good is associated with the positive externality.

In the neoclassical model, differences in income between different countries must be a reflection of differences in the capital–output ratio. These differences imply large differences in the rates of return to capital across countries. To emphasize just how large, suppose that the coefficient on capital is 0.4 and consider a country in Figure 2.5 with per capita income of one-tenth that in the United States. Using the formula $y = k^{0.4}$, it follows that capital in the United States must be larger by a factor $10^{2.5}$ and interest rates must be lower by a factor $10^{1.9}$. It would take an unbelievably high tax rate on foreign capital or probability of expropriation in the less-developed country for investment in the United States to be sensible if this were the only reason for the income differential. Going outside of the model proper, the income differential might be a reflection of differences in the technology in use in the two countries, but in this case there would seem to be comparable profits from exporting the technology to the small country. In this kind of model, the persistence of large income differentials seems to imply that there are large, persistent, unexploited profit opportunities.

The Uzawa model explains income differences with no unexploited profit opportunities. Low-income countries have less of both K and H, but in the same ratio as high-income countries. In a sense this goes too far. There is little evidence of overwhelming barriers to capital flows, but there are binding constraints on migration. The Lucas model reaches an intermediate conclusion. Rates of return to capital can be equalized across countries; but if they are, payments to human capital will be higher in the high-income country, and workers would be better off if they could move there.

If increasing returns are present and if barriers to flows of both capital and labor are removed, both capital and workers would move to the high-income region. This may seem implausible at first, until one contemplates the distribution of capital and workers within a country where no barriers are present. In fact, they are not spread evenly across the available land, as a constant returns model would imply. As Lucas emphasizes, they are highly concentrated in a few locations, cities. In less-developed countries where communication and transportation are costly, this process of concentration in just a few locations or even a single location is even more pronounced than it is in developed countries.

2.3.3. Linear Growth Models

Following up on Lucas's interpretation of the Uzawa model in terms of human capital, King and Rebelo (1988) argued that the version of this model with no increasing returns or externalities is of interest on its own.

They focus on the variables H and K and assume that $F(K,H)$ exhibits constant returns. This approach is useful, they argue, because a stochastic version provides a tractable framework for analyzing aggregate time series data that can accommodate both short-run business cycle variation and long-run trend behavior. Virtually all other theoretical frameworks for data analysis do not treat one of these sources of variation in the data seriously. Traditional business cycle models remove the trend behavior by some ad hoc means. Growth models average out the business cycle variation.

The full force of their argument is directed at macroeconomics. For the study of growth theory, throwing out the high-frequency variation in the data may be inefficient, but there is little evidence that how one does this will prejudice the conclusions one draws. Regardless of how one chooses to smooth the data, the long-run trends are clear. In contrast, the inferences for business cycle frequencies are more delicate. The answers to important questions about business cycles are often highly sensitive to how one detrends the time series. Moreover, most of the variation in aggregate data (measured in the sense of the magnitude of the matrix $X'X$ in a regression equation) comes from the trend behavior of the series. Throwing away the trends may sacrifice more information than throwing away the high frequencies.

One of the attractive properties that King and Rebelo emphasize about a stochastic version of the Uzawa model is that it can generate aggregate time series that have a unit root, that is, are stationary in first differences. This result contrasts with that for the Solow model with exogenous exponential technological change, in which aggregate series are stationary after exponential detrending. Now these two alternative methods for detrending data can be treated symmetrically from a theoretical point of view as well as from an econometric point of view.

The Uzawa model is a linear growth model in the sense that the rate of growth of the key state variable H is linear in H. Rebelo (1988) observes that this kind of linearity can be generalized to the case where H is a vector of state variables and the rate of growth of each component of H is a constant returns to scale function of H. The linearity of these models is part of what makes them so easy to work with. They have a balanced growth path along which the growth rate (or the expected growth rate in a stochastic version) is constant. Because the model does not rely on any form of increasing returns, the equilibrium is Pareto optimal and can be found by solving a social planning problem.

Jones and Manuelli (1988) go one step further and observe that linearity is not necessary for Pareto optimal, persistent growth. All that is required is asymptotic linearity. For example, in a one state variable neoclassical model, let production take a constant returns to scale form like $F(K,L) = K^\alpha L^{1-\alpha} + \rho K$ or $F(K,L) = [L^\phi + \rho^\phi K^\phi]^{1/\phi}$ for $\phi > 0$. As always, let $f(k) = F(K,1)$ denote per capita output. For each of these functional forms, per capita output is approximately of the form $f(k) = a + \rho k$ as k gets large. This formulation lets labor be a fixed factor, and the presence of this fixed factor implies that the marginal product of capital falls as the amount of capital increases. Like any model with a falling marginal product of capital, this kind of model will tend to have a rate of growth that decreases with the accumulation of capital. The observation made here is that the marginal product of capital is bounded away from zero, so the lower bound for the growth rate can be positive. During the 1960s, these kinds of models were viewed as unattractive because they require that the share of capital in total income increase over time, asymptotically approaching 1, but Jones and Manuelli argue that it is possible to reinterpret capital as a combination of physical capital and human capital and that the usual measure of income shares is not relevant.

The linear growth models are less ambitious than the models that try to explain the increasing long-run trend in growth rates, the presence of migration, or the effects of international trade or population growth on output growth. Their advantage is that they generate growth in very simple settings without relying on exogenous technological change, and for some purposes this advantage may be quite important. In the macroeconomic application pursued by King and Rebelo, the simplicity of the model is crucial. Linear models may increasingly be used as a complement to a Solow-style model with exogenous technological change whenever an economist wants to test a proposition in the context of a baseline model with growth.

2.3.4. The Krugman-Lucas Model

The second model in the Lucas paper is very similar to a model that was first worked out by Paul Krugman (1988). These models place less emphasis on the details of growth and more on the interaction of growth with trade. The key point here is that increasing returns can dramatically overturn the usual presumptions about the positive and normative effects of trade.

As described by Krugman, the model is stated in terms of labor L and the technology A and assumes that aggregate production $F(L,A)$ exhibits increasing returns. Like the Arrow-Romer model, the benefits of increases in A are enjoyed by all, so the increasing returns are external. Since there is no capital, A cannot be a function of investment. Here, it is assumed to depend on previous output, which is equivalent to making it depend on labor inputs. The twist on the model here is that there are many possible goods that can be produced, each with its own level of the technology A_i. For simplicity, output of good i is $y_i = A_i L_i$, and the technological coefficient A_i evolves according to a linear differential equation in previous production:[23]

$$\dot{A}_i = -\delta_i y_i.$$

Lucas uses an equivalent formulation in terms of labor L and the human capital H. Output of good i depends on the amount of human capital (H_i/L_i) per worker in the i industry and is multiplied by the amount of labor devoted to production of this good. Human capital H grows with previous output, but the effects are purely external. In either form, this captures what most economists think of when they describe learning by doing.

The implications for trade and welfare follow from the fact that the decisions about production made in the market will depend only on the relative magnitudes of the input coefficients, A_i or H_i/L_i in different countries, with no regard for the learning or growth coefficients δ_i. Suppose for simplicity that there are two goods. The good in which a country has cost advantage relative to a trading partner may not be the good with the high rate of learning, that is, a large δ_i. Under appropriate assumptions about preferences, it will be better to be in an industry with rapid learning and rapidly increasing output. In this case, opening a country to trade, which can lead to specialization in the industry with a slow rate of learning, can make a country worse off than it would be under autarky, where domestic production of both kinds of goods will take place.

This model has an obvious appeal at a time of increased tension over patterns of trade. It also suggests the direction that models of growth must pursue if they are to have anything to say about growth and trade. There must be more than one good in a model, and there must be some reason to trade. The model of increasing returns, dynamics, and external effects used here is simple and effective for pointing out the potential for conflict that is present if there are increasing returns, but it needs to be elaborated before it can address questions about issues like private savings and investment.

2.3.5. The Marshall-Young-Romer Model

One model that tries to introduce many goods and maintain an explicit dynamic model of accumulation is Romer (1987). This model differs from the others that contemplate increasing returns because it does not rely on external effects to support a decentralized equilibrium. Rather, it uses a model of monopolistic competition. Nonetheless, the dynamic equilibrium can be computed using the same techniques as those used for computing the externality and tax distortion models.

This model is based on the second of two sources of external economies cited by Marshall (1961), and emphasized by Allyn Young (1928). They suggested that trade among different firms offering unique specialized goods causes a form of increasing returns that is external to individual firms. The degree of specialization, or equivalently, the number of different firms that are available at any point in time or location, is limited by the presence of fixed costs. In this model, these different goods are assumed to be intermediate inputs into production, and the technology is such that having more available goods is useful. Surely a large part of what distinguishes Silicon Valley from a crossroads in Nebraska is the set of specialized goods and services immediately available for sale at each point. If you wanted to set up a business to produce new computer chips, land in Nebraska would be cheaper, but just try to find a firm nearby with the right equipment for baking, etching, and testing silicon wafers. If there were no fixed costs, one could imagine little infinitesimal versions of such firms spread smoothly over the entire surface area of the United States (or the world).

Although Marshall and Young choose to describe specialization in terms of a competitive equilibrium with externalities, it is now clear that a more rigorous way to capture the effects they had in mind is in a model with fixed costs. In an equilibrium with nonnegative profits, price must exceed marginal cost to be able to recover these fixed costs, so the model must therefore contemplate some form of market power.

Models of price setting behavior are always more difficult to describe than models of price taking behavior, but the basic idea can be described heuristically. Suppose that output of aggregate consumption goods can be written as a function $Y(\mathbf{x},L)$ that depends on labor L and on a list of intermediate inputs $\mathbf{x} = \{x_i\}_{i=0}^{\infty}$ that is potentially infinitely long. This input list describes all the inputs that could conceivably be used in production. One simple form for Y is

$$Y(\mathbf{x},L) = L^{1-\alpha} \sum_{i=1}^{\infty} x_i^{\alpha}.$$

This functional form is attractive primarily because of its simplicity.[24] At any point in time, only a finite number of goods x_i will be available for use by such firms, but the list of potential goods is unbounded. Because Y is a constant returns to scale production function, the industry that buys goods x_i and labor and sells final output Y will be a conventional competitive industry. This form of production is important because it captures the idea that there is a large and continually growing variety of inputs into production and that these inputs are not close substitutes. Increasing the quantity of one input does not reduce the marginal productivity of the others, so increasing the set of available inputs is always useful.

To avoid issues about integer constraints, it is easier to take a continuous version of this kind of production. Thus, suppose that the range of goods can be drawn from the entire real line, so $x(i)$ is now a function defined on $[0,\infty)$ and output Y takes the form

$$Y(\mathbf{x},L) = L^{1-\alpha} \int_0^{\infty} x(i)^{\alpha} di.$$

As before, the set of values for which $x(i)$ is greater than 0 will be finite at any point in time. For simplicity, one can denote this set as an interval $[0,M]$. To see how output increases with the range of inputs that are available, suppose that all intermediate inputs could be produced at a constant cost of 1 measured in terms of forgone resources. Then Z units of resources could be used to produce an input list $x_i = Z/M$ for all i between 0 and M. This would yield output

$$Y = L^{1-\alpha} M(Z/M)^{\alpha} = L^{1-\alpha} Z^{\alpha} M^{1-\alpha}.$$

Holding the amount of initial resources Z constant, output could be increased indefinitely by increasing the range M of different specialized inputs that are used.

What keeps this from being relevant is the presence of fixed costs. Producing new goods is assumed to involve a fixed cost, and this constraint limits the feasible range of goods that can be produced. Average cost curves will then be U-shaped, and for simplicity are assumed to be the same for all the different types of inputs. Ultimately, one would like a formulation that distinguishes new inputs from old inputs; but for the purposes here, it is easier to preserve the symmetry among the inputs. The fixed costs in the production of the goods x_i mean that the firms supplying these goods will not be price takers. A firm selling an intermediate input i will be the only firm producing that input and will explicitly face a downward sloping derived demand for the input from the competitive firms that produce the final output goods. The equilibrium will be one in which entry of additional firms producing additional intermediate inputs continues until profits for all firms are zero. Given some level of the resources Z devoted to the production of intermediate inputs, the equilibrium will have positive output for a finite range of inputs of length M. By symmetry, the same quantity $\bar{x}$ of each of these inputs will be produced. Given an explicit functional form for the cost function for producing x, the values for M and $\bar{x}$ can be explicitly calculated in terms of Z by solving the profit maximization problem for each of the individual monopolists and then allowing entry until zero profit is achieved.

Suppose that one chooses units such that 1 is the average cost of producing a unit of x from forgone consumption that is achieved in equilibrium. Then Z, $\bar{x}$, and M are related by $\bar{x} = x_i = Z/M$ for all i, and output takes the form

$$(2.15) \qquad Y = L^{1-\alpha}M(Z/M)^\alpha = L^{1-\alpha}Z^\alpha M^{1-\alpha}.$$

Now ask what would happen if the quantity of Z were to double. Consideration of the zero profit conditions shows that twice as many intermediate goods-producing firms would enter, demanding twice as much of the primary resource, with the per firm quantity $\bar{x}$ and the average cost Z/M left unchanged. (This simple result follows from the additive separability of the production function in the different intermediate goods.) Thus, the equilibrium quantity of goods M is proportional to Z. If one chooses units such that $\bar{x}$ is also equal to 1, then $M = Z$. Thus, the reduced-form expression for aggregate output in terms of the primary resource Z and labor L is

$$(2.16) \qquad Y = L^{1-\alpha}Z.$$

This equation describes a kind of reduced-form production function. It relates final output to L and to the amount of resources Z devoted to production of intermediate goods. It closely resembles the previous descriptions of aggregate output as an increasing returns to scale function of capital and labor. This resemblance extends to the interpretation of this kind of function in terms of externalities.

Suppose that the good Z merely represents cumulative forgone consumption, that is, resources that could have been consumed but were instead devoted to producing goods x_i. Thus, the evolution equation for Z is

(2.17) $\dot{Z} = Y - c.$

Suppose preferences take the usual discounted form in continuous time.

$$\int_0^\infty u(c)e^{-\rho t}dt.$$

The social planning problem for this economy would be to maximize these preferences subject to the constraints imposed by Equations (2.16) and (2.17), but the monopolistically competitive equilibrium described here will not support this optimum for reasons that appear to be very similar to those for the equilibrium with externalities. One can show (and a demonstration takes more than just the kind of hand waving offered here) that in this equilibrium, agents forgo current consumption in favor of future consumption as if they take account of the direct effect that this has on output—that is, taking account of the term Z^α in Equation (2.15)—but without taking account of the indirect effect this has on the range of goods produced M. In this sense, it is just like the externality model where agents choose $K(t)$, taking K(t) as given.

Using this intuition, it is possible to explicitly solve for the dynamic equilibrium with monopolistic competition. Mathematically, it turns out to be identical to problem P7 solved in Section 2.2.4. Formally, one chooses a path for $Z(t)$ to maximize utility, taking a path for $M(t)$ as given. One then imposes the equilibrium condition that $M(t) = Z(t)$. Note that this is just what one would expect from the previously noted result in Hart (1980). The monopolistically competitive equilibrium may not get the set of goods that are produced right, but it is optimal, taking the set of goods as given.

In the equilibrium for this model, growth takes place at a constant exponential rate. This rate of growth is too low relative to the rate a social planner could achieve, and it increases with any intervention that increases savings. The main value of this model is that it offers a different interpretation from the previous one, which relies on growth with spillovers of knowledge. What keeps growth going and avoids the problem of diminishing returns to capital accumulation is the continual introduction of new goods. The models can be related in the sense that the fixed cost in the introduction of a new good could be research and development costs needed to produce the knowledge *A* required to make the physical good. Thus, for producers of final output, one can still think of knowledge as an input into his production, but now it comes embodied in new inputs and can no longer be copied for free. In the aggregate, savings still has social benefits that are larger than the private benefits, but here the distortion arises because of departures from price taking, not from externalities or true spillovers. For comparisons across regions or countries, the relevant measure of the area over which one firm's actions affect other firms is no longer defined by how far knowledge can travel (the effect emphasized in the Arrow-Romer model and the Krugman version of the learning-by-doing model) nor by the necessity of direct contact between co-workers and colleagues (as in the Lucas models). Rather, it is determined by transportation costs and by how far goods can travel.

This model has immediate implications for trade. Removing barriers to trade increases total output in each country and, more important, raises the returns to savings and the amount of savings in each country and therefore raises growth rates in each country. Compared with the learning-by-doing models of Krugman and Lucas, it is more suggestive of the gains from trade than the potential for conflict. Nonetheless, if transportation costs are high, there is still some potential for conflict or rivalry. If all goods produced anywhere can be traded worldwide, all regions benefit equally from the introduction of goods in any location. As a result, advanced countries have no natural advantage over less-advanced countries, and the latter should tend to catch up with the former. On the other hand, if there is a significant range of goods that are too expensive to transport and trade outside of a limited area, developed areas will tend to have a built-in advantage over the less-developed areas. Under these circumstances, convergence will fail. Starting from symmetric positions for two different countries, the country that can first take the lead may have a permanent advantage over the other.

This model is useful for illustrating the kind of behavior that can arise in a model that departs from the assumption of competitive behavior, but in some ways it is too simple. According to this model, there is a one-for-one trade-off between introducing a new intermediate input in production and increasing the quantity produced of existing goods. Either kind of increased output merely requires additional capital in the form of forgone consumption. A more realistic formulation would take seriously the idea that new goods embody new knowledge and therefore require explicit research before they can be produced. This extension is pursued in Romer (1988). The main difference introduced by letting the fixed cost be a research cost instead of a capital cost is that it is knowledge A rather than capital K that is most seriously underaccumulated. The policy prescription suggested in this case is to subsidize research rather than physical capital accumulation. The presence of pure knowledge A also raises the possibility of knowledge spillovers that was not present in the model outlined above. Despite these differences, many of the predictions carry over. In particular, increases in the degree of worldwide integration increase the rate of introduction of new goods, and in this sense, trade encourages growth.

2.3.6. Endogenous Population Growth and Preferences for Children

All of the models so far neglect population growth as an endogenous variable. The key issue in modeling population growth is how to value the trade-off between more goods per person and more people. In the optimal planning literature of the 1960s and 1970s, three different strategies for dealing with a growing population were suggested. Let C_t denote aggregate consumption at time t, and let N_t denote the population. A planner could maximize the discounted sum of a utility function depending on C_t, $U = \Sigma \beta^t u(C_t)$, ignoring the size of the population. Alternatively, the planner could maximize some notion of average utility, letting $u(\cdot)$ depend on per capita consumption rather than on aggregate consumption, $U = \Sigma \beta^t u(C_t/N_t)$. Finally, the planner could maximize some notion of total utility received by individuals, multiplying individual utility $u(C_t/N_t)$ by the population N_t, $U = \Sigma \beta^t N_t u(C_t/N_t)$.

For the qualitative features of a model in which the path for N_t is taken as given, the choice does not matter very much. However, once population growth is allowed to be endogenous, these different specifications matter a great deal. Consider the thought experiment of holding aggregate consumption C_t constant and freely choosing N_t for each of these specifications of the objective function. In the first case, N_t has no effect. In the second, it is optimal to drive N_t to zero. In the third, it is optimal to drive N_t to infinity [so long as $u(\cdot)$ is strictly concave]. When production is added to the model, these conclusions are modified only slightly. The first case becomes like a model of a profit-maximizing slave owner who sells output C_t. Additional bodies are valuable as long as they are net producers of output. In the second and third cases, N_t will generally tend toward zero or infinity asymptotically. As long as the question of how people should be valued is put in moral or ethical terms, it is hard to know how to come to any resolution of this question. Maybe population really "ought" to go to zero or infinity.[25]

As macroeconomists pushed the equilibrium interpretation of Ramsey-type models, emphasizing the idea that the objective function comes from the preferences of individuals, the treatment of population growth became more positive and less normative. Nerlove (1974) was one of the first economists to suggest that the emerging theory of household decision-making be used to examine choices about fertility and that this analysis could be applied to questions about long-run growth. Razin and Ben-Zion (1975) gave one of the first explicit treatments of this approach. To do this, they had to face the same questions about functional form raised above, but in doing so, they were guided by evidence on the preferences of parents. Their solution was to take the second form, so what mattered was the average utility of future generations. By itself, this would imply that families would choose to have very few children, but they also added the idea that parents get direct utility from the presence of children. If n_t represents the reproduction rate of the family, the utility U_t of the parental decision-making unit at generation t takes the form $U_t = v(c_t,n_t) + \beta U_{t+1}$.[26] U_{t+1} is the utility of each of the children in the next generation. Thus, consumption c_{t+1} per child (or really per parental decision-making unit) rather than consumption C_{t+1} is what enters in $v_{t+1} = v(c_{t+1},n_{t+1})$. Because of the recursive form used here, this functional form says that parents care about the utility from per capita consumption of all of their descendants. Solving forward gives an implicit form of preferences for the head of a family at time zero,

$$U_0 = \sum \beta^t v(C_t/N_t,n_t).$$

Population does not go to zero because the direct value of children to parents from the term n_t in $v(c_t,n_t)$ offsets the increases in per capita quantities that reductions in family size would permit.

Robert Barro and Gary Becker extend this analysis to allow for the possibility that having more children has value that goes beyond the direct consumption value (Barro and Becker, 1986; Becker and Barro, 1987). In effect, these authors argue that parents may care not only about whether or not their children are successful and happy (that is, have C_t/N_t large) but also about how many happy and successful children they have. What Barro and Becker propose is an intermediate solution between case two above, which discounts $u(C_t/N_t)$, and case three, which discounts $N_t u(C_t/N_t)$. Suppose, they suggest, that a parent receives utility of the form

$$U_t = v(c_t) + \beta n_t^\chi U_{t+1},$$

where χ can lie between the values 0 and 1, which represent the two extreme forms of the objective function described above. In principle, their formulation can also accommodate a direct effect of n_t on current utility $v(\cdot)$, but much of their analysis ignores this effect since it is no longer needed to keep n_t from going to zero. When these preferences are solved forward, they imply infinite horizon preferences of the form

$$U_0 = \sum \beta^t N_t^\chi v(c_t),$$

where $c_t = C_t/N_t$ is per capita consumption. In the special case where the growth rate of the population n can be taken to be a constant, this reduces to

(2.18) $\qquad U_0 = \sum (\beta n^\chi)^t v(c_t).$

Both the Barro and Becker and the Razin and Ben-Zion formulations introduce a positive effect of n_t, but it makes a difference how this dependence enters. In the Barro-Becker preferences, changing the rate of reproduction is mathematically like changing the discount rate, and this property can lead to important effects on growth that are not present in the Razin and Ben-Zion model. To see this, confront the preferences in Equation (2.18) with a linear technology that depends only on physical capital K_t. Thus,

$$C_t = \rho K_t - K_{t+1}.$$

Restated in per capita terms, this expression becomes

(2.19) $\qquad c_t = \rho k_t - n_t k_{t+1}.$

If n is treated as a constant, it is a simple matter to use the techniques from Section 2.2 to maximize the objective (2.18) subject to the constraint (2.19). Call this problem P9, and let $\mathscr{L}9$ denote the associated Lagrangian:

$$\mathscr{L}9(\mathbf{K}, \boldsymbol{\lambda}) = \sum_{t=0}^{\infty} (\beta n^\chi)^t v(c_t) + \lambda_t[\rho k_t - n k_{t+1} - c_t].$$

Differentiating this expression with respect to k_t, it follows that the multiplier λ will grow at the rate n/ρ. The first-order condition for per capita consumption becomes $v'(c_t) = \lambda_t (\beta n^x)^{-t}$. Thus, $v'(\cdot)$ will fall over time and c_t will increase if the inequality

$$\frac{n^{1-x}}{\rho\beta} < 1$$

is satisfied. This result suggests that whether or not there is accumulation and growth on a per capita basis depends on the size of n, which now must be determined endogenously. This effect can lead to an interesting connection between per capita income growth and population growth. A value of the population growth rate n that is low will lead to unlimited accumulation and growth in per capita terms. A value that is too high will cause dissavings.

This kind of possibility is exploited by Tamura (1988) in a paper using a more complicated technology that depends on human capital accumulation instead of physical capital accumulation and that takes account of the fact that there are important time costs to raising children. Thus, the larger the human capital of the parents, the higher the cost of a child. In that model, the determination of the population growth rates $\{n_t\}_{t=0}^{\infty}$ depends on the initial stock of human capital per person. If it is too low, it is optimal to have high values of n_t and therefore to dissave. If the initial stock of human capital is above some critical level, it is optimal to have the growth rates n_t be small and to accumulate more and more human capital per capita. Thus, depending on the initial conditions, one family or country might be stuck in a permanent state of low per capita income with no per capita income growth and high population growth, while another might be in an equilibrium with low population growth and high per capita income growth. This description is suggestive of the observed pattern of cross-sectional variation in population growth rates and the level of per capita income (recall Figure 2.8) and justifies further work with this form of preferences.

2.4. Conclusion

The facts described in Section 2.1 do not exhaust the set of observations that are relevant for growth; nor do the models described in Section 2.3 exhaust the set of theoretical issues that are relevant. For example, observations about the growth rates of individual firms and industrial organization are directly relevant for any model with increasing returns or spillovers of information; these observations are modeled in Prescott and Boyd (1988). Growth driven by the creation of new goods and invention are closely related to the legal status of patents, issues that are modeled in Judd (1985). Interactions between product innovation and population size are considered in Schmitz (1986). The fact that some goods disappear as others are introduced is unquestionably a feature of long-run growth, one that is captured in Stokey (1986). The fact that goods can be ranked, with some of them introduced only after their prerequisites are available, is modeled in Vassilakis (1986).

Even within the restricted set of facts considered in Section 2.1, none of the models described in Section 2.3 is dominant. Each model emphasizes a different issue, and only after more experience with the models and the data will it become clear what the most important issues are and how these issues can be combined into a single model. As they stand, the models merely suggest how theory can begin to address the questions suggested by these facts: What explains growth rates that over the course of a century have increased per capita output by a factor of 10 or more in the most advanced economies in the world? Does a high rate of investment cause a high rate of growth or vice versa? Why are growth rates so different in different countries? What influence does international trade have on growth rates? Why has fertility fallen so dramatically in some countries but not in others? Why does labor try to move toward capital instead of vice versa? And most important of all, what policies influence the rate of per capita income growth in a country?

These are the kinds of questions that someone who is not an academic economist would like to have answers to, and if economists are to earn their keep, they must ultimately be able to address them. Twenty years ago, very little explicit attention was given to these questions, but this does not mean that the growth theory of this era was useless. As suggested in the introduction and in the double entendre in the title, growth theory was engaged in intellectual capital accumulation. Because of the insights developed into the connection between equilibrium theory, constrained optimization, and convex analysis, there now exist tractable general equilibrium models that economists can use for thinking about these questions and for analyzing data in an attempt to answer them. More and better models will no doubt follow, as will a consensus about what the right answers are.

Appendix. Proof of Proposition 2.1

Competitive Equilibrium Implies Saddle Point

Suppose that $(\hat{x}, \hat{p})$ is a competitive equilibrium. Since $\hat{x}$ is a solution to $PC(\hat{p}, \pi)$ and since the Slater condition holds for this problem, one can apply the necessary conditions from the Kuhn-Tucker theorem to conclude that there exists some $\hat{\gamma} \geq 0$ such that $(\hat{x}, \hat{\gamma})$ is a saddle point of the Lagrangian $\mathscr{L}C$ for PC $(\hat{p}, \pi)$:[27]

$$\mathscr{L}C1(x, \gamma) = U(x_1, x_2) + \gamma[\pi + \hat{p}_1(e - x_1) - \hat{p}_2 x_2].$$

Thus, $(\hat{x}_1, \hat{x}_2)$ maximizes $\mathscr{L}C_{\hat{\gamma}}(x)$. Similarly, one can (trivially) invoke the Kuhn-Tucker theorem for the problem of the firm to conclude that $\hat{x}_3$ maximizes the Lagrangian $\mathscr{L}F(\hat{p})$, where

$$\mathscr{L}F(x) = \hat{p}_2 f(x_3) - \hat{p}_1 x_3.$$

This will still be true if one replaces $\hat{p}$ by $\hat{\gamma}\hat{p}$. Since $\mathscr{L}1(x, \gamma\hat{p}) = \mathscr{L}C(x, \gamma) + \gamma\mathscr{L}F(x)$, it follows that $\hat{x}$ maximizes $\mathscr{L}1_{\hat{p}}(\cdot)$. Since $\hat{\gamma}$ minimizes $\mathscr{L}C_{\hat{x}}(\gamma)$ over nonnegative scalars, it follows that

$$\hat{\gamma}[\pi + \hat{p}_1(e - \hat{x}_1) - \hat{p}_2 \hat{x}_2] = 0.$$

Combining the preceding statement with the fact that

$$\pi = \Pi(\hat{p}) = \hat{p}_2 f(\hat{x}_3) - \hat{p}_1 \hat{x}_3,$$

implies that

$$\hat{\gamma}[\hat{p}_2(f(\hat{x}_3) - \hat{x}_2) + \hat{p}_1(e - \hat{x}_1 - \hat{x}_3)] = 0.$$

Since the expression on the left-hand side contains all the terms from $\mathscr{L}1(\hat{x}, \hat{\gamma}\hat{p})$ containing $\hat{\gamma}\hat{p}$, $\hat{\gamma}\hat{p}$ minimizes $\mathscr{L}1_{\hat{x}}(\cdot)$. Then $(\hat{x}, \hat{\gamma}\hat{p})$ is a saddle point of $\mathscr{L}1(x, \lambda)$.

Saddle Point Implies Competitive Equilibrium

Now suppose that $(\hat{x}, \hat{p})$ is a saddle point of $\mathscr{L}1(x, \lambda)$. From the definition of $\mathscr{L}1$, the constraints on the problem must be satisfied. Thus, $e - \hat{x}_1 - \hat{x}_3 \geq 0$, $f(\hat{x}_3) - \hat{x}_2 \geq 0$. This result implies that supply in each market will be greater than demand. It remains to show that $\hat{x}$ solves $PF(\hat{p})$ and $PC(\hat{p}, \pi)$, where $\pi = \Pi(\hat{p})$. By the sufficient conditions from the Kuhn-Tucker theorem, it is sufficient to show that there is a value γ such that $(\hat{x}, \gamma)$ is a saddle point to $\mathscr{L}C(x, \gamma)$ and that $\hat{x}$ maximizes $\mathscr{L}F(\cdot)$. Since $\mathscr{L}C(x, 1) +$

$\mathscr{L}F(x)$ is equal to $\mathscr{L}1(x,\hat{p})$, and since $\mathscr{L}C_\gamma(\cdot)$ depends on only the first two components of x, whereas $\mathscr{L}F(\cdot)$ depends on only the third component of x, it follows immediately that $\hat{x}$ maximizes $\mathscr{L}C_{\gamma=1}(\cdot)$ and that $\hat{x}$ maximizes $\mathscr{L}F(\cdot)$. Since $\hat{p}$ minimizes $\mathscr{L}1_{\hat{x}}(\cdot)$,

$$\pi + \hat{p}_1(e - \hat{x}_1) - \hat{p}_2\hat{x}_2 = \hat{p}_2(f(\hat{x}_3) - \hat{x}_2) + \hat{p}_1(e - \hat{x}_1 - \hat{x}_3) = 0,$$

so $\gamma = 1$ minimizes $\mathscr{L}C_{\hat{x}}(\cdot)$. Thus, $(\hat{x},1)$ is a saddle point for $\mathscr{L}C$. $\diamond$

Acknowledgments

In the preparation of this chapter I received helpful comments from Robert Barro, Michael Dotsey, Marvin Goodfriend, Robert King, Sergio Rebelo, Danyang Xie, and the students at the universities of Rochester and Chicago. Support from National Science Foundation grant #SES8618325 is gratefully acknowledged.

Notes

1. Anyone interested in a more detailed overview of the literature on growth through the 1970s can consult Hahn and Matthews (1964), Stiglitz and Uzawa (1969), Burmeister and Dobell (1970), Solow (1970), Hahn (1972), or Jones (1975).
2. The data for productivity used here attempt to track the private business sector data used in the postwar sample as closely as possible. For the postwar period, the source is the same as that for Figure 2.1. From 1890 to 1950, data for the private business sector are taken from Kendrick (1961). Prior to 1890, the basic data on output come from the work of Robert Gallman but must be retrieved from three different sources: summaries given in Gallman (1966), augmented with raw data from Gallman's work sheets that are published in Friedman and Schwartz (1982), and an estimate for growth during the decade of the 1860s reported in Kuznets (1971). Data on employment are from Lebergott (1966). In this early period, average hours worked per employee are assumed to have remained constant. To the extent that average hours in this period fell, as they did in subsequent periods, the reported rates of productivity growth are too low. Population data for the per capita series are taken from Maddison (1982).
3. The basic data are from the published source, but the actual data used here go beyond these in two senses. First, the published article gives data only through 1980, whereas the data used here came from a tape that was updated to include 1981. Second, the estimates of relative income for the African countries in the article and on the tape were recently found to have been overstated to a significant extent. Thus, the data used here for African countries make use of a rough correction provided by Robert Summers. By the

time this chapter appears in print, a much more comprehensive revision of the basic Summers and Heston data set will be available in the March 1988 issue of the *Review of Income and Wealth.*

4. Another way to address the question of convergence is to consider changes over time in the world distribution of income, an approach that was followed by Summers, Heston, and Kravis (1984). Their finding that world inequality income did not decrease in the postwar years is another way to describe the result illustrated in Figures 2.5 and 2.6.

5. This point was made with different data in Romer (1986) and is dismissed as unimportant in a footnote in Baumol (1986). Delong (1987) made the same point, but rather than starting in 1950, started in 1870 as Baumol did. This change makes little difference, for all of the action is in the postwar period. As was shown in Abramowitz (1986), even in Maddison's sample of countries the convergence with the United States took place only after 1950. From 1870 to 1950, the United States pulled ahead of the other countries. Even within the remaining set of countries, there was no tendency for income to converge.

6. For proofs of these and other assertions made in the text, see Rockafellar (1972).

7. Throughout, $Df(x)$ will denote the derivative of a function defined on $\mathbb{R}^n$ and $D_i f(x)$ will denote the partial derivative of f with respect to its ith argument. For functions defined on the real line, the usual prime notation for a derivative, $f'(x)$, will generally be used.

8. There is a technical point here. Concave functions are always continuous on the interior of the domain on which they are defined. The assumption of continuity here is necessary only to ensure that these functions do not have any jumps on any boundary points in Ω.

9. Here $\mathbb{R}^2_{++}$ denotes the strictly positive orthant in $\mathbb{R}^2$. This domain is used instead of the nonnegative orthant to accommodate functions like logarithmic utility that are widely used in practice. What follows could easily be modified to allow for consumption equal to zero.

10. See Ekeland and Teman (1976) for a general treatment of convex analysis and the Kuhn-Tucker theorem in an infinite dimensional space. Araujo and Scheinkman (1983) applied this kind of framework to derive necessary conditions for a continuous-time problem. Romer and Shinotsuka (1988) gave an explicit derivation of a Lagrangian for this kind of discrete-time model.

11. Specifying what the Slater condition is here is complicated, because one must define an interior point in an infinite dimensional space. For a general discussion of this issue, see Romer and Shinotsuka (1988). For this particular problem, let $(\hat{c}_0, \hat{k})$ denote the optimal quantities. If it is possible to construct a path $(\bar{c}_0, \bar{k})$ such that $\bar{c}_0 < \hat{c}_0$ and $\bar{k}_t > a\hat{k}_t$ for some $a > 1$, this problem can be shown to satisfy the Slater condition in the relevant sense. In the Solow-Swan model, this will be true as long as $\bar{c}_t$ is bounded below from the maximum sustainable value for consumption, $c_{\max} = \max_k f(k) - k$.

12. Many papers from macroeconomics have used Ramsey preferences to calculate a positive model of a decentralized equilibrium. In a partial equilibrium setting with constant interest rates, Lucas and Prescott (1971) showed that these preferences could be interpreted as a description of a market demand curve without invoking a representative agent. Of the papers that invoke a representative agent, three of the most influential are Barro (1974), Hall (1978), and Lucas (1978).

13. For a derivation of this Lagrangian, see Romer and Shinotsuka (1988).

14. For this result, see Ekeland and Scheinkman (1986).

15. This is also known as an Euler equation, or sometimes as an Euler-Lagrange equation. In classical notation this is often written as

$$\frac{\partial}{\partial k} M(k,\dot{k},t) - \frac{d}{dt}\left[\frac{\partial}{\partial \dot{k}} M(k,\dot{k},t)\right] = 0.$$

The notation used in the text is more explicit about what the time derivative refers to and why the meaning would be so different if d/dt were replaced by $\partial/\partial t$. For a proof, see any text that covers dynamic optimization, for example, Intriligator (1971) or Luenberger (1976).

16. The use of an uppercase letter K that is not italicized to distinguish aggregate quantities from firm quantities is unavoidable because uppercase and lowercase letters have already been used to indicate the distinction between total capital for a firm K and capital per worker k.

17. Since the number of workers is assumed to be equal to the number of firms, there is one worker per firm and the equilibrium condition is still $K = Nk$.

18. The 3% growth rate for output and capital follows from a growth rate of 2% per year in labor augmenting technological change and a growth rate of 1% per year in total quality adjusted labor.

19. The suggestion that innovation might move together with investment in physical capital is not entirely hypothetical. Schmookler (1966) presents detailed evidence from several industries that patents are closely correlated with investment in physical capital. The patents follow investment with a lag, and the number of patents in technologically unrelated areas, e.g., track and nontrack patents for railroads, show the same comovement with physical investment. These pieces of evidence suggest that the causation may not merely run from exogenous discoveries to new investment.

20. Arrow added an irrelevant fixed coefficients technology on top of his external effect. The result is a paper that is difficult to read and easy to misunderstand. Many economists seem to have the mistaken impression that this paper is concerned with on-the-job learning-by-doing by workers. Levhari (1966a,b) and especially Sheshinski (1967) offered simpler versions of Arrow's analysis that captured the essentials, but these papers seem to have received relatively little attention.

21. Lucas's paper actually considers two different models. The second is discussed below.
22. Uzawa's original interpretation of his model was one with endogenous accumulation of technology A rather than of human capital H. Lucas emphasizes the interpretation used here in terms of human capital.
23. Krugman actually allowed A_i in one country to depend on output in the foreign country as well as in the home country, so there are international spillovers from the learning-by-doing. So long as domestic output has a stronger effect than foreign output, the qualitative results described here will hold.
24. When this functional form is used to describe preferences, it is commonly referred to as the Dixit-Stiglitz preferences, based on their article of 1977. A continuous form of these preferences was used by Joseph Ostroy (1973). For the use of this form as a production function depending on intermediate inputs, see Ethier (1982).
25. See Pitchford (1974) for a defense of the second form for the objective function. Meade (1955) was influential in convincing economists to use the third formulation.
26. All of the analysis here abstracts from the fact that it takes two parents to raise a family. Treating this issue seriously requires more than multiplication by a factor of 2, because marriage leads to links between different families. For an exploration of the implications of these links, see Bernheim and Bagwell (1988).
27. Implicitly, the function $\mathcal{L}C1\ (x,\gamma)$ depends on the value of p that is used in the definition of the problem $PC1(p)$. For notational simplicity, this dependence is suppressed.

References

Abramowitz, M. 1986. Catching Up, Forging Ahead, and Falling Behind. *Journal of Economic History* 46(2): 385–406.

Araujo, A., and J. A. Scheinkman. 1983. Maximum Principle and Transversality Condition for Concave Infinite Horizon Economic Models. *Journal of Economic Theory* 30 (June): 1–16.

Arrow, K. J. 1962. The Economic Implications of Learning by Doing. *Review of Economic Studies* 29 (June): 155–173.

Barro, R. J. 1974. Are Government Bonds Net Wealth? *Journal of Political Economy* 82: 1095–117.

Barro, R. J., and G. S. Becker. 1986. Fertility Choice in a Model of Economic Growth. Unpublished paper, University of Chicago.

Baumol, W. J. 1986. Productivity Growth, Convergence, and Welfare: What the Long-Run Data Show. *American Economic Review* 76 (December): 1072–85.

Becker, G. S., and R. J. Barro. 1987. A Reformulation of the Economic Theory of Fertility. Working paper 26, Rochester Center for Economic Research.

Bernheim, D. B., and K. Bagwell. 1988. Is Everything Neutral? *Journal of Political Economy*.

Brock, W. 1975. A Simple Perfect Foresight Monetary Model. *Journal of Monetary Economics* 1: 133–150.

——— 1977. A Polluted Golden Age. *In* V. Smith (ed.), *Economics of Natural and Environmental Resources*. New York: Gordon and Breach.

Burmeister, E., and A. R. Dobell. 1970. *Mathematical Theories of Economic Growth*. New York: Collier-Macmillan.

Cass, D. 1965. Optimum Growth in an Aggregative Model of Capital Accumulation. *Review of Economic Studies* 32: 233–240.

Danthine, J.-P., J. B. Donaldson, and L. Smith. 1987. On the Superneutrality of Money in a Stochastic Dynamic Macroeconomic Model. *Journal of Monetary Economics* 20 (December): 475–501.

Delong, B. 1987. Have Productivity Levels Converged? Unpublished working paper, Massachusetts Institute of Technology.

Diamond, P. A. 1965. National Debt in a Neo-classical Growth Model. *American Economic Review* 55 (December): 1126–50.

Dixit, A. K., and J. P. Stiglitz. 1977. Monopolistic Competition and Optimum Product Diversity. *American Economic Review* 67 (June): 297–308.

Ethier, W. J. 1982. National and International Returns to Scale in the Modern Theory of International Trade. *American Economic Review* 72 (June): 389–405.

Ekeland, I., and R. Temem. 1976. *Convex Analysis and Variational Problems*. Amsterdam: North-Holland.

Ekeland, I., and J. A. Scheinkman. 1986. Transversality Conditions for Some Infinite Horizon Discrete Time Optimization Problems. *Mathematics of Operations Research* 11 (May): 216–229.

Friedman, M., and A. J. Schwartz. 1982. *Monetary Trends in the United States and the United Kingdom: Their Relation to Income, Prices, and Interest Rates, 1867–1975*. Chicago and London: The University of Chicago Press.

Gallman, R. E. 1966. Gross National Product in the United States, 1834–1909. *In Output, Employment, and Productivity in the United States After 1800*. New York: National Bureau of Economic Research, pp. 3–90.

Greenwood, M. J., and J. M. McDowell. 1986. The Factor Market Consequences of U.S. Immigration. *Journal of Economic Literature* 24 (December): 1738–72.

Hahn, F. H. 1972. *Readings in the Theory of Economic Growth*. London: Macmillan.

Hahn, F. H., and R. C. O. Matthews. 1964. The Theory of Economic Growth: A Survey. *Economic Journal* 74 (December): 779–902.

Hall, R. E. 1978. Stochastic Implications of the Life Cycle-Permanent Income Hypothesis: Theory and Evidence. *Journal of Political Economy* 86 (December): 971–987.

Hart, O. D. 1980. Perfect Competition and Optimum Product Differentiation. *Journal of Economic Theory* 22: 279–312.

Intriligator, M. D. 1971. *Mathematical Optimization and Economic Theory*. Englewood Cliffs, New Jersey: Prentice Hall.

Jones, H. G. 1975. *An Introduction to Modern Theories of Economic Growth*. New York: McGraw-Hill.

Jones, L., and R. Manuelli. 1988. A Model of Optimal Equilibrium Growth. Unpublished paper, Stanford University.

Jorgenson, D. W. 1987. The Economic Impact of Tax Reform. Unpublished working paper, Harvard University.

Judd, K. L. 1985. On the Performance of Patents. *Econometrica* 53 (May): 567–585.

Kaldor, N. 1961. Capital Accumulation and Economic Growth. *In* F. A. Lutz and D. C. Hague (eds.), *The Theory of Capital*. New York: St. Martin's Press, pp. 177–222.

Kendrick, J. W. 1961. *Productivity Trends in the United States*. Princeton, New Jersey: Princeton University Press.

——— 1973. *Postwar Productivity Trends in the United States, 1948–1969*. New York: NBER and Columbia University Press.

King, R. G., and S. Rebelo. 1988. Business Cycles with Endogenous Growth. Unpublished working paper, University of Rochester.

Koopmans, T. C. 1965. On the Concept of Optimal Economic Growth. *In The Econometric Approach to Economic Planning*. Amsterdam: North-Holland (for Pontific Acad. Sci.).

Krugman, P. 1988. The Narrow Moving Band, the Dutch Disease, and the Competitive Consequences of Mrs. Thatcher: Notes on Trade in the Presence of Dynamic Scale Economies. *Journal of Development Economics*.

Kuhn, H. W., and A. W. Tucker. 1951. Non-linear Programming. *In* J. Neyman (ed.), *Proceedings of the Second Berkeley Symposium on Mathematical Statistics and Probability*. Berkeley, California: University of California Press.

Kuznets, S. 1971. Notes on the Pattern of U.S. Economic Growth. *In* R. W. Fogel and S. L. Engerman (eds.), *The Reinterpretation of American Economic History*. New York: Harper & Row.

Lebergott, S. 1966. Labor Force and Employment, 1800–1960. *In Output, Employment, and Productivity in the United States After 1800*. New York: National Bureau of Economic Research, pp. 117–204.

Levhari, D. 1966a. Further Implications of 'Learning by Doing.' *Review of Economic Studies* 33 (January): 31–39.

——— 1966b. Extensions of Arrow's 'Learning by Doing.' *Review of Economic Studies* 33 (April): 117–132.

Lucas, R. E. 1988. On the Mechanics of Economic Development. *Journal of Monetary Economics*.

——— 1978. Asset Prices in an Exchange Economy. *Econometrica* 46 (November): 1429–47.

Lucas, R. E., and E. C. Prescott. 1971. Investment under Uncertainty. *Econometrica* 39 (September): 659–681.

Lucas, R. E., and N. L. Stokey. 1984. Optimal Growth with Many Consumers. *Journal of Economic Theory* 32: 139–171.

—— 1987. Money and Interest in a Cash-in-Advance Economy. *Econometrica* 55 (May): 491–515.

Luenberger, D. G. 1976. *Optimization by Vector Space Methods.* New York: John Wiley & Sons.

Maddison, A. 1982. *Phases of Capitalist Development.* Oxford: Oxford University Press.

—— 1987. Growth and Slowdown in Advanced Capitalist Economies: Techniques of Quantitative Assessment. *Journal of Economic Literature* 25 (June): 649–698.

Marshall, A. 1961. *Principles of Economics,* 9th Ed. London: Macmillan.

Matthews, R. C. O., C. H. Feinstein, and J. C. Odling-Smee. 1982. *British Economic Growth 1856–1973.* Oxford: Clarendon Press.

Meade, J. E. 1955. *Trade and Welfare.* Oxford: Oxford University Press.

Nerlove, M. 1974. Household and Economy: Toward a New Theory of Population and Economic Growth. *Journal of Political Economy* 82 (March/April): S200–S218.

Norsworthy, J. R. 1984. Growth Accounting and Productivity Measurement. *Review of Income and Wealth* 30 (June): 309–329.

Ohkawa, K., and H. Rosovsky. 1973. *Japanese Economic Growth.* Stanford, California: Stanford University Press.

Ostroy, J. 1973. Representation of Large Economies: The Equivalence Theorem. Paper presented at the winter meetings of the Econometric Society.

Phelps, E. S. 1966. Models of Technical Progress and the Golden Rule of Research. *Review of Economic Studies* 33 (April): 133–145.

J. D. Pitchford. 1974. *Population in Economic Growth.* New York: Elsevier.

Prescott, E. C., and J. H. Boyd. 1987. Dynamic Coalitions, Growth, and the Firm. *In* E. C. Prescott and N. Wallace (eds.), *Minnesota Studies in Macroeconomics* 1. Minneapolis: University of Minnesota Press.

Prescott, E. C., and R. M. Townsend. 1984. General Competitive Analysis in an Economy with Private Information. *International Economic Review* 25 (February): 1–20.

Ramsey, F. P. 1928. A Mathematical Theory of Savings. *The Economic Journal* 38 (December): 543–559.

Razin, A., and U. Ben-Zion. 1975. An Intergenerational Model of Population Growth. *American Economic Review* 65 (December): 923–933.

Rebelo, S. 1988. Long Run Policy Analysis and Long Run Growth. Unpublished paper, University of Rochester.

Rockafellar, R. T. 1970. *Convex Analysis.* Princeton, New Jersey: Princeton University Press.

Romer, P. M. 1983. Dynamic Competitive Equilibria with Externalities, Increasing Returns, and Unbounded Growth. Unpublished doctoral dissertation, University of Chicago.

——— 1986. Increasing Returns and Long-Run Growth. *Journal of Political Economy* 94 (October): 1002–37.

——— 1987. Growth Based on Increasing Returns Due to Specialization. *American Economic Review* 77 (May): 56–62.

——— 1988. Endogenous Technological Change. Unpublished paper, University of Rochester.

Romer, P. M., and T. Shinotsuka. 1988. The Kuhn-Tucker Theorem and Transversality Conditions at Infinity. Unpublished working paper, University of Rochester.

Samuelson, P. A. 1958. An Extract Consumption-Loan Model of Interest with or without the Social Contrivance of Money. *Journal of Political Economy* 66 (December): 467–482.

Samuelson, P. A., and R. M. Solow. 1956. A Complete Capital Model Involving Heterogeneous Capital Goods. *The Quarterly Journal of Economics* 70 (November): 537–562.

Schmitz, J. 1986. Optimal Growth and Product Innovation. Working paper, University of Wisconsin.

Schmookler, J. 1966. *Invention and Economic Growth*. Cambridge, Massachusetts: Harvard University Press.

Shell, K. 1967. A Model of Inventive Activity and Capital Accumulation. *In* K. Shell (ed.), *Essays in the Theory of Optimal Economic Growth*. Cambridge, Massachusetts: MIT Press.

Sheshinski, E. 1967. Optimal Accumulation with Learning by Doing. *In* K. Shell (ed.), *Essays on the Theory of Optimal Economic Growth*. Cambridge, Massachusetts: MIT Press.

Solow, R. M. 1956. A Contribution to the Theory of Economic Growth. *The Quarterly Journal of Economics* 70 (February): 65–94.

——— 1970. *Growth Theory: An Exposition*. New York and Oxford: Oxford University Press.

Stiglitz, J. E., and H. Uzawa. 1969. *Readings in the Modern Theory of Economic Growth*. Cambridge, Massachusetts: MIT Press.

Stokey, N. L. 1986. Learning by Doing and the Introduction of New Goods. Working paper, Northwestern University.

Stokey, N., R. E. Lucas, Jr., and E. C. Prescott. 1989. *Recursive Methods in Economic Dynamics*. Cambridge, Massachusetts: Harvard University Press.

Summers, R., and A. Heston. 1984. Improved International Comparisons of Real Product and Its Composition: 1950–1980. *Review of Income and Wealth* 30 (June): 207–262.

——— 1988. A New Set of International Comparisons of Real Product and Prices: Estimates for 130 Countries, 1950–1985. *Review of Income and Wealth* 34 (March): 1–26.

Summers, R., A. Heston, and A. Kravis. 1984. Changes in the World Income Distribution. *Journal of Policy Modeling* 6, 237–269.

Swan, T. W. 1956. Economic Growth and Capital Accumulation. *The Economic Record* 32 (November): 334–361.

Tamura, R. 1988. Fertility, Human Capital, and the 'Wealth of Nations.' Unpublished paper, University of Chicago.

Uzawa, H. 1965. Optimum Technical Change in an Aggregative Model of Economic Growth. *International Economic Review* 6 (January): 18–31.

Vassilakis, Spyros. 1986. Increasing Returns and Strategic Behavior. Unpublished doctoral dissertation, Johns Hopkins University.

von Weizsacker, C. C. 1966. Tentative Notes on a Two-Sector Model with Induced Technological Progress. *Review of Economic Studies* 33 (July): 245–251.

Young, A. A. 1928. Increasing Returns and Economic Progress. *Economic Journal* 38 (December): 527–542.

3 Rational Expectations and the Informational Role of Prices

Sanford J. Grossman

A prominent feature of competitive prices is their guidance of the allocation of resources. People would rather produce the commodity that will bring a high price than some other commodity that for the same production cost brings a low price. Thus resources are drawn into the production of the relatively scarce commodity. Unfortunately, this *allocative* role of prices is confused with an informational role. The neoclassical model of competitive equilibrium prices associated with Marshall or Walras can model the allocative role of prices, but as is shown below, the model is inadequate for handling situations where information is dispersed. The Rational Expectations model is a generalization of the Walrasian model to economies where information is dispersed. Individuals, in forming their demands, take into account the fact that the price at which they can effect a trade is determined by information that is possessed by others but is relevant to their own demand at the given price. This situation radically alters the meanings of demand, of supply, and of equilibrium. This chapter is a short introduction to Rational Expectations models of markets where information is dispersed. The reader is referred to Grossman (1981) for a detailed introduction.

The Walrasian model assumes that the only thing an individual need know about the rest of the economy is the prices of the goods and services he is going to be trading. Each consumer trades at known prices p to buy the consumption basket x, a transaction that maximizes his utility $u(x)$ subject to a budget constraint $px \leq$ wealth. No feature of the preferences, technology, or information of other people enters a consumer's optimization problem other than the prices at which he can trade. Similarly, producers use prices to compute the net market value of their production plans and to find the best technologically feasible plan. Again, the external economy is irrelevant; once prices are known, no producer need be concerned about any consumer's information or preferences. I shall argue that when information is dispersed markets will not clear at the Walrasian prices and, further, the allocations of the Walrasian model are not efficient.

I offer the following example to illustrate the inadequacies of the Walrasian model. Recall that according to the Walrasian model a consumer's demand depends only on his own information and the prices he observes. If his private information is unchanged but the price of a commodity goes down, then he will tend to buy more of the commodity; his budget constraint has shifted, but his preferences are unchanged. Now imagine that the commodity in question is a security traded on a stock market. A typical consumer goes to work during the day on some activity that may provide him with no information about a particular security he owns. Suppose he comes home at the end of the day to find that the price has fallen. One surely does not suppose that he then increases his demand for the security, as if his preferences were unchanged and his budget constraint has made the holding of the security cheaper. In fact, he may decide to keep his security holding unchanged on the basis of the observation that the price fell because other people had unfavorable information regarding the security's payoff. Indeed, some writers have characterized an informationally efficient market as one in which a change in the equilibrium price would not cause a person to alter his demand for a security. (See Fama, 1970, for a discussion of informational efficiency.) The formal model behind this intuition is not that of the Walrasian model, according to which consumers' preferences are independent of prices; it is as if the consumer changes his preference for the security when the price changes.

The Walrasian model also fails to predict market-clearing allocations. Suppose that consumer i has private information denoted by y_i. I shall denote his demand for the security by $X_i(p; y_i)$. This demand is formed by maximizing his utility using his private information y_i subject to a budget constraint involving p. Let $y = (y_1, y_2, \ldots)$ be the list of everyone's private information. A Walrasian equilibrium is a price $p(y)$ such that $\Sigma_i X_i = X^s$, where X^s is the total supply of the security. If this is indeed an "equilibrium," then there should be no desire to recontract at the price $p(y)$. But clearly there will be a desire to recontract at $p(y)$ if everyone knows that the price is indeed determined by the demands of all traders. To see the desire to recontract, recall that each trader i based his demand on his private information alone. Suppose that trader 1 observed a y_1, which indicated that the payoff on the security is likely to be unusually low. His Walrasian demand would then specify that at each price p only a small amount of the security was desired. But suppose that other traders observe very good news about the payoff on the security; then their demands will be very high, so the market clearing price will be high. Trader 1, after observing the market clearing price, would realize that his information was an outlier and that the security is a better investment than his private information indicates. He would then reenter the market and seek to buy more than indicated by his Walrasian demand function.

It is a fact that the price at which the market clears conveys information. This means that rational traders will adjust their demand functions to reflect the fact that if the market clears at a price p, then this price tells them something about how much of the security they would want to hold. Formally this means that the "demand" by trader i, when the price is $p = p(y)$, is $X_i[p; y_i, p(y)]$. The trader reasons that his demand at price p should be based on the information y_i as well as on the information contained in the event that the price is $p(y)$. An ordinary Walrasian demand function specifies what a consumer would desire to hold at a particular price p irrespective of whether p is a market-clearing price. In a market with dispersed information, such a demand function is irrelevant. The demand at p is not specifiable without reference to the information contained in the event that the price is p. To construct an equilibrium price at which no recontracting is desired, one must know the desired holding for each individual at each price p that is market clearing for some information y, that is, $p(y) = p$ for some y.

A Rational Expectations (R.E.) price function $p(y)$ has the property that, for each y, when $p(y) = p$ the total market demand equals supply, given that each individual chooses his demand at p to maximize his expected utility and that his choice is conditioned on his private information and on the information contained in the event that p is a market-clearing price (that is, $p(y) = p$). A crucial characteristic of R.E. allocations is that each individual forms his demand as if he had much more than his private information. In the next sections I shall show that $p(y)$ can be a sufficient statistic for the information of all traders, that is, observing the market-clearing price allows each trader to achieve the allocations that would have been achieved if each trader could have observed the whole economy's information. Thus, the R.E. model can formalize the notion that in a decentralized economy prices convey and aggregate information. In particular, in Section 3.2 I shall show that if markets are complete, then an R.E. equilibrium that is a sufficient statistic for all of the economy's information exists. An immediate consequence is that the R.E. allocations for an economy with a complete set of markets but dispersed information cannot be Pareto dominated by a central planner in possession of all of the economy's information.

The organization of this chapter is as follows. Section 3.1 analyzes a simple model in which production decisions are affected by the information contained in a futures price. Section 3.2 presents a general equilibrium model in which securities prices convey information. Therein, conditions are given under which prices perfectly aggregate dispersed information. Section 3.3 contains conclusions and empirical evidence on the informativeness of securities prices. Section 3.4 discusses some implications of R.E. models for the analysis of business cycles. In the R.E. models in Section 3.4 consumers receive poor information from prices regarding economywide shocks. By this mechanism, shocks that would have a small effect on aggregate employment under homogeneous information have a large effect under dispersed information. In Section 3.4 I shall also discuss implicit contract models in which consumers receive good information about economywide shocks, but prices provide poor information about their own productivity. In such a situation, R.E. under asymmetric information and optimal contracting imply that output will respond more to observable aggregate shocks than would be the case if all consumers know their own productivity.

3.1. A Simple Model in Which Prices Convey Information

The ideas raised in the preceding section can be clarified by a simple example. Consider an economy where an investment at time $t - 1$ yields a random reward per unit denoted by $\tilde{D}$ at time t. Let $C(q)$ be the cost of producing investment; and let this investment yield the random reward $q\tilde{D}$. In other words, let $q\tilde{D}$ represent the total amount of a commodity produced by the investment. To model the informational role of markets, I shall introduce a futures market, where p_f is the price at $t - 1$ for one unit of the commodity to be delivered at date t.

A way to model information is to imagine that trader i observes at $t - 1$ a signal $\tilde{y}_i$ that tells him something about the realization of $\tilde{D}$ in period t. (For example, if $\tilde{D}$ is determined by tomorrow's rainfall, then $\tilde{y}_i$ can be the current wind velocity and humidity observed by agent *i*.) Let $\bar{\mathbf{y}} = (\bar{y}_1, \bar{y}_2, \bar{y}_3, \ldots)$ be the vector of all traders' information.

Suppose for the moment that all traders are risk neutral. If x_i denotes the amount sold forward by trader *i*, then his expected profit is

$$(3.1) \qquad p_f x_i + E[\tilde{D}|y_i](q_i - x_i) - C(q_i)$$

where $E[\tilde{D}|y_i]$ denotes the conditional expectation of $\tilde{D}$ given the private information of trader *i*, namely, y_i. From (3.1) it is clear that each trader will want to increase his forward sales as long as $p_f > E[\tilde{D}|y_i]$ and decrease his sales as long as $p_f < E[\tilde{D}|y_i]$. If there is no constraint on short sales or long positions, then no equilibrium forward price will exist when $E[\tilde{D}|y_i] \neq E[\tilde{D}|y_j]$. That is, the statement that in a Walrasian equilibrium futures prices reflect people's beliefs about the future is meaningless when people have different beliefs.

The above result is, of course, extreme and due to the assumption of risk neutrality. However, the point that the Walrasian competitive equilibrium does not transmit information can be seen more clearly if one assumes that trader *i* is risk averse with Von Neumann-Morgenstern utility function

$$(3.2) \qquad U_i(W) = 1 - e^{-a_i W} \qquad a_i > 0,$$

and further, assume that $(\tilde{D}, \bar{\mathbf{y}})$ are jointly normally distributed.

It is useful to record some facts about normal distributions. If $\tilde{Z}$ is normal with mean *m* and variance *v*, and $t > 0$, then $Ee^{-t\tilde{Z}} = \exp\{-tm + t^2 v/2\}$. Thus if $\tilde{W} = p_f x_i + \tilde{D}(q_i - x_i) - C(q_i)$, then the fact that $\tilde{W}$ is normally distributed with mean $= p_f x_i + (q_i - x_i)E[\tilde{D}|y_i] - C(q_i)$ and variance $= (q_i - x_i)^2 \text{Var}(\tilde{D}|y_i)$ can be used to compute $Ee^{-a_i \tilde{W}}$. If $(\tilde{Z}_1, \tilde{Z}_2)$ are jointly normal, then $E[\tilde{Z}_1|\tilde{Z}_2 = Z]$ is a linear function of *Z*, and $\text{Var}[\tilde{Z}_1|\tilde{Z}_2 = Z]$ is a constant independent of the value of *Z*.

If trader *i* chooses q_i and x_i to maximize $E[U_i(p_f x_i + (q_i - x_i)\tilde{D} - C(q_i))|y_i]$, it is as if he were interested only in the mean and variance of wealth. The solutions can be shown to satisfy

$$(3.3) \qquad x_i = q_i + \frac{p_f - E[\tilde{D}|y_i]}{a_i \text{Var}(\tilde{D}|y_i)} \qquad C'(q_i) = p_f.$$

Assume that the *N* firms are the only ones operating in the futures market. The equilibrium in the futures market requires that p_f make

$\sum_{i=1}^{N} x_i = 0$. If one assumes that $C'(q_i) = cq_i$ for some $c > 0$, then (3.3) can be used to solve for the market-clearing price p_f^0 (writing it as a function of **y**):

$$(3.4) \qquad p_f^0(\mathbf{y}) = \sum_i \frac{E[\tilde{D}|y_i]}{a_i \text{Var}(\tilde{D}|y_i)} \cdot \left[\sum_j (a_j \text{Var}(\tilde{D}|y_j))^{-1} + \frac{N}{c} \right]^{-1}.$$

Equation (3.4) shows that the market-clearing price p_f^0 is a complicated function of **y**. It is some kind of weighted average of the expectations of different traders, where the weights are the product of risk aversion (that is, a_i) and the precision of the information (that is, $\text{Var}(\tilde{D}|y_i)$). Although some writers have suggested that equations like (3.4) show the aggregative ability of competitive prices, (3.4) shows quite the reverse. In particular, one can seen how bad (3.4) does by comparing the allocations obtainable with what would arise in an imaginary fully informed *artificial* economy where *each* trader i had *all* of the economy's information **y**. Consider the case where knowing **y** identifies $\tilde{D}$ exactly, so that $\text{Var}(\tilde{D}|\mathbf{y}) = 0$. That is, there exists a function $g(\cdot)$ such that $\tilde{D} = g(\mathbf{y})$. If each trader has some piece of information about the state of demand in his neighborhood and if total market demand is the sum of neighborhood states of demand, then $\tilde{D} = y_1 + y_2 + \ldots + y_N$. Thus, when each trader possesses **y**, he would face no risk, and hence the only market-clearing futures price would be

$$(3.5) \qquad p_f(\mathbf{y}) = E[\tilde{D}|\mathbf{y}] = \tilde{D}.$$

Equation (3.5) is clearly different from (3.4). Furthermore, it is easy to show that a planner with all the information **y** could reallocate the x_i and change the production decisions q_i to make everyone better off than they would be with the allocations generated by the ordinary competitive equilibrium in (3.4) [since in (3.4), (a) traders bear excess risk and (b) investment should continue to the point where $cq_i = E[\tilde{D}|\mathbf{y}]$]. If prices and allocations were generated as in the artificial economy where each trader observes **y**, then a planner who knows **y** will not be able to Pareto dominate the competitive allocations.

There is something very wrong with the ordinary Walrasian equilibrium when traders have different information. One can see this by imagining that (3.4) is fine and that the economy described above is replicated many times so that each trader i observes many realizations of $(p_f^0(\tilde{\mathbf{y}}), \tilde{y}_i, \tilde{D})$. Then each trader will come to know the joint distribution of $(p_f^0, \tilde{y}_i, \tilde{D})$.

Hence each trader is able to learn the conditional distribution of $\tilde{D}$ given $\bar{y}_i$, p_f^0. A trader will in general find that $E[\tilde{D}|y_i] \neq E[\tilde{D}|y_i, p_f^0]$; that is, observing p_f^0 will lead each trader to change his beliefs because it gives him new information. After traders learn this, they will desire to recontract after observing $p_f^0(\mathbf{y})$. [A smart trader might even say to himself: "Let all the other traders trade naively using their own information. I will wait until the market clears, and after observing the current realization of $p_f^0(\mathbf{y})$, I will make my purchases of x_i and q_i to maximize $E[U_i|p_f^0(y), y_i]$. Since I am a price taker, I will expect to do better than by trading now and maximizing $E[U_i|y_i]$."]

When traders observe $p_f^0(\mathbf{y})$ and then compute their optimal choices to maximize $E[U_i|y_i, p_f^0]$, $p_f^0(y)$ will no longer, in general, be the market-clearing price that corresponds to $\bar{\mathbf{y}} = \mathbf{y}$, because $p_f^0(\mathbf{y})$ is the market-clearing price when each trader forms his demands naively looking only at his own information, that is, maximizing $E[U_i|y_i]$. It is important to note that in an economy *where all traders have the same information,* there is no desire to recontract at the Walrasian equilibrium price. That is exactly why one thinks of it as a true equilibrium. However, if traders come to the market with different information, the price at which the market clears is itself a very important piece of information to each trader (in that it reveals the information of other traders).

A proper definition of an equilibrium price is one at which there is no desire to recontract when each trader gets what he demands at that price. At what price $p_f^e(\mathbf{y})$ will there be no desire to recontract after traders observe p_f^e? This price must have the property that, when traders form their demands by conditioning on p_f^e (that is, choosing x_i, q_i to max $E[U_i|y_i, p_f^e(\mathbf{y})])$, $p_f^e(\mathbf{y})$ will indeed be the market-clearing price.

Formally $p_f^e(\mathbf{y})$ is an R.E. equilibrium:

(3.6a) if $x_i(p_f, y_i)$, $q_i(p_f, y_i)$ solves
$$\max_{x_i, q_i} E[U_i \left(p_f x_i + (q_i - x_i)\tilde{D} - C(q_i))|y_i, p_f^e(\mathbf{y})], \quad \text{and}$$

(3.6b) $\displaystyle\sum_{i=1}^{N} x_i(p_f^e(\mathbf{y}), y_i) = 0$ for all $\mathbf{y}$.

One can see why $p_f^e(\mathbf{y})$ is called an R.E. equilibrium by considering the view taken earlier. Traders who observe the futures price know that it is in some way a reflection of the information possessed by other traders. They know that price will be high when traders have good news about $\tilde{D}$.

Thus, traders attempt to invert $p_f(\mathbf{y})$ and go from an observation of the endogenous variable p_f to learn about the exogenous variable $\mathbf{y}$. Of course, when all traders do this, that affects the price at which the market will clear. The price $p_f^e(\mathbf{y})$ is an equilibrium point of the above process. When prices are generated by $p_f^e(\mathbf{y})$ and when traders use this price function to learn about $\mathbf{y}$, then the market will clear at $p_f^e(\mathbf{y})$ when $\tilde{\mathbf{y}} = \mathbf{y}$. Again, one sees that Rational Expectations is an equilibrium concept rather than a condition of individual rationality.

Recall that for the example in (3.1)–(3.4), the ordinary competitive equilibrium price did not transmit any information to traders; no trader formed his demand as if the price at which a trade takes place informs him of the worth of the trade. In particular, there was no relationship between it and the equilibrium allocations that occur in the artificial economy where each trader has all the economy's information. Grossman (1976) has shown that the R.E. equilibrium does an extraordinary thing. For the above example (and in a large class of models given below), the R.E. equilibrium is exactly the same as in the fully informed artificial economy. The above remark is particularly easy to prove in the case where $\mathbf{y}$ provides perfect information about $\tilde{D}$, that is, where $\mathrm{Var}(\tilde{D}|\mathbf{y}) = 0$. In this case

$$(3.7) \qquad p_f^e(\mathbf{y}) = \mathrm{E}[\tilde{D}|\mathbf{y}] = \tilde{D}$$

is an R.E. equilibrium. I must show that markets will clear at $p_f^e(\mathbf{y})$ when $\tilde{\mathbf{y}} = \mathbf{y}$. This result can be seen by noting that $\mathrm{Var}(\tilde{D}|\mathbf{y}) = 0$ implies that $\mathrm{Var}(\tilde{D}|p_f^e(\mathbf{y})) = 0$; hence each consumer in (3.6) has perfect information about $\tilde{D}$ and thus acts as if he were risk neutral. When all traders are risk neutral, $p_f = \mathrm{E}[\tilde{D}|p_f^e(\mathbf{y})]$ is a market-clearing futures price.

I made the unnecessarily strong assumption that $\mathrm{Var}(D|\mathbf{y}) = 0$ in order to show how in an R.E. model the futures price can equal the expected spot price *conditional on all the economy's information*, even though traders have different beliefs $\mathrm{E}[\tilde{D}|y_i]$. Although traders come to the market with different information, they leave the market with allocations that are as if they all had the same information and their common information is the best available, namely, $\mathbf{y}$. From (3.6a), the reader may verify that producers set q_i so that $C'(q_i) = p_f^e \equiv \mathrm{E}[\tilde{D}|\mathbf{y}]$. Thus production decisions are guided by all the economy's information (that is, it is as if each trader had all the economy's information).

These results are unobtainable in a standard Walrasian equilibrium; there, price is a weighted average of people's information rather than a sufficient statistic for that information [see (3.4)]. Note also that traders will face risk using only their own information in the standard Walrasian equilibrium, even when there is no social risk [for example, when $\text{Var}(\tilde{D}|\mathbf{y}) = 0$].

The above results were derived from the assumption that $\text{Var}(\tilde{D}|\mathbf{y}) = 0$. Suppose I drop that assumption but maintain the assumption that $(\tilde{D}, \tilde{y})$ are jointly normal. Then the following expression is an R.E. equilibrium:

$$(3.8) \qquad p_f^e(\mathbf{y}) = \sum_{i=1}^{N} \frac{E[\tilde{D}|\mathbf{y}]}{a_i \text{Var}(\tilde{D}|\mathbf{y})} \cdot \left[\sum_j (a_j \text{Var}(\tilde{D}|\mathbf{y}))^{-1} + \frac{N}{c} \right]^{-1}.$$

To show this, I shall introduce more notation. Given any two vector random variables $\tilde{z}_1$, $\tilde{z}_2$, let $F(z_1|z_2)$ denote the conditional probability that $\tilde{z}_1 \leq z_1$ given that it is observed that $\tilde{z}_2 = z_2$. It serves my purpose to say that a statistic $t(z_2)$ is *sufficient* for the information in z_2 concerning z_1 if $F(z_1|z_2) = F(z_1|t(z_2))$.[1] This statement captures the idea that inferences about z_1 based upon observing $t(z_2)$ will be the same as those based upon observing z_2. It is a fact that for normal distributions the conditional mean $E[\tilde{D}|\mathbf{y}] \equiv t(\mathbf{y})$ is sufficient for the information in $\mathbf{y}$ concerning $\tilde{D}$ (see Mood, Graybill, Boes, 1974, pp. 306–310). Furthermore, any invertible function of a sufficient statistic is itself a sufficient statistic. Thus, if $p_f^e(\mathbf{y})$ in (3.8) is an invertible function of $E[\tilde{D}|\mathbf{y}]$, then $p_f^e(\mathbf{y})$ is a sufficient statistic regarding $\tilde{D}$. A fact about normal distributions is that the conditional variance of $\tilde{A}$ given $\tilde{B} = B$, $\text{Var}(\tilde{A}|\tilde{B} = B)$, is the same for all realizations of B if $\tilde{A}$, $\tilde{B}$ are jointly normal. Thus, $\text{Var}(\tilde{D}|\mathbf{y})$ is constant for all realizations $\mathbf{y}$ of $\tilde{y}$. Therefore, (3.8) states that $p_f^e(\mathbf{y})$ is a linear function of $E[\tilde{D}|\mathbf{y}]$, which is clearly an invertible function of $E[\tilde{D}|\mathbf{y}]$; that is, any trader who observes $p_f^e(\mathbf{y})$ can infer $E[\tilde{D}|\mathbf{y}]$. I conclude that $p_f^e(\mathbf{y})$ is a sufficient statistic.

I must show that $p_f^e(\mathbf{y})$ is an R.E. equilibrium, that is, solves (3.6). The proof is immediate since $p_f^e(\mathbf{y})$ gives traders the same beliefs about $\tilde{D}$ that they would have if they observed $\mathbf{y}$. That is, (3.8) is the solution for the ordinary competitive equilibrium in the "artificial" economy where all traders observe everything. This statement can be seen from (3.4), which gives the ordinary Walrasian equilibrium when each trader observes y_i. If $\mathbf{y}$ is substituted for y_i and y_j in (3.4), then I get the competitive equilibrium for the economy where everyone observes everything. The fact that $p_f^e(\mathbf{y})$ is also a sufficient statistic means that in the economy where traders come to the market with diverse private information but also observe the price $p_f^e(\mathbf{y})$, their information will be as if each trader knew all the economy's information. By construction, $p_f^e(\mathbf{y})$ clears the market if each trader knows all the economy's information.

The above argument shows that even if traders are risk averse and the aggregate information $\mathbf{y}$ is imperfect (that is, $\mathrm{Var}(\tilde{D}|\mathbf{y}) \neq 0$), then the R.E. price produces allocations that behave as if each trader had all the economy's information. (In Section 3.2 I shall consider a general equilibrium model where welfare propositions can be proved about the R.E. equilibrium.)

For an R.E. price to be a sufficient statistic for all the economy's information, it is necessary and sufficient that the ordinary Walrasian equilibrium price for the artificial economy $p_A(\mathbf{y})$ (where all traders are assumed to know everything) be itself a sufficient statistic for the information. As can be seen from the above example, this condition requires that $p_A(\mathbf{y})$ be an invertible function of all the relevant information in the economy. This, in turn, requires that there be at least as many prices (that is, markets) as pieces of information. For example, if there are two "factors" of information that determine the future price of wheat, it will be quite difficult to invert this simple price for its two determining factors. This difference can be seen in the following example.

Consider a modification of the problem in (3.1); instead of q_i being endogenous, it is exogenous for a group of traders, called nonproducers. These traders have existing stocks of the commodity that they desire to hedge in the futures market. For such traders, (3.3) gives their demand for futures, except that q_i is exogenously given. Denote these traders by $i = N + 1, N + 2, \ldots, N + H$. The aggregate demand for futures is given by summing (3.3) over all traders:

$$(3.9) \qquad 0 = \sum X_i = \sum_{i=1}^{N} \left(\frac{P_f}{c} + \frac{P_f - \mathrm{E}[\tilde{D}|y_i, P_f]}{a_i \, \mathrm{Var}(\tilde{D}|y_i, P_f)} \right)$$

$$+ \sum_{i=N+1}^{N+H} \left(q_i + \frac{P_f - \mathrm{E}[\tilde{D}|y_i, P_f]}{a_i \, \mathrm{Var}(\tilde{D}|y_i, P_f)} \right).$$

A particularly simple case to consider is where the traders $i = N + 1, \ldots, N + H$ are very risk averse, that is, $a_i = +\infty$ for $i = N + 1, N + 2, \ldots, N + H$. In this case the nonproducers sell futures inelastically of size q_i on the market.

Let $Q \equiv \sum_{i=N+1}^{N+H} q_i$, so (3.9) becomes

(3.10) $$0 = \sum_{i=1}^{N} \left(\frac{P_f}{c} + \frac{P_f - E[\tilde{D}|y_i, P_f]}{a_i \mathrm{Var}(\tilde{D}|y_i, P_f)} \right) + Q.$$

Next, suppose that the producers do not know Q. In particular, suppose Q is random, independent, and jointly normally distributed with $\mathbf{y}$ and D. It can now easily be seen that there does not exist an R.E. equilibrium that is a sufficient statistic for all of the economy's information. To see this, suppose to the contrary that there exists a function $P_f(\mathbf{y}, Q)$ such that for all realizations of $\mathbf{y}$, Q, the conditional distribution of D given y_i, $P_f(\mathbf{y}, Q)$ equals the conditional distribution of D given $\mathbf{y}$. Then (3.10) can be solved for $P_f(\mathbf{y}, Q)$ as

(3.11) $$P_f(\mathbf{y}, Q) = \left(-Q + \sum_{i=1}^{N} \frac{E[\tilde{D}|\mathbf{y}]}{a_i \mathrm{Var}(\tilde{D}|\mathbf{y})} \right) \left(\sum_{i=1}^{N} \frac{1}{c} + \frac{1}{a_i \mathrm{Var}(\tilde{D}|\mathbf{y})} \right)^{-1}.$$

However, by the joint normality of $\tilde{D}$, $\mathbf{y}$, it is the case that $\mathrm{Var}(\tilde{D}|\mathbf{y})$ is a constant independent of the realization of $\mathbf{y}$. Therefore, the right-hand side of (3.11) is a linear function of Q and $E[\tilde{D}|\mathbf{y}]$. But since Q is random, $P_f(\mathbf{y}, Q)$ cannot completely reveal $E[\tilde{D}|\mathbf{y}]$. Thus, $P_f(\mathbf{y}, Q)$ is not a sufficient statistic for $\mathbf{y}$.

Indeed, it can be shown that there is a solution to (3.10) of the form

(3.12) $$P_f(\mathbf{y}, Q) = \sum_{i=1}^{N} b_i y_i + b_0 Q,$$

where the b_i are coefficients chosen to make (3.10) an identity (see Diamond and Verrecchia, 1981). It can be shown that as the variance of Q goes to zero, $P_f(\mathbf{y}, Q)$ becomes a sufficient statistic for $\mathbf{y}$.

Equation (3.12) shows that there are two factors affecting the price, where one factor, Q, causes random variation in the price that disguises the information that the price contains about the information possessed by other traders. Intuitively, a trader does not know whether P_f is high because traders have received good news about D or whether it is high because Q is low. A given trader wants to distinguish between these two factors, because a low value of Q is irrelevant to him, whereas good news about D indicates that he should hold more futures contracts.

In the next section I shall show that if markets are complete then there is an R.E. equilibrium at which price is a sufficient statistic for the economy's information.

3.2. The Role of Prices in Allocating Resources

The example of the previous section shows that in an economy subject to uncertainty traders are forced to think about the characteristics of other traders; in a Walrasian model prices do not summarize all relevant aspects of a trader's environment. This view is in contrast to another, widely held view, obtained from the study of economies where information is not dispersed, that prices are signals providing all the information about other traders that an individual trader needs to know.

Although prices are often referred to as signals in nonstochastic economies, they clearly play no formal role in transferring information. No one learns anything from prices. People are *constrained* by prices (often in just the right way so that individual rationality is transformed into collective rationality); however, they are not *informed* by prices in the classical Walrasian or Marshallian models. It is an old idea that prices contain information. Perhaps the clearest statement appeared in Hayek (1945, p. 527): "We must look at the price system as . . . a mechanism for communicating information if we want to understand its real function . . . The most significant fact about this system is the economy of knowledge with which it operates, or how little the individual participants need to know in order to be able to take the right action . . . by a kind of symbol, only the most essential information is passed on."

Hayek wrote the above in criticism of the planning literature of the 1940s. That literature, taking the mathematical models of Walras and the welfare theorems of Lange literally, assumed that the State could set prices in such a way as to induce an efficient allocation and also the income distribution desired by the leaders of the State. (The fundamental theorem of welfare economics assures us that, assuming convexity, any Pareto optimum can be supported by a competitive price system.) Hayek argued (in a vague way) that such arguments miss the point of price competition and the invisible hand. Each trader knows something about his own customers and neighborhood. No one knows everything about the economy. Each individual's little piece of information gets aggregated and transmitted to others via trading. The final competitive allocations are as if an invisible hand *with all the economy's information* allocated resources. However, a planner without all of that information could not have done as well.

In this section I shall show that the R.E. model is capable of capturing the above ideas. I shall show how the fundamental theorem of welfare economics can be extended to economies with dispersed information, in such a way that Hayek's conjecture is true in an R.E. equilibrium. I shall also further clarify the role of speculative markets as aggregators and transmitters of information.

The discussion in Section 3.1 suggests that if there are futures states of nature (which I denote by $\tilde{s}$) about which traders have different information, then the opening of enough speculative markets will create a price system that can be a sufficient statistic for all the information. In this section I shall make that more precise. To do so, it is notationally convenient to consider a pure exchange economy rather than one with production. Suppose that the state of nature each trader is uncertain about concerns his endowment of commodities next period. Thus, I assume that consumer h has an endowment $\tilde{e}_h$ of (for simplicity) a single commodity that is random. Let $\tilde{s}$ denote the social state that determines all traders' endowments. Let e_{hs} denote what trader h's actual endowment is if $\tilde{s} = s$. Since each trader's endowment is random, his consumption will in general also be a function of the state of nature c_{hs}. Let $\tilde{c}_h$ be the random variable that denotes trader h's consumption. I assume there are only a finite number of social states n, so $\tilde{s}$ takes on n values. Thus, every random variable can be written as a vector where the sth element of the vector is the realization of the random variable in state s, for example, $\tilde{c}_h = (c_{h1}, c_{h2}, \ldots, c_{hn}) \equiv (c_{hs})_{s=1}^n$.

I assume that consumers are able to get information about $\tilde{s}$ in the current period before $\tilde{s}$ is realized and before markets open. That is, I assume that before markets open, consumer h observes the realization of a random variable $\tilde{y}_h$ that is correlated with $\tilde{s}$. Let Y_h denote the range of $\tilde{y}_h$. Let $\tilde{y} \equiv (\tilde{y}_h)_{h=1}^H$ denote all of the information possessed by all traders. Let Y denote the range of $\tilde{y}$.

In order to model the situation where there is a complete set of speculative markets, I assume that traders can exchange promises to deliver (or take delivery) of the commodity contingent on the occurrence of the event $\tilde{s} = s$, that is, that there is a complete set of Arrow-Debreu securities.

An Arrow-Debreu equilibrium for the above economy (which is just the Walrasian equilibrium for an economy where the "goods" are $\tilde{c}_h$ and endowments are $\bar{e}_h$), is a price vector $\bar{p}^w = (p_s^w)_{s=1}^n$ and consumption allocations $\bar{c}^w = (\bar{c}_h^w)_{h=1}^H$, such that

(3.13) $\bar{c}_h^w$ solves $\max_{\bar{c}_h} \sum_s U_h(\bar{c}_{hs})\text{Prob}(\bar{s} = s | \bar{y}_h = y_h)$

         s.t. $\bar{p}^w \cdot \bar{c}_h \le \bar{p}^w \cdot \bar{e}_h$,   and

(3.14) $\sum_h \bar{c}_h^w \le \sum_h \bar{e}_h$.

In (3.13) each trader maximizes his expected utility subject to a budget constraint. Note that each trader's beliefs about $\bar{s}$ depend on his information y_h, so his optimal consumption bundle $\bar{c}_h^w(p, y_h)$ depends on the price and his information. Thus, the price at which supply equals demand $\bar{p}^w(\mathbf{y})$ will depend on everyone's information.

It is useful to define the Walrasian equilibrium for the *artificial economy* where each trader observes all the information $\mathbf{y}$. Thus, let $\bar{p}^a(\mathbf{y})$ and $\bar{c}^a(\mathbf{y})$ be the Walrasian equilibrium in (3.13) and (3.14) when $\text{Prob}(\bar{s} = s | \bar{y}_h = y_h)$ is replaced by $\text{Prob}(\bar{s} = s | \bar{\mathbf{y}} = \mathbf{y})$ in (3.13). That is, each consumer maximizes his expected utility conditional on *all* the economy's information. The allocations in the artificial economy correspond to the Walrasian equilibrium in which each consumer's preferences over the commodity vector $\bar{c}_h$ is derived from $\sum_s U_h(c_{hs})\text{Prob}(\bar{s} = s | \bar{\mathbf{y}} = \mathbf{y})$. If all traders observe all the information $\mathbf{y}$, then the first-order conditions for (3.13) can be written as

(3.15) $\dfrac{p_s^a(\mathbf{y})}{p_1^a(\mathbf{y})} = \dfrac{U_h'(c_{hs})}{U_h'(c_{h1})} \dfrac{\pi_s(\mathbf{y})}{\pi_1(\mathbf{y})}$ $s = 2, 3, \ldots, n$,

(3.16)   where $\dfrac{\pi_s(\mathbf{y})}{\pi_s(\mathbf{y})} \equiv \dfrac{\text{Prob}(\bar{s} = s | \bar{\mathbf{y}} = \mathbf{y})}{\text{Prob}(\bar{s} = s_1 | \bar{\mathbf{y}} = \mathbf{y})}$.

I shall show that $p_s^a(\mathbf{y})$ reveals $\pi_s(\mathbf{y})$ and use this fact to show that there exists an R.E. equilibrium for the economy where each trader h observes only y_h, which is a sufficient statistic for all the information $\mathbf{y}$. Thus, the artificial economy yields the same allocations as an R.E. equilibrium. One can see why this is important by noting that by the fundamental theorem of welfare economics a central planner with all the economy's information $\mathbf{y}$ could *not* find a feasible allocation $\bar{c}(\mathbf{y}) = (\bar{c}_h(\mathbf{y}))$ such that

(3.17) $E[U_h(\bar{c}_h(\mathbf{y})) | \mathbf{y}] \ge E[U_h(\bar{c}_h^a(\mathbf{y})) | \mathbf{y}]$ for all h and $\mathbf{y}$,

with strict inequality for some h. Condition (3.17) is true because the Walrasian equilibrium for the artificial economy induces a Pareto optimal allocation of the commodity vector $(\tilde{c}_h)$ relative to the preferences $\sum_s U_h(c_{hs}) \text{Prob}(\tilde{s} = s|\tilde{\mathbf{y}} = \mathbf{y})$.

However, the actual Walrasian equilibrium $\tilde{p}^w$, $\tilde{c}^w$ can, in general, be Pareto dominated by a central planner who knows all the information $\mathbf{y}$ (that is, a feasible allocation $\tilde{c}_h(\mathbf{y})$ will exist so that $E[U_h(\tilde{c}_h(\mathbf{y}))|\mathbf{y}] \geq E[U_h(\tilde{c}_h(\tilde{p}^w(\mathbf{y}),\mathbf{y}))|\mathbf{y}]$ for all h and $\mathbf{y}$ with strict inequality for some h). This outcome is exactly what I illustrated in the example in the previous section. As in that section, I can define an R.E. equilibrium. I shall prove that as long as markets are complete (in the sense that consumers can buy and sell $\tilde{c}_h$ freely), there exists an R.E. equilibrium for the economy where each trader has his own information, which cannot be Pareto dominated by a central planner who has all the economy's information. This model formalizes the idea that the prices have an explicit informational role.

To prove the above theorem, I need only prove that the Walrasian equilibrium to the artificial economy $\tilde{p}^a(\mathbf{y})$, $\tilde{c}^a(\mathbf{y})$ is an R.E. equilibrium. In this context, an R.E. equilibrium is a pair $(\tilde{c}^0, \tilde{P}^0(y))$ such that $\tilde{c}^0 \equiv (\tilde{c}_h^0(y_h, P))_{h=1}^H$, $\tilde{c}_h^0(y_h, P) \equiv (c_{hs}^0(y_h, P))_{s=1}^n$, $\tilde{P}^0 = (P_s^0(y))_{s=1}^n$ where

(3.18a) $c_h^0(y_h, P^0)$ solves $\displaystyle\max_{c_h} \sum_s U_h(c_{hs})\text{Prob}(\tilde{s} = s|\tilde{y}_h = y_h, \tilde{P}^0 = P^0)$

s.t. $P^0 \cdot c_h \leq P^0 \cdot e_h$ and

(3.18b) $\displaystyle\sum_h \tilde{c}_h^0(y_h, \tilde{P}^0(y)) = \sum_h \tilde{e}_h$ for all $\mathbf{y}$.

If one considers the *artificial* economy where each consumer h has the information $\tilde{\mathbf{y}}$ rather than $(\tilde{y}_h, \tilde{P}^0)$, then an equilibrium to the artificial economy that is an invertible function of $\{\text{Prob}(\tilde{s} = s|\tilde{\mathbf{y}} = \mathbf{y})\}_{s=1}^n \equiv \pi(\mathbf{y})$ will be a Rational Expectations equilibrium, because $\pi(\mathbf{y})$ is a sufficient statistic for the information in $\mathbf{y}$ regarding $\tilde{s}$.[2] Thus, a consumer who conditions on any invertible function of $\pi(\mathbf{y})$ has the same beliefs as a consumer who conditions on $\mathbf{y}$. Hence in (3.18a), when a consumer conditions on y_h and on $\tilde{P}^0$, which is an invertible function of $\pi(\mathbf{y})$, he will have the same demands as a consumer in the artificial economy who conditions on $\mathbf{y}$.

If I show that $\tilde{p}^a(\mathbf{y})$ is an invertible function of $\pi(\mathbf{y})$, then $\tilde{p}^a(\mathbf{y})$ will be an R.E. equilibrium; that is, it will solve (3.18). Grossman (1981) examines this for an economy that is a special case of the one studied here (in particular, there are production, multiple periods, and state-dependent utility). Therein, it is shown that $\tilde{p}^a(\mathbf{y})$ is an R.E. equilibrium. This result can be understood using (3.15). Make the state 1 commodity the numeraire, that is, set $p_1^a(\mathbf{y}) \equiv 1$. Since there are n states, there are $n - 1$

relative prices. Note that since $\sum_{s=1}^{n} \pi_s(\mathbf{y}) = 1$, there are $n - 1$ probabilities. Also note that consumption c_h^s is just a function of prices p^a and probabilities π. Assume that $U_h(\cdot)$ is strictly concave. For $p^a(\mathbf{y})$ not to be an invertible function of $\pi(\mathbf{y})$, it would have to be the case that (3.15) could hold at the same p^a for different values of π. But if p^a stays constant and π_s rises, this will tend to make everyone want to consume more of c_s. (Note that it is not optimal for a consumer to reduce c_s and c_1, when $n = 2$, since this reduces his utility at an unchanged level of wealth.) But *all* consumers cannot buy more of c_s since its supply is fixed. Thus the market cannot clear at the same p^a for different values of π. This argument is literally correct if there are two states ($n = 2$); however, a more elaborate argument is required for $n > 2$ (and is presented in Grossman, 1981), since more than just one probability can change.

An immediate consequence of the fact that there exists an R.E. equilibrium that is a sufficient statistic for all the economy's information is that there exists an R.E. equilibrium ($\bar{P}^0$, $\bar{c}^0$) that cannot be Pareto dominated by a central planner with all the economy's information. Formally,

THEOREM. There exists an R.E. equilibrium ($\bar{P}^0(\mathbf{y})$, $c^0(\mathbf{y})$) such that if $\bar{c}(\mathbf{y}) = (\bar{c}_h(\mathbf{y}))_h$ is any other feasible allocation (that is, $\sum_h [c_h(\mathbf{y}) - e_h(\mathbf{y})] \leq 0$ for all $\mathbf{y}$), then for each $\mathbf{y}$, it is impossible to have

$$(3.19) \qquad \sum_s U_h(c_{hs}(\mathbf{y}))\text{Prob}(s|\mathbf{y}) \geq \sum_s U_h(c_{hs}^0(\mathbf{y}))\text{Prob}(s|\mathbf{y})$$

for all h and strict inequality for some h.

The theorem is a much stronger statement about the optimality of competitive allocations than the usual theorem. The standard optimality result essentially says that in an economy where markets are complete and all consumers have identical information, then a planner with the same information cannot Pareto dominate the competitive allocations. This theorem states that in an economy where traders may have arbitrarily diverse information, the allocations brought about by competitive prices are as if each trader had all the information. Hence these allocations cannot be Pareto dominated.

In the above economy, there are n commodities $(c_{hs})_{s=1}^{n}$ and, thus, n prices that consumers observe to get information about $\mathbf{y}$ $(P_s^0(\mathbf{y}))_{s=1}^{n}$. Note that the information in $\mathbf{y}$ is summarized by the n vector $\pi(\mathbf{y}) = (\pi_s(\mathbf{y}))_{s=1}^{n} = (\text{Prob}(\tilde{s} = s|\tilde{\mathbf{y}} = \mathbf{y}))_{s=1}^{n}$. From the previous discussion, it is clear that $P^a(\mathbf{y})$

$\equiv \bar{P}^a(\pi(y))$, that is, $P^a(\mathbf{y})$ depends on $\mathbf{y}$ only through $\pi(\mathbf{y})$. Theorem 1 in Grossman (1981) showed that $\bar{P}^a(\pi)$ is essentially an invertible function of π. The n-vector $\pi(\mathbf{y})$ is a sufficient statistic for $\mathbf{y}$, and there are n traded speculative commodities. That is, there are enough prices around so that all the information relevant to consumers can be extracted from $P^a(\mathbf{y})$. If there are fewer markets, this would not, in general, be true, as was seen in the example at the end of Section 3.1. The next section discusses how the informativeness of speculative markets is determined by incentives for information collection.

3.3. Conclusions Regarding the Informativeness of Securities Prices

In the previous sections I have demonstrated that the Walrasian model requires a generalization in order to provide a model of market prices at which traders do not want to recontract. The R.E. equilibrium generates such prices. This generalization of the Walrasian equilibrium to situations where information is dispersed permits an extension of the fundamental theorem of welfare economics. The new theorem states that if markets are complete then each individual acting in his own self-interest in an economy where information is dispersed is able to achieve allocations that are as if each individual had access to all of the economy's information.

I have suggested that financial markets are a natural aggregator of information. They serve as a place where traders can attempt to earn a return for private information collection and in the process transfer valuable information to other people. Financial markets are thus the likely candidates for clarification of the predictive superiority of the R.E. model over the Walrasian model. Furthermore, by examining the mechanics of trade on financial markets, one can better understand how R.E. allocations are implemented.

Recall that the trader conditions his "demand" at P on the information in the event that P is the equilibrium price. It is not clear how a P comes about that is indeed the equilibrium price when information is y, given that each trader only has a "demand" at the equilibrium price and no single trader observes y. In most financial markets traders are able to submit demand curves in the form of limit orders to their brokers on the trading "floor." Traders can also submit "market orders" to their brokers, which state that a certain quantity should be bought (or sold) immediately irrespective of price. In the notation of Section 3.1, this mechanism makes the market clearing price $P(y,q)$ a function of the information

y of traders with limit orders and the total number of market orders to be executed—say, q. Traders who submit limit orders take account of the fact that if their order gets executed at a particular price P_0, then this transaction occurs because other traders have submitted particular limit orders based upon their information, which when combined with the flow of market orders has caused supply to equal demand at $P(y,q) = P_0$. For example, a trader who was willing to buy only at a very low price realizes that his limit order will get executed only if other traders receive very negative news or if there is a large inflow of market orders to sell. These calculations mimic the calculations required in an R.E. equilibrium (see Kyle, 1985).

The R.E. model also helps one appreciate the idea of an informationally efficient financial market. In such a market, most traders do not collect information because they know that the price system is already aggregating the information of all traders. Of course, it could not be an equilibrium for everyone to think that someone else has collected information. Grossman and Stiglitz (1980) have shown that there will be an equilibrium level of "noise" in prices that sufficiently disguises the information of those traders who do collect information so that they earn a return for information collection. Thus markets cannot perfectly aggregate information that is costly to collect. The cost of information collection and the benefit of having a little better information than the next person determine how close a market can be to a perfect aggregator of information.

Huberman and Schwert (1985) have estimated the degree to which a market aggregates information. They tested the aggregation theory on data involving bonds indexed to Israel's inflation rate. Trading on an indexed bond market causes dispersed information about inflation to be aggregated in much the same way as a futures market or a contingent claims market. Forecasting the inflation rate involves forecasting the prices of goods in various industries. Thus, the inflation rate for month t is publicly announced about 15 days after month t. The announcement basically states information that was dispersed in private hands 15 days before the announcement, since the producers and consumers of a particular industry's products knew the price of the products at the time they were set in the industry. If trading in indexed bonds and other securities aggregated this dispersed information in the period before the announcement, then the price of indexed bonds should not change very much on the basis of the public announcement of the inflation rate. Huberman and Schwert found that about 85% of the news in the inflation announcement is reflected in indexed bond prices before the announcement. Thus only 15% of the unanticipated inflation information was not aggregated by securities prices.

3.4. Heterogeneous Information and Macroeconomics

3.4.1. Rational Expectations Models

In the previous sections I have discussed the logic of Rational Expectations models for economies where information is dispersed. I have emphasized that such models are essential for understanding the informational role and efficiency of securities markets. Another major use can be made of these ideas, however—in attempts to explain business cycles.

The models of Barro (1976) and Lucas (1973) assumed that agents know more about the nominal price of the products they produce than they know about either the economywide price level or the size of the aggregate monetary injection. An agent's supply of goods of type i is shown to depend on $P_i - E[P|P_i]$, where P_i is the price of good i and P is the economywide price level. Furthermore, $P_i = P + \varepsilon_i$, where $E[\varepsilon_i|P] = 0$, and ε_i represents a real relative shock. It follows that if a monetary injection occurs (which is not directly observable) then agent i will observe a high P_i, which he will (rationally) attribute partially to ε_i being high. Hence $P_i - E[P|P_i]$ will be high, and output will be high. That is, an unobserved shock to the economywide price level will (rationally) cause each agent i to think that demand has shifted toward the product he produces.

It is crucial to understand that under complete information (that is, where P is directly observable) the nominal shock would have no effect on supply: $P_i - E[P|P_i, P] = P + \varepsilon_i - P = \varepsilon_i$. It is only the relative demand shock to i's product that would affect his output. Thus, dispersed information and rational expectations cause the nominal shock to have a larger effect on output than would occur under homogeneous information. Dispersed information creates a "multiplier" whereby shocks, which would otherwise have a small effect, cause correlated (across individuals) errors of expectations, and thus have a much larger effect.

Unfortunately, there is little empirical evidence in favor of the above transmission mechanism for nominal shocks. The Huberman and Schwert study has already shown that the existence of economywide securities markets will cause securities prices to aggregate and reveal information about economywide shocks. Furthermore, there is no evidence showing that unanticipated inflation is positively related to aggregate output (see Fair, 1979).

The above evidence should be combined with facts like (1) consumers purchase market baskets of goods and this necessarily gives them information about the prices of goods other than those they produce; (2) monetary injections occur via open-market operations on economywide capital markets; (3) the money supply is publicly announced and generally available with a very short lag; and (4) the economywide price level is made publicly available by the Bureau of Labor Statistics with only a slightly longer lag. The evidence suggests that asymmetric information about monetary factors is not a route by which nominal shocks have a large effect on output. However, the fact that dispersed information causes errors that are correlated across people can be used to construct theories of business cycles that explain why small unobserved shocks to the economy can have large effects on aggregate output.

Grossman and Weiss (1982) presented such a model. In that model agents have private information about the real productivity of their investments. The price level P and the money supply are public information, and there is an economywide nominal bond market with an interest rate denoted by r. However, prices and interest rates do not completely reveal to each agent the extent of the economywide shock to real productivity, denoted by n. Each agent i uses his own productivity, denoted by $n + \varepsilon_i$, and the observed prices to estimate n. Agents are interested in n because it is the real shadow cost of their own private investments, that is, an effective real interest cost of investment. Thus, agent i's investment is a function of $n + \varepsilon_i - \mathrm{E}[n|n + \varepsilon_i, P, r]$. Given that P and r do not reveal n (because of other private factors such as random money demand which make P and r noisy functions of n), it is shown that investment will vary more with n than would be the case if n were public information.

3.4.2. Implicit Contract Models

An unsatisfactory feature of the above models is that only *unobservable* aggregate shocks cause output to fluctuate by more than would be predicted by a homogeneous information Walrasian model. To the extent that output and employment fluctuate by more than can be explained by a homogeneous information model, it is important to see if this can be explained by a model in which *observable* aggregate shocks cause excessive fluctuations. The enormous supply of aggregate data provided by news services and the government, and the large body of evidence that securities prices quickly react to public news, make it difficult to accept (without substantial empirical evidence) a theory of aggregate fluctuations based upon aggregate shocks that are unobserved.

Grossman, Hart, and Maskin (1983) developed a model in which *observed* aggregate shocks make prices a noisier signal, a feature that, in turn, causes excessive aggregate fluctuations. Their model is based upon the asymmetric information implicit contract model of Azariades (1983) and Grossman and Hart (1981).

The implicit contract model posits a risk averse employer, for whom the marginal and average productivity of an input (for example, labor) varies positively with a state of nature $\bar{s}$. A risk sharing contract is signed between the employer and a supplier of risk sharing (which may also be the supplier of the input, although this is not necessary) before $\bar{s}$ is observed by anyone. It is assumed, however, that when $\bar{s}$ is realized, only the employer can observe its realization directly; the supplier of risk sharing cannot observe s directly. This situation makes ordinary insurance impossible. Normally the employer would receive a large payment in states where s is low and small payments where s is high; but this is now infeasible since the insurer cannot observe s. Nevertheless, since the marginal productivity of the input varies positively with s, the risk sharer can use the employment of the input as a screening device. That is, before s is realized, the risk sharer and the employer can agree that the insurance payments to the firm will be low in states in which the firm uses a lot of the input (since those are states in which s is high).

Grossman and Hart proved that if the parties to the contract optimally use input utilization as a screening device to improve risk sharing, then this practice will lead to underutilization of the inputs in all states except the best possible state $\bar{s}$ in which it is utilized correctly. That is, if R is the actual cost of the input l and if $w(l)$ is the employer's total cost of using the input (inclusive of insurance payments conditioned on input usage), then the optimal contract will specify that $w'(l) > R$ for all l except for the l associated with the best state of nature $\bar{s}$, and $w'(l(\bar{s})) = R$. Thus the marginal cost of utilization faced by the firm is higher than the actual input cost. The idea of the proof is as follows: for input utilization to screen for realizations of $\bar{s}$, it must be the case that the insurance received by the employer fall when l rises, that is, $-(w(l) - Rl)$ must fall as l rises, since $-(w(l) - Rl)$ is the insurance payment received by the firm.

Consider this example. Suppose that there are only two states s_1 and s_2 and that the input's marginal and average product are higher in state 1 than in state 2. Let $l^*(s)$ denote the input usage that would be chosen in state s if s could be publicly observed, that is, if l did not have to serve a screening function. Then the above result implies that $l(s_1) = l^*(s_1)$ while l will be underutilized in state 2, that is, $l(s_2) < l^*(s_2)$.

Now consider the case where a public shock causes an increase in the dispersion of s across firms. Suppose that prior to a shock all firms have the same s—say, $\bar{s}$. Suppose, further, that there is a publicly observed shock that raises the s of, say, 1/2 the firms and lowers it for the other 1/2 of firms in such a way that under homogeneous information input utilization would be unchanged, that is, $(1/2)l^*(s_1) + (1/2)l^*(s_2) = l^*(\bar{s})$. If I let $\bar{s}$ represent the *cross-sectional* distribution of s after the shock and assume that each employer knows his s but shares risk with an organization that only knows the cross-sectional distribution of s, then this model of cross-sectional dispersion is formally identical to the previous contractual model of risk sharing where $\bar{s}$ represented temporal uncertainty in an economy in which only one realization of $\bar{s}$ occurs at a time. It follows that the lucky firms with a high s will choose the same utilization as under homogeneous information, whereas the unlucky employers (with a low s) will have to signal that their realization of s is low by choosing a lower input utilization than they would have under homogeneous information. Hence, an optimal risk sharing arrangement implies that an increase in the dispersion of productivity will cause total input utilization to fall.

Grossman, Hart, and Maskin used this idea to model the effect on employment of a publicly observed shock. They considered an economy in which labor is the input utilized to produce intermediate goods. The intermediate goods are used to produce final goods. The price vector P of final goods is public information. The productivity of a particular intermediate good is affected by a nonpublic random variable $\tilde{\Theta}$. In particular, the realizations of $\tilde{\Theta}$ determine how intensively a particular intermediate good is utilized by a final goods industry. Finally, the publicly observed shock is a shock that shifts demand from one final good toward another final good. In the absence of shocks to final demand, the $\tilde{\Theta}$ shocks are constructed to have no effect on employment; the realizations of $\tilde{\Theta}$ determine which final good utilizes a particular firm's intermediate good, but the marginal value product of intermediate good labor is unaffected by which final good sector utilizes its output. However, a random observed shock to final demand disrupts this equality of marginal value products, creating cross-sectional dispersion in the marginal value product of labor in the intermediate goods industries. For example, a publicly observed demand shift from small cars to large cars will adversely affect those intermediate goods producers whose goods are used relatively intensively in the production of small cars. In the absence of the final demand shock, a particular intermediate goods producer will not care whether small cars or large cars use his hardware intensively; in a stationary state resources will have flowed across sectors to equalize the profitability of factor usage in both final goods industries. However, after the unanticipated shift in demand toward large cars, the rise in the relative price of large cars will cause the marginal value product of labor to rise in those firms for which Θ is such that they supply large car firms rather than small car firms.

A worker in an intermediate goods industry who observes a final demand shock but does not know how this affects the firm he works in will face an increase in uncertainty about his marginal value productivity. In particular, if n is the public shock and $\tilde{s}$ is a random variable describing the cross-sectional distribution of marginal value productivities of labor in intermediate goods industries, then this framework can be placed into the one analyzed earlier to conclude that those firms adversely affected by the shock will have lower employment than if workers' marginal products were public, whereas firms that are affected positively will choose the level of employment that would occur if their inputs' marginal products were public. However, a general equilibrium analysis that takes into account how the lost income from underemployment adversely affects the industry *toward which* the relative demand shock occurs, shows that *all* industries will have lower employment than would occur in a world in which marginal value products are public information.

Grossman, Hart, and Maskin discussed an example and provided some empirical evidence for a relative demand shock caused by an unanticipated inflation that redistributes wealth between nominal creditors and nominal debtors. If age differences between nominal creditors and debtors cause the groups to have different wealth elasticities of demand for final goods, then the wealth redistribution will cause a change in the relative demand for final goods. Since workers in intermediate goods industries will be unable to determine the effect on their own marginal value product by observing final goods prices, this shock will exacerbate the asymmetric information between employers and employees and cause a rise in aggregate unemployment (in an implicit contract model).

The implicit contract model is thus able to propose an explanation for excessive employment fluctuations that is consistent with a world where workers receive very good information on economywide shocks and consumers goods prices but poor information about their own marginal value productivity. This model stands in sharp contrast to the Lucas and Barro models, where it is assumed that workers have very good information about their own marginal value productivity but very poor information about the prices of consumer goods and economywide shocks.

Notes

1. This statement is equivalent to the usual definition that involves the factorization of the likelihood function of z_1 given z_2; see the Appendix in Grossman (1978).

2. Note that $\text{Prob}(\bar{s} = s|\mathbf{y}) = \text{Prob}(\bar{s} = s|\pi(\mathbf{y}))$. This statement can be proved as follows: let $F(s)$ be any function of s and let $\bar{Q}(\mathbf{y}) = E[F(s)|\mathbf{y}] = \Sigma_s F(s)\text{Prob}(s|\mathbf{y}) \equiv Q(\pi(\mathbf{y}))$. Hence $E[F(s)|\mathbf{y}]$ depends on $\mathbf{y}$ only through $\pi(\mathbf{y})$. But $E[F(s)|\pi(\mathbf{y})] = E\{E[F(s)|\mathbf{y}]|\pi(\mathbf{y})\} = E[Q(\pi(\mathbf{y}))|\pi(\mathbf{y})] = Q(\pi(\mathbf{y})) \equiv E[F(s)|\mathbf{y}]$. The result now follows if I set $F_i(s) = 1$ if $s = s_i$, and $F_i(s) = 0$ otherwise.

References

Azariades, C. 1983. Employment with Asymmetric Information. *Quarterly Journal of Economics* 98 (suppl.): 157–172.

Barro, R. 1976. Rational Expectations and the Role of Monetary Policy. *Journal of Monetary Economics* 2: 1–32.

Diamond, D., and R. Verrecchia. 1981. Information Aggregation in a Noisy Rational Expectations Model. *Journal of Financial Economics* 9: 221–235.

Fair, R. 1979. An Analysis of the Accuracy of Four Macroeconomic Models. *Journal of Political Economy* (August).

Fama, E. 1970. Efficient Capital Markets: A Review of Theory and Empirical Work. *Journal of Finance* 25: 383–417.

Grossman, S. 1976. On the Efficiency of Competitive Stock Markets Where Traders Have Diverse Information. *Journal of Finance* 31(2): 573–585.

——— 1978. Further Results on the Informational Efficiency of Competitive Stock Markets. *Journal of Economic Theory* 18(1): 81–101.

——— 1981. An Introduction to the Theory of Rational Expectations under Asymmetric Information. *Review of Economic Studies* 68: 541–559.

Grossman, S., and O. Hart. 1981. Implicit Contracts, Moral Hazard, and Unemployment. *American Economic Review* 71 (May): 301–307.

Grossman, S., O. Hart, and E. Maskin. 1983. Unemployment with Observable Aggregate Shocks. *Journal of Political Economy* 91(6): 907–928.

Grossman, S., and J. Stiglitz. 1980. On the Impossibility of Informationally Efficient Markets. *American Economic Review* 70(3): 393–408.

Grossman, S., and L. Weiss. 1982. Heterogeneous Information and the Theory of the Business Cycle. *Journal of Political Economy* 90 (August): 699–727.

Hayek, F. H. 1945. The Use of Knowledge in Society. *American Economic Review* (September).

Huberman, G., and G. Schwert. 1985. Information Aggregation, Inflation, and the Pricing of Indexed Bonds. *Journal of Political Economy* 93(1): 92–114.

Kyle, P. 1985. Informed Speculation with Imperfect Competition. Unpublished paper, Princeton University.

Lucas, R. 1973. Some International Evidence on Output-Inflation Tradeoffs. *American Economic Review* (June): 326–334.

Mood, A., F. Graybill, and D. Boes. 1974. *Introduction to the Theory of Statistics,* 3rd Ed. New York: McGraw-Hill.

4   Consumption

Robert E. Hall

No specialty in macroeconomics has been more profoundly influenced by the rational expectations revolution than has the study of consumption. From the early 1950s, when the life cycle-permanent income hypothesis came to dominate the profession's thinking about consumption, until the late 1970s, the consumption field was largely dormant. In the following decade, however, a substantial upsurge of new work has occurred. Although almost all of the new work embodies the hypothesis of rational expectations, much more has been added to our thinking than just the simple idea that consumers make consumption plans on the basis of all available information about future income.

My survey of this work will start with the initial impact of rational expectations—the development of the Euler equation characterization of optimal consumption behavior and the empirical tests of it. Tests have been applied by a number of authors using data for the United States and for a number of other countries. Roughly speaking, the Euler equation says that consumption should evolve as a random walk; that is, the change in consumption should not be predictable. The empirical work testing this proposition says, in sum, that consumption is fairly close to a random walk, but certain variables have enough predictive power that the hypothesis is rejected in formal statistical tests.

One interesting branch of the ensuing research has asked whether the predictability of the change in consumption can be explained by the inability of consumers to borrow when income is temporarily low. The investigation of "liquidity constraints" has occupied quite a number of investigators, most of whom have reached the conclusion that liquidity constraints do help to explain aspects of the data not explained by the simple rational expectations life cycle-permanent income hypothesis.

They typically find that most of the movements of consumption are consistent with the simple model; only a minority of consumers are constrained.

Another branch has sought to explain departures from the simple random walk by examining the implications of the durability of consumption goods. Durability turns out to compete with liquidity constraints, in that models containing both features do not rely very heavily on liquidity constraints to explain the predictability of consumption.

The third branch of the literature I shall examine considers a more refined version of the Euler equation. Theoretically, changes in expected real returns should influence the rate of change of consumption. When asset markets offer high returns, consumers should defer consumption. That is, the rate of growth of consumption of individual households should be positively correlated with the expected return. Rejection of the simple random walk model might be the result of this correlation. However, the aggregation of interest-rate effects is a complicated issue; there is no simple relation between expected real returns and the rate of growth of aggregate consumption.

There are some important topics related to consumption that I have excluded from this discussion. In particular, the literature stimulated by Robert Barro's work on Ricardian equivalence is outside my domain. On this, see Bernheim's (1987) survey and synthesis.

4.1. Rational Expectations and the Euler Equation

Work on consumption from the time of Keynes's *General Theory* focused on the development of a consumption function, that is, a structural relation between income (and possibly the interest rate) and consumption. Friedman's permanent income hypothesis and Modigliani's life-cycle hypothesis were seen as suggestions about the way that income variables might enter the consumption function. The main point was that temporary changes in income should have less impact on consumption than should permanent changes. Probably the most impressive evidence on the point was in Friedman's examination of cross-sectional data on family income and consumption. When it came to building a consumption function, however, Friedman and his followers (such as Darby, 1972) made consumption a distributed lag of current and past income. Muth (1960) had shown that a geometric distributed lag was optimal under rational expectations only with a certain special stochastic process for income, but the consumption function literature did not pursue this point until many years later. In aggregate U.S. data, the distributed lag from income to consumption had a peculiar feature—either most of the weight applied to current income or the lag came out to be almost infinitely long.

Ando and Modigliani's empirical consumption function (1963) took a more structural view of expectations. They reasoned that the unemployment rate was an additional variable that the public might consider in deciding whether the current level of real income was representative of its permanent level.

The opening shot in the rational expectations revolution was Robert Lucas's (1976) famous critique of econometric policy models that was presented in 1973. The models he criticized consisted of sets of structural equations. One of the three structural equations he found wanting was the consumption function. And his criticism was profound. It was not that the typical consumption function was misspecified. Rather, he said, there is no such thing as a consumption function. There is a structural relation between permanent income and consumption, but the consumption function asserts a structural relation between observed income and permanent income, and there is no reason to expect a stable relation of that type. Changes elsewhere in the economy—for example, in stabilization policy—could alter the optimal way for a consumer to make an inference about permanent income from observed income. Development of consumption functions has little purpose. In particular, a model for policy analysis based on a consumption function is self-defeating.

Although Lucas was scornful of existing econometric policy evaluation models, his message was not completely destructive of all model-building or empirical research. There are structural relationships in the economy, but the consumption function is not among them. For consumption, the structural relation, invariant to policy interventions and other shifts elsewhere in the economy, is the intertemporal preference ordering. The view of consumption that flowed from Lucas's work is that today's level of consumption is the level chosen by consumers to maximize expected lifetime utility, given all available information about current and future income and prices. The consumer uses all available knowledge about the behavior of other actors in the economy, including the government, in processing the information.

Lucas's critique of the consumption function was overshadowed by his critique of the Phillips curve, where he generalized and formalized a point made very effectively several years earlier by Friedman (1968). The next step in the development of the rational expectations view of consumption was Hall's (1978) test of a general implication of Lucas's view. Hall neither tried to repair the traditional consumption function nor tried to estimate the deep parameters of utility. Rather, he formulated a simple empirical test of the idea that consumers maximize the expected value of lifetime utility subject to an unchanging real interest rate. The basic idea is to look at the Euler equation describing the optimal behavior of such a consumer. The Euler equation characterizes the equality of the marginal rate of substitution between consumption this year and consumption next year to the relative price of the two. That relative price is simply the present discounted cost of a unit of future consumption. Mathematically, the consumer seeks to maximize

$$E_t \sum_s \left(\frac{1}{1 + \delta}\right)^s u(c_{t+s})$$

$$\text{s.t.} \sum_s \left(\frac{1}{1 + r}\right)^s (c_{t+s} - w_{t+s}) = A_t.$$

The notation is

E_t = mathematical expectation conditional on all information in t

δ = rate of subjective time preference

r = real rate of interest, a constant over time

$u(\cdot)$ = one-period utility function, strictly concave

c_t = consumption

w_t = earnings from sources other than savings

A_t = assets apart from human capital

On the possible relaxation of the assumption of intertemporal separability, see Browning (1986b). Derivation of results with constant expected real interest rates in general equilibrium appears in Christiano, Eichenbaum, and Marshall (1987).

The Euler equation expressing the equality of the marginal rate of substitution to the price ratio is

$$E_t u'(c_{t+1}) = \frac{1 + \delta}{1 + r} u'(c_t).$$

That is, marginal utility next year is expected to be the same as marginal utility this year, except for a trend associated with the constant rate of time preference δ and the constant real interest rate r. Another way to express the same idea is

$$u'(c_{t+1}) = \frac{1 + \delta}{1 + r} u'(c_t) + \varepsilon_t.$$

Here ε is a random variable whose expectation at time t (when consumption c_t is being chosen) is zero. In particular, ε is uncorrelated with $u'(c_t)$, so this equation is a regression. If the functional form of $u(\cdot)$ were known, this equation could be the basis of a test of optimization. For the optimizing consumer, no variable observed in year t would receive a nonzero coefficient if added to the equation. If a variable were found that helped predict next year's marginal utility and if that variable were known to the consumer at the time c_t was chosen, then the consumer would be shown to have failed to optimize.

Hall's original work did not try to make use of information about the functional form of the utility function. Instead, he argued that the Euler equation could be approximated closely by assuming a quadratic utility function, in which case it could be written as

$$c_{t+1} = \lambda c_t + \varepsilon_t.$$

In this framework, the basic test of optimization involves placing additional variables on the right-hand side and computing the t- or F-test for their exclusion.

Chang (1987) considered the issue of when simple random walk relations hold exactly. Zeldes (1986) computed consumption functions numerically with nonnegativity constraints and concluded that the quadratic specification can be misleading in some circumstances.

Hall found that lagged real disposable income had little predictive power for consumption; the hypothesis that only c_t helped predict c_{t+1} among variables dated t and earlier was accepted. However, he showed that the Euler-equation restriction was rejected for the stock market. The recent change in the real value of the stock market has statistically significant predictive power for the future change in consumption.

Flavin (1981) examined the relation between income and consumption in the rational expectations framework and found sufficient predictive power to reject the strict optimization hypothesis. Her theoretical work involved the development of an explicit structural consumption function, based on the hypothesis that real income obeys a stable stochastic process. Thus her model itself is subject to Lucas's criticism, which points out that the stochastic process of income is a result of the interaction of all the actors in the economy and is not a deep structural characteristic of the consumer alone. However, her test turned out to be identical to the type of test proposed by Hall. She found rejection of optimization because she included more lagged values of income than Hall had tried and because of a few other minor changes.

Flavin's structural model enabled her to interpret her findings quantitatively. In her results, the parameter describing the excess response of consumption to the contemporaneous change in income is about 0.36. She pointed out that the relatively small values of coefficients found by Hall on lagged income in the reduced-form consumption regression signify much larger structural coefficients. As a general matter, Flavin found even more evidence than did Hall to reject the pure optimization model with a constant real interest rate.

Goodfriend (1986) pointed out that Flavin's procedure rests on the hypothesis that aggregate income is immediately observable. If, instead, there is a one-quarter lag before aggregate income becomes public, one would expect rejection roughly along the lines found by Flavin.

Mankiw and Shapiro (1985b) criticized Flavin's work on the grounds that her detrending procedure would induce the finding of excess sensitivity even if it were absent from the original data. They considered an example in which income is a random walk. Optimal consumption is also a random walk. Hall's test applied to the original data will not reject optimization. However, with detrended data, income and consumption will be cyclical and will flunk Hall's test. They noted that Flavin's test is indecisive in the original data, because income is essentially a random walk before detrending.

Stock and West (1987) challenged Mankiw and Shapiro's interpretation of excess sensitivity as arising from a spuriously detrended random walk. They argued that by detrending a random walk with drift, Flavin induced a change in the large sample distribution from a normal to a nonstandard distribution of the type associated with an ARIMA process with unit roots. Using theoretical results of Sims, Stock, and Watson (1987), they noted that, in contrast, Hall's original tests based on lagged consumption were valid even with preliminary detrending of the data. The key difference between Hall's and Flavin's procedure is that Hall included lagged consumption as a regressor, whereas Flavin did not. Stock and West presented the results of Monte Carlo experiments to support their argument, which is otherwise based on asymptotic theory. In addition, results obtained by Deaton (1986) cast doubt on the hypothesis that the bias identified by Mankiw and Shapiro can fully explain the finding of excess sensitivity of consumption to income.

Deaton's work also casts doubt on the likelihood of success of models that try to fit a stochastic process to income and then infer the appropriate response of consumption to the innovations in that process. He noted that a nonstationary process for real income—specifically, a first-order autoregressive process in the first difference—seems to provide a reasonable description of the income process. But for that process, the observed response of consumption to an income innovation is much too small rather than too big. Subtle differences in the income process have major implications for the consumption response. Accordingly, results obtained within a restricted class of income processes may not give reliable statistical tests of the hypothesis of excess sensitivity. Campbell and Deaton (1987) pursued the idea and fitted a number of low-order ARIMA models of income. Most of them have the property that the innovation in consumption should have a larger variance than the innovation in income. They also reached the same conclusion by examining the autocorrelations of income. However, both of their procedures are biased toward the conclusion that consumption is excessively smooth, so their findings are inconclusive.

West (1986) used a variance bounds technique to examine the question of the relative variabilities of consumption and income. He concluded that the evidence is ambiguous, though possibly it favors excess smoothness of consumption. In a related paper, Christiano (1987) finds that small influences on consumption through intertemporal substitution associated with variations in real returns could explain an apparent excess smoothness of consumption.

Nelson (1987) reexamined Hall's original empirical results and Flavin's later work. He argued that a more reasonable approximation could be achieved by assuming logarithmic utility and a log-normal distribution for later consumption given earlier consumption. He demonstrated that the current change in income is a statistically significant predictor of the coming change in consumption in that framework. Nelson also confirmed that Flavin's strong results on excess sensitivity may be the result of her procedure for detrending the data.

Jacobson (1981) showed that measures of consumer attitudes had predictive power even in the presence of the stock-market value included in Hall's original study.

Miron (1986) showed that the results obtained by Flavin and others rejecting the simple random walk hypothesis could be reversed by using seasonally unadjusted data and an explicit model of seasonal effects rather than by using seasonally adjusted data.

Kormendi and LaHaye (1986) carried out tests of the explanatory power of lagged income changes for the current change in consumption for a panel of 30 countries. They failed to reject the hypothesis of no explanatory power for the panel as a whole. Using Flavin's approach, they found that consumption appears to be undersensitive to changes in permanent income.

4.1.1. Time Aggregation

Evans (1982), Christiano (1984), and others have pointed out that the data employed to test the Euler equation are time averages, whereas the theory deals with consumption chosen at isolated points in time. Working (1960) derived the time series properties of a time average of a random walk. The first difference of the time average is a first-order moving average process with a serial correlation of about 0.25. Tests of the Euler equation can be modified to take account of this property—it implies particular coefficients for lagged consumption and invalidates the most recent observation on real income in the test regression. Hall (1988) treated the time aggregation problem at some length, but neither he nor any other author has repeated the Euler equation tests to take account of time aggregation. Estimation problems with time-aggregated data are discussed in detail in Hansen and Singleton (1986).

4.1.2. Findings of Countries Other than the United States

Daly and Hadjimatheou (1981) repeated Hall's basic Euler equation test using data for the United Kingdom. They found substantial predictive power for lagged disposable income and lagged liquid assets; they rejected the exclusion of those variables from the Euler equation unambiguously. Their work was criticized by Cuddington and Hurd (1981) on the grounds that they presented only the final results of an extensive search for successful predictors. However, Muellbauer (1983) found a similar rejection for the United Kingdom using only consumption lagged once and income lagged once and twice.

Cuddington (1982) examined Canadian data and found significant predictive power for real money balances, real private wealth, real GNP, and the unemployment rate.

Johnson (1983) rejected the Euler equation optimization condition with Australian data. He found predictive power for certain measures of lagged income and the unemployment rate.

4.1.3. Findings in Cross-Sectional Data

In principle, variations in income and consumption experienced by individual families should provide more powerful tests of models of consumption. However, some of the advantages of the proliferation of observations available in cross sections are lost because of measurement problems. In the United States, for example, there is no body of data that reports on the total consumption of families in successive years. Much of the research on U.S. data has been done with data on income and food consumption from the Panel Study of Income Dynamics.

Hall and Mishkin (1982) examined this body of data within the framework of a rational expectations theory of consumption. Their model hypothesizes that consumption at the level of the individual family has a transitory measurement error or other source of noise not explained by the theory. In the presence of such an error, the simple regression test of the Euler equation is restricted: it must impose a unit coefficient on lagged consumption and cannot use further lags of consumption as candidates for failure of the hypothesis of unpredictability. Hall and Mishkin regressed the first difference of food consumption on the lagged change in income and found a coefficient of -0.010 with a standard error of 0.002. The rejection of optimization is strong statistically, although the magnitude of the departure from the theoretical value of zero is small.

Hall and Mishkin also estimated a structural model of consumption similar to Flavin's. Their model departs from hers in two ways. First, it permits current consumption to respond to the immediate future innovation in income. This modification is suggested by the timing of the data and also by the possibility that families have some advance information about income changes. The results confirm that such advance information is available to families. Second, the model permits a fraction of consumption to move in proportion to actual current income instead of permanent income. If a fraction of the sample is liquidity constrained, their income will move in this way. The results suggest that about 20% of consumption is linked to current rather than permanent income. With these two modifications, the model is successful in explaining the entire pattern of covariances of income and food consumption found in the data.

Hayashi (1985) studied a panel of Japanese households in a similar framework. In addition to food consumption, the panel reports data on four other categories of consumption. Hayashi found that lagged income has significant predictive power for the change in consumption, in contradiction to the Euler equation characterization of optimization. He formulated a more general model to explain the predictive power of income, which included the possibility of liquidity constraints and also the possibility that consumption in one period provides satisfaction in succeeding periods. He incorporated the latter effect by making the utility function depend on a distributed lag of past expenditures. His results show that the durability of consumption is an important part of the explanation of the failure of the simple Euler equation. After taking account of durability, he found a sharp estimate that 15% of households are liquidity constrained.

Altonji and Siow (1987) considered the problem of errors in measuring income in panel studies. They show that income measurement errors are important quantitatively but that the generally favorable findings in panel studies of the life cycle-permanent income model are confirmed when the errors are considered explicitly.

Working with highly detailed data from a Norwegian panel, Mork and Smith (1986) found results generally favorable to the life cycle-permanent income model.

4.1.4. Restrictions Imposed by the Rational Expectations Permanent Income Model on the Joint Behavior of Income and Consumption

Sargent (1978) was the first to investigate the problem of formulating optimal consumption behavior as a restriction on a general time series model of income and consumption. However, as pointed out by Flavin (1981), Sargent's version of the permanent income model did not take account of the fact that current saving finances future consumption. As a result, the restrictions he derived and tested were not a satisfactory characterization of optimal consumption. Flavin derived the restrictions implied by the standard permanent income model. The cross-equation restrictions on the coefficients of lagged variables turn out to be exactly those tested by Hall (1978)—the exclusion of all variables other than lagged consumption in the autoregressive representation for consumption. She showed that there are no restrictions operating across the coefficients of the two autoregressions. However, if one interprets the univariate time series model of income literally, in the sense that no lagged variable other than income is useful in forecasting income, the model also implies an important restriction on the covariance matrix of the innovations of consumption and income. That matrix is singular; the two innovations are proportional to one another and the theory relates their constant of proportionality to the coefficients of the income process. Sargent did not consider the restrictions on the covariance matrix. Flavin argued that the singularity should not be expected in actual data, where a more elaborate model would be appropriate. In that model, consumers use information to forecast future income that is not conveyed by the current and past levels of income. Then the innovation in consumption is not perfectly correlated with the innovation in income, nor does theory prescribe the numerical relation between the two innovations. If people respond to the information contained in other variables in addition to income, the measured correlation of the innovations in income and in consumption should be less than one. It is tempting to interpret the residual in an income autoregression as proportional to the innovation in permanent income. However, if people respond to variables in addition to the ones in the econometrician's right-hand variables, the residual in an income equation will be an error-ridden measure of the innovation in permanent income. Flavin's analysis of the covariance matrix of the income and consumption residuals indicates that the magnitude of the measurement error is far from negligible.

The issue of the singularity of the covariance matrix of a set of variables under certain information assumptions with rational expectations was also considered at a more general level by Sargent and Hansen (1981).

John Campbell (1986) considered the restrictions imposed by optimal consumption behavior on a three-variable system comprising consumption, labor income, and capital income (the latter defined as the constant expected real interest rate times the level of assets). He showed that the restrictions implied by theory can be stated as parameter restrictions on a vector autoregression. The first restriction is that capital income evolves according to the intertemporal budget constraint with constant expected real interest rate (the actual return ex post can be random). This restriction is a statement about the technology, not about consumption behavior.

The second restriction is that either the change in consumption, or, equivalently, the statistic

$$s_t - \Delta x_t - (1 + r)\, s_{t-1}$$

(where s_t is saving and x_t is labor income) is unpredictable. This statistic is the innovation in consumption plus the innovation in capital income, so it is unpredictable for essentially the same reasons that the change in consumption is unpredictable.

Campbell's test is close to a test of the unpredictability of consumption changes and has the same partial equilibrium character because he does not test the constancy of expected real rates. The advantage of his framework is that it can be used to assess the quantitative importance for savings behavior of deviations from the permanent income theory.

Campbell also made the interesting observation that the level of saving can be written as the present discounted value of expected future declines in noncapital income. That is, the permanent income model explains saving only through the income-smoothing motive. In the model, saving is positive only when income exceeds its permanent level and is consequently expected to decline in the future. In fact, average saving is higher than the model predicts.

The movements of saving also differ somewhat from those of the optimal forecast of the decline in labor income, but the two variables have about the same standard deviations. Campbell argued that if consumption were excessively sensitive to income, then saving would have a lower standard deviation than would the optimal forecast. He concluded that the failure of the permanent income model should not be described as excess sensitivity.

Campbell and Clarida (1986) obtained results for Canada and Britain that are quite similar to those for the United States.

4.1.5. Liquidity Constraints

The notion that the sensitivity of consumption to income is greater than that predicted by the permanent income hypothesis has long been associated with the idea that households are unable to dissave during periods of abnormally low income. Instead of continuing a normal level of consumption by drawing down financial assets or borrowing, they must reduce consumption. Such households face liquidity constraints because they do not hold liquid assets or collateral suitable for borrowing.

Hayashi (1987) has provided a very complete survey of the literature on liquidity constraints. My remarks here are selective.

Muellbauer (1983) and Zeldes (1985) developed the theory of the response of consumers to liquidity constraints within the framework of the rational expectations permanent income model. As they noted, it is an oversimplification to say that liquidity-constrained consumers simply spend all of their disposable income. Rather, the liquidity constraint has a shadow price that functions as an interest rate. In circumstances where an unconstrained consumer would maintain consumption by dissaving, a consumer influenced by liquidity constraints will behave as if he faced a higher interest rate. The consumer will substitute away from current consumption because it is, in effect, more expensive. Although an Euler equation can be derived for the consumer facing a liquidity constraint, it includes a term involving the shadow price of the constraint. The determination of that shadow price involves a consideration of the entire intertemporal planning problem of the consumer and does not decompose in a simple way. Because the current shadow price is almost certainly correlated with current and past income, the simple Euler equation proposition of unpredictable changes in consumption does not hold for the liquidity-constrained consumer.

Runkle (1983) and Zeldes examined liquidity constraints in panel data for individual households. They applied the simple Euler equation test in log form; that is, they tested the hypothesis that the rate of growth of consumption is unpredictable except for a term involving market interest rates. They showed that for households with low net worth, who are candidates for liquidity constraints, the hypothesis is rejected. Runkle found that the rate of growth of consumption is positively related to net worth in families with assets below $1500, whereas Zeldes found that consumption growth is negatively related to real disposable income. The latter finding was also reported by Hall and Mishkin (1982) and other authors who interpreted their findings as supporting liquidity constraints but did not develop a formal model of the effect of the constraints.

Flavin (1985) examined the issue of liquidity constraints in time series data in an extended version of her earlier model. She considered two explanations of her earlier finding that the innovation in consumption is excessively sensitive to the innovation in income. First, consumers may be myopic—that is, they may behave as if they faced extremely high interest rates at all times. Second, some consumers at some times may face liquidity constraints. She noted that the two alternative explanations can be distinguished by studying the relation of excess sensitivity to variables that measure the incidence of liquidity constraints. For this purpose, she used the unemployment rate. In the null hypothesis derived from the rational expectations-permanent income hypothesis, the unemployment rate helps predict future income but has no direct influence on consumption in the absence of liquidity constraints. Flavin found that when the unemployment rate is included in the model as an additional variable to forecast income but is constrained to have no direct effect on consumption, the excess sensitivity of consumption to current income is large and statistically significant, as before. However, when the unemployment rate, interpreted as an indicator of liquidity constraints, is permitted to have a direct impact on consumption, the measured excess sensitivity of consumption to income falls substantially in magnitude and becomes insignificant. Because of the high degree of correlation between the unemployment rate and income, the empirical results do not provide clear-cut conclusions, but Flavin interpreted the results as providing some support for a role of liquidity constraints.

Muellbauer and Bover (1986) developed a more elaborate model of liquidity constraints in time series data and concluded that the model provides a good description of U.S. data.

Browning (1987) tested for liquidity constraints in a novel way. Under the assumptions that married couples plan to have children sooner or later and that there is no shift of preferences for drinking and smoking as a result of the arrival of children, life-cycle theory predicts that there should be no change in alcohol and tobacco consumption when children arrive. British panel data support this proposition.

4.1.6. Durable Goods

At the most basic level, the theory of durables consumption is no different from the theory of nondurables consumption. Households consume a flow of services from durables and that flow should be determined in the same way as the flow of other types of consumption. However, a number of authors have gone beyond this simple statement to build and estimate models that deal with the joint behavior of income and the acquisition of stocks of durables.

Mankiw (1982) developed the most basic model in a time series setting. He noted that the stock of durables should evolve according to the same Euler equation as the flow of consumption of nondurables. If the deterioration of the stock of durables occurs at a constant rate, the purchases of durables should obey a first-order autoregressive, first-order moving average process; the parameter of the moving average process depends only on the rate of deterioration. He obtained strong rejection of that hypothesis. He found that the stochastic process for durables purchases is close to a random walk, a finding that implies that the quarterly deterioration rate for durables is about 100%. Although he did not pursue the idea, he noted that it appears that a model with adjustment costs would also be rejected by the data.

Bernanke (1984) examined purchases of automobiles within a four-year panel of households. He assumes that households choose an optimal stock of autos through the standard rational expectations permanent income model and then purchase autos at a rate given by a partial adjustment process. He did not try to justify the partial adjustment assumption through consideration of optimization, although a model of adjustment costs probably could yield his model as the outcome of optimization. The estimation method is similar to the one used by Hall and Mishkin (1982). His empirical findings reveal an adjustment rate of about 70% per year. His most interesting finding is that there is no evidence of excess sensitivity of auto purchases to transitory income. It appears that partial adjustment of consumption to current income is a competing explanation of facts that lead other investigators to conclude that liquidity constraints are important.

Bernanke (1985) developed a complete model with adjustment costs. Using quarterly U.S. data for durables, nondurables, and income, he found substantial excess sensitivity of both durables and nondurables within a model that posits constant real interest rates.

Mankiw (1985) studied durables in a framework that considers substitution between durables and nondurables and also intertemporal substitution. He found evidence of high elasticities of substitution in both dimensions. As a result, movements of real interest rates are an important influence making durables purchases depart from the predictions of a model that assumes constant real interest rates. He was unable to reject the hypothesis that income and consumption have the relation predicted by the simple rational expectations permanent income model.

Bar-Ilan and Blinder (1987) developed a theory of durables purchases that takes explicit account of the lumpiness of durables. They showed that individual households will determine a range for the stock of each type of durable and make purchases or sell existing durables if the stock falls

outside the range. They tackled the difficult problem of developing implications of the model for aggregate data, with somewhat mixed results.

4.1.7. Intertemporal Substitution

The effect of changes in interest rates on consumption and saving has
always been an important topic of research on consumption. With the
exception of Boskin (1978), there has been relatively little research on the
traditional question of the role of the interest rate in the consumption
function. The answer to that question is complicated because changes in
the interest rate have both an income and a substitution effect. By contrast, the Euler equation formulation that has dominated research since
the rational expectations revolution provides a way to measure the pure
substitution effect of changes in interest rates.

The Euler equation for consumption with a variable real interest rate
first appeared in the finance literature. Rubinstein (1976) contributed most
of the basic model. The marriage of a constant-elasticity utility function
with log-normally distributed returns provides a first-order condition in a
highly tractable form. Breeden (1977, 1979) developed the intertemporal
consumption model in the form that has been employed by countless
authors in the past decade. The basic relation derived by Breeden can be
written as

$$\Delta \log c_t = \frac{1}{\alpha} r_t + k + \varepsilon_t.$$

Here α is the coefficient of relative risk aversion, r_t is the mean of the
distribution of the log of the value in $t + 1$ of a unit investment made at t,
ε_t is a normally distributed disturbance, and k is a constant related to the
covariance of r_t and $\Delta \log c_t$, to the variances of both variables, and to the
rate of time preference. Breeden and his successors in the finance literature (Grossman and Shiller, 1982a,b; Shiller, 1982; Ferson, 1980;
Breeden, 1983; and many others, many cited in the last reference) considered this equation to be part of a system with one equation for each type
of investment. They defined the consumption beta of an investment as a
normalization of the covariance of its return with the change in the log of
consumption. Most of the literature in finance in this area has been devoted to measuring consumption betas and testing the relations among the
betas and the mean returns of different investments.

Within the macroeconomic literature on consumption, the finance paper that has had the greatest influence is that by Hansen and Singleton (1983). They estimated both single equations and systems of equations for multiple investments, using monthly consumption and returns data. Their estimates of the coefficient of relative risk aversion, α, span a range centered on unity. They also tested and rejected the restrictions among the constants and the covariances, but this finding has more relevance for finance than for consumption. Additional results along this line appeared in Eichenbaum, Hansen, and Singleton (1986).

Hansen and Singleton's framework has been adopted by Summers (1982), Mankiw, Rotemberg, and Summers (1985), and Bean (1986) with similar results. Browning (1986a) has reached a similar specification by a somewhat different route. However, these subsequent papers have interpreted the coefficient of the expected real interest rate, r_t, on the right-hand side of a consumption growth equation as dealing with the propensity of consumers to substitute intertemporally from one period to the next. That is, they think of the equation in the form,

$$\Delta \log c_t = \sigma r_t + k + \varepsilon_t.$$

Here σ is the intertemporal elasticity of substitution. A 1% rise in the expected real interest rate, r_t, causes the consumer to substitute σ percent of consumption from this year to the next. Formally, the difference is just the replacement of the reciprocal of the coefficient of relative risk aversion, $1/\alpha$, by σ, but a large difference of interpretation goes with that change.

Hall (1988) considered the question of the relation between these interpretations. The model underlying both the finance research and the macroeconomic research is founded upon an intertemporally separable utility function,

$$\sum e^{-\delta t} c_t^{1-\alpha}.$$

The parameter α controls the curvature of the one-period utility function and hence controls both the degree of risk aversion (the higher α is, the less willing the consumer is to substitute consumption among states of the world) and the degree of intertemporal substitution (the higher α is, the less willing the consumer is to substitute consumption among time periods). It is known that additive separability of the utility function together with the maximization of expected utility means that risk aversion and intertemporal substitution are controlled together by the curvature of the one-period utility function (Selden, 1978).

Hall argued that the coefficient in an equation with the growth of consumption on the left and the expected real return from a particular investment on the right is the intertemporal elasticity of substitution, not the reciprocal of the coefficient of relative risk aversion. Risk aversion can be estimated using a system of two or more equations with investments of different riskiness, in which case the coefficient of relative risk aversion can be measured from the differences in the constants (as in Grossman and Shiller 1982a).

Hall's argument on this point is not conclusive, because there does not seem to be a convenient class of utility functions in which the two parameters are cleanly separated, except in the special case of only two periods. For the special case, Selden's results show that it is unambiguously the elasticity of intertemporal substitution and not the reciprocal of the coefficient of relative risk aversion that appears as the coefficient of the expected real interest rate in the consumption growth equation.

Viewed in this light, the previous research has found intertemporal elasticities of around one. Fluctuations in expected interest rates are a prime source of movements in consumption, according to the results. However, Hall questioned the finding of a substantial elasticity. Through the use of additional data for the interwar period and for the 1980s, when fluctuations in expected real rates were larger, and through a choice of instrumental variables that considers the timing of the data, he found values of the intertemporal elasticity close to zero, with reasonably small standard errors.

Muellbauer and Bover (1986) suggested a possible source of a downward bias in estimates of the intertemporal elasticity of substitution. They pointed out that aggregation may induce a negative correlation between the constant in the consumption growth equation and the interest rate—higher interest rates shift consumption toward groups, such as the elderly, with lower values of the constant.

Browning (1986c) took a very different approach to intertemporal substitution. He adapted nonparametric techniques developed by Varian to test the hypothesis that the observed sequence of consumption and interest rates are consistent with consumer choice under certainty. Under Browning's null hypothesis, all variations in consumption are attributed to intertemporal substitution and none to income surprises. He rejects the hypothesis for Canadian, U.K., and U.S. data, but there are extended subperiods when the hypothesis cannot be rejected.

4.1.8. Transitory Consumption and Shifts in Preferences

Flavin (1981), Hall and Mishkin (1982), and numerous other authors have noted that consumption may have a stochastic component not explained by the permanent income hypothesis. In panel data, the evidence for such a component is overwhelming; the component accounts for more of the variation of the first difference of consumption than does the component associated with changes in permanent income. Furthermore, in panel data, there is a presumption that at least part of the component is truly transitory consumption, because it arises from measuring consumption over a fairly brief period, so that changes in household inventories and the lumpiness of many purchases influences measured consumption.

In time series data, where a general equilibrium analysis is mandatory, the diagnosis and treatment of transitory consumption is a much more difficult issue. Garber and King (1984) pointed out just how strong are the identifying assumptions needed to validate Euler-equation models in time series data. In effect, either shifts in preferences or other sources of changes in consumption other than changes in income or wealth must be assumed away, or special and questionable assumptions must be made about their stochastic properties. The easiest assumption, although very special, is that shifts in preferences occur as a random walk, so that the corresponding stochastic component in the first difference of consumption is unpredictable. Then the Euler equation has an extra stochastic term that satisfies the assumptions already made about the term that comes from the innovation in income or wealth. MaCurdy (1987) has set up a framework for studying consumption and labor supply in the presence of stochastic shifts of a very general type.

If shifts in preferences are anything but a random walk, then the Euler equation is probably not identified. Certainly the methods generally used for estimating the Euler equation are no longer valid. If shifts in preferences are stationary, although possibly serially correlated, then the first difference of consumption will have a component that is negatively serially correlated. The disturbance in period t will include the innovation in preferences in period $t - 1$ and possibly earlier as well. Because the earlier innovation shifted consumption, and a shift in consumption feeds back into income, variables dated $t - 1$ are no longer uncorrelated with the disturbance. In simple regression tests of the Euler equation with a fixed real interest rate, lagged income is no longer an appropriate regressor. The finding of significant coefficients for lagged income is no longer evidence against the rational expectations permanent income model. In more elaborate tests with variable expected real returns, lagged income is no longer eligible as an instrumental variable.

Hall (1986) attacked this problem by using an instrument that he considers truly exogenous: military spending. His objective was to isolate shifts in consumption associated with preference shifts from those associated with changes in well-being. He reasoned that changes in well-being cause movements along an expansion path for consumption of goods and leisure. The slope of the expansion path is revealed by the changes in the two variables brought about by changes in military spending. Then random shifts in preferences cause the two variables to depart from the expansion path. In other words, the residuals in the estimated consumption-work effort relation are a measure of the stochastic component of consumption associated with preference shifts. He found that the residuals are a dominant source of fluctuations in consumption itself and account for an important but not dominant fraction of fluctuations in total GNP. The only support in the work for the Euler equation approach is that the random shifts are at least approximately a random walk.

4.2. Conclusions

It is reasonably well established that the simple conclusion from the rational expectations permanent income model with constant expected real interest rate is inconsistent with the data: The rate of change of consumption can be predicted by past values of real income and past values of a number of financial variables. Much of the recent literature on the macroeconomics of consumption can be seen as attempts to explain this finding.

Durable goods and the durability of consumption seem to explain the finding reasonably well. Hayashi's model with durable consumption leaves only a small role for liquidity constraints, and Mankiw's and Bernanke's models with durable goods accept the hypothesis of no explanatory power from lagged income.

Liquidity constraints can also explain the finding in a reasonably convincing way. Not only is the predictive power of income rationalized by only a modest incidence of liquidity constraints, but ancillary tests give reasonable results as well—for example, the predictive power of lagged income is concentrated among households with few liquid assets, according to Runkle and Zeldes, and unemployment displaces income as a predictor, according to Flavin. However, a model combining liquidity constraints and durable goods assigns all of the explanation for the predictive power of lagged income to durability and none to liquidity constraints, according to Bernanke.

Intertemporal substitution does not seem to be an important part of the explanation of the predictive power of lagged income and other variables. There is controversy about whether or not the intertemporal elasticity of substitution is large enough to make changes in expected interest rates an important factor in fluctuations in consumption growth. Nevertheless, no author has been able to show that the predictive power of other variables disappears when intertemporal substitution is considered.

Acknowledgments

I am grateful to David Bizer for outstanding assistance. This research was supported by the National Science Foundation and is part of the NBER's program on economic fluctuations.

References

Altonji, J., and Aloysius Siow. 1987. Testing the Response of Consumption to Income Changes with (Noisy) Panel Data. *Quarterly Journal of Economics* 102: 293–328.

Ando, A., and F. Modigliani. 1963. The Life-Cycle Hypothesis of Saving: Aggregate Implications and Tests. *American Economic Review* 53: 55–84.

Bar-Ilan, A., and A. S. Blinder. 1987. The Life-Cycle Permanent-Income Model and Consumer Durables. Working paper 2149, National Bureau of Economic Research.

Bean, C. 1986. The Estimation of 'Surprise' Models and the 'Surprise' Consumption Function. *Review of Economic Studies* 53: 497–516.

Bernanke, B. S. 1984. Permanent Income, Liquidity, and Expenditure on Automobiles: Evidence from Panel Data. *Quarterly Journal of Economics* 99(3): 587–614.

———— 1985. Adjustment Costs, Durables, and Aggregate Consumption. *Journal of Monetary Economics* 15 (January): 41–68.

Bernheim, B. D. 1987. Ricardian Equivalence: An Evaluation of Theory and Evidence. *In* S. Fischer (ed.), *NBER Macroeconomics Annual 1987.* Cambridge, Massachusetts: MIT Press, pp. 263–304.

Boskin, M. J. 1978. Taxation, Saving, and the Rate of Interest. *Journal of Political Economy* 86(2): S3–S27.

Breeden, D. T. 1977. Changing Consumption and Investment Opportunities and the Valuation of Securities. Unpublished doctoral dissertation, Stanford Graduate School of Business.

——— 1979. An Intertemporal Asset Pricing Model with Stochastic Consumption and Investment Opportunities. *Journal of Financial Economics* 7: 265–296.

——— 1983. Consumption, Production and Interest Rates: A Synthesis. Unpublished paper, Stanford University.

Browning, M. 1986a. The Intertemporal Allocation of Expenditure of Non-Durables, Services, and Durables. Unpublished paper, McMaster University.

——— 1986b. Testing Intertemporal Separability in Models of Household Behaviour. Unpublished paper, McMaster University.

——— 1986c. A Non-Parametric Test of the Life-Cycle Rational Expectations Hypothesis. Unpublished paper, McMaster University.

——— 1987. Eating, Drinking, Smoking, and Testing the Life-Cycle Hypothesis. *Quarterly Journal of Economics* 102: 329–345.

Campbell, J. Y. 1986. Does Saving Anticipate Declining Labor Income? An Alternative Test of the Permanent Income Hypothesis. Unpublished paper, Princeton University.

Campbell, J. Y., and R. H. Clarida. 1986. Household Saving and Permanent Income in Canada and the United Kingdom. Unpublished paper.

Campbell, J. Y., and A. Deaton. 1987. Is Consumption Too Smooth? Working paper 2134, National Bureau of Economic Research.

Chang, F.-R. 1987. A Theory of the Consumption Function with Wage Fluctuations. Unpublished paper, Indiana University.

Christiano, L. J. 1984. The Effects of Aggregation over Time on Tests of the Representative Agent Model of Consumption. Unpublished paper, University of Chicago and Carnegie Mellon University.

——— 1987. Is Consumption Insufficiently Sensitive to Innovations in Income? Working paper 333, Research Department, Federal Reserve Bank of Minneapolis.

Christiano, L. J., M. Eichenbaum, and D. Marshall. 1987. The Permanent Income Hypothesis Revisited. Working paper 335, Research Department, Federal Reserve Bank of Minneapolis.

Cuddington, J. T. 1982. Canadian Evidence on the Permanent Income–Rational Expectations Hypothesis. *Canadian Journal of Economics* 15(2): 331–335.

Cuddington, J. T., and Hurd, M. D. 1981. Valid Statistical Tests of the Permanent Income–Rational Expectations Hypothesis. Unpublished paper.

Daly, V., and Hadjimatheou, G. 1981. Stochastic Implications of the Life Cycle–Permanent Income Hypothesis: Evidence for the U.K. Economy. *Journal of Political Economy* 89(3): 596–599.

Darby, M. R. 1972. The Allocation of Transitory Income among Consumers' Assets. *American Economic Review* 62(4): 928–941.

Deaton, A. 1986. Life-Cycle Models of Consumption: Is the Evidence Consistent with the Theory? Working paper 1910, National Bureau of Economic Research.

Eichenbaum, M. S., L. P. Hansen, and K. J. Singleton. 1986. A Time Series Analysis of Representative Agent Models of Consumption and Leisure Choice under Uncertainty. Working paper 1981, National Bureau of Economic Research.

Evans, O. 1982. The Life Cycle Inheritance: Theoretical and Empirical Essays on the Life Cycle Hypothesis of Saving. Unpublished doctoral dissertation, University of Pennsylvania.

Ferson, W. 1980. Consumption, Inflation, and the Term Structure of Interest Rates. Unpublished paper.

Ferson, W. E., and J. J. Merrick, Jr. Forthcoming. Nonstationarity and Stage-of-the-Business-Cycle Effects in Consumption-Based Asset Pricing Relations. *Journal of Financial Economics*.

Flavin, M. A. 1981. The Adjustment of Consumption to Changing Expectations about Future Income. *Journal of Political Economy* 89(5): 1020–37.

——— 1985. Excess Sensitivity of Consumption to Current Income: Liquidity Constraints or Myopia? *Canadian Journal of Economics* 18 (February): 117–136.

Friedman, M. 1968. The Role of Monetary Policy. *American Economic Review* 58: 1–17.

Garber, P., and R. King. 1984. Deep Structural Excavation? A Critique of Euler Equation Methods. Presented at NBER Research Program on Economic Fluctuations Macro Conference.

Goodfriend, M. 1986. Information-Aggregation Bias: The Case of Consumption. Unpublished paper, Federal Reserve Bank of Richmond and University of Rochester.

Grossman, S. J., A. Melino, and R. J. Shiller. 1985. Estimating the Continuous Time Consumption Based Asset Pricing Model. Working paper 1643, National Bureau of Economic Research.

Grossman, S. J., and R. J. Shiller. 1982a. The Determinants of the Variability of Stock Market Prices. *American Economic Review* 71(2): 222–227.

——— 1982b. Consumption Correlatedness and Risk Measurement in Economies with Non-Traded Assets, and Heterogeneous Information. *Journal of Financial Economics* 10(2): 195–210.

Hall, R. E. 1978. Stochastic Implications of the Life Cycle-Permanent Income Hypothesis: Theory and Evidence. *Journal of Political Economy* 86(6): 971–987.

——— 1986. The Role of Consumption in Economic Fluctuations. *In* R. J. Gordon (ed.), *The American Business Cycle: Continuity and Change*. Chicago: The University of Chicago Press, 237–255.

——— 1988. Intertemporal Substitution in Consumption, *Journal of Political Economy* 96: 339–357.

Hall, R. E., and F. S. Mishkin. 1982. The Sensitivity of Consumption to Transitory Income: Estimates from Panel Data on Households. *Econometrica* 50(2): 461–481.

Hansen, L. P., S. F. Richard, and K. J. Singleton. 1981. Econometric Implications of the Intertemporal Capital Asset Pricing Model. Unpublished paper, Carnegie Mellon University.

Hansen, L. P., and K. J. Singleton. 1983. Stochastic Consumption, Risk Aversion, and the Temporal Behavior of Stock Market Returns. *Journal of Political Economy* 91(2): 249–265.

———— 1986. Efficient Estimation of Linear Asset Pricing Models with Moving Average Errors. Unpublished paper, University of Chicago, Harvard University, and Carnegie Mellon University.

Hayashi, F. 1985. The Permanent Income Hypothesis and Consumption Durability: Analysis Based on Japanese Panel Data. *Quarterly Journal of Economics* 100 (November): 1083–113.

———— 1987. Tests for Liquidity Constraints: A Critical Survey and Some New Observations. *In* T. Bewley (ed.), *Advances in Econometrics, Fifth World Congress,* vol. 2. Cambridge: Cambridge University Press, pp. 91–120.

Jacobson, R. 1981. Testing the Implications of the Life Cycle–Permanent Income Hypothesis. Unpublished paper, University of California, Berkeley.

Johnson, P. 1983. Life-Cycle Consumption under Rational Expectations: Some Australian Evidence. *Economic Record* 59: 345–350.

Kormendi, R. C., and L. LaHaye. 1986. Cross-Regime Tests of the Permanent Income Hypothesis. Working paper, University of Michigan.

Lucas, R. E. 1976. Econometric Policy Evaluation: A Critique. *In* K. Brunner and A. H. Meltzer (eds.), *Carnegie-Rochester Series on Public Policy,* vol. 1. Amsterdam: North-Holland.

MaCurdy, T. E. 1987. Modeling the Time Series Implications of Life-cycle Theory. Unpublished paper, Stanford University.

Mankiw, G. N. 1982. Hall's Consumption Hypothesis and Durable Goods. *Journal of Monetary Economics* 10(3): 417–425.

———— 1985. Consumer Durables and the Real Interest Rate. *The Review of Economics and Statistics* 67(3): 353–362.

Mankiw, G. N., J. Rotemberg, and L. Summers. 1985. Intertemporal Substitution in Macroeconomics. *Quarterly Journal of Economics* 100(1): 225–251.

Mankiw, G. N., and M. D. Shapiro, 1985a. Risk and Return: Consumption Beta Versus Market Beta. Discussion Paper No. 738, Cowles Foundation.

———— 1985b. Trends, Random Walks, and Tests of the Permanent Income Hypothesis. *Journal of Monetary Economics* 16(2): 165–174.

Marsh, T. A. 1984. On Euler-Equation Restrictions on the Temporal Behavior of Asset Returns. Working paper 1619-84, Alfred P. Sloan School of Management.

Miron, J. A. 1986. Seasonal Fluctuations and the Life Cycle-Permanent Income Model of Consumption. *Journal of Political Economy* 94 (December): 1258–79.

Mork, K. A., and V. K. Smith. 1986. Another Test of the Life-Cycle Hypothesis, but with Much Improved Panel Data. Unpublished paper, Vanderbilt University.

Muellbauer, J. 1983. Surprises in the Consumption Function. *Economic Journal* 93 (suppl.): 34–40.

Muellbauer, J., and O. Bover. 1986. Liquidity Constraints and Aggregation in the Consumption Function under Uncertainty. Discussion paper 12, Oxford Institute of Economics and Statistics.

Muth, J. 1960. Optimal Properties of Exponentially Weighted Forecasts. *Journal of the American Statistical Association* 55: 299–306.

Nelson, C. R. 1987. A Reappraisal of Recent Tests of the Permanent Income Hypothesis. *Journal of Political Economy* 95: 641–646.

Rubinstein, M. 1976. The Strong Case for the Generalized Logarithmic Utility Model as the Premier Model of Financial Markets. *The Journal of Finance* 31(2): 551–571.

Runkle, D. 1983. Liquidity Constraints and the Permanent Income Hypothesis: Evidence from Panel Data. Unpublished paper, Brown University.

Sargent, T. J. 1978. Rational Expectations, Econometric Exogeneity, and Consumption. *Journal of Political Economy* 86(4): 673–700.

Sargent, T. J., and L. P. Hansen. 1981. Formulating and Estimating Dynamic Linear Rational Expectations Models. *In* R. Lucas and T. Sargent (eds.), *Rational Expectations and Econometric Practice,* vol. 1. Minneapolis: University of Minneapolis Press, pp. 91–125.

Selden, L. 1978. A New Representation of Preferences over 'Certain X Uncertain' Consumption Pairs: The 'Ordinal Certainty Equivalent' Hypothesis. *Econometrica* 46 (September): 1045–60.

Shiller, R. J. 1982. Consumption, Asset Markets, and Macroeconomic Fluctuations. *Carnegie-Rochester Conference Series on Public Policy* 17 (Autumn): 203–238.

Sims, C., J. H. Stock, and M. W. Watson. 1987. Inference in Linear Time Series Models with Some Unit Roots. Hoover Working Papers in Economics E-87-1, Hoover Institution.

Stock, J. H., and K. D. West. 1987. Integrated Regressors and Tests of the Permanent Income Hypothesis. Unpublished paper, Harvard University, Princeton University, Stanford University, and the NBER.

Summers, L. 1982. Tax Policy, the Rate of Return, and Savings. Working paper 995, National Bureau of Economic Research.

West, K. D. 1986. The Insensitivity of Consumption to News about Income. Unpublished paper. Princeton University.

Working, H. 1960. Note on the Correlation of First Differences of Averages in a Random Chain. *Econometrica* 28: 916–918.

Zeldes, S. 1985. Consumption and Liquidity Constraints: An Empirical Investigation. Paper 24-85, Rodney L. White Center for Financial Research.

——— 1986. Optimal Consumption with Stochastic Income: Deviations from Certainty Equivalence. Unpublished paper, University of Pennsylvania.

5   The Neoclassical Approach to Fiscal Policy

Robert J. Barro

Recent developments in macroeconomics have been dominated by the neoclassical, or equilibrium, approach. This approach models the economy under the twin disciplines of individual rationality and cleared markets. However, the models allow for frictions by including incomplete information, mobility costs, distorting taxes, and so on. The early studies in this area focused on the real effects of monetary disturbances—see Friedman (1968), Phelps (1970), Lucas (1972, 1973), Sargent and Wallace (1975), and Barro (1976, 1977). In fact, despite the generality of Lucas's (1976) critique of policy evaluation, the neoclassical approach was sometimes viewed as nearly synonymous with some narrow findings about the relationship between nominal and real variables. For example, neoclassical macroeconomics was closely identified with the expectational Phillips curve under rational expectations, the ineffectiveness proposition on monetary policy, and the real effects of unanticipated money.

It turns out that pinning down the real consequences of money and monetary policy is a difficult problem with many loose ends. Therefore, it is fortunate that the neoclassical approach has also contributed substantially to macroeconomic analyses that have little or nothing to do with money. For example, the approach has been usefully applied to purely real models that feature shocks to technology and preferences; that is, "real business cycle theories," as surveyed in Chapter 1 by Bennett McCallum. In this chapter I shall examine another area of fruitful application, namely, the macroeconomic effects of the government's expenditures, taxation, and debt issue.

In Section 5.1 I develop a simple model of saving and investment. In this model there is a representative, infinite-lived consumer, and production is neoclassical with variable capital and labor. I use the model developed in Section 5.1 to analyze government purchases of goods and services in Section 5.2. Particular attention is given to permanent versus temporary changes in purchases, to the role of public services in utility and production functions, and to empirical evidence. In Section 5.3 I extend the analysis to allow for distorting taxation, first on labor income, and then on capital income.

In Section 5.4 I introduce deficit finance and the public debt. The discussion focuses on the Ricardian equivalence theorem for taxes versus debt. After deriving the theorem in a simple framework, I consider various issues, such as finite lifetimes, imperfect credit markets, and the timing of distorting taxes, that are thought to influence the conclusions. This section concludes with empirical evidence on the relation of budget deficits to interest rates, saving, and the current-account balance.

5.1. A Model of Saving and Capital Accumulation

The simple dynamic model of a closed economy developed in this section will be used for the subsequent analysis of government spending, taxes, and debt issue. The representative person, who can be viewed as the head of the representative extended family, seeks to maximize total utility, U, as given by

$$(5.1) \qquad U = u(c_1, n_1) + \frac{1}{(1 + \rho)} u(c_2, n_2) + \frac{1}{(1 + \rho)^2} u(c_3, n_3) + \ldots$$

$$= \sum_1^\infty \left[\frac{u(c_t, n_t)}{(1 + \rho)^{t-1}} \right],$$

where c_t is consumption per person in period t, n_t is the amount of work effort, and ρ is the rate of time preference on utility. The utility function, u, satisfies the usual concavity conditions, with $\partial u/\partial c_t > 0$, $\partial u/\partial n_t < 0$, and $0 < \rho < \infty$.

Equation (5.1) assumes that there is no change over time in the size of the representative family; that is, population growth is zero. (The number of families is also constant.) The specification uses an infinite horizon, which can be viewed as reflecting altruistic linkages from parents to children to grandchildren, and so on. Then the discount on future utility, $\rho > 0$, can be interpreted as reflecting the lesser weight attached to children's consumption relative to own consumption when the levels of per capita consumption across generations are the same. It is convenient to start by treating work effort as given and constant over time, although the analysis can readily be extended to incorporate the work-leisure choice. Since work is constant, we can normalize by setting $n_t = 1$ in each period.

The real wage rate—and, hence, real labor income—for period t is given to the family as the amount w_t. The family holds the amount of real assets, k_t, at the end of period t, where a negative value signifies borrowing. Assets pay the real rate of return r_t in period $t + 1$. Therefore the budget constraint for each period is

(5.2) $k_{t-1}(1 + r_{t-1}) + w_t = c_t + k_t.$

The initial stock of assets, k_0, is given to the family.

Define the present-value factor d_t by

(5.3) $d_t = d_{t-1}/(1 + r_{t-1}),$ for $t = 1, 2, \ldots,$ and $d_0 = 1.$

Then, using Equation (5.2) for each period starting from $t = 1$, the budget constraint in present-value form is

(5.4) $k_0 + \sum_1^H d_t w_t = \sum_1^H d_t c_t + d_H k_H$

for any date $H \geq 1$. Now suppose that total utility in Equation (5.1) involved the finite horizon H, rather than an infinite horizon. That is, assume that people did not care about the utils generated after date H. (H would represent a person's expected remaining lifetime in models where parents were not linked altruistically to their children.) If it is infeasible to leave debts after date H (for example, after death), so that $k_H < 0$ is ruled out, then the maximization of utility entails setting $k_h = 0$ (which is a transversality condition for this problem). Otherwise people would leave behind some resources that could have been used to raise consumption and hence utility at an earlier date. (The assumption is that people cannot be satiated with consumption—that is, $\partial u/\partial c > 0$ if $c < \infty$.) The condition $k_H = 0$ in Equation (5.4) means that the total present value of consumption expenditure from dates 1 through H equals the total present value of labor income from dates 1 through H plus the initial assets, k_0.

The same kind of result applies when the horizon is infinite. In this case the transversality condition is that the term $d_H k_H$ approaches zero as H approaches infinity.[1] That is, the family does not leave over asymptotically any resources that have a finite, positive present value. The implication is that as H tends to infinity the final term on the right-hand side of Equation (5.4) approaches zero.[2] Accordingly, the present value of expenditures over an infinite horizon equals the present value of labor income plus the initial assets,

$$(5.5) \qquad k_0 + \sum_1^\infty d_t w_t = \sum_1^\infty d_t c_t.$$

Hence, the family's optimization problem amounts to maximizing U in Equation (5.1), subject to the present-value budget constraint in Equation (5.5) (and subject to $c_t \geq 0$ for all t).

The first-order conditions for the optimization are[3]

$$(5.6) \qquad \frac{\partial u/\partial c_t}{\partial u/\partial c_{t+1}} = \frac{1 + r_t}{1 + \rho}, \qquad t = 1, 2, \ldots$$

These conditions relate the time path of consumption to interest rates and the rate of time preference, ρ. A higher interest rate motivates people to postpone consumption, whereas a higher value of ρ has the opposite effect. Equation (5.6) implies that $c_{t+1} \gtreqless c_t$ as $r_t \gtreqless \rho$. Hence, in a steady state where consumption is constant, the interest rate is constant and equal to ρ.

Consider the special case where marginal utility has a constant elasticity with respect to consumption; that is,[4]

$$(5.7) \qquad u(c) = \frac{c^\gamma - 1}{\gamma}, \qquad \text{for} \quad \gamma < 1 \quad \text{and} \quad \gamma \neq 0.$$

Substituting into Equation (5.6) leads to

$$(5.8) \qquad \frac{c_{t+1}}{c_t} = \left[\frac{1 + r_t}{1 + \rho}\right]^{1/(1-\gamma)}.$$

Therefore, with this utility function, the first-order conditions imply a simple relation between the growth rate of consumption and the ratio of the interest-rate factor, $1 + r_t$, to the time-preference factor, $1 + \rho$.

The model is closed by incorporating a one-sector production function with constant returns to scale in capital and labor. When written in terms of output per worker, y_t, and capital per worker, k_t, the function is

$$(5.9) \qquad y_t = f(k_{t-1}),$$

where the derivatives are $f' > 0$ and $f'' < 0$. The present analysis neglects technological progress, although exogenous progress of the Harrod neutral form could readily be included. Competitive firms with the technology shown in Equation (5.9) maximize profits by equating the marginal product of capital to the interest rate and the marginal product of labor to the wage rate,

$$(5.10) \qquad f'(k_{t-1}) = r_{t-1}, \qquad f(k_{t-1}) - k_{t-1}f'(k_{t-1}) = w_t.$$

With constant returns to scale, the output per worker (and per person), $y_t = f(k_{t-1})$, equals the total income per person, $w_t + r_{t-1}k_{t-1}$. In a closed economy this income goes either to consumption, c_t, or investment, $k_t - k_{t-1}$, which implies[5]

$$(5.11) \qquad y_t = f(k_{t-1}) = c_t + k_t - k_{t-1}.$$

Net and gross investment (and net and gross output) coincide here, because there is no depreciation of capital.

The values of k_t and c_t follow from Equations (5.5), (5.6), (5.10), and (5.11). Since the steady state features constant values of k and c, Equation (5.6) implies that the steady-state interest rate is $r = \rho$. Hence, the steady-state capital stock must satisfy the condition

$$(5.12) \qquad f'(k) = r = \rho.$$

Since investment is zero in the steady state, Equation (5.11) implies that the steady-state level of consumption is $c = f(k)$.

It can be shown that the capital stock converges monotonically to the steady-state value determined from Equation (5.12).[6] For example, if $k_0 < k$, the initial interest rate is $r_1 = f'(k_0) > \rho$. The excess of output, $y_1 = f(k_0)$, over consumption, c_1, allows for positive investment, and hence for an increase in the capital stock over time. As k_t rises, r_t declines and eventually approaches the value ρ. Consumption grows over time as long as $r_t > \rho$ [see Equations (5.6) and (5.8)] but approaches a constant level as r_t approaches ρ. If the model is extended to include population growth or technological progress, then output and consumption can grow continually in the steady state.

5.2. Government Purchases and Public Services

Suppose that in period t the government buys the quantity of goods G_t from private producers,[7] financing these purchases with lump-sum taxes.

Hence, the government's budget constraint is $G_t = T_t$, where T_t is the real amount of tax revenues. (Later sections cover distorting taxation and budget deficits.)

The government uses its purchases to provide a flow of "free" public services to households and businesses. Consider first the effect of these services on utility. Assume that each person cares about the quantity of government purchases (and the associated amount of public services) per capita, denoted by g_t. This assumption neglects the public nature of some government spending, such as the space program and national defense. However, the general results go through if governmental services are public goods.

The representative family's total utility is now given by

$$(5.13) \qquad U = \sum_1^\infty [u(c_t + \alpha g_t, n_t)/(1 + \rho)^{t-1}] + \Phi(g_1, g_2, \ldots).$$

Thus, public expenditures g_t appear as part of the composite consumption flow, $c_t^* = c_t + \alpha g_t$. The greater the parameter α, the more closely public services substitute for a unit of contemporaneous private spending.[8] For example, α would be close to unity for school lunch programs, but close to zero for national defense. The analysis assumes that the substitution parameter satisfies the condition, $0 < \alpha < 1$. This condition turns out to deliver the standard results about interest rates and some other variables. One way to rationalize the constraint, $\alpha < 1$, is that (with lump-sum taxes) the representative person would end up at least as well off with a larger government if $\alpha \geq 1$ [assuming that g_t contributes nonnegatively to the term Φ in Equation (5.13)]. Then, if α declines with increases in the ratio of g_t to c_t and if the government raises g_t whenever $\alpha \geq 1$, the economy ends up operating where $\alpha < 1$. The subsequent analysis applies in this range.

Equation (5.13) allows for additional effects of public services in the additively separable term, $\Phi(\cdot)$. The point of this term is that the condition $\alpha < 1$ does not require the marginal unit of public spending to be valued by less than a unit of private spending. Since $\Phi(\cdot)$ enters separably in Equation (5.13), however, this term has no bearing on households' choices of consumption or labor supply. The term would matter if the model were used to derive optimal choices of government spending. But the present analysis assumes this optimizing behavior only to the extent of ensuring the condition $\alpha < 1$.

The representative household's present-value budget constraint from Equation (5.5) is now modified to include the present value of taxes, which equals the present value of per capita spending, $\sum_1^\infty d_t g_t$. In addition, since utility depends on $c_t^* = c_t + \alpha g_t$ in each period, it is useful to replace c_t by $c_t^* - \alpha g_t$ in the budget constraint. Carrying out these changes leads to

$$(5.14) \qquad k_0 + \sum_1^\infty d_t w_t = \sum_1^\infty d_t c_t^* + (1 - \alpha) \sum_1^\infty d_t g_t.$$

Note that with the c_t^*'s held fixed only the fraction $1 - \alpha$ of government purchases appears as a net expense for households. The fraction α of these purchases provides services that substitute directly for private spending.

5.2.1. Permanent Changes in Government Purchases

Suppose that the economy begins with no government purchases at the steady state described in Section 5.1. Hence, the capital stock per person is the amount k, the interest rate is $r = \rho$, and consumption per person is $c = f(k)$. Then consider a once-and-for-all increase of government purchases per person from 0 to the amount g. The assumption is that this change was unexpected beforehand but is perceived as permanent once it occurs.[9] In this case, if the interest rate is the constant r, wealth falls in accordance with the term on the far right of the budget constraint in Equation (5.14), which equals $(1 - \alpha)g/r$. Households react by reducing c_t^* in each period.[10] (With variable work effort, households would tend also to raise labor supply in each period.)

Consider how government spending affects the steady state of the economy. Since the rate of time preference, ρ, is fixed, the steady-state interest rate is still $r = \rho$. Therefore, with no change in the production function, the condition $f'(k) = r = \rho$ determines the same value of k as before. To see the effect on consumption, note that total output now equals consumption plus investment plus government purchases,

$$(5.15) \qquad y_t = f(k_{t-1}) = c_t + k_t - k_{t-1} + g_t.$$

Therefore, in the steady state, in which investment is zero,

$$(5.16) \qquad c = f(k) - g, \quad \text{and} \quad c^* = c + \alpha g = f(k) - (1 - \alpha)g.$$

Given k, an increase in g reduces c one-to-one, and reduces c^* by the fraction $1 - \alpha$.

Since the steady-state capital stock does not change, there is no dynamic adjustment to a permanent (but unanticipated) increase in government purchases. When g rises, "permanent income" falls sufficiently to crowd out enough private consumer spending to accommodate the extra government spending—that is, c^* falls by $(1 - \alpha)g$ because wealth falls by the amount $(1 - \alpha)g/r$. Therefore the permanent increase in government purchases has no effect on real interest rates.[11]

Although these results pertained to a closed economy, the conclusions would be the same in this case for an open economy. In particular, a permanent shift in government purchases would not induce changes in the current-account balance.

5.2.2. Temporary Changes in Government Purchases

Assume now that the changes in government purchases are temporary rather than permanent. Empirically, the clearest example is military expenditure during wartime. Figure 5.1 shows that purchases rise at the start of a war at time t_1 from the value associated with peacetime, g^{peace}, to that associated with war, g^{war}. (For convenience, this figure and the next one ignore the discrete length of periods.) The high level of spending lasts until time t_2, when the war ends. Then spending returns to the value g^{peace}. The assumption is that the start of the war at time t_1 was a surprise but that the end of the war—that is, the date t_2—is known once the war begins. (The general idea is that people know that wartime spending is temporary—that is, that wars do not last forever.)

Suppose again that the economy begins at a steady state, so that $r_t = \rho$ before time t_1. Pretend for the moment that, as in the case of a permanent shift, the temporary change in government purchases has no effect on capital stocks. With no change in investment (and work effort still treated as fixed), Equation (5.15) implies that c_t falls one-to-one with the increase in g_t during the war and rises correspondingly at time t_2. Figure 5.1 shows this conjectural path for consumption.

For this path to be an equilibrium, the interest rate must follow a path that induces optimizing households to choose these values for consumption. The solution for the interest rate appears also in Figure 5.1. Since consumption is constant—although at a depressed level—between times

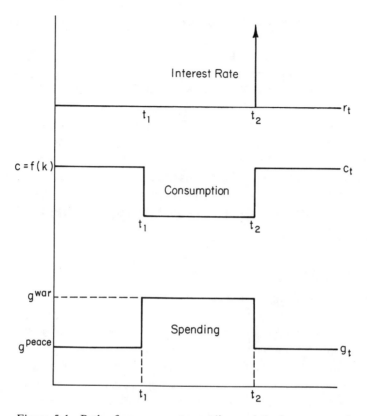

Figure 5.1   Path of government spending and the interest rate in war
and peace.

t_1 and t_2, $r_t = \rho$ applies at these times [see Equations (5.6) and (5.8)]. Given that the war was a surprise at t_1, $r_t = \rho$ applies also at this date.[12] Furthermore, $r_t = \rho$ would apply after date t_2 when c_t was again constant, although at the higher peacetime level. But consumption rises discretely at time t_2. Since people anticipate this change—because they expect the war to end—the interest rate at t_2 must be high enough to motivate the sharp gradient in consumption [see Equations (5.6) and (5.8)].

From the standpoint of the wartime period—say, just after t_1—short-term real interest rates do not change, but longer term rates (of maturity greater than $t_2 - t_1$) increase. These changes reflect the emergency that occurs when the government's demand for goods is temporarily high.

People who defer spending from the wartime period to after the war's end receive a premium in the form of a high real interest rate. Short-term rates do not change because they relate to different dates within the war and hence to times of equally severe emergencies.[13]

The sharp distinction between short- and long-term interest rates does not hold with a variable capital stock.[14] The path for c_t and r_t in Figure 5.1 is no longer an equilibrium because the high real interest rate at time t_2 exceeds the marginal product of capital, $f'(k) = \rho$. Therefore people would attempt to liquidate their capital stocks just prior to the war's end. This liquidation means that consumption would rise before t_2. Therefore the interest rate must increase earlier. But this process continues backward all the way to the start of the war at time t_1.

The equilibrium with variable capital appears in Figure 5.2. The real interest rate, r_t, rises gradually from t_1 to t_2, along with the declining stock of capital per worker, to maintain equality between r_t and $f'(k_t)$.[15] Then the process reverses after the war's end. One conclusion is that the short-term interest rate now depends on current and lagged values of temporary government purchases. The lagged values matter because they contributed to the decline of the capital stock and, hence, to the higher current marginal product of capital.

The path of consumption in Figure 5.2 conforms to that of the interest rate—namely (after a discrete fall at t_1), c_t rises in accordance with the excess of r_t over ρ [see Equations (5.6) and (5.8)]. The declining stock of capital corresponds to negative (or, more generally, reduced) investment, which combines with the lower level of consumption to accommodate the government's high wartime demand for goods. Thus, temporary government purchases now crowd out both types of private spending.

If the marginal product of capital rises slowly with reductions in the capital stock—that is, if $|f''(k)|$ is small—then most of the crowding out during wartime shows up in investment. In Figure 5.2 the interest rate would then rise only by a small amount between dates t_1 and t_2. Correspondingly, the path of consumption during wartime would be relatively flat, with only a small downward movement at time t_1. In fact, this pattern accords broadly with the U.S. data for World War II and the Korean War. At these times the wartime crowding out showed up mainly as reduced private investment (including purchases of consumer durables) rather than as lower consumer expenditures on nondurables and services.[16]

For an open economy, the major difference is the tendency for a

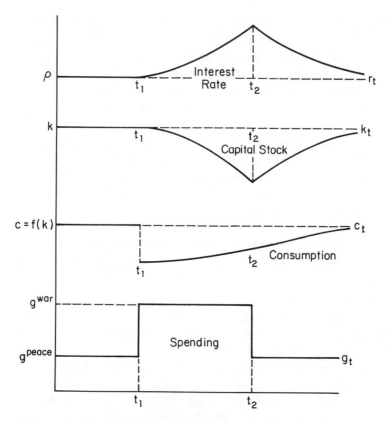

Figure 5.2 Path of government spending and the interest rate in war and
peace, allowing for investment goods.

current-account deficit to substitute for a higher real interest rate. That is,
the economy tends to borrow from abroad to finance temporary government purchases (see Ahmed, 1986, 1987, for a discussion and some empirical evidence for the United Kingdom). The use of external debt means
that the government's expenditures crowd out less private domestic
spending in the short run. In this setting temporary government purchases
in one country raise real interest rates only to the extent that the country
is large or that its marginal borrowing rate increases with the amount
borrowed. But if government purchases rise simultaneously in other
countries—as in a world war—then real interest rates increase as in the
model of a closed economy.

5.2.3. Effects of Government Purchases on Production

Incentives for labor supply. Thus far the changes in government purchases affect production only to the extent that the capital stock changes. In this section I shall consider other avenues for effects on output. The first possibility is that changes in purchases influence the amount of work effort.

A permanent increase in government purchases amounts, as noted before, to a reduction in wealth. With variable work effort, the reduction in wealth tends to raise the supply of labor. (The assumption is that leisure, like consumption, is a normal good.) The increase in labor supply leads to an expansion of employment and hence to greater production. But these results hold unambiguously only with lump-sum taxes. If the extra government expenditure is financed by raising the tax rate on labor income, then the substitution effect from the higher tax rate favors leisure over work. (I shall consider these effects in detail in Section 5.3.) With an income tax—or other types of distorting taxes—the net impact of a permanent increase in government purchases on labor supply is ambiguous.

For a temporary increase in government purchases, the wealth effect is relatively minor. However, the higher interest rate exerts intertemporal-substitution effects on leisure that mirror those on consumption (see Figures 5.1 and 5.2). Thus, people are motivated to work an unusually large amount during wartime or other emergencies.[17] Since the higher interest rate crowds out private spending for consumption and investment, there is no multiplier in the model. That is, the increase in output must fall short of the rise in government purchases.

Barro and King (1984, pp. 825–828) compared a temporary increase in government purchases with an equal-size, but permanent increase. (In both cases the changes were unanticipated beforehand.) If the response of the capital stock is neglected (as in Figure 5.1), and if taxes are lump sum, then the changes in work effort and production are the same in each case. That is because, with additively separable utility over time [as assumed in Equation (5.1)] and no variability of capital, there is no tie of the current period to the future. Expectations about future levels of government purchases, which differentiate permanent from temporary changes, do not matter for current choices in this setting.[18]

For a temporary change in purchases, the inclusion of variable capital, as in Figure 5.2, means that investment absorbs some of the reductions that otherwise show up in consumption and leisure. Therefore the short-run declines in consumption and leisure tend to be less than before—in particular, less than that when the change in purchases is permanent. This result suggests that the short-run effect on work and production would be larger when the change in government purchases is permanent. However, this conclusion need not follow when taxes are distorting. Recall that an increase in the tax rate on labor income tends to reduce work and production. Furthermore, as discussed in Section 5.4, governments typically finance temporary increases in expenditures with budget deficits instead of taxes. Therefore, the contractionary effect from a higher tax rate tends to be smaller when the change in purchases is temporary. This force offsets the effects of investment and leaves as ambiguous the comparison between temporary and permanent changes in government purchases.

Effects of public services on production. So far, public services were a source of utility for households. But many governmental activities, such as a legal system and police protection, function also as inputs to private production. It is straightforward to include this element if the quantity of public services does not influence the marginal products of capital and labor; otherwise the analysis is more complicated.

Let β be the marginal product of public services,[19] where β would tend to decline as the quantity of government purchases rises. One new consideration is that the wealth effect from an expansion of purchases takes account of the increase in output, and hence real income, by β units. Therefore, instead of falling by the fraction $1 - \alpha$ of an increase in purchases, permanent income now falls by the fraction $1 - \alpha - \beta$. Thus, wealth still declines when purchases rise if $\alpha + \beta < 1$. That is, the condition is that the direct substitution for contemporaneous consumption, α, plus the effect on contemporaneous private output, β, be less than unity. Given this condition, the results from before for interest rates and effective consumption still hold with $\alpha + \beta$ substituted for the previous coefficient α.[20]

Some differences arise for measured GNP, which includes government purchases at cost. As an input to private production, these services represent intermediate goods that should not be double-counted in GNP.[21] But the conventional practice includes these goods when the government buys them and includes them again when the goods as inputs lead to an increase in private production. An example is police protection; a shift from guards employed by private businesses to public police raises measured GNP if the private and public personnel are equally productive.

For the case of a permanent increase in government purchases, there is still no effect on the steady-state values of k and r. However, abstracting from changes in labor supply, the direct effect of public services on production means that an increase by 1 unit in purchases leads to an increase by β units in the measured value of steady-state real GNP.

If public services influence the marginal product of labor, then a new substitution effect arises on the work-leisure choice. There are examples, however, where labor's marginal product falls at a given quantity of private employment (as when public police substitute for private guards) and others where labor's marginal product rises (as with improvements in the economy's infrastructure, such as a more efficient legal system and enhanced national security). Unfortunately, the overall effect of government purchases on work effort remains ambiguous.

Government purchases may also affect the marginal product of private capital (see Aschauer, 1988). A straightforward case is where public investments are close substitutes for potential private projects. Then an expansion of government capital amounts to an increase in total capital, and hence, with diminishing marginal productivity, to a reduction in $f'(k)$ for a given quantity of private capital, k. In this case there is direct crowding out of private investment by public investment. It is also possible, however, that public infrastructure, such as the legal system and highways, can raise the productivity of private capital. Then public investment could encourage private investment.

5.2.4. Empirical Evidence on the Effects of Government Purchases

Interest rates. One prediction is that temporary increases in government purchases raise real interest rates. A test of this proposition requires a data set in which some changes in purchases are identifiable ex ante as temporary. Empirically, the clearest examples of these changes are the variations in military spending during wartime. This consideration makes wartime experiences attractive for tests of theories about the effects of temporary government purchases. However, this advantage is offset by the many other aspects of war that can affect real interest rates.

One complication is the possibility of defeat, which affects the default premium on government bonds and may also influence the security of property rights in private bonds and capital stocks. If the threat to all assets is the same, then a greater probability of default raises real interest rates and reduces capital intensity. (Consumption is higher than otherwise because of the chance of confiscation of capital.) If the threat applies more to government bonds than to other assets, then the real interest rate on these bonds rises by correspondingly more.[22] Another consideration is that wartime may involve destruction of capital; hence, production declines and real interest rates rise. Finally, wartime controls in the form of rationing and production directives can substitute for movements in interest rates as devices for crowding out private spending. For example, the command economy aspects of World Wars I and II meant that real interest rates would rise less than under free-market conditions.

Some interesting evidence on the relation between temporary government spending and interest rates comes from the long-term British data. (See Benjamin and Kochin, 1984, and Barro, 1987b, for the details.) Especially during the eighteenth century and through 1815, the United Kingdom was involved in numerous wars, which caused substantial temporary variations in government purchases. Furthermore, the British economy before World War I was free of most other governmental interventions, such as price and interest-rate controls, that often accompany wars. The nature of the positive relation between military spending and interest rates shows up in Figure 5.3. The variable R_t is the long-term nominal interest rate on British consols (meaningful short-term rates are unavailable for much of this period), and the variable $\bar{g}_t$ is a measure of temporary spending, expressed as a ratio to trend GNP. A regression equation covering the interval from 1730 to 1913 is

(5.17)
$$R_t = 3.54 + 6.1\bar{g}_t$$
$$(0.20)\quad(1.3)$$

$AR(1)$ coefficient for error term $= 0.91$,
$$(0.03)$$

where standard errors are in parentheses. Hence the effect of temporary spending on the long-term interest rate is significantly positive; a 1 percentage point increase in the ratio of temporary spending to GNP raises the interest rate by about six basis points. There is also evidence of lagged, mostly positive effects of $\bar{g}$ on R, as predicted by the theory (see Figure 5.2).

One problem with Equation (5.17) is that it applies to nominal interest rates, which include a premium for long-term expected inflation. (However, the average of actual inflation in the United Kingdom was virtually zero from 1730 to 1913.) Another problem is that temporary military expenditures in the United Kingdom were typically accompanied by

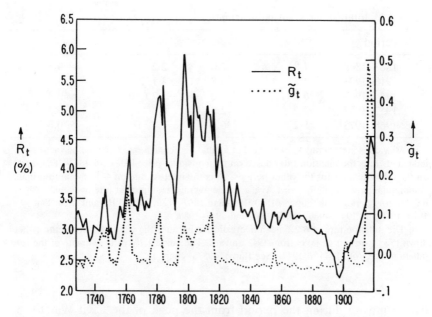

Figure 5.3 Temporary military spending and interest rates in the United Kingdom, 1729–1918. R_t, interest rate on British consols; $\tilde{g}_t$, temporary military spending as a ratio to trend GNP.

budget deficits (see Section 5.4). Therefore, it is not possible to tell clearly from these data whether interest rates rose because of temporary government purchases or because of the associated deficits (or some combination of the two).

For the United States, there is not much evidence for a positive effect of wartime spending on real interest rates. Table 5.1 (based on Barro, 1987a, Chap. 12) shows the realizations for inflation and short-term nominal interest rates for the five main wars since the Civil War. In each case the variables are averages over an interval from the peak of military spending to a peacetime period five years later. If normal real interest rates are identified with values in neighboring peacetime periods, then realized real interest rates were lower than normal during the Civil War, World War I, and World War II, and slightly above normal for the Korean and Vietnam Wars. As mentioned earlier, the failure of real interest rates to rise during the world wars could reflect the influence of the command economy. But it is surprising that the nominal, short-term interest rate

Table 5.1   Interest rates during wartime[a]

Period	π_t	R_t	r_t	Avg. r_t
1863–1868	4.8	7.0	2.2	9.1
1918–1923	2.7	5.8	3.1	4.0
1944–1949	6.2 (1.1)[b]	1.0	−5.2 (−0.1)	2.3
1952–1957	2.2	2.6	0.4	−0.2
1968–1973	5.2	6.6	1.4	0.6

a. All values are averages, expressed at annual percentage rates, for the periods indicated. π_t is the inflation rate, based on the consumer price index for 1863–1868, and on the GNP deflator for the other periods. R_t is the interest rate on 4- to 6-month prime commercial paper. $r_t = R_t - \pi_t$. Avg. r_t is the average real interest rate over the neighboring periods, as follows, 1840–1860 and 1867–1880, 1900–1916 and 1920–1940, 1920–1940 and 1947–1960, 1947–1960, and 1947–1980.

b. The inflation rate of 6.2% is an overestimate because the wartime price controls held down the "true" price level from 1942 onward. The value 1.1% is an estimate of the true inflation rate from 1944 to 1949. (See Barro, 1987a, chap. 12.)

barely moved during the period from the peak of the Civil War to the subsequent peacetime years, despite an inflation rate (4.8%) that was much higher than the negative values experienced in adjacent periods.

Plosser (1987) found that shocks to military spending are positively related to real interest rates in the United States for the period 1968–1976. But there is no significant relation in the period after 1976.

Evans (1987a, tables 1–6), using U.S. data since 1908, found a tendency for interest rates to be positively related to current and lagged changes in federal expenditures and federal purchases. However, the results are sensitive to the sample period, estimation technique, and the distinction between nominal and real interest rates. Evans (1987b) showed that some positive relation between government purchases and interest rates arises also in the period 1974–1985 for Canada, France, Germany, Japan, and the United Kingdom.

Effects on output and employment. The results in Barro (1981, pp. 1114–15) for the United States from 1942 to 1978 indicate that a 1-unit, temporary increase in military purchases raises real GNP 0.6 to 0.8 units (based on a 95% confidence interval). But a permanent increase in military spending of 1 unit raises real GNP 0.2 to 0.6 units. The response to temporary changes is significantly larger than that to permanent changes; recall that this comparison was theoretically ambiguous. The pattern of results is similar when the sample begins after World War II. For the case of nondefense purchases, the data do not allow isolation of temporary changes. The impact on output of permanent changes in nondefense purchases is imprecisely determined, with a 95% confidence interval of $(-0.9, 1.2)$. Overall, the results for military spending support the hypothesis that increases in government purchases lead to increases in real GNP, but by less than one-to-one.

Ahmed (1986, Tables 1 and 3) found for the United Kingdom from 1908 to 1980 that a temporary increase of 1 unit in military purchases raised real GNP 0.2 to 0.6 units (based on a 95% confidence interval). The results for permanent changes, which combined military and nonmilitary purchases, are less well determined and more sensitive to other aspects of the specification. Typical results show a 95% confidence interval of $(0.0, 1.0)$. Thus, Ahmed's results also support the idea that government purchases increase real GNP, but by less than one-to-one. The relative importance of temporary versus permanent changes is unclear here.

Hall (1980, p. 19) found that employment (measured as total employee-hours) increases along with military purchases. He interpreted this response in terms of an intertemporal-substitution variable that combines the 1-year real interest rate and the level of the real wage rate. The expansion of total employment is consistent with the results described earlier for real GNP.

Aschauer (1985) studied the behavior of consumption (measured as consumer expenditures on nondurables and services) in the post-World War II United States. He used the consumer's optimization condition over time—as shown in Equation (5.6)—based on the augmented consumption flow, $c_t^* = c_t + \alpha g_t$. From this condition he obtained an estimate for the parameter α, which measures the direct substitution between public services and private consumer spending. The results (Aschauer, 1985, table 2—his parameter θ) show a 95% confidence interval of $(0.0, 0.4)$. Thus, the substitution appears to be nonnegligible but substantially less than one-to-one. (See Section 5.4.5 for further discussion of these results.) Kormendi (1983) reached similar conclusions from direct estimation of a consumption function.

Aschauer (1988) found, for a given rate of return on capital, that public, nonmilitary investment crowds out private investment nearly one-to-one. He also found, however, that an increase in public, nonmilitary capital raises the productivity of capital, and thereby encourages private investment. The last effect seems to reflect the role of public capital as infrastructure. Overall, Aschauer concluded that public investment had a small effect on private investment and, therefore, a positive effect on national investment.

5.3. Tax Rates

5.3.1. Taxes on Labor Income

Most of the previous discussion assumed that government expenditures were financed by lump-sum taxes. Now I shall make the analysis more realistic by allowing for distorting taxation. I shall assume that expenditures are financed by an income tax. It would be possible, however, to allow for expenditure taxes, the inflation tax, and so on.

As already noted, a tax on labor income implies a substitution effect for work versus leisure (or other nontaxed activities, such as the underground economy). The relevant substitution variable is the marginal tax rate—that is, the increase in tax (or reduction in transfers) implied by an addition to labor income. Figure 5.4, based on Barro and Sahasakul (1986), shows a measure of some components of the marginal tax rate for the U.S. economy. The values are averages of individual rates, when weighted by each household's adjusted gross income. The variable τ_I refers to the federal individual income tax, τ_S to the social security payroll tax,[23] and τ to the sum of the two taxes. In the main the upward movements in the average marginal tax rates parallel the increases in overall federal spending. The sharp increase in τ_I during World War II—from 4% in 1939 to 26% in 1945—reflects increases in tax rates and the extension of the federal income tax to a wide array of households. Two interesting examples of reductions in tax rates are the Kennedy–Johnson cuts, which reduced τ_I from 24.7% in 1963 to 21.2% in 1965, and the Reagan tax cuts, which lowered τ_I from 31.3% in 1981 to 27.2% in 1983.

Typically, an increase in government purchases, G, is accompanied by a rise in the average marginal tax rate, τ. But the wealth effect from more G (described earlier) implies more labor supply, whereas the substitution effect from a higher τ implies less labor supply. Consequently, the overall effect of government purchases on work effort is ambiguous. It is also possible, however, to alter the composition of taxes and thereby change τ without shifting the level of spending, G, and real tax revenues, T. For example, a movement toward the social security tax—which is basically a flat-rate levy on labor earnings—and away from the graduated income tax would lower τ for a given total of revenue collected. Since G is held fixed,

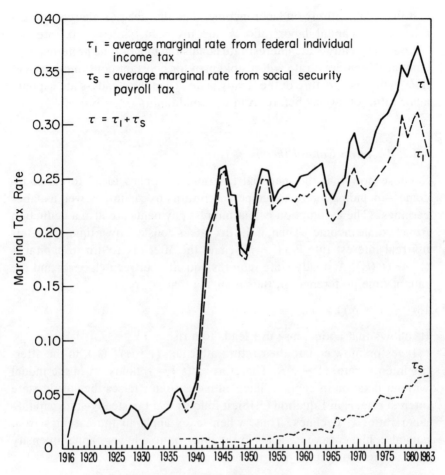

Figure 5.4   Average marginal tax rates, 1916–1983. τ_I, average marginal rate from federal individual income tax; τ_S, average marginal rate from social security payroll tax; $\tau = \tau_I + \tau_S$.

the response of labor supply now reflects only the positive substitution effect from a lower τ. Similarly, by varying the budget deficit (discussed in the next section), it is possible to shift the relative values of tax rates, τ_t, in different periods without changing the pattern of expenditures. Again the responses reflect substitution effects—in this case intertemporal effects that favor more work and production in the periods with relatively low tax rates.

If taxes fall entirely on labor income, then the steady-state real interest rate, r, and capital–labor ratio, k, are invariant with the tax rate. As before, the steady-state interest rate equals the rate of time preference, ρ. Only at this interest rate will people plan for constant consumption over time, which is a feature of the steady state. Then the steady-state capital–labor ratio follows as before from the condition, $f'(k) = r = \rho$.

5.3.2. Taxes on Capital Income

Suppose now that the marginal tax rate, τ, applies to all forms of income—including interest income and returns to capital, as well as labor earnings. (The assumption is that interest payments are also a deduction from taxable income.) Then, if the tax rate is constant over time, the after-tax real interest rate is $(1 - \tau)r_t$, and the after-tax return to capital is $(1 - \tau)f'(k_t)$. A steady state requires equality between $(1 - \tau)r$ and the rate of time preference, ρ, thus implying that

$$(5.18) \qquad r = \rho/(1 - \tau).$$

It follows that an increase in τ leads to a rise in r.

Investors now equate their return after tax, $(1 - \tau)f'(k_t)$, to the after-tax interest rate, $(1 - \tau)r_t$. Therefore, $f'(k_t) = r_t$ holds, as in the model without taxation of capital. Since an increase in τ raises the steady-state interest rate, r, in Equation (5.18), it follows that the steady-state capital–labor ratio, k, declines. Thus, when taxes apply to the earnings from capital, a higher tax rate leads in the long run to a lower capital intensity (and in the short run to less investment).

5.3.3. Effects of Inflation

In some types of tax systems marginal tax rates interact with inflation (see Feldstein and Summers, 1979). For example, with historical-cost depreciation and first-in/first-out inventory accounting, an increase in inflation raises the effective tax rate on earnings from capital. The effect is greater the longer the life of the capital. Similarly, the failure to index nominal capital gains for inflation raises the effective tax rate on capital. Other effects of inflation can arise from the specification of bracket limits, exemptions, and other factors in nominal terms.

In the cases mentioned above, the tax law can be changed (even if not through explicit indexation) to compensate for inflation. For example, the government can allow for accelerated depreciation and investment tax credits—as it did in the United States—to compensate (imperfectly) for the smaller real value of depreciation allowances. Similarly, the nominal values of bracket limits and other factors can be changed through direct legislation. Because of these endogenous responses by the government, it is unclear whether a net linkage between inflation and effective marginal tax rates exists.

If the tax rate τ applies to the nominal interest rate, R, then the after-tax nominal rate is $(1 - \tau)R$. Hence the after-tax real rate is

$$(5.19) \qquad (1 - \tau)R - \pi = (1 - \tau)r - \tau\pi,$$

where $r = R - \pi$ is the gross-of-tax real interest rate. Accordingly, for a given value of r, an increase in π implies a decline in the after-tax real interest rate. In effect, the unindexed tax system imposes the levy, $\tau\pi$, on the inflation part of the nominal interest rate.

On the other hand, if interest payments are tax deductible, then for a given r inflation reduces the after-tax real borrowing rate along with the after-tax real lending rate. It is then possible for the equilibrium after-tax real interest rate to be invariant with inflation. From Equation (5.19) the nominal interest rate, R, must move by the factor $1/(1 - \tau)$ of changes in π—that is, nominal interest rates must adjust by more than one-for-one with inflation. However, there seems to be no empirical evidence that verifies this relationship.

5.3.4. Transfers and Marginal Tax Rates

The marginal tax rate on income considers not only the behavior of taxes but also any interactions with transfer payments. For example, the amounts paid for welfare, for unemployment compensation, and in some cases for social security are inversely related to a person's earnings. The negative effect of income on transfers amounts to an addition to the marginal tax rate. Overall estimates for this effect in the United States are unavailable. Its impact is important for low-income persons, however. For example, the Council of Economic Advisers (1982 report, p. 129) estimated that "typical welfare recipients, namely single mothers with children, face marginal tax rates in excess of 75%."

5.3.5. Laffer Curves

With a balanced budget, an increase in government expenditures requires an increase in government revenues. For a given composition of taxes (including the inflation tax), the assumption has been that an increase in revenues requires an increase in the average marginal tax rate on income, τ. But a higher marginal tax rate motivates reductions in labor and capital, so the fall in the tax base offsets the positive effect of a higher τ on revenues. If labor and capital fall by enough—so that the proportionate fall in the tax base exceeds the proportionate rise in the tax rate—then government revenues decline on net.

Labor and capital respond to the term, $1 - \tau$, which is the fraction of before-tax income that an individual retains at the margin. [Recall that, in the long run, the capital–labor ratio is determined from the condition $f'(k) = r = \rho/(1 - \tau)$.] Furthermore, the term $1 - \tau$ becomes more sensitive to changes in τ as τ rises—that is,

$$(5.20) \qquad \frac{d(1 - \tau)}{(1 - \tau)} = - \left(\frac{\tau}{1 - \tau}\right)\left(\frac{d\tau}{\tau}\right).$$

Thus, given the responses of labor and capital to $1 - \tau$, the condition in Equation (5.20) implies that the positive effect of τ on government revenues diminishes as τ rises. This result is often called a Laffer curve (Figure 5.5). Note that revenues are maximized when the average marginal tax rate attains the value τ^*. For $\tau > \tau^*$, the proportionate decline in the tax base exceeds the proportionate rise in τ; hence, revenue declines with further increases in τ.

Stuart (1981) estimated that τ^* for Sweden was about 70%. Moreover, he argued that the actual average marginal tax rate in Sweden rose above 70% during the 1970s and subsequently reached a value as high as 80%. Thus, Sweden was operating on the falling portion of the Laffer curve in the 1970s. Given the smaller size of the government, however, it is likely that $\tau < \tau^*$ applies currently in the United States. Nevertheless, it is possible that targeted reductions in tax rates—rather than across-the-board cuts—would lead to increases in revenues. For example, Lindsey (1987, table 2) estimated that the cuts in income tax rates in 1982 led overall to a reduction in revenues but that the amounts collected rose on net in the top income brackets.

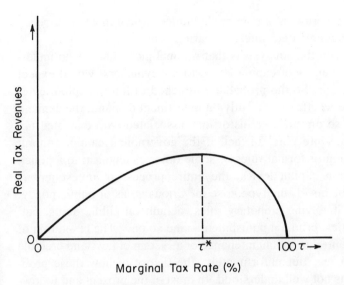

Figure 5.5   The relation of tax receipts to the tax rate (a Laffer curve).
From Barro (1987a, fig. 13.9).

5.3.6. Capital Levies

The distorting effects of income taxes involve the tax rate that people expect to pay when they earn income. For example, when evaluating an investment, a producer considers the anticipated tax rate on future income from capital. Similarly, when deciding how much to work, people take into account the expected tax rate on labor earnings. Since distortions depend on expected tax rates, governments find it tempting to surprise people ex post. For instance, governments may levy a high tax on capital (a "capital levy") after the investment has already been made. Such a tax appears to be nondistorting if the investment is irreversible.

The same argument applies to the inflation tax. Distortions, such as transaction costs associated with economizing on cash holdings, depend on the nominal interest rate, which incorporates the expected rate of inflation. Therefore, given inflationary expectations, surprise increases in money and prices generate government revenue without causing the usual distortions. In effect, these surprises are capital levies on the public's holdings of the government's nominal liabilities, which include currency and nominally denominated, interest-bearing debt.

The problem with this analysis is that rational individuals, who understand the attractiveness of capital levies to policymakers, would expect such levies to occur. So the probability attached to future capital levies would have adverse effects currently on investment demand, the demand for money, and so on, and the distortions associated with expected tax rates would come into play. In fact, if the government cannot commit itself by reputation or formal rules or some other mechanism to a policy that abstains from capital levies, the entire process of investment is threatened. Problems of this type arise in various areas of public policy, including those involving monetary rules, default on public debts, patents, tax amnesties, criminal punishments, and so on.[24] The resolution of these issues is central to the maintenance of a system of laws and credible government policies. But unfortunately, the theory of how these problems are solved is not well understood. In most of the present and following section—and in much of the existing theory of public finance—the problem of capital levies is ignored.

5.4. Budget Deficits and the Public Debt

Suppose now that the government can finance expenditures by issuing interest-bearing public debt. Assume that this debt has a maturity of one period and that the government's interest rate coincides with private rates. Then the government's budget constraint in real terms becomes

$$(5.21) \qquad G_t + r_{t-1}B_{t-1} = T_t + (B_t - B_{t-1}),$$

where G_t is real purchases (to which one could add real transfer payments), B_{t-1} is the real public debt outstanding at the end of period $t - 1$, r_{t-1} is the real interest rate on this debt, and T_t is real tax revenues. The taxes are again treated as lump-sum. As before, money creation does not appear in the government's budget constraint as a separate form of revenue. This revenue corresponds to a particular type of distorting tax (the inflation tax) and is best viewed as an alternative to other distorting taxes, which are reintroduced below. The new elements in Equation (5.21) are the interest payments on the left-hand side and the change in the debt on the right-hand side.

The representative person's wealth depends on his or her share of the initial public debt, B_0, less his or her share of the present value of current and prospective taxes. (The analysis abstracts from the value attached to public services, which is fixed by the path of G_t.) If each person has an infinite horizon and faces the same real interest rate as the government, then the relevant magnitude for the representative person as of date 1 is

$$B_0 - \sum_1^\infty d_t T_t,$$

where d_t is again the present-value factor, as given in Equation (5.3).

A crucial point is that, for a given path of G_t, this net wealth term is invariant with B_0, or the entire path of current and future budget deficits. To demonstrate this invariance, consider the present-value sum of taxes over a finite horizon H [with substitution for T_t from Equation (5.21) and for d_t from Equation (5.3)],

$$\sum_1^H d_t T_t = \sum_1^H \{d_t[G_t + (1 + r_{t-1})B_{t-1} - B_t]\}$$

$$= \sum_1^H d_t G_t + \sum_1^H d_t(1 + r_{t-1})B_{t-1} - \sum_1^H d_t B_t$$

$$= \sum_1^H d_t G_t + B_0 + \sum_2^H d_{t-1}B_{t-1} - \sum_1^H d_t B_t$$

$$= \sum_1^H d_t G_t + B_0 - d_H B_H.$$

Letting H approach infinity leads to

(5.22) $$\sum_1^\infty d_t T_t = \sum_1^\infty d_t G_t + B_0 - \lim_{H \to \infty}(d_H B_H).$$

In Section 5.1 the transversality condition for an individual's optimization problem, $\lim_{H \to \infty}(d_H k_H) = 0$, ensured that people did not leave over any resources that asymptotically had positive present value. But the public debt is held by individuals as part of their assets; so it follows from the same argument that $d_H B_H$ must approach zero asymptotically.[25] In other words, individuals who optimize over an infinite horizon would not hold public debt that grows asymptotically at a rate as high as the interest rate. [If the debt grew this fast asymptotically, then $d_H B_H$ would not remain finite as H tended to infinity—see the definition of d_t in Equation

(5.3).] This condition rules out Ponzi games or chain letters where the government issues debt and finances the payments of interest and principal by perpetual issues of new debt.[26]

Setting the last term to zero in Equation (5.22) implies

$$(5.23) \qquad \sum_1^\infty d_t T_t = \sum_1^\infty d_t G_t + B_0.$$

The present value of taxes is pegged by the present value of spending plus the initial debt; the government must pay for what it gets (in a present-value sense) either now or later. Hence, the relevant term for the representative household's wealth is

$$(5.24) \qquad B_0 - \sum_1^\infty d_t T_t = - \sum_1^\infty d_t G_t,$$

which means that wealth is invariant with B_0 and the entire subsequent path of budget deficits (except that the path of debt is constrained to satisfy the condition that $d_H B_H$ approach zero asymptotically). Household wealth does vary inversely with shifts in the present value of government purchases, $\sum_1^\infty d_t G_t$ (which would be adjusted as before for the service value attached to public spending).

The result implies a version of the Ricardian equivalence theorem on the public debt.[27] Assume that

a. The economy contains a representative individual with an infinite horizon.
b. Individuals borrow and lend at the same real interest rate as the government.
c. Future taxes are perfectly foreseen.
d. Taxes are lump sum.
e. The path of government purchases (and transfer payments), G_t, is given.

Under these conditions, the economy's path of real interest rates, investment, consumption, and so on is invariant with shifts between taxes and budget deficits or with changes in the initial stock of public debt. With lump-sum taxes, budget deficits can matter directly to households only through wealth effects, which involve the term $B_0 - \sum_1^\infty d_t T_t$. But the previous analysis showed that this term is invariant with B_0, or the entire path of subsequent budget deficits. Therefore the equilibrium path for r_t, k_t, c_t, and so on does not change with shifts in B_0 or in budget deficits.

Consider this example. Suppose that the government cuts current taxes, T_1, by 1 unit and runs a larger deficit, so that B_1 is higher by 1 unit. The Ricardian result implies that households use their tax cut to absorb the larger public debt without any changes in interest rates. Households save more without an increase in interest rates because the current tax cut by 1 unit implies (with a given path of government purchases and transfers) an increase by 1 unit in the present value of future taxes. Thus, today's extra private saving generates just enough future private assets to pay the extra future taxes. In this way the entire path of consumption (as well as that of work effort) does not change. To put the result another way, the increase in private saving exactly offsets the fall in public saving so as to maintain the total of national saving.[28]

Meaningful criticisms of the Ricardian result amount to deviations from the assumptions set out above. In the following discussion I shall maintain the assumption of a fixed path of government purchases and transfers [assumption (e)] and shall evaluate in turn the arguments that have been raised concerning (a) through (d). In each case it is important to consider not only whether the Ricardian view remains intact but also what alternative conclusions emerge. Many economists tend to raise points that invalidate strict Ricardian equivalence and then simply assume that the points support a specific alternative—usually the standard view that a budget deficit lowers desired national saving and thereby drives up real interest rates. Many criticisms of the Ricardian position turn out also to be inconsistent with this standard view.

5.4.1. Finite Horizons and Related Issues

The idea of finite horizons, motivated by the finiteness of life, is central to life-cycle models (see, for example, Modigliani and Brumberg, 1954, and Ando and Modigliani, 1963). In these models, individuals capitalize only the taxes that they expect to face before dying. Consider again a deficit-financed tax cut and assume that the higher future taxes occur partly during the typical person's expected lifetime and partly afterward. Then the present value of the first portion must fall short of the initial tax cut, because a full balance results only if the second portion is included. The increase in net wealth of persons currently alive motivates an increase in consumption demand (and a decline in labor supply). The rise in consumer demand means that private saving does not rise by enough to offset fully the decline in government saving—hence, desired national saving falls. The resulting increase in the current real interest rate reduces investment demand in the short run and the stock of capital in the long run. Modigliani (1961) referred to this outcome as a "burden of the public debt," in the sense that future generations are burdened by having less capital to work with.

Feldstein (1974) showed that similar results occur with a pay-as-you-go social security program. An increase in the scale of the program is good for the currently old, who receive more benefits without paying for them. The currently young pay more taxes but recoup part of these expenses later from the higher benefits that are financed by taxes on the next generation. As with a budget deficit, the net effects of the pay-as-you-go system are a decrease in desired national saving, an increase in real interest rates, and crowding-out of private capital.

These results about budget deficits and social security can be derived in the overlapping-generations model of Diamond (1965), which was an extension of the Samuelson (1958) model to include reproducible capital. In the Diamond model people live for two periods, corresponding to one period of work and one of retirement. Blanchard (1985) obtained similar results in a model where individuals die off stochastically. The advantages of the Blanchard model over the overlapping-generations framework are that, first, the horizon can be treated as a continuous parameter (related to the probability of dying per unit of time) and, second, some comparative-statics exercises are more tractable.

Basically, a finite horizon generates the standard results about budget deficits: real interest rates rise and private capital is crowded out. However, the argument works only if the typical person feels better off when the government shifts a tax burden to his or her descendants. The argument fails if the typical person is already giving to his or her children out of altruism. In this case people react to the government's imposed intergenerational transfers, which are implied by budget deficits or social security, with a compensating increase in voluntary transfers (see Barro, 1974). For example, parents adjust their bequests or the amounts given to children while the parents are still living (or, equivalently, children raise their transfers to aged parents). Empirically, the most important example of intergenerational transfers is probably the financing of children's education (see Drazen, 1978, for a discussion).

The main point is that a network of intergenerational transfers makes the typical person a part of an extended family that goes on indefinitely. In this setting households capitalize the entire array of expected future taxes and thereby plan effectively with an infinite horizon. In other words, the

Ricardian results, which depended on infinite horizons, can remain valid even in a model with finite lifetimes.

Two important points should be stressed. First, intergenerational transfers do not have to be "large"; what is necessary is that transfers based on altruism be operative at the margin for the typical person. Specifically, most people must be away from the corner solution of zero transfers, where they would, if permitted, opt for negative payments to their children. (However, the results also go through if children typically support their aged parents.) Second, the transfers do not have to show up as bequests at death. Other forms of intergenerational transfers work in a similar manner.

Buiter (1980) and Weil (1987a) worked out the conditions necessary for bequests to be operative for the representative family. One result is that an equilibrium with operative bequests cannot exhibit the type of inefficient oversaving that is possible in the models of Diamond (1965) and others, in which finite-lived persons have no concern for subsequent generations. Basically, bequests arise if parents "love their children enough"—a condition made plausible by the fact that the parents decided to have the children in the first place (see Becker and Barro, 1988). Buiter (1980), Kimball (1987), and Kanaya (1986, chap. 1) allowed also for gifts from children to parents. A principal finding is that child-to-parent transfers would not arise for the representative family in an equilibrium with efficient saving. However, the potential for these gifts limits the extent of inefficient oversaving that can occur.

One objection to Ricardian equivalence is that some persons, such as those without children, are not connected to future generations (see Tobin and Buiter, 1980, pp. 86ff.). Persons in this situation tend to be made wealthier when the government substitutes a deficit for taxes. At least this conclusion obtains to the extent that the interest and principal payments on the extra public debt are not financed by higher taxes during the remaining lifetimes of people currently alive. However, the quantitative effects on consumption tend to be small. For example, for someone who has 30 years of life remaining and consumes at a constant rate, a one-time budget deficit of $1 would increase real consumption demand by 1.4 cents per year if the annual real interest rate is 5%, and by 2.1 cents per year if the real interest rate is 3%.[29]

The aggregate effect from the existence of childless persons is even smaller, because people with more than the average number of descendants experience a decrease in wealth when taxes are replaced by budget deficits. (In effect, although some people have no children, all children must have parents.) The presumption for a net effect on aggregate consumer demand depends on different propensities to consume out of wealth for people with and without children. Since the propensity for those without children tends to be larger (because of the shorter horizon), a positive net effect on aggregate consumer demand would be predicted. However, the quantitative effect is likely to be trivial. Making the same assumptions as in the previous example, including the constancy of consumption over time for each family, a budget deficit of $1 would raise aggregate real consumption demand by 0.3 cents per year if the real interest rate is 5%, and by 0.9 cents if the real interest rate is 3%.

In general, the crucial consideration for Ricardian equivalence is not finite horizons per se but the extent to which members of current generations are connected to those in future generations. For example, Weil (1987b) shows that effects of the finite-life type can arise in models where individuals have infinite horizons if new agents with infinite horizons enter the economy in future periods. These new persons can be interpreted as unloved children or as immigrants. Budget deficits matter here because they shift part of the future tax burden to these unloved children and immigrants.[30]

Feldstein (1988) points out that uncertainty about future income means that bequests are also uncertain—in particular, the typical person has a nonzero probability of being at a corner where the bequest is zero. In this situation budget deficits affect the consumption choices of all persons— even those who turn out to leave bequests, ex post. However, in the aggregate, the conclusions are similar to those from a deterministic setting where some fraction of persons are at the corner of zero bequests. Also, persons whose income turns out to be low enough to trigger zero bequests may move into the region where they receive transfers from their children, a shift that works toward restoring the Ricardian results.

Darby (1979, chap. 3) and Kotlikoff and Summers (1981) calculated that the accumulation of households' assets in the United States for the purpose of intergenerational transfers is far more important than that associated with the life cycle. This observation suggests that intergenerational transfers would be operative for most people, a suggestion that supports the Ricardian position as noted above.

Bernheim, Shleifer, and Summers (1985) noted that the motivation behind intergenerational transfers also matters for the results. These authors considered the possibility that bequests, instead of being driven by altruism, are a strategic device whereby parents induce their children to be-have properly. Some imaginative evidence is presented (involving how often children visit and communicate with their parents) to document the importance of strategic bequests. Some related evidence about the moti-vation for transfers appeared in Cox (1987).

This enforcement theory of giving has different implications for the effects of budget deficits and social security. If the government redistrib-utes income from young to old (by running a deficit or raising social security benefits), then the old have no reason in this model to raise transfers to offset fully the government's actions. Instead, the old end up better off at the expense of the young, and aggregate consumer demand rises. Then, as in the standard approach, real interest rates increase and private capital is crowded out.

One shortcoming of this approach is that it treats the interaction be-tween parents and children as equivalent to the purchases of services on markets. In this setting parents would tend to pay wages to children rather than using bequests or other forms of intergenerational transfers. These features—as well as the observation that most parents seem to care about their children's welfare—can be better explained by introducing altruism along with a desire to influence children's behavior.[31] In this case Ricardian equivalence may or may not hold. Consider the utility that a parent would allocate to his or her child if there were no difficulty in motivating the child to perform properly. Suppose that the parent can design a credible threat involving bequests that entails the loss of some part of the child's utility. (Note that if no threats are credible, the whole point of strategic bequests disappears.) If the threat is large enough to induce the behavior that the parent desires, Ricardian equivalence still holds. For example, if the government runs a budget deficit, the parent increases transfers to the child and thereby preserves the child's level of utility, as well as the desired form of behavior. On the other hand, to secure the desired performance, the parent may have initially allowed excess utility to the child. Then a budget deficit enables the parent to reduce the child's utility (as desired) while maintaining or even enhancing the threat that influences the child's behavior. In this case Ricardian equivalence does not hold.

Bernheim and Bagwell (1988) argued that the linkages implied by altru-istic transfers imply too much neutrality. If parents give to their children, then marriage creates connections between unrelated members of the same generation; for example, between two sets of in-laws. If the groups become large enough, then even an income tax may become neutral. (The result holds for a variety of solution concepts for the interaction among individuals.) In the usual public-finance analysis, individuals neglect the parts of their marginal products that go to increased tax revenues for the government. Then the insufficient private incentives to work and produce generate inefficient outcomes. However, suppose that the proceeds from the tax payments benefit someone to whom the taxpayer is connected via altruistic transfers. Then people treat their tax payments as equivalent to extra disposable income. When almost everyone is connected to almost everyone else via altruistic linkages—as in the Bernheim–Bagwell analysis—the taxes are fully internalized. Hence, the usual distortions implied by taxation do not arise.

To evaluate this argument, begin by numbering the presently living generations, starting from the oldest, as 1, 2, . . . Suppose that all persons marry and have two children (although the number of children can be allowed to vary across families and also average something other than two). Assume that half of the children are male and half female. Assume also that spouses are linked altruistically to each other and that parents provide altruistic transfers to each child. Then, by considering prospective marriages and children in future generations, Bernheim and Bagwell (1988, sect. 4) showed that the typical person ends up linked to almost everyone else by a complex network of altruistic transfers. At least this result holds if each male has about the same probability of marrying each female. However, this outcome cannot be an equilibrium because each individual—say, in generation 1—would find it advantageous to curtail his or her giving. In a fully interconnected situation, giving to another person—including one's child—is equivalent to giving to the whole of society. Weak conditions on preferences ensure that the typical person prefers own consumption to this gift to society, which amounts to a voluntary tax. Therefore, given the assumptions made before, equilibria must involve some parents not giving altruistically to all of their children.

From the perspective of generation 1, the incentive to give to someone in generation 2—say, to a child and his or her spouse—is diminished when the recipient also gets transfers from others, including his or her in-laws. The existence of multiple donors creates a free-rider problem—each potential giver would like to commit to providing less or nothing to induce other potential givers to provide more. In the absence of cooperative agreements, one possible equilibrium occurs when no couple in generation 2 receives altruistic transfers from more than one couple in generation 1. (Other equilibria could feature multiple giving as long as it was not pervasive enough to generate the sort of interconnectedness that was ruled out above.) With multiple giving eliminated, each couple in generation 2 may be linked altruistically to one set of parents from generation 1, but not to both sets. From the perspective of generation 1, some couples give to both children, some to 1 child, and some to neither. But on average each couple in generation 1 is linked to no more than one couple in generation 2.

For the Ricardian analysis, it is important to consider whether there exist many persons in generation 2 who receive no altruistic transfers from anyone in generation 1. As in the models that ignored marriage, the answer depends on the strength of caring from parents to children. If this caring is strong for the typical parents and child (again, a proposition supported by the parents' choice to have the child), an equilibrium will not feature many people in generation 2 who receive nothing from someone in generation 1. In equilibrium the average couple in generation 1 would be linked with roughly 1 couple in generation 2. In fact, one simple system that automatically generates this outcome is the one in which parents give to children of one sex but not to children of the other (see Kanaya, 1986, sects. II.5 and III.4).

The linkage of the typical couple in each generation to one couple in the next is a pattern that produces Ricardian equivalence. Budget deficits and social security are then offset by changes in private transfers, just as in the model without marriage. However, two caveats are worth mentioning. First, some couples may give to no one in the next generation, while others give to more than one couple. Then the results are similar to those described earlier for the situation in which some persons are childless and others have more than the average number of children. In this case strict Ricardian equivalence fails, but—as also argued before—the departures tend to be quantitatively insignificant. The only new aspect of marriage here is that the incidence of persons who do not give to children is greater than the number who are literally childless. The second caveat is that the free-rider problem associated with multiple giving means that intergenerational transfers tend to be smaller than the Pareto optimal amount that would be attained with perfect cooperation (see Nerlove, Razin and Sadka, 1984; Kanaya, 1986, chaps. II and III). Therefore the incidence of couples in generation 2 who receive nothing from someone in generation 1 tends to be larger than it would be if this coordination problem were absent.

5.4.2. Imperfect Loan Markets

Many economists argue that the imperfection of private credit markets is central to an analysis of the public debt (see, for example, Mundell, 1971). To incorporate this element, assume that the economy consists of two types of infinite-lived economic agents—those of group A who have the same discount rate, r, as the government (and are therefore willing to hold the government's debt), and those of group B who have the higher discount rate, $\bar{r} > r$. The constituents of group A would include many large businesses and some individuals. The members of group B, for example, small businesses and many households, possess poor collateral; therefore, loans to these people imply large costs of evaluation and enforcement. It follows that the members of group B face higher borrowing rates (even after an allowance for default risk) than the government does. The discount rate $\bar{r}$ equals the marginal borrowing rate for those who are actually borrowing. Otherwise the discount rate equals the consumption rate of time preference, which lies somewhere between the rate r and the marginal borrowing rate (which conceivably would be infinity). A small business (and also a household contemplating a purchase of consumer durables) adjusts its investment so that the marginal rate of return to investment equals the discount rate $\bar{r}$.

Suppose that the government cuts current taxes and runs a budget deficit. Further, assume that the division of the tax cut between groups A and B—say, fifty–fifty—is the same as the division of the higher future taxes needed to service the extra debt. As in the standard Ricardian case, those from group A experience no net change in wealth. But since $\bar{r} > r$, the present value of group B's extra future taxes falls short of that group's share of the tax cut. So those from group B react to their increased wealth by raising consumption demand; and, as current consumption increases, the discount rate $\bar{r}$ tends to fall, which motivates small businesses and households to increase investment demand. For example, if a business uses its tax cut to raise current investment, the fall in $\bar{r}$ reflects the diminishing marginal return to investment.

In the aggregate, a budget deficit now raises aggregate demand; or equivalently, the aggregate of desired private saving increases by less than one-to-one with the government's deficit. It follows that the real interest rate r, which applies to group A and the government, rises to induce people to hold the extra public debt. There is crowding out of consumption and investment by members of group A. But since the discount rate $\bar{r}$ for group B declines on net, the expenditures of this group are encouraged. The main result is a diversion of expenditures from group A to group B and a corresponding narrowing of the spread between the two discount rates, r and $\bar{r}$. In the aggregate, investment may either rise or fall, and the long-term effect on the capital stock is uncertain. The major change, however, is a better channeling of resources to their ultimate uses—namely, the persons from group B, who have relatively high values for rates of time preference and for marginal returns to investment, command a greater share of current output. In any event the outcomes are nonneutral, and in that sense non-Ricardian.

The important finding from the inclusion of imperfect loan markets is that the government's issue of public debt can amount to a useful form of financial intermediation. The government induces people with good access to credit markets (group A) to hold more than their share of the extra public debt. Those with poor access (group B) hold less than their share and thereby effectively receive loans from the first group. This process works because the government implicitly guarantees the repayment of loans through its tax collections and debt payments. Thus, loans between A and B take place even though such loans were not viable (because of "transaction costs") on the imperfect private credit market.

This much of the argument may be valid, although it credits the government with too much skill in the collection of taxes from people with poor collateral (which is the underlying problem for private lenders). But even if the government is more efficient, the conclusions do not resemble those from the standard analysis. As discussed before, budget deficits can amount to more financial intermediation and are in that sense equivalent to a technological advance that improves the functioning of loan markets. From this perspective it is reasonable to find a reduced spread between various discount rates and an improvement in the allocation of resources. If the government really is better at the process of intermediating, then more of this activity—that is, more public debt—raises perceived wealth because it actually improves the workings of the economy.

Instead of introducing costs of enforcing the collection of loans, Yotsuzuka (1987) extended the analysis of King (1984) and Hayashi (1987) by allowing for adverse selection among borrowers with different risk characteristics. Individuals know their probabilities of default, but the lenders' only possibility for learning these probabilities comes from observing the chosen levels of borrowing at going interest rates. In this setting the government's borrowing amounts to a loan to a group that pools the various risk classes. Such borrowing matters if the private equilibrium does not involve similar pooling. However, by considering the incentives of lenders to exchange or not exchange information about their customers, Yotsuzuka argues that the private equilibrium typically involves a pooled loan of limited quantity at a relatively low interest rate. Then the high-risk types may borrow additional amounts at a high interest rate. In this case the government's borrowing replaces the private pooled lending and leads to no real effects. That is, Ricardian equivalence holds despite the imperfect private loan market where high-risk people face high marginal borrowing rates. The general lesson again is that Ricardian equivalence fails because of imperfect credit markets only if the government does things in the loan market that are different from, and perhaps better than, those carried out privately.

5.4.3. Uncertainty about Future Taxes and Incomes

Some economists have argued that the uncertainty about individuals' future taxes—or the complexity in estimating them—implies a high rate of discount in capitalizing these future liabilities (see Bailey, 1971, pp. 157–158; Buchanan and Wagner, 1977, pp. 17, 101, 130; Feldstein, 1976, p. 335). In this case a substitution of a budget deficit for current taxes raises net wealth because the present value of the higher expected future taxes falls short of the current tax cut. It then follows that budget deficits raise aggregate consumer demand and lower desired national saving.

A proper treatment of uncertainty leads to different conclusions. Chan (1983) first considered the case of lump-sum taxes that have a known distribution across households. However, the aggregate of future taxes and the real value of future payments on public debt are subject to uncertainty. In this case a deficit-financed tax cut has no real effects. Individuals hold their share of the extra debt because the debt is a perfect hedge against the uncertainty of the future taxes. (This analysis assumes that private credit markets have no "imperfections" of the sort discussed earlier.)

Suppose now that future taxes are still lump-sum but have an uncertain incidence across individuals. Furthermore, assume that there are no insurance markets for relative tax risks. Then a budget deficit tends to increase the uncertainty about each individual's future disposable income. Chan (1983, p. 363) showed for the "usual case" (of nonincreasing absolute risk aversion) that people react by reducing current consumption and raising current saving. Consequently, the effects on real interest rates, investment, and so on are the opposite of the standard ones.

The results are different for an income tax (Chan, 1983, pp. 364–366; Barsky, Mankiw, and Zeldes, 1986). Suppose that each person pays the tax τy_i, where y_i is the person's uncertain future income. Suppose that there are no insurance markets for individual income risks and that τ is known. (The analysis thus abstracts from uncertainties in relative tax rates across individuals.) In this case a budget deficit raises the future value of τ and thereby reduces the uncertainty about each individual's future disposable income. In effect, the government shares the risks about individual disposable income to a greater extent. It follows that the results are opposite to those found before—namely, a budget deficit tends to raise current consumption and reduce current saving.

Overall, the conclusions depend on the net effect of higher mean future tax collections on the uncertainty associated with individuals' future disposable incomes. Desired national saving tends to rise with a budget deficit if this uncertainty increases, and vice versa.

5.4.4. The Timing of Taxes

Departures from Ricardian equivalence arise also if taxes are not lump-sum—for example, with an income tax. In this situation budget deficits change the timing of income taxes and thereby affect people's incentives to work and produce in different periods. It follows that variations in deficits are nonneutral, although the results tend also to be inconsistent with the standard view.

Suppose, for example, that the current income tax rate, τ_1, declines and the next period's rate, τ_2, rises. To simplify matters, assume that today's budget deficit is matched by enough of a surplus next period so that the public debt does not change from date 3 onward. Because the tax rate applies to income, people are motivated to work and produce more than usual in period 1 and less than usual in period 2. Since the tax rate does not apply to expenditures (and since wealth effects are negligible here), it follows that desired national saving rises in period 1 and falls in period 2. Therefore, after-tax real interest rates tend to be relatively low in period 1—along with the budget deficit—and relatively high in period 2—along with the surplus. At least these results follow if the effects on investment demand are small because of adjustment costs (which were omitted for simplicity in the model developed in Section 5.1). The main point is that the results are not only non-Ricardian but also counter to the standard view. (Temporary variations in consumption taxes tend to generate the standard pattern where real interest rates and budget deficits are positively correlated.)

In the Ricardian case where debt and deficits do not matter, it is not possible to determine the optimal path of the budget deficit. But in a world of distorting taxes, that path can be determined and corresponds to the optimal time pattern of taxes. In effect, the theory of debt management becomes a branch of public finance, specifically, an application of the theory of optimal taxation.

One important observation is that budget deficits can be used to smooth tax rates over time, despite fluctuations in government expenditures and the tax base. For example, if time periods are identical except for the quantity of government purchases—which are assumed not to interact directly with labor supply decisions—then optimality dictates uniform taxation of labor income over time. This constancy of tax rates requires budget deficits when government spending is unusually high and surpluses when spending is unusually low.

Constant tax rates over time will not be optimal in general;[32] for example, optimal tax rates on labor income may vary over the business cycle. To the extent that some smoothing is called for, budget deficits would occur in recessions and surpluses in booms. If optimal tax rates are lower than normal in recessions and higher than normal in booms, then the countercyclical pattern of budget deficits is even more vigorous.

To see the implications of tax smoothing for budget deficits, use Equation (5.23) to get the government's present-value budget constraint, starting from date i,

$$(5.25) \qquad \sum_{t=i}^{\infty} (d_t/d_{i-1}) T_t = \sum_{t=i}^{\infty} (d_t/d_{i-1}) G_t + B_{i-1}.$$

Now, assume a proportional income tax, $T_t = \tau_t Y_t$, where τ_t is the tax rate and Y_t is the tax base—assumed to correspond to real GNP. Then the smoothing condition, $\tau_t = \tau_i$ for all $t \geq i$, implies that the tax rate is

$$(5.26) \qquad \tau_i = \frac{\sum_{t=i}^{\infty} (d_t/d_{i-1}) G_t + B_{i-1}}{\sum_{t=i}^{\infty} (d_t/d_{i-1}) Y_t}.$$

Suppose in the steady state that G_t and Y_t each grow at the rate n (so that the ratio, G_t/Y_t, has no drift). Then "normal" spending, G_i^*, and GNP, Y_i^*, can be defined as the values—constant for $t \geq i$—that satisfy the relations,

$$(5.27) \qquad G_i^* \sum_{t=i}^{\infty} (d_t/d_{i-1})(1 + n)^{t-i} = \sum_{t=i}^{\infty} (d_t/d_{i-1})G_t,$$

$$Y_i^* \sum_{t=i}^{\infty} (d_t/d_{i-1})(1 + n)^{t-i} = \sum_{t=i}^{\infty} (d_t/d_{i-1})Y_t.$$

The variable Y_i^* corresponds to trend-adjusted permanent income and G_i^* to trend-adjusted permanent government purchases (plus transfers).

Substituting from Equation (5.27) into Equation (5.26) leads to the formula for the tax rate,

$$(5.28) \qquad \tau_i = \frac{G_i^* + (r_{i-1} - n)B_{i-1}}{Y_i^*}.$$

This result applies with constant interest rates, $r_t = r_{i-1}$ for $t \geq i$. Otherwise the term $(r_{i-1} - n)B_{i-1}$ is replaced by a more general measure of trend-adjusted interest payments. Equation (5.28) says that the constant tax rate equals the ratio of permanent spending—G_i^* plus trend-adjusted interest payments—to permanent income.

The government's budget constraint implies that the deficit is

$$B_i - B_{i-1} = G_i + r_{i-1}B_{i-1} - \tau_i Y_i.$$

Substituting for τ_i from Equation (5.28) and rearranging terms lead to the condition[33]

$$(5.29) \qquad B_i - B_{i-1} = G_i - G_i^* + [(Y_i^* - Y_i)/Y_i^*]$$
$$\cdot [G_i^* + (r_{i-1} - n)B_{i-1}] + nB_{i-1}.$$

Hence tax smoothing has the following implications for budget deficits:

1. The deficit rises one-to-one with temporary spending, $G_i - G_i^*$. In particular, deficits are positive in wartime, where $G_i > G_i^*$, and negative in peacetime, where $G_i < G_i^*$.

2. The deficit rises with the shortfall of current output from normal, $Y_i^* - Y_i$, where the coefficient is the ratio of normal spending—G_i^* plus trend-adjusted interest payments—to normal GNP. To put the result another way, with a proportional income tax and a constant tax rate, tax

revenues fall in the same proportion as GNP. Hence the shortfall in revenues—which equals the budget deficit—is the product of the proportionate fall in receipts and the normal amount of receipts, which equals the normal amount of spending. The result implies deficits during recessions and surpluses during booms. [The standard full-employment deficit, as discussed in Brown (1956) and Council of Economic Advisers (1962, pp. 78–82), adjusts for this behavior of deficits.]

3. When spending and GNP are at their normal values, the government runs a deficit (if $B_{i-1} > 0$) of size nB_{i-1}. The growth in debt, other things equal, at rate n maintains the ratio of the debt to GNP. Otherwise the tendency of interest payments to rise or fall relative to GNP would be inconsistent with stabilization of the tax rate.

Equation (5.29) involves all variables in real terms. If the debt is denominated in nominal units, then—assuming that inflation is perfectly anticipated—the left-hand side becomes the change in the real debt. Hence, other things equal, the nominal debt grows in the same proportion as the price level to maintain the real value of the debt. It follows that expected inflation can account for a significant portion of the budget deficit, when it is measured in the standard way as the change in the government's nominal obligations. (The recent practice of adjusting deficits for inflation is a response to this element.)

Under conditions of perfect foresight, the tax rate determined in Equation (5.28) remains constant over time. (The accumulated debt varies in just the right way to offset changes in G_i^* and Y_i^*, which need not be constant even under conditions of perfect foresight.) New information about the path of G_t or Y_t would imply revisions to the tax rate calculated in Equation (5.28), but the sign of these revisions is not predictable ex ante. Thus, in the presence of uncertainty the tax rate behaves like a random walk (or, more precisely, a Martingale) instead of remaining constant.

Changes in the real value of the outstanding debt, B_{i-1}, affect the tax rate in the same direction. Thus, unexpected inflation or default on existing obligations leads to a fall in the tax rate. In particular, unlike expected inflation, a surprise increase in the price level does not lead to an increase of the nominal debt in the same proportion. In the tax-smoothing model there is no target for the real debt or the debt–GNP ratio to which the government tends to return.

It is possible to use the tax-smoothing approach as a positive theory of how the government operates rather than as a normative model of how it should act.[34] Barro (1979, 1986b) showed that this framework explains much of the behavior of U.S. federal deficits from 1916 to 1983, although the deficits for 1984–1987 turn out to be higher than predicted. Over the full sample, the major departures from the theory are an excessive reaction of deficits to the business cycle (so that tax rates fall below "normal" during recessions) and an insufficient reaction to temporary military spending (so that tax rates rise above normal during wars). These departures were found also by Sahasakul (1986), who looked directly at the behavior of average marginal tax rates. Barro (1987b, sect. 3) found for the British data from the early 1700s through 1918 that temporary military spending is the major determinant of budget deficits. Also, unlike the results of the U.S. case, these results indicate a one-to-one response of budget deficits to temporary spending.

Hercowitz (1986a) applied a similar analysis to the evolution of Israel's foreign debt. He found that temporary military spending, net of the foreign transfers to Israel that are stimulated by that spending, was financed roughly one-to-one by foreign debt. However, the countercyclical response of the debt was weaker than that predicted by the theory.

Mankiw (1987b) used the tax-smoothing model for a joint analysis of the inflation tax and other taxes. This perspective can explain why short-term nominal interest rates, which are the tax rate associated with money, have been close to a random walk since the founding of the Federal Reserve System in 1914 (see Mankiw and Miron, 1986). Moreover, Mankiw (1987b) found for the United States from 1952 to 1985 that changes in interest rates are positively associated with changes in the ratio of federal tax receipts to GNP, or with changes in average marginal tax rates. These results accord with a model where interest rates and other tax rates are jointly determined from an optimal-tax perspective.

The tax-smoothing approach provides a positive theory of public debt and budget deficits while retaining the modeling device of a representative private agent. Another approach attempts to explain debt issue as the outcome of a conflict between groups with different interests. For example, Cukierman and Meltzer (1987) brought in distributional considerations by assuming that some fraction of the population is currently or prospectively at a corner solution with respect to private intergenerational transfers. In a political equilibrium determined by the position of the median voter, the quantity of public debt depends on the distribution of the corner constraints, which depends in turn on the distribution of income and other variables. Persson and Svensson (1987) and Alesina and

Tabellini (1987) considered a division of political parties and the electorate in terms of the desired size or composition of public expenditures. Then the accumulation of national debt can be a device whereby a government influences its successor's choices about public expenditures. From a positive standpoint, the quantity of public debt depends on the degree of political polarization, on factors that determine the stability of governments, and so on.

Lucas and Stokey (1983) and Persson and Svensson (1984) showed that the debt-management problem involves capital-levy problems, which are similar to those discussed earlier. One aspect concerns incentives to wipe out the existing real debt, either by formal default or—for nominally denominated debt—by unanticipated inflation. Since a higher initial real debt requires a higher tax rate in Equation (5.28), and since taxation entails deadweight losses, there appears to be a welfare gain for the representative person from the government's canceling the existing debt and "starting over." Of course, such behavior compromises the government's ability to issue new debt and therefore tends to eliminate the feasibility of using debt management to smooth out the pattern of tax rates. Avoidance of this outcome requires the government to follow rules that overcome the temptation to place capital levies on the outstanding debt.

A more subtle time-consistency problem involves the term structure of real interest rates, which the government can influence through its choices of tax rates over time. Lucas and Stokey (1983) and Persson and Svensson (1984) show that the maturity structure of the public debt can be designed to avoid this problem. That is, with the correct maturity structure, the government is automatically motivated to follow through on its previous plans for tax rates.

5.4.5. Empirical Evidence on the Economic Effects of Budget Deficits

The Ricardian and standard views have different predictions about the effects of fiscal policy on a number of economic variables. In the next sections I shall summarize the empirical evidence on interest rates, saving, and the current-account balance.

Interest rates. The Ricardian view predicts no effect of budget deficits on real interest rates, whereas the standard view predicts a positive effect, at least in the context of a closed economy. Many economists have tested these propositions empirically (for a summary, see U.S. Treasury

Department, 1984). Typical results show little relationship between budget deficits and interest rates. For example, Plosser (1982, p. 339) finds for quarterly U.S. data from 1954 (or 1959 or 1964) to 1978 that unexpected movements in privately held federal debt do not raise the nominal yield on government securities of various maturities. In fact, there is a weak tendency for yields to decline with innovations in federal debt. Plosser (1987, tables VIII and XI), in his later study that included data through 1985, reached similar conclusions for nominal and expected real yields. Evans (1987b) obtained similar results for nominal yields with quarterly data from 1974 to 1985 for Canada, France, Germany, Japan, the United Kingdom, and the United States.

Evans (1987a, tables 4–6) found from annual U.S. data for 1931 to 1979 that current and past real federal deficits have no significant association with nominal interest rates on commercial paper or corporate bonds or with realized real interest rates on commercial paper. Over the longer period from 1908 to 1984, analysis of monthly data indicated a negative relation between deficits and nominal or real interest rates (Evans, 1987a, tables 1–3). Evans also explored the effects of expected future budget deficits or surpluses. He assumed that people would have expected future deficits in advance of tax cuts, like those in 1981, and future surpluses in advance of tax hikes. But interest rates turned out typically not to rise in advance of tax cuts and not to fall in advance of tax hikes. If anything, interest rates tended to move with the opposite pattern. Mankiw's (1987b) analysis, which viewed interest rates as a form of tax rate, is consistent with these findings.

Overall, the empirical results on interest rates support the Ricardian view. Given these findings, it is remarkable that most macroeconomists remain confident that budget deficits raise interest rates.

Consumption and saving. Most empirical results on the interplay between budget deficits and saving come from the estimated coefficients of fiscal variables in consumption or saving functions. Examples of this work are found in papers by Kochin (1974), Tanner (1979), Feldstein (1982), Kormendi (1983), Seater and Mariano (1985), and Modigliani and Sterling (1986). The majority of these (selected) studies found that fiscal policy has little effect on consumer demand, but Feldstein and Modigliani/Sterling reached opposite conclusions.

The consumption-function approach has also been used to assess the effect of retirement programs under social security. When funded on a pay-as-you-go basis, such programs are similar to budget deficits in terms of their theoretical effects on national saving. Feldstein (1974, 1977) initially concluded that more generous social security programs depressed national saving. However, this finding was contested in subsequent research (see, for example, Barro, 1978; Darby, 1979; Esposito, 1978; Sterling, 1977; Barro and MacDonald, 1979; and Leimer and Lesnoy, 1982). Overall, the evidence from the U.S. time series and from a cross-section of countries failed to demonstrate a clear link between social security and national saving.

The empirical studies mentioned above relied on estimates of consumption functions, which involve well-known identification problems. For example, the approach does not deal satisfactorily with the simultaneity among consumption, income, and real interest rates. Another difficulty concerns the definitions of wealth and income; the inclusion of capital gains has substantial effects on measures of U.S. saving (see Poterba and Summers, 1986, app. table A-2). Other problems concern the fiscal variables that enter as regressors. The potential signaling role of these variables for future income or government expenditure affects the interpretation of estimated coefficients. For example, if the government adjusts its budget deficits to smooth out tax rates (as suggested in Section 5.4.4), then the current tax rate proxies for the expected long-run ratio of government expenditure to income, which influences current consumption demand (see Kochin, Benjamin, and Meador, 1985). Similarly, the correlation of the deficit with recessions, wars, and so on affects the analysis.

Carroll and Summers (1987) compared private saving in the United States and Canada. They note that the private saving rates were similar in the two countries until the early 1970s, but have since diverged—for 1983–1985, the Canadian rate was higher by about 6 percentage points. After holding fixed some macroeconomic variables and aspects of the tax systems that influenced saving, the authors isolated a roughly one-to-one, positive effect of government budget deficits on private saving. That is, as implied by the Ricardian view, the relative values of net national saving in Canada and the United States appeared to be invariant with the relative values of the budget deficits. The results indicated that the increase in the relative value of the Canadian private saving rate since the early 1970s reflected in part the stronger Canadian shift toward budget deficits.

Aschauer (1985) avoided the problem of estimating consumption or saving functions by using the "Euler-equation" approach applied previously by Hall (1978) and others. Assuming a fixed real interest rate and quadratic utility for a representative consumer, Aschauer showed that the Ricardian view implies

$$(5.30) \qquad c_t = a + b(c_{t-1} + \alpha g_{t-1}) - \alpha g_t^e + u_t,$$

where c is consumption, g is government purchases, u is a classical error term, and the parameter α is the extent to which g_t substitutes for c_t in households' utility. Equation (5.30) implies that lagged budget deficits (or other lagged variables) would matter for c_t only to the extent that they affect the forecast of purchases, g_t^e. The results on deficits turn out to accord with the implied restrictions. In particular, the lagged deficit enters significantly along with c_{t-1} and lagged values of g in a regression for c_t, but only because the lagged deficit (and the lags of g) have some predictive power for g_t.

Current-account deficits. Popular opinion attributes the large current-account deficits in the United States since 1983 to the effects of budget deficits. There has been no careful analysis of this relationship over long time periods or across countries. The U.S. data, however, reveal a positive association between budget and current-account deficits only if the experience since 1983 is included.

Figure 5.6 shows the values since 1948 of the ratio of the total government budget surplus to GNP (solid line) and the ratio of net foreign investment to GNP (dotted line).[35] Through 1982 there is no association between these two variables (correlation = −0.04). But including the data since 1983 raises the correlation to 0.41. In effect, the U.S. data since World War II reveal just a single incident—the period since 1983—when budget and current-account deficits were high at the same time. While this recent comovement is interesting, it does not provide strong support for the view that budget deficits cause current-account deficits.

Part of the agenda for empirical research is to investigate the relationship between the two deficits over longer periods of time and for a variety of countries. As with the studies of consumption and interest rates, it will be important to discover whether the exogenous part of shifts in budget deficits has a systematic effect on the current-account balance.

5.5. Concluding Observations

The neoclassical approach provides a coherent framework for theorizing about the macroeconomic effects of government spending, taxes, and

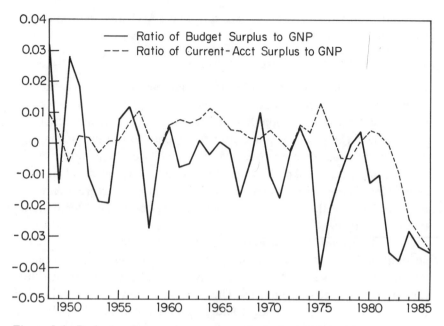

Figure 5.6   Budget and current-account surpluses in the United States.

debt. The approach has numerous empirical implications, which are thus far not sharply at odds with the limited evidence that is available.

The macroeconomics of fiscal policy is a promising area for further theoretical and empirical research. One interesting extension concerns the role of fiscal influences in long-term economic growth. A study of this type requires a framework in which disturbances, such as changes in tax rates or government purchases, have long-term implications for growth rates. Some new approaches to technology and growth, as described in Romer (1986; and Chapter 2) and King and Rebelo (1986), allow for effects like these.

Further results could be derived in the application of optimal taxation theory to the positive analysis of public debt management. Under what circumstances is tax-rate smoothing—as expressed by a Martingale property for tax rates—a close approximation to optimal behavior? To the extent that temporary variations in tax rates are justified, how would these variations match up with aggregate business conditions, wartime, and so on?

In general, it would be useful to have more quantitative information about the consequences of fiscal policy. This information could take the form of additional empirical evidence, but it might also be derivable from simulation of calibrated equilibrium models. In particular, the approach of Kydland and Prescott (1988) could be usefully applied to the influence of fiscal policy.

Acknowledgments

I am grateful for suggestions from Alan Auerbach, Marty Feldstein, Bob King, Greg Mankiw, Torsten Persson, Richard Rogerson, Paul Romer, Alan Stockman, Larry Summers, and Philippe Weil. The National Science Foundation has supported this research.

Notes

1. For an analysis of these conditions, see Weitzman (1973) and Ekeland and Scheinkman (1986).
2. With an infinite horizon, the limitation on borrowing is that $d_H k_h$ must approach a nonnegative quantity as $H \to \infty$. That is, debt must grow asymptotically at a rate lower than the interest rate [see the definition of d_t in Equation (5.3)]. This restriction rules out Ponzi games where an individual borrows and then finances the interest by a perpetual stream of new borrowings.
3. The second-order conditions for a maximum are satisfied if $\partial^2 u / \partial (c_t)^2 < 0$.
4. As $\gamma \to 0$, $u(c) \to \log(c)$. One feature of Equation (5.7) is that it allows for steady states where consumption per person grows at a constant rate. However, the present analysis abstracts from steady-state growth.
5. Recall that population is constant, so it is not necessary to provide capital for a growing population.
6. For an analysis of a related model and its stability properties, see Blanchard and Fischer (1986).
7. Public production would lead to different results if the government's technology, management ability, and so on differed from that of private producers. Analysis of these differences involves the incentives associated with private versus public ownership. For a recent discussion in the context of privatization, see Yarrow (1986).
8. This analysis follows the approach pioneered by Bailey (1971, chap. 9).
9. For an analysis of permanent fiscal changes that were anticipated in advance, see Hall (1971, sect. 2) and Judd (1985).
10. The term $\Phi(\cdot)$ in Equation (5.13) does not affect households' choices. Therefore "wealth" falls, although utility may rise because of this term. Wealth and

welfare do not correspond in the sense of Hicks (1946, chap. 2) because the movement in Φ amounts to a shift in preferences.

11. Mankiw (1987a) argues that an unanticipated, permanent increase in government purchases lowers the real interest in the short run in a model with consumer durables. The result comes from the assumption that the goods demanded by government are produced with a technology that is labor intensive relative to that for the services of consumer durables (transportation, housing, etc.). Hence, an increase in government purchases, which lowers households' demand for durables services (through the negative income effect), amounts to a reduction in the demand for capital. If durables services were produced by a technology with the same capital intensity as that for other goods, then this effect would no longer arise.

12. If the war were anticipated, people would expect a discrete fall in consumption at time t_1. Then the interest rate would have to be sharply negative at this time. More generally, the interest rate during peacetime would equal ρ less an amount related to the probability that a war would start. If this probability varies, then interest rates can vary without any changes in the realized values of government purchases.

13. These results appear in Benjamin and Kochin (1984, pp. 593–596).

14. Uncertainty about the war's duration also changes the results. Short-term rates now rise to reflect the probability of the war's end during the current period.

15. The fall in capital occurs through literal eating up of stocks in this simple model. More generally, capital per worker can fall because of depreciation of existing stocks, reduced net investment (which would be positive in the steady state of a model with growth in population or technology), or increases in the labor force. These features are ignored here for simplicity.

16. See Barro (1987a, chap. 12). The data for World War II also indicate crowding out of nonmilitary government purchases.

17. See Hall (1980) for a discussion of intertemporal substitution of labor supply. If the utilization rate of capital were variable, then capital services would tend to rise currently along with labor services. The higher interest rate motivates producers to use their capital more intensively, even though such utilization entails greater user costs or higher depreciation rates of capital. For an analysis of variable utilization, see Merrick (1984) and Greenwood, Hercowitz, and Huffman (1988).

18. If production takes time, then variations in labor input have a capital-like element (see Hercowitz, 1986b, sect. 2). In this case, it matters whether the change in government purchases is temporary or permanent. The results are similar to those with variable capital, as discussed earlier.

19. As in the specification for households, the assumption is that the quantity of government purchases per firm is the amount that matters for an individual producer. For a discussion of public services as an input to production, see Grossman and Lucas (1974).

20. As before (with lump-sum taxes), if $\alpha + \beta \geq 1$, the representative person would be at least as well off if g_t increases. If the government raises g_t in such situations, and if α and β fall as g_t rises, then $\alpha + \beta < 1$ applies in the relevant range.
21. For related discussions of the treatment of government purchases in the national accounts, see Kuznets (1948, pp. 156–157) and Musgrave (1959, pp. 186–188).
22. Victory or defeat may have additional effects that involve future flows of income or opportunities for investment. If these flows are just transfers to the victor, then a greater probability of victory tends to raise current real interest rates (because it stimulates current consumption). This effect offsets the one described in the text.
23. No adjustment is made for the effect of social security "contributions" on an individual's subsequent benefits. In principle, any increase in benefits represents a subtraction from the marginal tax rate. For an argument that this effect is important for people close to retirement age, see Gordon (1982).
24. For discussions in the context of macroeconomic policy see Kydland and Prescott (1977), Barro (1986a), Fischer (1986), and Rogoff (Chapter 6).
25. For a formal demonstration, see McCallum (1984).
26. As noted by Weil (1987b), this result depends on the existence of a representative family with an infinite horizon. However, the condition $\lim_{H\to\infty}(d_H B_H) = 0$ follows also if people would not hold public debt in excess of the government's "collateral," assuming that this collateral grows asymptotically at a rate lower than the interest rate.
27. For discussions, see Ricardo (1951), Buchanan (1958), Hall (1967), Barro (1974), and O'Driscoll (1977). At least for macroeconomists, the term *Ricardian equivalence theorem* comes from Buchanan (1976). As to whether the presence of this idea in Ricardo's work is important, I can only quote Rosenberg (1976, p. 79): "what often happens in economics is that, as concern mounts over a particular problem . . . an increasing number of professionals commit their time and energies to it. We then eventually realize that there were all sorts of treatments of the subject in the earlier literature . . . We then proceed to read much of our more sophisticated present-day understanding back into the work of earlier writers whose analysis was inevitably more fragmentary and incomplete than the later achievement. It was this retrospective view which doubtless inspired Whitehead to say somewhere that everything of importance has been said before—but by someone who did not discover it."
28. The invariance result holds also for an open economy. The budget deficit motivates enough extra private saving by domestic residents to keep national saving intact—hence there is no effect on the current-account balance. A shift in B_0, with some of this debt held by foreigners, would matter. This change amounts to giving more claims to foreigners without allowing for the goods that foreigners gave up to acquire these claims.

29. The assumption is that the real debt remains permanently higher by $1. For some related calculations, see Miller and Upton (1974, chap. 8) and Poterba and Summers (1987, sect. I).
30. However, if immigrants are already charged an optimal entrance fee, then this fee would adjust for budget deficits and Ricardian equivalence would be preserved.
31. The same issues arise in theories of population growth. Easterlin (1973) and Becker and Barro (1988) use a framework of altruism to determine optimizing choices of fertility. Other authors, such as Sundstrom and David (1985), relate decisions on fertility to the service value of children. This approach parallels the treatment of intergenerational transfers by Bernheim, Shleifer, and Summers (1985).
32. The conditions for optimality, based on results from optimal taxation theory, appear in Kremers (1985) and Aschauer and Greenwood (1985). On the notion of tax smoothing, see Pigou (1928, chap. 6), Barro (1979, 1986b), Kydland and Prescott (1980), and Flemming (1987).
33. If the interest rate is not constant, the main change is that temporary government spending includes also temporary interest payments, $(r_{i-1} - r_{i-1}^*)B_{i-1}$, where $r_{i-1}^* \equiv 1/[\Sigma_{t=i}^{\infty}(d_t/d_{i-1})]$ is the permanent interest rate (in the sense that an asset that paid the constant coupon r_{i-1}^* in each period $t \geq i$ has the same present value as an asset that pays the stream of coupons, $r_{i-1}, r_i, \ . \ . \ .$).
34. An anonymous colleague suggests that a normative theory is one that fits the data badly.
35. The data are quarterly, seasonally adjusted values from Citibase. The budget surplus is on a national accounts' basis. Results are similar if the federal surplus is used instead of the total government surplus.

References

Ahmed, S. 1986. Temporary and Permanent Government Spending in an Open Economy: Some Evidence for the U.K. *Journal of Monetary Economics* 17 (March): 197–224.

——— 1987. Government Spending, the Balance of Trade, and the Terms of Trade in British History. *Journal of Monetary Economics* 20 (September): 195–220.

Alesina, A., and G. Tabellini. 1987. A Positive Theory of Fiscal Deficits and Government Debt. Unpublished paper, Carnegie Mellon University.

Ando, A., and F. Modigliani. 1963. The 'Life Cycle' Hypothesis of Saving: Aggregate Implications and Tests. *American Economic Review* 53 (March): 55–84.

Aschauer, D. A. 1985. Fiscal Policy and Aggregate Demand. *American Economic Review* 75 (March): 117–127.

——— 1988. Does Public Capital Crowd Out Private Capital? Unpublished paper, Federal Reserve Bank of Chicago.

Aschauer, D. A., and J. Greenwood. 1985. Macroeconomic Effects of Fiscal Policy. *Carnegie-Rochester Conference Series on Public Policy* 23 (Autumn): 91–138.

Bailey, M. J. 1971. *National Income and the Price Level,* 2nd Edition. New York: McGraw-Hill.

Barro, R. J. 1974. Are Government Bonds Net Wealth? *Journal of Political Economy* 82 (November/December): 1095–1117.

—— 1976. Rational Expectations and the Role of Monetary Policy. *Journal of Monetary Economics* 2 (January): 1–32.

—— 1977. Unanticipated Money Growth and Unemployment in the United States. *American Economic Review* 67 (March): 101–115.

—— 1978. *The Impact of Social Security on Private Saving: Evidence from the U.S. Time Series.* Washington, D.C.: American Enterprise Institute.

—— 1979. On the Determination of the Public Debt. *Journal of Political Economy* 87 (October): 940–971.

—— 1981. Output Effects of Government Purchases. *Journal of Political Economy* 89 (December): 1086–1121.

—— 1986a. Recent Developments in the Theory of Rules versus Discretion. *Economic Journal* 95 (Suppl): 23–37.

—— 1986b. U.S. Deficits since World War I. *Scandinavian Journal of Economics* 88(1): 195–222.

—— 1987a. *Macroeconomics,* 2nd Edition. New York: John Wiley & Sons.

—— 1987b. Government Spending, Interest Rates, Prices, and Budget Deficits in the United Kingdom, 1701–1918. *Journal of Monetary Economics* 20 (September): 221–247.

Barro, R. J., and R. G. King. 1984. Time-Separable Preferences and Intertemporal-Substitution Models of Business Cycles. *Quarterly Journal of Economics* 99 (November): 817–839.

Barro, R. J., and G. M. MacDonald. 1979. Social Security and Consumer Spending in an International Cross Section. *Journal of Public Economics* 11: 275–289.

Barro, R. J., and C. Sahasakul. 1986. Average Marginal Tax Rates from Social Security and the Individual Income Tax. *Journal of Business* 59 (October): 555–566.

Barsky, R. B., N. G. Mankiw, and S. P. Zeldes. 1986. Ricardian Consumers with Keynesian Propensities. *American Economic Review* 76 (September): 676–691.

Becker, G. S., and R. J. Barro. 1988. A Reformulation of the Economic Theory of Fertility. *Quarterly Journal of Economics* 103 (February): 1–25.

Benjamin, D. K., and L. A. Kochin. 1984. War, Prices, and Interest Rates: A Martial Solution to Gibson's Paradox. *In* M. D. Bordo and A. J. Schwartz (eds.), *A Retrospective on the Classical Gold Standard.* Chicago: The University of Chicago Press.

Bernheim, B. D., and K. Bagwell. 1988. Is Everything Neutral? *Journal of Political Economy* 96 (April): 308–338.

Bernheim, B. D., A. Shleifer, and L. H. Summers. 1985. The Strategic Bequest Motive. *Journal of Political Economy* 93 (December): 1045–76.

Blanchard, O. J. 1985. Debt, Deficits, and Finite Horizons. *Journal of Political Economy* 93 (April): 223–247.

Blanchard, O. J., and S. Fischer. 1986. Consumption and Investment: Basic Infinite Horizon Models. Chapter 2 of unpublished manuscript on macroeconomic theory.

Brown, E. C. 1956. Fiscal Policy in the 'Thirties: A Reappraisal. *Journal of Political Economy* 46 (December): 857–879.

Buchanan, J. M. 1958. *Public Principles of Public Debt*. Homewood, Illinois: Irwin.

—— 1976. Barro on the Ricardian Equivalence Theorem. *Journal of Political Economy* 84 (April): 337–342.

Buchanan, J. M., and R. E. Wagner. 1977. *Democracy in Deficit*. New York: Academic Press.

Buiter, W. H. 1980. Crowding Out of Private Capital Formation by Government Borrowing in the Presence of Intergenerational Gifts and Bequests. *Greek Economic Review* 2 (August): 111–142.

Carroll, C., and L. H. Summers. 1987. Why Have Private Savings Rates in the United States and Canada Diverged? *Journal of Monetary Economics* 20 (September): 249–279.

Chan, L. K. C. 1983. Uncertainty and the Neutrality of Government Financing Policy. *Journal of Monetary Economics* 11 (May): 351–372.

Council of Economic Advisers. 1962, 1982. *Annual Report*. Washington, D.C.: U.S. Government Printing Office.

Cox, D. 1987. Motives for Private Income Transfers. *Journal of Political Economy* 95 (June): 508–546.

Cukierman, A., and A. H. Meltzer. 1987. A Political Theory of Government Debt and Deficits in a Neo Ricardian Framework. Unpublished paper, Carnegie Mellon University.

Darby, M. R. 1979. *The Effects of Social Security on Income and the Capital Stock*. Washington, D.C.: American Enterprise Institute.

Diamond, P. A. 1965. National Debt in a Neoclassical Growth Model. *American Economic Review* 55 (December): 1126–50.

Drazen, A. 1978. Government Debt, Human Capital, and Bequests in a Life-Cycle Model. *Journal of Political Economy* 86 (June): 505–516.

Easterlin, R. A. 1973. Relative Economic Status and the American Fertility Swing. *In* E. B. Sheldon (ed.), *Family Economic Behavior: Problems and Prospects*. Philadelphia: Lippincott.

Ekeland, I., and J. A. Scheinkman. 1986. Transversality Conditions for Some Infinite Horizon Discrete Time Optimization Problems. *Mathematics of Operations Research* 11 (May): 216–229.

Esposito, L. 1978. Effect of Social Security on Saving: Review of Studies Using U.S. Time-Series Data. *Social Security Bulletin* 41 (May): 9–17.

Evans, P. 1987a. Interest Rates and Expected Future Budget Deficits in the United States. *Journal of Political Economy* 95 (February): 34–58.

—— 1987b. Do Budget Deficits Raise Nominal Interest Rates? Evidence from Six Industrial Countries. *Journal of Monetary Economics* 20 (September): 281–300.

Feldstein, M. S. 1974. Social Security, Induced Retirement, and Aggregate Capital Accumulation. *Journal of Political Economy* 82 (September/October): 905–926.

—— 1976. Perceived Wealth in Bonds and Social Security: A Comment. *Journal of Political Economy* 84 (April): 331–336.

—— 1977. Social Security and Private Savings; International Evidence in an Extended Life Cycle Model. *In* M. S. Feldstein and R. Inman (eds.), *The Economics of Public Services*. London: Macmillan.

—— 1982. Government Deficits and Aggregate Demand. *Journal of Monetary Economics* 9 (January): 1–20.

—— 1988. The Effects of Fiscal Policies When Incomes Are Uncertain: A Contradiction to Ricardian Equivalence. *American Economic Review* 78 (March): 14–23.

Feldstein, M. S., and L. H. Summers. 1979. Inflation and the Taxation of Capital Income in the Corporate Sector. *National Tax Journal* 32 (December): 445–470.

Fischer, S. 1986. Time Consistent Monetary and Fiscal Policies: A Survey. Unpublished paper, Massachusetts Institute of Technology.

Flemming, J. S. 1987. Debt and Taxes in War and Peace: The Case of a Small Open Economy. *In* M. J. Boskin, J. S. Flemming, and S. Gorini (eds.), *Private Saving and Public Debt*. Oxford: Basil Blackwell.

Friedman, M. 1968. The Role of Monetary Policy. *American Economic Review* 58 (March): 1–17.

Gordon, R. H. 1982. Social Security and Labor Supply Incentives. Working paper 986, National Bureau of Economic Research.

Greenwood, J., Z. Hercowitz, and G. W. Huffman. 1988. Investment, Capacity Utilization, and the Real Business Cycle. *American Economic Review* 78 (June): 402–417.

Grossman, H. I., and R. F. Lucas. 1974. The Macro-Economic Effects of Productive Public Expenditures. *The Manchester School* 42 (June): 162–170.

Hall, R. E. 1967. The Allocation of Wealth among the Generations of a Family Which Lasts Forever—a Theory of Inheritance. Chapter 1 of unpublished doctoral dissertation, Massachusetts Institute of Technology.

—— 1971. The Dynamic Effects of Fiscal Policy in an Economy with Foresight. *Review of Economic Studies* 38 (April): 229–244.

—— 1978. Stochastic Implications of the Life Cycle-Permanent Income Hypothesis: Theory and Evidence. *Journal of Political Economy* 86 (December): 971–987.

—— 1980. Labor Supply and Aggregate Fluctuations. *Carnegie-Rochester Conference Series on Public Policy* 12 (Spring): 7–33.

Hayashi, F. 1987. Tests for Liquidity Constraints: A Critical Survey and Some New Observations. *In* T. F. Bewley (ed.), Advances in Econometrics, Fifth World Congress. Cambridge: Cambridge University Press.

Hercowitz, Z. 1986a. On the Determination of the External Debt: The Case of Israel. *Journal of International Money and Finance* 5: 315–334.

—— 1986b. The Real Interest Rate and Aggregate Supply. *Journal of Monetary Economics* 18 (September): 121–145.

Hicks, J. 1946. *Value and Capital,* 2nd Edition. Oxford: Oxford University Press.

Judd, K. L. 1985. Short-Run Analysis of Fiscal Policy in a Simple Perfect Foresight Model. *Journal of Political Economy* 93 (April): 298–319.

Kanaya, S. 1986. Four Essays on Macroeconomics. Unpublished doctoral dissertation, University of Rochester.

Kimball, M. S. Making Sense of Two-Sided Altruism. *Journal of Monetary Economics* 20 (September): 301–326.

King, M. A. 1984. Tax Policy and Consumption Smoothing. Unpublished paper, London School of Economics.

King, R. G., and S. Rebelo. 1986. Business Cycles with Endogenous Growth. Unpublished paper, University of Rochester.

Kochin, L. A. 1974. Are Future Taxes Anticipated by Consumers? *Journal of Money, Credit, and Banking* 6 (August): 385–394.

Kochin, L. A., D. K. Benjamin, and M. Meador. 1985. The Observational Equivalence of Rational and Irrational Consumers If Taxation Is Efficient. *In* Federal Reserve Bank of San Francisco, *Seventh West Coast Academic Conference*.

Kormendi, R. C. 1983. Government Debt, Government Spending, and Private Sector Behavior. *American Economic Review* 73 (December): 994–1010.

Kotlikoff, L. J., and L. H. Summers. 1981. The Role of Intergenerational Transfers in Aggregate Capital Accumulation. *Journal of Political Economy* 89 (August): 706–732.

Kremers, J. J. M. 1985. Is Dynamic Tax Smoothing an Optimal Public Financial Policy? Unpublished paper, Oxford University.

Kuznets, S. 1948. Discussion of the New Department of Commerce Income Series. *Review of Economics and Statistics* 30 (August): 151–179.

Kydland, F. E., and E. C. Prescott. 1977. Rules Rather Than Discretion: The Inconsistency of Optimal Plans. *Journal of Political Economy* 85 (June): 473–491.

—— 1980. A Competitive Theory of Fluctuations and the Feasibility and Desirability of Stabilization Policy. *In* S. Fischer (ed.), *Rational Expectations and Economic Policy*. Chicago: The University of Chicago Press.

—— 1988. The Work Week of Capital and Its Cyclical Implications. *Journal of Monetary Economics* 21 (March/May): 343–360.

Leimer, D. R., and S. D. Lesnoy. 1982. Social Security and Private Saving: New Time-Series Evidence. *Journal of Political Economy* 90 (June): 606–629.

Lindsey, L. B. 1987. Individual Taxpayer Response to Tax Cuts: 1982–1984. *Journal of Public Economics* 33 (July): 173–206.

Lucas, R. E. 1972. Expectations and the Neutrality of Money. *Journal of Economic Theory* 4 (April): 103–124.

—— 1973. Some International Evidence on Output-Inflation Tradeoffs. *American Economic Review* 63 (June): 326–334.

—— 1976. Econometric Policy Evaluation: A Critique. *Carnegie-Rochester Conference Series on Public Policy* 1: 19–46.

Lucas, R. E., and N. L. Stokey. 1983. Optimal Fiscal and Monetary Policy in an Economy without Capital. *Journal of Monetary Economics* 12 (July): 55–93.

Mankiw, N. G. 1987a. Government Purchases and Real Interest Rates. *Journal of Political Economy* 95 (April): 407–419.

—— 1987b. The Optimal Collection of Seigniorage: Theory and Evidence. *Journal of Monetary Economics* 20 (September): 327–341.

Mankiw, N. G., and J. A. Miron. 1986. The Changing Behavior of the Term Structure of Interest Rates. *Quarterly Journal of Economics* 101 (May): 211–228.

McCallum, B. T. 1984. Are Bond-Financed Deficits Inflationary? A Ricardian Analysis. *Journal of Political Economy* 92 (February): 123–135.

Merrick, J. J. 1984. The Anticipated Real Interest Rate, Capital Utilization, and the Cyclical Pattern of Real Wages. *Journal of Monetary Economics* 13 (January): 17–30.

Miller, M. H., and C. W. Upton. 1974. *Macroeconomics, A Neoclassical Introduction*. Homewood, Illinois: Irwin.

Modigliani, F. 1961. Long-run Implications of Alternative Fiscal Policies and the Burden of the National Debt. *Economic Journal* 71 (December): 730–755.

Modigliani, F., and R. Brumberg. 1954. Utility Analysis and the Consumption Function: An Interpretation of Cross-Section Data. *In* K. H. Kurihara (ed.), *Post-Keynesian Economics*. New Brunswick, New Jersey: Rutgers University Press.

Modigliani, F., and A. Sterling. 1986. Government Debt, Government Spending, and Private Sector Behavior: A Comment. *American Economic Review* 76 (December): 1168–79.

Mundell, R. A. 1971. Money, Debt, and the Rate of Interest. *In* R. A. Mundell, *Monetary Theory*. Pacific Palisades, California: Goodyear.

Musgrave, R. 1959. *Theory of Public Finance*. New York: McGraw-Hill.

Nerlove, M., A. Razin, and E. Sadka. 1984. Bequests and the Size of Population When Population Is Endogenous. *Journal of Political Economy* 92 (June): 527–531.

O'Driscoll, G. P. 1977. The Ricardian Nonequivalence Theorem. *Journal of Political Economy* 85 (February): 207–210.

Persson, T., and L. E. O. Svensson. 1984. Time-Consistent Fiscal Policy and Government Cash-Flow. *Journal of Monetary Economics* 14 (November): 365–374.

——— 1987. Why a Stubborn Conservative Would Run a Deficit: Policy with Time-Inconsistent Preferences. Unpublished paper, University of Rochester.

Phelps, E. S. 1970. The New Microeconomics in Employment and Inflation Theory. *In* E. S. Phelps (ed.), *Microeconomic Foundations of Employment and Inflation Theory*. New York: Norton.

Pigou, A. C. 1928. *A Study in Public Finance*. London: Macmillan.

Plosser, C. I. 1982. Government Financing Decisions and Asset Returns. *Journal of Monetary Economics* 9 (May): 325–352.

——— 1987. Further Evidence on the Relation between Fiscal Policy and the Term Structure. *Journal of Monetary Economics* 20 (September): 343–367.

Poterba, J. M., and L. H. Summers. 1986. Finite Lifetimes and the Savings Effects of Budget Deficits. Unpublished paper, Harvard University.

——— 1987. Finite Lifetimes and the Savings Effects of Budget Deficits. *Journal of Monetary Economics* 20 (September): 369–391.

Ricardo, D. 1951. Funding System. *In* P. Sraffa (ed.), *The Works and Correspondence of David Ricardo,* Vol. IV, *Pamphlets and Papers, 1815–1823.* Cambridge: Cambridge University Press.

Romer, P. M. 1986. Increasing Returns and Long-Run Growth. *Journal of Political Economy* 94 (October): 1002–37.

Rosenberg, N. 1976. *Perspectives on Technology*. Cambridge: Cambridge University Press.

Sahasakul, C. 1986. The U.S. Evidence on Optimal Taxation over Time. *Journal of Monetary Economics* 18 (November): 251–275.

Samuelson, P. A. 1958. An Exact Consumption-Loan Model of Interest with or without the Social Contrivance of Money. *Journal of Political Economy* 66 (December): 467–482.

Sargent, T. J., and N. Wallace. 1975. Rational Expectations, the Optimal Monetary Instrument, and the Optimal Money Supply Rule. *Journal of Political Economy* 83 (April): 241–254.

Seater, J. J., and R. S. Mariano. 1985. New Tests of the Life Cycle and Tax Discounting Hypotheses. *Journal of Monetary Economics* 15 (March): 195–215.

Sterling, A. G. 1977. An Investigation of the Determinants of the Long-Run Savings Ratio. Unpublished paper, Massachusetts Institute of Technology.

Stuart, C. E. 1981. Swedish Tax Rates, Labor Supply, and Tax Revenues. *Journal of Political Economy* 89 (October): 1020–38.

Sundstrom, W. A., and P. A. David. 1985. Old-Age Security Motives, Labor Markets, and Farm Family Fertility in Antebellum America. Unpublished paper, Stanford University. Forthcoming in *Explorations in Economic History*.

Tanner, J. E. 1979. An Empirical Investigation of Tax Discounting. *Journal of Money, Credit, and Banking* 11 (May): 214–218.

Tobin, J., and W. Buiter. 1980. Fiscal and Monetary Policies, Capital Formation, and Economic Activity. *In* G. M. von Furstenberg (ed.), *The Government and Capital Formation.* Cambridge, Massachusetts: Ballinger.

U.S. Treasury Department. 1984. *The Effect of Deficits on Prices of Financial Assets: Theory and Evidence.* Washington, D.C.: U.S. Government Printing Office.

Weil, P. 1987a. Love Thy Children: Reflections on the Barro Debt Neutrality Theorem. *Journal of Monetary Economics* 19 (May): 377–391.

——— 1987b. Permanent Budget Deficits and Inflation. *Journal of Monetary Economics* 20 (September): 393–410.

Weitzman, M. 1973. Duality Theory for Infinite Horizon Convex Models. *Management Science* 19 (March): 783–789.

Yarrow, G. 1986. Privatization in Theory and Practice. *Economic Policy* 1 (April): 324–377.

Yotsuzuka, T. 1987. Ricardian Equivalence in the Presence of Capital Market Imperfections. *Journal of Monetary Economics* 20 (September): 411–436.

6   Reputation, Coordination, and Monetary Policy

Kenneth Rogoff

One of the most exciting developments in macroeconomics over the past decade has been the application of game theory to the study of government policy. Although this research is still in its infancy, early results offer the promise of formalizing political and institutional issues that until now could only be analyzed using nonquantitative methods. The purpose of this chapter is not to survey the numerous interesting applications of "strategic macroeconomics." Rather I intend to discuss a critical unresolved issue in this literature: to what extent can reputation substitute for legal constraints on macroeconomic policy?

The analysis in this chapter will focus on reputation and monetary policy partly because that is the concern of much of the extant literature. Monetary policy presents an especially dramatic example of the government's inability to make even short-term commitments; there is really no technological constraint on how quickly the government can renege on a commitment not to inflate. Even if there are temporary limitations on the number of printing presses available, the government can always step on the gas by printing currency in higher denominations.

Early analyses of the "time-consistency" problem of monetary policy revealed the possibility that a government might be able to increase its own welfare—and in some instances, social welfare—if only it could tie its hands and precommit to a (perhaps state-contingent) path for the money supply.[1] This problem can arise even if there are no exogenous disturbances, and even if the government is trying to maximize the welfare of the representative individual. Recent literature shows that early analyses may have overstated the government's credibility problems by focusing on "one-shot" games (or more generally, by implicitly ruling out certain classes of history-dependent strategies). Because monetary policy involves repeated interactions between the government and the public, reputational considerations can mitigate or even eliminate the time-consistency problem. (Henceforth, I shall use the more precise term *subgame perfect* in place of the macroeconomic theory jargon term *time-consistent*).[2]

Whereas the current generation of reputational models have a number of appealing features, they also have one fundamental limitation. Typically the models yield either a multiplicity of equilibria or an equilibrium that is extremely sensitive to the public's beliefs about the monetary authority's preferences. This limitation, which is inherited from the antecedent game-theory models, is well known to careful readers of the policy credibility literature. But because many authors focus on the most efficient attainable equilibria in their models, casual readers may not appreciate the significance of the nonuniqueness question. It is true that the new reputational models suggest ways to induce "cooperative" behavior between the public and the private sector, even in the absence of any method for writing binding contracts. But there is as yet no convincing argument for why, out of the continuum of reputational equilibria, the economy will coordinate on a "good" equilibrium and not on a "bad" equilibrium. There is a real sense in which repeated game models replace a cooperation problem with a coordination problem. This coordination problem would seem to be particularly compelling in a macroeconomic context with a large number of agents. Of course, if it is indeed possible to rely on reputation to enforce optimal policy rules, then a very good case can be made for preferring this solution to one involving written legal contracts (constitutional amendments). It is virtually impossible to foresee every type of problem that society may face and to design a fully contingent law. Reputation provides a far more flexible mechanism for dealing with circumstances that could not have been imagined (or would have been prohibitively expensive to think about carefully) at the time the law was written.

In Section 6.1 I shall review the model of central bank reputation developed by Barro and Gordon (1983a). Their reputation mechanism is a variant of the infinite-horizon trigger-strategy equilibrium first proposed by J. Friedman (1971). I shall then extend Barro and Gordon's analysis to allow for equilibria analogous to the "severe punishment" equilibria of Abreu (1988), and I shall also demonstrate conditions under which their infinite-horizon analysis carries over to a finite-horizon setting. In Section

6.2 I shall consider Canzoneri's extension of the Barro-Gordon model, which allows for the possibility that the central bank has private information about its money supply forecasts. Canzoneri argued that such private information underlies the government's and private sector's inability to focus on a zero inflation equilibrium. Following Green and Porter (1984), he showed that reputation can still operate in a private-information environment, although there will be periodic reversions to a high-inflation equilibrium. Like the models in Section 6.1, Canzoneri's model has a continuum of equilibria. It would seem that the coordination problems involved in achieving the most favorable equilibrium in the private-information case are even more severe than in the complete information case.

In the models of Sections 6.1 and 6.2, the public knows the central bank's abilities and objectives from the outset. Section 6.3 will deal with the case where the public is unsure either about the policymaker's preferences or about his cost to breaking commitments. These analyses involve applications of Kreps and Wilson (1982) and Milgrom and Roberts (1982). I shall consider in some detail the model of Rogoff (1987), which extends the model of Barro (1986) to allow for a continuum of types. The types differ in the cost they bear to reneging on a commitment not to inflate. In contrast with the models considered in earlier sections, this model has a unique equilibrium. The policymaker sticks to his zero-inflation commitment early in his term, even if he would bear no direct cost by reneging. However, the equilibrium can be quite sensitive to the specification of the public's beliefs. In Vickers's (1986) and Driffill's (1986) variant of this model, it may pay for types who are extremely concerned with inflation to take actions to signal their type, thereby immediately demonstrating that they are not soft-money types. Section 6.4 will deal with Cukierman and Meltzer's (1986) model, in which the policymaker's type is subject to serially correlated disturbances. They suggest that a policymaker may actually have some incentive to adopt an inefficient targeting procedure, to obscure his actions. In Section 6.5 I shall briefly touch on some related research; and Section 6.6 contains my conclusions.

6.1. Trigger-Strategy Models of Monetary Policy Credibility

In this section I shall consider a model in which private agents know the monetary authorities' objective function exactly, can monitor their actions perfectly, and can observe (possibly with a lag) all the same information. It may seem odd that there can be any discussion of reputation in this context, but as Barro and Gordon (1983a) demonstrated, such a model can indeed yield equilibria in which the central bank rationally believes that its actions today will affect the public's expectations about what it will do in the future.

The framework for analyzing monetary policy credibility employed here (and throughout the chapter) is a slight variant of a popular example due to Kydland and Prescott (1977). This extremely simple and easily tractable model forms the basis for virtually all the literature surveyed below. The main limitation of the model is that it treats the government as maximizing an objective function that may or may not correspond to the objective function of a representative private agent. However, the Kydland and Prescott example does make explicit the objectives and possible moves of all the players, and it is useful for illustrating strategic factors that may easily be obscured in a more complex dynamic model.[3]

Monetary policy can have real effects in the model because private agents form expectations of period t inflation, π_t, on the basis of $t - 1$ information.[4] It is important to emphasize that the atomistic agents are "expectations takers." The aggregate inflation rate, π, is exogenous to the individual; he can only affect his own price prediction error, $\pi_t - \pi_t^{ei}$. I stress this point, because in the analysis below it is easy to become confused and mistakenly think that individuals are setting their expectations strategically. What is true is that there are equilibria in which the collective actions of private agents have a strategic effect on the government's choice of monetary policy. But these equilibria do not require any explicit cooperation within the private sector. Any individual who "defects" and tries setting his expectations differently will only be punishing himself.

The fact that the individual cannot affect the aggregate inflation rate or the aggregate prediction error does not necessarily imply that these factors do not enter his utility function.[5] Consider the case, for example, where there is an externality arising from income taxation. If all citizens are "tricked" into working too much or into holding too high a level of real money balances, the individual gains on net because government revenues rise. But, it never pays for an individual to intentionally guess wrong himself. Thus an individual attempts to minimize

(6.1) $\qquad J_t = (\pi_t - \pi_t^{ei})^2.$

In most of the monetary policy credibility literature, it is assumed that unanticipated inflation increases output (via a contracts or an island model). Many parallel issues arise when unanticipated inflation matters, because the government issues currency or nonindexed nominal bonds.[6] I shall assume that the loss function of the monetary authorities is given by

(6.2a) $$\Omega_t = \sum_t^T L_s \beta^{s-t},$$

(6.2b) $$L_s = f(\pi_s - \pi_s^e - k) + g(\pi_s),$$

where $k > 0, f'(\cdot), g'(\cdot) \gtreqless 0$ as $(\cdot) \gtreqless 0$, and $f'(\cdot), g'(\cdot) \to 0$ as $(\cdot) \to 0$. The variable β is the monetary authorities' subjective discount rate, and T is their time horizon. The difference $\pi - \pi^e$ is the average level of private sector price prediction errors. For now, I shall assume that T is infinite and that $f''(\cdot), g''(\cdot) > 0$; both assumptions will be relaxed later in this section. The basic structure underlying Equations (6.1) and (6.2) has been extensively examined (see Barro and Gordon, 1983a,b; Canzoneri, 1985; Rogoff, 1985b, or Tabellini, 1983). Barro and Gordon discuss how, in the presence of externalities such as income taxation (my example above), the government's objective function can be interpreted as the social welfare function, even though $k > 0$. Later it will become clear that if $k = 0$ (there is no externality) then the optimal monetary rule (zero inflation) is subgame perfe t.

Before considering repeated-game reputational equilibria, it is necessary to first examine equilibria of the "one-shot" game (there is only one period). Because the private sector forms expectations about period t inflation based on $t - 1$ information, the central bank treats π_t^e as given when setting π_t. Minimizing Ω over π, one obtains the first-order condition for the central bank's maximization problem, $-f'(\pi - \pi^e - k) = g'(\pi)$. Provided individuals form expectations rationally, then $\pi = \pi^e$ in equilibrium. Hence, a necessary condition for a subgame perfect equilibrium in the one-shot game is

(6.3) $$-f'(-k) = g'(\pi^*),$$

where π^* is the one-shot game equilibrium inflation rate. Given the assumption that $f'', g'' > 0$, it is straightforward to show that the second-order conditions hold and that $\pi^* > 0$ is unique. The logic underlying the equilibrium characterized by (6.3) is well known. The central bank always has the ability to inflict price prediction errors on the private sector. But when $\pi^e = \pi^*$, it will never choose to do so.[7] As inflation rises, so too does the marginal cost of inflating. The time-consistent equilibrium level of inflation, π^*, is sufficiently high that the marginal gain from surprise inflation equals the marginal cost.

In this nonstochastic model, the fact that the central bank can exercise discretion brings it no benefits and only leads to a high rate of inflation. The same equilibrium arises even when aggregate inflation enters directly into private agents' utility functions. Because an individual's actions have only an infinitesimal effect on the aggregate price level, each agent will still act as if he were only concerned with his own price-prediction error. Determining whether or not there exists some mechanism by which the economy can coordinate on a more favorable equilibrium (without imposing legal restraints) is the main focus of our investigation. The equilibrium characterized by (6.3) is of interest for a number of reasons. First, it is the unique subgame perfect equilibrium when the monetary authorities maximize over any finite horizon (*if*, as in the above example, the equilibrium of the one-shot game is unique). Second, π^* remains an equilibrium when their horizon is infinite and can serve as a credible threat to induce more "cooperative" behavior from the monetary authorities. I shall now illustrate this point, beginning with the class of reputational equilibria demonstrated by Barro and Gordon (1983a).

Consider a level of inflation, $\tilde{\pi}$, such that $0 \le \tilde{\pi} < \pi^*$, and suppose that each individual forms expectations according to

(6.4) $\pi_t^{ei} = \begin{cases} \tilde{\pi} & \text{if } \pi_{t-1} = \pi_{t-1}^e, \\ \pi^* & \text{otherwise.} \end{cases}$

Thus if $\pi_{t-1}^e = \tilde{\pi} < \pi^*$, then individuals will continue expecting low inflation as long as the central bank "cooperates" and does not try to fool them.[8] If the central bank ever does inflate beyond $\tilde{\pi}$, the economy will be subjected to "punishment" for one period. (When $\pi_{t-1} > \tilde{\pi} = \pi_{t-1}^e$, π^e reverts to π^*. If the central bank then sets $\pi_t = \pi^*$, π_{t+1}^e reverts back to $\tilde{\pi}$.) It is important to recognize that the public's expectations are rational in the subgame that would occur if the central bank were ever to "cheat." The central bank has absolutely no incentive to surprise private agents during a punishment period. For by setting $\pi = \pi^*$ during a punishment period, it minimizes both this period's loss function and next period's inflationary expectations.

I shall now confirm that there are indeed equilibria where the public forms its expectations according to (6.4) and where $\tilde{\pi} < \pi^*$. To determine whether a particular value for $\tilde{\pi}$ is a *trigger-strategy equilibrium* level of inflation under (6.4), it is necessary to consider whether the central bank will have any incentive to *defect* and set $\pi \neq \tilde{\pi}$. This question turns on the magnitude of the maximum current-period gain from defecting, $B(\tilde{\pi})$, in comparison with the expected future cost to defecting, $C(\tilde{\pi})$. These magnitudes are given by

(6.5) $B(\tilde{\pi}) = f(-k) + g(\tilde{\pi}) - f[\pi^D(\tilde{\pi}) - \tilde{\pi} - k] - g[\pi^D(\tilde{\pi})] > 0,$

where $\pi^D(\tilde{\pi}) = \text{argmin}[f(\pi - \tilde{\pi} - k) + g(\pi)]$, and

(6.6) $C(\tilde{\pi}) = \beta[g(\pi^*) - g(\tilde{\pi})] > 0.$

For a given level of $\tilde{\pi}$ to be an equilibrium, it is necessary that $B(\tilde{\pi}) \leq C(\tilde{\pi})$; otherwise the central bank will always choose to defect. Although $\tilde{\pi} = 0$ may not be an equilibrium,[9] it is possible to prove that there always exists some $\tilde{\pi}$ such that $0 \leq \tilde{\pi} < \pi^*$ and $B(\tilde{\pi}) \leq C(\tilde{\pi})$. [*Proof:* $\tilde{\pi} < \pi^D(\tilde{\pi})$ $< \pi^*$ by f'', $g'' > 0$. Let $\tilde{\pi} = \pi^* - \varepsilon$. Since $-f'(\pi^D - \tilde{\pi} - k) = g'(\pi^D)$, and since $\pi^D - \tilde{\pi} < \varepsilon$, then $B(\pi^* - \varepsilon)$ must become second order as ε becomes small (by an envelope theorem argument). Since $C(\pi^* - \varepsilon)$ remains first order for small ε, then, by the continuity of f and g, there must exist some $\varepsilon > 0$ such that $B(\pi^* - \varepsilon) < C(\pi^* - \varepsilon)$.]

Denote $\hat{\pi}$ as the lowest (positive) inflation rate that can be a trigger-strategy equilibrium level of inflation under (6.4). It is trivial to show that $\hat{\pi}$ is nonincreasing in β, the central bank's discount rate, and that any $\tilde{\pi}$ such that $\hat{\pi} \leq \tilde{\pi} \leq \pi^*$ can be an equilibrium. This multiplicity of equilibria, which was noted by Barro and Gordon, is an issue I shall return to later in this section. It is also simple to show that if $\hat{\pi} > 0$, then it would be possible to have a lower equilibrium rate of inflation if the expectations mechanism of the public embodied a punishment interval longer than just one period. If the central bank's discount rate β is small, however, even an infinite punishment interval may not be enough to sustain zero inflation.[10]

When $\hat{\pi} > 0$, there is another mechanism for sustaining a lower inflation rate, one that does not involve extending the punishment period. The alternative mechanism involves having a more severe punishment instead of a more prolonged one. The more severe punishment consists of reverting to an inflation rate higher than π^* whenever the central bank defects. In some applications, this alternative mechanism may be important because it is not intuitively appealing to have a long or infinite punishment interval. Also, severe punishments can play a role in the optimal equilibrium of the model with private information, a situation that will be studied in Section 6.2. I do not regard severe punishment equilibria as being particularly plausible in the present context, however. My primary motivation for introducing this alternative class of equilibria here is to underscore the severity of the multiple equilibrium problem. Thus it is sufficient merely to illustrate the equilibria, so I shall not derive the optimal severe punishment equilibrium.

To make the mechanism underlying severe punishment equilibria more transparent, it is helpful first to demonstrate why it is possible for inflationary expectations to rise *temporarily* above π^*. Let $\delta > 0$, and consider the following (nonstationary) path of expectations initiating in period t. (Since $\pi^{ei} = \pi^e$ in equilibrium, I henceforth ignore the distinction between the two):

(6.7) $$\pi_t^e = \pi^* + \delta$$

$$\pi_{t+i}^e = \begin{cases} \hat{\pi} & \text{if } \pi_{t+i-1} = \pi_{t+i-1}^e, \quad i \geq 1 \\ \pi^* & \text{otherwise.} \end{cases}$$

Since $g(\pi^*) - g(\hat{\pi})$ is finite, it is clearly possible to choose a δ small enough so that $\pi^* + \delta$ is an equilibrium for period t, provided the public's expectations are governed by (6.7). It is true that at $\pi^* + \delta$, the central bank would be willing to let output drop below the natural rate to achieve lower current-period inflation. But the central bank knows that it must be willing to suffer through exceptionally high inflation in period t if it wants inflation in $t + 1$ to be $\hat{\pi}$, and not π^*. The fact that $\pi^* + \delta$ can be made a credible threat implies that it is possible to attain an inflation rate lower than $\hat{\pi}$ without extending the punishment interval. For example, consider an equilibrium analogous to (6.4):[11]

(6.8) $$\pi_t^e = \begin{cases} \tilde{\pi}' & \text{if } \pi_{t-1} = \pi_{t-1}^e, \\ \pi^* + \delta & \text{otherwise.} \end{cases}$$

It is clear that the lowest attainable inflation rate under (6.8) is lower than the lowest attainable inflation rate under (6.4), $\hat{\pi}$, if $\hat{\pi} > 0$.

The trigger-strategy equilibria discussed thus far break down if the monetary authorities maximize over a finite horizon (say, because the policymaker has only a finite term in office). Since the unique one-shot game equilibrium must obtain in the last period, trigger strategies "unravel" backward. If, however, there are multiple equilibria in the one-shot game, then there can exist trigger-strategy equilibria in the finite-horizon case. Benoit and Krishna (1985) and Friedman (1985) have demonstrated this general principle. In fact, even if only a narrow range of high inflation rates are equilibria in the one-shot game, it still may be possible to sustain zero inflation rates early in the policymaker's term (if his term is long enough and his discount factor low enough). Let $\pi_1 > 0$ be the lowest equilibrium inflation rate in the one-shot game and let π_2 be the highest. During the policymaker's final period in office, period T, the range of equilibria is of course the same as in the one-shot game. Hence, $\pi_1 \leq \pi_T \leq \pi_2$. However, in period $T - 1$, it may be perfectly rational for the public to believe that $\pi_{T-1}^e = \pi_1 - \varepsilon$, $\varepsilon > 0$. For small enough ε, these expectations can be supported by the belief that if the government does not defect in $T - 1$ ($\pi_{T-1} = \pi_1 - \varepsilon$), then $\pi_T^e = \pi_1$. If it defects ($\pi_{T-1} \neq \pi_1 - \varepsilon$), then $\pi_T^e = \pi_2$. Hence defection is punished by going to the "bad" Nash equilibrium in the final period. Let π_s' denote the lowest subgame perfect equilibrium that can be attained in period s. It is straightforward to show that if $\pi_s' > 0$, then $\pi_s' - \pi_{s-1}' > 0$. (The assumption that the discount rate β is constant is a sufficient condition for this result.) The more periods that remain, the longer the punishment interval can be. Also, as one moves back from date T, the maximum one-period punishment, $\pi_2 - \pi_{s'}'$ rises.

Consider the following concrete example. Suppose one replaces the central bank's inflation loss function, $g(\pi)$ [see Equation (6.2b)], with the following (nonconvex) loss function

(6.9) $\qquad h(\pi) = \begin{cases} g(\pi) & \text{for } \pi \leq \pi^* + k, \\ g(\pi^* + k) & \text{for } \pi^* + k < \pi \leq z, \\ g(\pi^* + k) + g(\pi - z) & \text{for } z < \pi, \end{cases}$

—where z is a sufficiently large constant such that $-f'[-(k + z)] \geq g'(\pi^* + k)$. If one replaces $g(\cdot)$ with $h(\cdot)$ in Equation (6.2b) then, as one can easily confirm, there are two equilibria in the one-shot game, π^* and $\pi^* + z$. Now assume that the central bank maximizes over a two-period horizon and that it does not discount second-period welfare ($\beta = 1$). Consider what happens if the public forms expectations of π as follows:

(6.10) $\qquad \pi_{T-1}^e = 0$

$\qquad \pi_T^e = \begin{cases} \pi^* & \text{if } \pi_{T-1} \leq 0, \\ \pi^* + z & \text{otherwise.} \end{cases}$

One can easily show that when confronted with the inflation expectations mechanism (6.10), the central bank will ratify the public's beliefs and set $\pi_{T-1} = 0$. [If it sets $\pi_{T-1} > 0$, then it will bear a cost in period T of

$h(\pi^* + z) - h(\pi^*)$ which, by construction of h, is equal to $g(\pi^* + k)$. This cost outweighs any possible gain. The gain to inflating in period $T - 1$ is strictly less than $f(-k) - f(0)$, which is strictly less than $g(\pi^* + k) - g(\pi^*)$. Hence $\pi^e = 0$ is a subgame perfect equilibrium for period $T - 1$.] As in the infinite-horizon case, there are a multiplicity of equilibria. For example, any inflation rate less than π^* but greater than zero can be equilibrium for period $T - 1$.

It is interesting to observe that one can construct an analogous equilibrium in the case where (1) the one-shot game equilibrium is unique, and (2) the policymaker does not literally have a finite horizon but heavily discounts events that will occur after he leaves office. Suppose, for example, that one replaces the policymaker's loss function, (6.2a), with the alternative function

$$(6.11) \qquad \Omega_t = \sum_t^{\infty} L_s \beta(s)^{s-t},$$

where L_s is again given by Equation (6.2b), but now $\beta(s) = 1$ for $s \leq T$, and $\beta(s) = \varepsilon$ for $s > T$, with ε being very small. In his final period in office, T, the lowest attainable trigger-strategy equilibrium level of π, $\hat{\pi}_T$, will be very close to π^*, since future periods are discounted very heavily. (This assertion is easily confirmed.) Nevertheless, the small wedge between $\hat{\pi}_T$ and π^* is sufficient to support a level of inflation $\hat{\pi}_{T-1} < \hat{\pi}_T$ via the same general argument as above. If the policymaker's term is long enough, it will be possible to credibly sustain a very low inflation rate during his initial periods in office.

The analysis above is readily generalized to the stochastic case, if information is symmetric. (In the next section, I shall consider the case of asymmetric information.) Barro and Gordon (1983a) have illustrated some of the possibilities that can arise. The optimal trigger-strategy equilibria will involve having the public make (unforecastable) price-prediction errors. When a disturbance causes the benefits of unanticipated inflation to be unusually high, the monetary authorities engineer a surprise inflation. The public's expectations of inflation are still correct, on average, because the monetary authorities spring surprise deflations when the benefits are low. It should be noted that, because the models studied in this section have multiple equilibria, they can generate variable or stochastic inflation even in a completely unchanging environment. It is possible to have trigger-strategy equilibria that bounce back and forth between different points either with certainty, or with reference to an extrinsic random variable (sunspots).

The trigger-strategy equilibria I have been analyzing do not require any explicit cooperation between private agents, or between the private sector and the central bank. If an atomistic private agent believes that other agents form inflationary expectations according to (6.4) [or (6.8)], then it is only rational for him to form expectations the same way (if the equilibrium is subgame perfect).[12] However, although these low-inflation equilibria do not require explicit cooperation across individual agents, there is a serious question of how agents coordinate on a particular equilibrium. First, what is the length of the punishment interval going to be? Given the length of the punishment interval, is there any reason to suppose that the public will expect the lowest equilibrium inflation rate corresponding to this punishment interval? Even if one assumes that the public can coordinate on the punishment interval and can agree to expect the lowest credible level of inflation, there is still a degree of indeterminacy. Will $\pi^e = \hat{\pi}$, the lowest attainable inflation rate under (6.4), or will the public expect the lower inflation rate attainable under a severe punishment strategy such as (6.8)?

It might be argued that by making announcements concerning its future monetary policies, the government can focus the private sector's expectations on a particular equilibrium. But I am uneasy with pushing this line of reasoning too far. For the government to coordinate the public's expectations on a particular equilibrium inflation rate, it is necessary for it to coordinate the public's expectations about what will happen if it defects. Ex ante, the government wants to convince the public that it has a great deal to lose by defecting, that is, that the punishment interval will be long and severe. But after a defection, it has every incentive to try to persuade private agents that the punishment interval should be short.

But there is a broader problem. It is extremely difficult for a large number of agents to communicate with one another and to observe one another's actions. Even if trigger-strategy expectations have some practical importance, it seems difficult to argue that the economy should always succeed in focusing on the first-best trigger-strategy equilibrium. Clearly the government can focus expectations if it has some way of legally precommitting itself (a constitutional amendment governing monetary policy) or if it can precommit to penalties it will suffer by inflating (say, by going long in nominal bonds). These resolutions, of course, really amount to changing the structure of the game in a way that allows the government some ability to precommit.

Another somewhat implausible feature of the equilibria considered in this section is that (except for the one-shot game equilibrium), they generally require that the public's expectations about future inflation be discontinuous functions of current inflation. If the government defects by a small amount, expected inflation rises by just as much as if the government were to inflate massively. It would seem worthwhile exploring assumptions implying that continuous changes in the environment lead to continuous changes in the public's beliefs about future inflation. Whereas it may still be possible to have reputational equilibria with continuous reaction functions, the severity of the multiple equilibrium problem might be significantly diminished. (Stanford, 1986, provides some suggestive results.) Yet another approach to placing restrictions on the possible equilibria is to recognize that agents cannot make an unlimited number of calculations (see, for example, Rubinstein, 1986).

6.2. Private Information

Thus far, I have assumed that the public can perfectly monitor the central bank's actions. Canzoneri (1985) has analyzed the implications of relaxing this assumption, while retaining the assumption that the public knows the central bank's objective function. In this case, achieving the coordination necessary to attain optimal reputational equilibria seems even more problematic.

Canzoneri analyzes an infinite-horizon model similar to the model of the preceding section. He assumes that the central bank does not discount the future ($\beta = 1$), so in the absence of private information (and for a long enough punishment interval) there always exists a trigger-strategy equilibrium in which expected inflation is zero. He then introduces money demand shocks into the model. These shocks are observed only after the central bank has set the money supply. But the central bank is able to condition its actions on a forecast of the money demand disturbance. Its forecast is imperfect, so the central bank would be unable to completely damp out price fluctuations even if it were trying to minimize the price-prediction errors of private agents.

If the public is able to observe both the money demand disturbance and the central bank's forecast of it, then no new conceptual issues arise.

There are trigger-strategy equilibria analogous to those of Section 6.1 (for stochastic versions of the model). As long as the public can always directly confirm that any unanticipated inflation is entirely attributable to an error the central bank made in forecasting, there is no need to "execute" any punishment. (Technically, of course, private agents do not act strategically, and there is no explicit cooperation among them.) Canzoneri argues, however, that it might be very difficult for the public to directly confirm the central bank's forecast and that this forecast should be treated as private information.[13] He then shows, by applying Green and Porter's (1984) extension of Friedman's trigger-strategy model, that it is still possible to have an equilibrium that improves on the outcome of the one-shot game.[14]

In the equilibrium Canzoneri analyses, the public sets expected inflation equal to zero, as long as the economy is not entering a reversionary (punishment) period. The public then observes actual inflation and employes a one-tailed test. If inflation is above a certain threshold value, then there will be a one-period reversion to the inflation-rate expectations of the one-shot game. If the threshold is set at just the right level, the central bank can be induced to target zero inflation. (In setting the level of the money supply, the central bank must trade off increases in current employment with increases in the probability of entering a reversionary period.) Even though the central bank does not cheat (in equilibrium), large money demand forecast errors still occur periodically, thereby throwing the economy into periods of high expected inflation.

Like the model of Section 6.1, this model yields a multiplicity of other equilibria; and it is not clear how or why the public would coordinate on this particular one. It is not satisfactory to argue that this equilibrium is somehow "focal" because it is optimal. For one thing, the optimal equilibrium does not, in general, have such a simple structure. (Note that punishments actually occur in this model. So even if different punishment strategies yield the same level of expected inflation, they do not necessarily yield the same level of welfare.) Abreu, Pierce, and Stacchetti (1985) have shown that optimal punishment strategies in the Green-Porter model typically involve an analogue of the severe punishment strategies discussed in Section 6.1. They also show that the optimal strategies are not, in general, based on a simple one-tailed test (although the one-tailed test equilibrium is intuitively appealing). That the optimal trigger strategies can be so complicated, even when the underlying model has a relatively simple structure, is further reason to avoid loose arguments that the public will coordinate on the best equilibrium.

Canzoneri's model has some attractive features and some, at least superficially, odd features. By introducing private information, Canzoneri is able to explain why there must be some inflationary bias (on average) even if the public can coordinate on the best attainable equilibrium. Also, the model illustrates how serially uncorrelated forecast errors can produce serially correlated inflation rates: reversionary periods follow a cooperative period in which inflation was high. On the negative side, the public's expectations mechanism does not seem particularly plausible. The public finds itself punishing the central bank periodically, even though it knows that the central bank would never cheat (in equilibrium). Whenever the central bank inadvertently allows inflation to slip above its threshold value, the public must punish it by discontinuously raising inflation-rate expectations. The punishment is necessary to induce the central bank to continue to target low inflation in the future. Note that the public never actually learns anything about the policymaker's type; it knows everything at the outset and knows that it would never pay for the central bank to defect from the equilibrium. Thus Canzoneri's model should not be interpreted as one in which the central bank has private information about its preferences. His model has properties quite different from those of the models I shall discuss next in Section 6.3.

6.3. Reputation Building When the Private Sector Is Unsure of the Central Bank's Objectives

In the trigger-strategy models of Sections 6.1 and 6.2, the public knows the central bank's objectives and abilities at the outset. Therefore it is debatable whether these can really be interpreted as models of central bank "reputation." Partly for this reason, and partly because of concern about the degree of coordination required in trigger-strategy models with large numbers of agents, some researchers have begun to explore frameworks in which the public is unsure either about the policymaker's preferences or about his cost of breaking commitments.[15] These analyses address a number of interesting and important issues but, as I shall show, they do not provide a fully satisfactory resolution of the coordination problem. The "commitments" approach will be considered first. The analysis below is based on Rogoff (1987), with some of the technical details omitted. The results are summarized in the last part of this section.

Assume that the policymaker's horizon [T in Equation (6.2a)] is finite and that upon entering office, the policymaker makes a commitment never to inflate. The public is unsure about the cost to the policymaker of breaking his commitment, and it is with this cost that one associates the different possible "types" of policymakers. Suppose, for example, that the policymaker's commitment takes the form of a law that proscribes certain direct penalties on the central bank if it inflates. The public may not know how costly the central bank regards these penalties, or it may not know how large a weight the policymaker places on his own individual welfare relative to the social welfare function, Equations (6.2). Specifically, the policymaker has a finite-horizon loss function given by

(6.12a) $$\Omega_0 = \sum_0^T L_s(\pi, \pi^e, c)\beta^s, \qquad 1/2 < \beta < 1,$$

(6.12b) $$L_t(\pi_t, \pi_t^e, c) = -(\pi_t - \pi_t^e) + (\pi_t)^2/2 \\ + Z(c, \pi_t, \pi_{t-1}, \pi_{t-2}, \ldots)/2,$$

where $Z = c$ if $\pi_t \neq 0$ *and* $\pi_{t-i} = 0$ for all $i > 0$; $Z_t = 0$ otherwise. In other words, the central bank bears a fixed one-time cost to reneging on its commitment never to inflate.[16] The central bank's cost of breaking its commitment is private information. At time zero, the public only knows that $c \in [0,\mu]$, where $\mu > 1$; it has uniform priors over this interval. In subsequent periods, the public uses Bayes' rule to update its priors in a manner I shall specify shortly. [The use of Bayes' rule is consistent with *sequential* equilibrium (see Kreps and Wilson, 1982). Sequential equilibrium provides a natural generalization of subgame perfection to the present private information environment.]

Given the information structure and the special functional form embodied in (6.12b), one can readily deduce

PROPOSITION 6.1. In any (sequential) equilibrium, $\pi_t = 0$ or $\pi_t = 1$ for all t.

Trivially $\pi_t = 0$ in all periods before the policymaker breaks his commitment. And once he does inflate, there is no longer any further cost to inflating, so thereafter inflation must rise to $\pi = 1$, the unique equilibrium for any finite horizon. With a little further calculation, one can confirm that $\pi = 1$ will also be the policymaker's choice in the first period he inflates, regardless of c or π^e.

The interesting question is how the public's inflationary expectations evolve during the periods before the policymaker reneges, when they are guessing whether and when the commitment will be broken. It is useful to define

$$\sigma_t \equiv \{\pi_t^e | \pi_{t-1}, \pi_{t-2}, \ldots = 0\}$$

as the public's expectation of inflation in period t, given that the central bank has not broken its commitment prior to t. Clearly $\sigma_t \leq 1$, since by Proposition 6.1, π will equal zero or one in any period t. Proposition 6.2 below states that all types with sufficiently low costs of reneging ($c < 1$) will certainly renege in the last period if they have not done so previously, but no type ($c > 1$) will inflate for the first time in the last period.

PROPOSITION 6.2. If $\pi_t = 0$ for all $t < T$, then $\pi_T = 1$ if $c < 1$, and $\pi_T = 0$ if $c \geq 1$.

Proposition 6.2 is readily confirmed by calculating how the central bank would fare if it set $\pi = 0$ in periods zero through $t - 1$, and $\pi = 1$ in periods t through T (note that it takes $\{\sigma_s\}$ as given):

$$(6.13) \qquad \Gamma(t,c) = \sum_0^{t-1} \beta^s \sigma_s + \beta^t[(c - 1)/2 + \sigma_t] + \sum_{t+1}^{T} \beta^s/2.$$

Proposition 6.2 follows since $\Gamma(T,c) \gtreqless \sum_0^T \beta^s \sigma_s$ as $c \gtreqless 1$. Note that $\Gamma(t,c)$ is continuous and monotonically increasing in c.

One can also deduce from (6.13) that a high-cost type would never begin inflating in an earlier period than a lower-cost type would. If one holds $\{\sigma_s\}$ fixed, one sees that the higher the cost to the central bank of breaking its commitment, the more incentive it has to wait to incur this cost.

PROPOSITION 6.3. $[\Gamma(t_1,c_2) - \Gamma(t_2,c_2)] > [\Gamma(t_1,c_1) - \Gamma(t_2,c_1)]$, for $c_2 > c_1$ and $t_2 > t_1$.

Proposition 6.3 follows immediately from the fact that

$$(6.14) \qquad [\Gamma(t_1,c_1) - \Gamma(t_2,c_1)] - [\Gamma(t_1,c_2) - \Gamma(t_2,c_1)]$$
$$= (1 - \beta^m)(c_1 - c_2) < 0,$$

for $\beta < 1$, where $m \equiv t_2 - t_1$.

With the above results, I am now prepared to discuss the evolution of σ_t. In a sequential equilibrium, the public's beliefs must evolve according to Bayes' rule, so

$$(6.15) \qquad \sigma_t = \frac{\hat{c}_t - \hat{c}_{t-1}}{\mu - \hat{c}_{t-1}},$$

where $\hat{c}_t \equiv \sup\{\hat{c} \in [0,\mu] | c < \hat{c}$ implies $\Gamma(t + i,c) > \Gamma(t,c)$ for all i such that $0 < i \le T - t\}$.

Thus $\hat{c}_t$ is the critical value of c such that all types $c < \hat{c}_t$ will begin inflating in period t if they have not already begun inflating in an earlier period. The denominator of (6.15) represents the range of cost types that the public believes would not have inflated prior to period t. The numerator represents the range of cost types that the public believes will inflate for the first time in period t (in which case, they will set $\pi = 1$). Since the public's initial priors over c are uniform, (6.15) gives the expected inflation rate conditional on past inflation being uniformly zero. Because Proposition 6.3 implies that $\hat{c}_t$ must be nondecreasing in t, (6.15) is the only possible form for rational expectations.

To fully characterize an equilibrium, it is necessary to solve for a path $\{\hat{c}_s\}$ such that the public's expectations are rational; that is, the public must be correct in its belief that a policymaker of cost type $\hat{c}_s$ will actually choose to first renege in period s.

Proposition 6.2 suggests that $\hat{c}_T$ must equal 1. Consider the case where there is only one period. Then by Proposition 6.2 and by (6.15), the unique sequential equilibrium would be $\sigma = 1/\mu$ and $\hat{c} = 1$. If the policymaker's cost to reneging is so high that he would be indifferent between reneging and not reneging in the final period ($c = 1$), then it seems reasonable to suppose that he wouldn't renege in an earlier period. For then the one-time gain would be the same, but there would be an additional cost of having to live with the maximum level of expected inflation ($\pi^e = 1$) in all future periods.

Taking $\hat{c}_T = 1$ as given, it is straightforward to show that a necessary and sufficient condition for a sequential equilibrium is that the path of $\hat{c}_t$ must be governed by the recursion

$$(6.16) \qquad \Gamma(t,\hat{c}_t) - \Gamma(t + 1,\hat{c}_t) > 0, \qquad \text{if} \quad \hat{c}_t = 0,$$

$$= 0, \qquad \text{if} \quad \hat{c}_t > 0.$$

(See Rogoff, 1987.) Equation (6.16) says simply that the highest-cost type who would first inflate in period t, $\hat{c}_t$, must be just indifferent between first inflating in period t and waiting until period $t + 1$. If, in contradiction to (6.16), $\hat{c}_t$ strictly preferred to inflate first in period t, then there would have to exist a slightly higher cost type who would also want to begin inflating at time t.

To find the difference equation that governs the evolution of $\hat{c}$ for all $\hat{c} > 0$, first combine (6.13) with the equality relationship in (6.16) to obtain

(6.17) $\quad [-1 + \hat{c}_t(1 - \beta)]/2 = \beta(\sigma_{t+1} - 1).$

Then substitute (6.15) into (6.17) to get

(6.18) $\quad \hat{c}_{t+1} = F(\hat{c}_t)$

$$= \frac{\beta - 1}{2\beta}\hat{c}_t^2 + \frac{\mu(1 - \beta) + 1}{2\beta}\hat{c}_t + \mu - \frac{\mu}{2\beta}.$$

For $\hat{c}_t > 0$, the equilibrium is governed by (6.18) with terminal condition $\hat{c}_T = 1$. To construct an equilibrium backward from the terminal condition, invert (6.18) for $\hat{c}_t$ in terms of $\hat{c}_{t+1}$:

(6.19) $\quad \hat{c}_t = F^{-1}(\hat{c}_{t+1})$

$$= \frac{\mu(1 - \beta) + 1}{2 - 2\beta}$$

$$\pm \frac{\{[\mu(1 - \beta) + 1]^2 - 4(1 - \beta)[2\beta\hat{c}_{t+1} - \mu(2\beta - 1)]\}^{1/2}}{2 - 2\beta}.$$

Given that $\mu > 1$ and $\beta > 1/2$, it is readily confirmed that for $0 \leq \hat{c}_{t+1} \leq 1$, F^{-1} has exactly one real root less than one, and that $F^{-1}(\hat{c}_{t+1}) < \hat{c}_{t+1}$. Hence there can only be one unique equilibrium path terminating at $\hat{c}_T = 1$, and along this path $\hat{c}_t$ is strictly increasing in t for $\hat{c}_t > 0$.

An important characteristic of the equilibrium path of $\hat{c}$ is obtained by twice differentiating (6.18) to obtain

(6.20) $\quad d^2\hat{c}_{t+1}/d\hat{c}_t^2 = -(1 - \beta)/\beta < 0,$

which implies that $F^{-1\prime\prime}(\hat{c}_{t+1}) > 0$. Thus $\hat{c}_{T-k} - \hat{c}_{T-k-1}$ is increasing in k, and, for some finite $\bar{k}$, the function F^{-1} must map a positive $\hat{c}_{T-\bar{k}}$ into a negative $\hat{c}_{T-\bar{k}-1}$. This is, of course, infeasible, but recall from (6.16) that (6.18) only governs the path of $\hat{c}_t$ for $\hat{c}_t > 0$. $\hat{c}_{T-\bar{k}-1}$ does not turn negative but becomes zero for all periods $s \leq T - \bar{k} - 1$.

To confirm that this is equilibrium, note that $F^{-1}(\hat{c}_{t+1}) < 0$ if and only if

(6.21) $\quad \hat{c}_{t+1} < \mu - \mu/2\beta.$

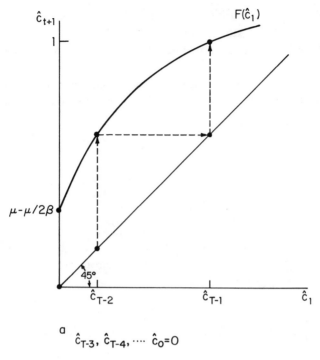

Figure 6.1   Equilibrium path of $\hat{c}$.

By setting $\hat{c}_t = 0$ and $\sigma_{t+1} = \hat{c}_{t+1}/\mu$ in (6.17), one can confirm that condition (6.21) provides the maximum level of $\hat{c}_{t+1}$ such that a type zero would not choose to inflate for the first time at t.

Figure 6.1 presents a graph of Equation (6.18) and constructs an equilibrium. The condition $\beta > 1/2$ ensures that the curve $F(\hat{c}_t)$ intersects the $\hat{c}_{t+1}$ axis at a positive value. The condition $1 > \mu - \mu/2\beta$ ensures that the $\hat{c}_{t+1}$ intercept is less than one (otherwise $\hat{c}_{T-1} = 0$). In the example in the figure, $\hat{c}_T, \hat{c}_{T-1}, \hat{c}_{T-2} > 0$ and $\hat{c}_{T-s} = 0$ for $s > 2$. Hence if T is large enough ($T \geq 3$), there will be an initial interval during which no type would renege. Over this interval, expected inflation is zero. In fact, inflation can only occur in the last three periods, so any increase in T beyond three only increases the length of the zero inflation phase.

I have shown that there exists a unique equilibrium with $\hat{c}_T = 1$. In Rogoff (1987), I showed that certain further restrictions are required to rule out "perverse" (sequential) equilibria in which types $c > 1$ may inflate; a sufficient condition involves having μ be large relative to T.

Let me now summarize the results. If the policymaker's term is long enough, he will not renege at first, regardless of his cost type. Expected inflation is zero. The longer the term, the longer this initial period of zero inflation. As the end of the policymaker's term nears, his temptation to inflate rises and he may decide to renege. If the policymaker has a low cost to reneging, he will inflate earlier than will a higher-cost type. If the policymaker's cost is sufficiently high, he will never renege. Once the economy enters the phase where reneging is possible, expected inflation begins to rise. The public overpredicts inflation in periods where the policymaker does not renege and underpredicts inflation in the period where reneging first occurs. As Barro (1986) pointed out in a closely related model, the public may actually be better off when facing a policymaker who can easily break his commitment. Intuitively, the lower his cost to reneging, the closer the policymaker's objective function is to the social welfare function (provided "inflation surprises" actually benefit the public by coordinating higher activity). However, the public is also better off the more likely it thinks, ex ante, that it is facing a high-cost type (high μ). The higher μ, the lower inflationary expectations. This result is closely related to the principal-agent result in Rogoff (1985b).

In the model just analyzed, policymakers differ in their cost of breaking a commitment. As Vickers (1986) has shown, quite different equilibria can arise if policymakers differ in the relative weights they place on inflation versus price-prediction errors. Suppose, for example, that there are two types: a "strong" type, who places a very high (but not infinite) weight on inflation, and a "weak" type, who places a low weight on inflation. The natural "pooling" equilibrium would involve having the weak type set low inflation to masquerade as a strong type. Only toward the final period would the weak type reveal himself. But, depending on the parameters, it is possible to have a *separating* equilibrium in which the strong type does something drastic immediately (sets inflation very low or in a sufficiently general setting, deflates) to set himself apart from the weak type. By taking an action that the weak type would not be willing to mimic, the strong type is able to enjoy lower expected inflation in later periods. In the separating equilibrium, the weak type can do no better than acting as he would in a one-shot game; he reveals himself immediately. Vickers's analysis also raises the broader question of whether, in a more general model, strong policymakers might have other ways to signal their type (that is, low budget deficits, low government spending, cheap cigars, and so on). The separating equilibrium just described cannot occur if the strong type cares *only* about inflation, as postulated in Backus and Driffill's (1985) original article. If the strong type does not care at all about price-prediction errors, then he will not care about inflationary expectations.

Driffill (1986) considered conditions under which pooling and separating equilibria (or both) can occur and also extended Vickers's analysis to allow for a continuum of types. Driffill briefly looked at the case where the policymaker has imperfect control over inflation; the public can directly observe inflation but not the random error causing actual inflation to deviate from target inflation. [This general class of problems is discussed in much more detail by Saloner (1984).] Here the public can no longer be certain that the policymaker is a weak type when high inflation is observed. In equilibrium, the weaker type may choose to target a somewhat higher level of inflation than he would if his actions could be observed.

Vickers and Driffill considered only two-period problems. This limitation may be important, because possibly the least robust results for the class of models considered in this section pertain to the "end play" of the model. These results can be sensitive to the assumption that the policymaker has a known finite horizon, an assumption that seems implausible if the policymaker genuinely cares about social welfare. It may be reasonable to assume that the policymaker will behave as if his actions have no effect beyond his term, provided his successor is drawn at random from a large population and provided the public has very strong priors about the distribution of types within this population. In this case, the policymaker's actions have no effect on the initial conditions (the public's priors) faced by his successor. But this is not the case if (as seems plausible) policymakers are chosen by some nonrandom process. For then, the observation that today's Fed chairman is a low-cost type ($c < 1$) ought to influence the public's priors as to the nature of his successor. These priors, in turn, affect future social welfare.

The analyses discussed in this section provide an interesting perspective on reputation building, but further investigation is needed to determine whether these models really describe how the economy resolves its coordination problem. Although the models yield a unique equilibrium in some cases, the equilibrium may be quite sensitive to the exact distribution of the public's priors. Fudenberg and Maskin (1986) have proved a folk theorem for this class of models; their results suggest that virtually any path of inflation can be an equilibrium given the right priors. Also, it is unrealistic to treat the policymaker's type as fixed, so that once revealed, it is known forever. In the next section, I shall consider models in which the policymaker's type can evolve over time.

6.4. Reputation When the Policymaker's Type Evolves over Time

Cukierman and Meltzer have investigated a model in which the policymaker's type is subject to serially correlated disturbances.[17] They argue that this formulation is realistic since monetary policy is set by a committee whose membership and political constituency change over time. They similarly rationalize why the monetary authority's type should be treated as private information. A second source of private information in their model is that the monetary authorities have only imperfect control over the money supply. Using Kalman filter techniques, Cukierman and Meltzer were able to prove that the model has a unique "linear" equilibrium in which the public updates its beliefs using a linear feedback rule. They showed that this equilibrium has a number of appealing properties. For example, the public's beliefs about the policymakers' current type (and hence expected inflation) are continuous in actual observed inflation, and a rise in the variance of the monetary control error raises the level and variance of inflation. However, because the model is quite complicated, Cukierman and Meltzer were not able to rule out the existence of other types of equilibria, such as equilibria with pooling or equilibria in which the public's updating mechanism is nonlinear. Given the pervasive information asymmetries in the model and the fact that the policymaker has an infinite horizon, the issue of multiple equilibria would seem potentially quite important.

It is not possible to present all the details of Cukierman and Meltzer's model in this survey. I shall try, however, to describe one of their main results. Cukierman and Meltzer suggested that the central bank may deliberately saddle itself with an inefficient forecasting technology to mask its intentions. The essence of this result can be presented in a one-shot game model. Let the central bank's objective function take the specific functional form

$$(6.22) \qquad L = -x(\pi - \pi^e) + \pi^2/2.$$

(Cukierman and Meltzer do not interpret this loss function as coinciding with the social welfare function.) It is easily seen that in a one-shot game, the central bank will set $\pi = x$ regardless of π^e; hence the unique equilibrium is $\pi^e = \pi = x$.

A key element of Cukierman and Meltzer's result is the assumption that the central bank's preferences are stochastic. Suppose, for example, that based on time $t - 1$ information, $x = 0$ in period t with probability 1/2, and that $x = 2$ in period t with probability 1/2. If the private sector is able to observe x before setting π^e, then $E_{t-1}(L_t) = (1/2)(0) + (1/2)(2) = 1$, where $E_{t-1}(L_t)$ is the expected value of the central bank's period t objective function, conditioned on information available prior to the realization of x. If, on the other hand, the private sector is unable to observe x before setting π^e, then $\pi^e = 1$, and $E_{t-1}(L_t) = (1/2)(0) + (1/2)(0) = 0$. Therefore if the central bank can precommit to not revealing x before the public sets π^e, it will choose to do so. The central bank cannot systematically fool the private sector by hiding its preferences. Private agents always still guess inflation correctly on average. However, the central bank still gains, because it is able to cause surprise inflation when the benefits to inflating are high and save surprise deflations for periods when the costs are low.

As described earlier, the full-blown Cukierman and Meltzer model involves an infinite-horizon dynamic game with serially correlated preference shocks. The public never directly observes the central bank's preferences but only infers them from the path of the money supply. By intentionally adopting an imprecise monetary control procedure, the central bank is able to obscure its preferences. The monetary authorities gain by means of the channel illustrated above but lose because inaccurate monetary control raises the variance of inflation.

The above result makes sense only if the monetary authorities actually have some way of precommitting to imprecise monetary control. Perhaps the monetary authorities can install an inadequate computer system that would take time to upgrade. On the other hand, it seems unlikely that the monetary authorities can accomplish anything by choosing a difficult-to-control intermediate target, since the targeting procedure can be changed overnight. The monetary authorities would have every incentive to change to an easy-to-control target in periods where they would benefit by having the public better observe their actions.

6.5. Related Research

I have restricted my attention to purely reputational constraints on monetary policy. There are a plethora of other channels for the government to (partially) precommit, although one might argue that reputation is ultimately involved in every case. Lucas and Stokey (1983) and Persson,

Persson, and Svensson (1987) have shown that *if* the government can precommit to paying its bonds, then it may be able to credibly precommit to the optimal time profile and composition of taxation. (As an example, the government can reduce its temptation to use the seigniorage tax by issuing real debt and relending the proceeds to the public in the form of loans with fixed nominal repayment schedules.)

Kotlikoff, Persson, and Svensson (1988) have suggested an interesting explanation for why governments may be able to commit to not taxing capital too heavily, even if the temptation is great because capital taxation has no short-term distortionary effects. They presented an overlapping-generations model in which each generation "sells" the optimal tax law to the next generation. An old generation that taxes its own capital holders too heavily finds itself with no tax law to sell the next generation. Whenever one generation compromises the existing law, the next generation sets up its own and restores the economy to an efficient path. The "trigger-strategy" equilibrium Kotlikoff, Persson, and Svensson considered is interesting in that punishments do not involve any deadweight costs.

Another channel for precommitment arises when there are multiple government controllers. Rogoff (1985a) illustrated how sovereign governments may be better off using competing monies (monetary policies) than by jointly controlling a common currency (fixed exchange rate). The threat of exchange rate depreciation can serve as a tempering influence on a sovereign who is contemplating unilateral inflation. Private agents recognize this tempering influence; and as a result, the time-consistent inflation rate is lower than under the common currency/fixed exchange rate regime. (This same argument can be made for having state-issued currencies in place of a national currency.)

6.6. Conclusions

There has been considerable progress toward introducing reputational considerations into models of monetary policy. But a number of important questions remain unanswered. The most disturbing feature of the models proposed to date is that either the equilibrium is very sensitive to changes in the information structure, or there are a multiplicity of equilibria, or both. In many cases there would appear to be substantial coordination problems in achieving the most favorable equilibria, particularly when one takes into account the scale of the coordination problem in a macroeconomic setting. Crawford (1985) has observed that in some situations, strategic uncertainty—uncertainty about which equilibrium strategy other agents are adopting—may be just as important as uncertainty about exogenous factors (see also Axelrod, 1984). A considerable amount of research is being devoted to this question, and it is quite possible that at some future date we will have a more definitive answer. But in the meantime, one must interpret with caution any prescriptions for monetary policy that rely heavily on supergame structures. It is certainly too soon to conclude that reputational constraints completely eliminate any case for imposing legal constraints on monetary policy, as some have inferred.

Strategic models of government policy certainly do represent a clear improvement over early rational expectations models, in which the government's behavior was treated as exogenous. It may be constructive to treat the government as a black box in studying certain phenomena, but it is hardly adequate as a framework for studying macroeconomic policy design.

Acknowledgments

An earlier version of this paper appeared in the Spring 1987 volume of the *Carnegie-Rochester Conference Series on Public Policy* (North-Holland, Amsterdam). This research was supported by the National Science Foundation and the Alfred P. Sloan Foundation.

Notes

1. See Kydland and Prescott (1977) and Calvo (1978). Phelps (1967) and Phelps and Pollak (1968) anticipated some of the basic themes underlying the modern time-consistency literature.
2. For a discussion of the relationship between time consistency and subgame perfection, see Fershtman (1986).
3. Atkeson (1986) illustrates trigger-strategy equilibria in an overlapping-generations model.
4. In the underlying structural model, money can have real effects either because of confusion between local and aggregate disturbances or because there are imperfectly indexed wage contracts. In the former case, there must be a temporal lag in the diffusion of aggregate information.
5. It is difficult to argue that anticipated inflation has an effect of the same order of magnitude as unanticipated inflation. (There are the "shoe-leather" costs resulting from lower holdings of real money balances. Also, there may be some activities, such as income tax accounting, which are costly to index

properly.) Our analysis does not require that the welfare effect of anticipated inflation be large.

6. See Calvo (1978), Barro (1983), or Grossman and Van Huyck (1986).

7. In a stochastic version of the model, the central bank may choose to cause price-prediction errors, although private sector agents will still be able to infer the mean inflation rate (see Barro and Gordon, 1983a, or Rogoff, 1985b).

8. Because f'', $g'' > 0$, one would obtain the same results if one replaced (6.4) with the weaker condition: $\pi_t^e = \bar{\pi}$ if $\pi_{t-1} \leq \pi_{t-1}^e$, and $\pi_t^e = \pi^*$ otherwise. In the private information example studied in Section 6.2, it will be necessary to make this modification.

9. If $f(\cdot) = (\pi - \pi^e - k)^2$, $g(\cdot) = \pi^2$, and $\beta = 1$, then $\bar{\pi} = 0$ is a trigger-strategy equilibrium under (6.4).

10. It is easy to prove that zero inflation is always attainable if the time interval between periods is small enough, provided that the length of the punishment interval is unrestricted. In (6.1) and (6.2), I have arbitrarily set the time interval at one. As the interval approaches zero, the transitory output gains from defecting become very short lived, whereas the punishment can be held constant. [Grossman and Van Huyck (1986) make this point in the context of an optimal seigniorage model.] Hence, if one chooses to rationalize (6.1) and (6.2) by means of an islands model, then a zero inflation rate is always attainable unless there is a discrete time lag in the diffusion of aggregate information.

11. Again, it is possible to define defections in terms of inequalities instead of equalities, but this does not make any qualitative difference in the case of symmetric information.

12. Some have criticized Barro and Gordon's trigger-strategy equilibrium as being subject to a "free-rider" problem. This criticism is not well founded. As the discussion in the text makes clear, the equilibrium is indeed Nash. There might be a free-rider problem if it were necessary to raise funds to improve coordination of private-sector expectations.

13. Whether the central bank actually has any private macroeconomic information is debatable. If the central bank's forecast of money demand is based entirely on publicly available data, then the private sector should be able to construct the same forecast. It might be argued that the central bank has much faster access to data on bank deposits and that this information is only released to the public with a long lag. Of course, if the central bank does not discount the future too heavily, then even the lagged release of data is still sufficient to allow trigger-strategy equilibria similar to those analyzed in Section 6.1.

14. The Keynesian flavor of Canzoneri's analysis is not an essential ingredient. Barro and Gordon (1983a) discuss how to extend their model to the case where the monetary authority has imperfect control over the inflation rate and where its control error is private information. In their paper, however, they do not present formal results.

15. See Backus and Driffill (1985), Horn and Persson (1985), Vickers (1986), and Driffill (1986) for the case where the public is uncertain about the weight the policymaker attaches to limiting inflation. See Tabellini (1983), Barro (1986), and Rogoff (1987) for the case where the public is unsure about the policymaker's cost of breaking commitments. See also Wood (1987) for an application to foreign exchange markets.

16. The analysis goes through with only slight modifications to the case where the fixed cost of inflating (breaking the commitment) has to be paid in every period the central bank inflates. See Rogoff (1987).

17. Rogoff and Sibert (1988) have also constructed a model in which the government's type changes over time, although their application is to electoral cycles in macroeconomic policy rather than to monetary policy credibility. In their model, an electoral cycle in inflations occurs as part of a signaling process in which incumbent politicians try to signal that they are able to administer the government more efficiently than would-be challengers.

References

Abreu, D. 1988. On the Theory of Infinitely Repeated Games with Discounting. *Econometrica* 56: 383–396.

Abreu, D., D. Pierce, and E. Stacchetti. 1985. Optimal Cartel Equilibria with Imperfect Monitoring. Unpublished paper, Harvard University.

Atkeson, A. 1986. Reputation and Time Consistency in a Macro Model. Unpublished paper, Stanford University.

Axelrod, R. 1984. *The Evolution of Cooperation.* New York: Basic Books.

Backus, D., and J. Driffill. 1985. Inflation and Reputation. *American Economic Review* 75: 530–538.

Barro, R. J. 1983. Inflationary Finance under Discretion and Rules. *Canadian Journal of Economics* 16: 1–16.

——— 1986. Reputation in a Model of Monetary Policy with Incomplete Information. *Journal of Monetary Economics* 17: 3–20.

Barro, R. J., and D. B. Gordon. 1983a. Rules, Discretion, and Reputation in a Model of Monetary Policy. *Journal of Monetary Economics* 12: 101–121.

——— 1983b. A Positive Theory of Monetary Policy in a Natural Rate Model. *Journal of Political Economy* 91: 589–610.

Benoit, J. P., and V. Krishna. 1985. Finitely Repeated Games. *Econometrica* 53: 905–922.

Calvo, G. 1978. On the Time Consistency of Optimal Policy in a Monetary Economy. *Econometrica* 46: 1411–28.

Canzoneri, M. B. 1985. Monetary Policy Games and the Role of Private Information. *American Economic Review* 75: 1056–70.

Crawford, V. P. 1985. Dynamic Games and Dynamic Contract Theory. *Journal of Conflict Resolution* 29: 195–224.

Cukierman, A., and A. H. Meltzer. 1986. A Theory of Ambiguity, Credibility, and Inflation under Discretion and Asymmetric Information. *Econometrica* 54: 1099–128.

Driffill, J. 1986. Macroeconomic Policy Games with Incomplete Information: Extensions and Generalizations. Unpublished paper, University of South Hampton.

Fershtman, C. 1986. Fixed Rules and Decision Rules: Time Consistency and Subgame Perfection. Unpublished paper, Hebrew University.

Friedman, J. W. 1971. A Noncooperative Equilibrium for Supergames. *Review of Economic Studies* 38: 861–874.

—— 1985. Cooperative Equilibria in Finite Horizon Noncooperative Supergames. *Journal of Economic Theory* 35: 390–398.

Fudenberg, D., and E. Maskin. 1986. The Folk Theorem in Repeated Games with Discounting and Incomplete Information. *Econometrica* 54: 533–554.

Green, E. J., and R. H. Porter. 1984. Noncooperative Collusion under Imperfect Price Information. *Econometrica* 52: 87–100.

Grossman, H. I., and J. B. Van Huyck. 1986. Seigniorage, Inflation, and Reputation. *Journal of Monetary Economics* 18: 21–31.

Horn, H., and T. Persson. 1985. Exchange Rate Policy, Wage Formation, and Credibility. *Institute for International Studies,* Seminar Paper No. 325, Stockholm.

Kotlikoff, L. J., T. Persson, and L. E. O. Svensson. 1988. Laws as Assets: A Possible Solution to the Time Consistency Problem. *American Economic Review* 78: 662–667.

Kreps, D. M., and R. Wilson. 1982. Reputation and Imperfect Information. *Journal of Economic Theory* 27: 253–279.

Kydland, F. E., and E. C. Prescott. 1977. Rules Rather than Discretion: The Inconsistency of Optimal Plans. *Journal of Political Economy* 85: 473–492.

Lucas, R. E., and N. Stokey. 1983. Optimal Fiscal and Monetary Policy in an Economy without Capital. *Journal of Monetary Economics* 12: 55–93.

Milgrom, P., and J. Roberts. 1982. Predation, Reputation, and Entry Deterrence. *Journal of Economic Theory* 27: 280–312.

Persson, M., T. Persson, and L. Svensson. 1987. Time-Consistency of Fiscal and Monetary Policy. *Econometrica* 55: 1419–31.

Phelps, E. S. 1967. Phillips Curves, Expectations of Inflation, and Optimal Employment over Time. *Economica* 34: 254–281.

Phelps, E. S., and R. A. Pollak. 1968. Second-Best National Saving and Game-Equilibrium Growth. *Review of Economic Studies* 2: 185–199.

Rogoff, K. 1985a. Can International Monetary Policy Cooperation Be Counterproductive? *Journal of International Economics* 18: 199–217.

—— 1985b. The Optimal Degree of Commitment to an Intermediate Monetary Target. *Quarterly Journal of Economics* 100: 1169–89.

—— 1987. Reputational Constraints on Monetary Policy. *In* K. Brunner and

A. H. Meltzer (eds.), *Carnegie-Rochester Conference Series on Public Policy* 26. Amsterdam: North-Holland.

Rogoff, K., and A. Sibert. 1988. Elections and Macroeconomic Policy Cycles. *Review of Economic Studies* 55: 1–16.

Rubinstein, A. 1986. Finite Automata Play the Repeated Prisoner's Dilemma. *Journal of Economic Theory* 39: 83–96.

Saloner, G. 1984. Dynamic Limit-Pricing in an Uncertain Environment. Working paper 342, Massachusetts Institute of Technology.

Stanford, W. G. 1986. On Continuous Reaction Function Equilibria in Duopoly Supergames with Mean Payoffs. *Journal of Economic Theory* 39: 233–250.

Tabellini, G. 1983. Accommodative Monetary Policy and Central Bank Reputation. Unpublished paper, University of California, Los Angeles.

Vickers, J. 1986. Signalling in a Model of Monetary Policy with Incomplete Information. *Oxford Economic Papers* 38.

Wood, P. R. 1987. Defending a Fixed Exchange Rate: The Central Bank's Reputation and the Deterrence of Speculative Attacks on Its Foreign Reserves. Unpublished doctoral dissertation, University of Wisconsin.

7   Time Consistency and Policy

V. V. Chari, Patrick J. Kehoe,
and Edward C. Prescott

The design of fiscal and monetary policy is a central concern in aggregative economics. A useful framework for thinking about optimal policy design is provided by the public finance tradition stemming from Ramsey (1927). Ramsey studied a static, representative consumer economy with many goods. A government requires fixed amounts of these goods, which are purchased at market prices and financed by proportional excise taxes. Given the excise taxes, prices and quantities are determined in a competitive equilibrium. The government's problem is to choose tax rates to maximize the welfare of the representative consumer. It is straightforward to extend Ramsey's formulation to study fiscal policy in dynamic models with uncertainty by reinterpreting the goods in the static problem as state-contingent commodities. In this context a policy for government is a rule specifying state-contingent tax rates. Given a policy, competitive equilibrium prices and allocations are defined as functions of the state of the economy. The design problem is to choose a policy that maximizes a social welfare function defined over the resulting competitive allocations. An optimal policy together with the resulting competitive equilibrium is called a *Ramsey equilibrium*.

In a Ramsey equilibrium, consumers make decisions once and for all at the beginning of time. But this equilibrium can also be interpreted as a one-time choice of government policy with consumers making decisions sequentially, given the policy. The Ramsey policies then solve the design problem in environments where societies have access to a commitment technology to bind the actions of future governments. In many situations, however, it is more appropriate to think of policies as being chosen at each date, with society having no ability to commit to future policies. In such environments, one is tempted to conclude that the resulting policy choices coincide with the Ramsey policies. This is not the case. Consider the policy choice problem at some date t, assuming that policies and allocations coincide with the Ramsey equilibrium until that date. The solution to the new policy choice problem typically does not coincide with the Ramsey policies from that date onward. Kydland and Prescott (1977), Prescott (1977), Calvo (1978), and Fischer (1980) have shown that this dynamic inconsistency of the Ramsey policies is pervasive in models of fiscal and monetary policy. This dynamic inconsistency means that the Ramsey policies are typically irrelevant in a world without commitment. Clearly, rational individuals will not base their decisions on the Ramsey policies if a different set of policies will be chosen in the future.

A solution to the design problem without commitment must therefore require that policies be *sequentially rational*. That is, the policy rules must maximize the social welfare function at each date given that private agents behave optimally. Likewise, optimality on the part of private agents requires that they forecast future policies as being sequentially rational for society. A sequence of policy rules, allocations, and prices satisfying these conditions is a *time-consistent equilibrium*. We say there is a time-consistency problem if the Ramsey equilibria differ from the time-consistent equilibria. It is worth remarking that time-consistency problems can arise in individual decision problems when preferences change over time (see Strotz, 1955). We shall therefore restrict our focus to situations where preferences are time consistent in Strotz's sense. The source of time-consistency problems cannot then lie in such preferences.

In Section 7.1, we shall argue that the source of time-consistency problems lies in conflict among agents. We shall show that in a team environment where all agents share a common objective function, there can be no time-consistency problems. Most models of fiscal and monetary policy use a representative agent construct and a social welfare function that coincides with the representative agent's utility function. The representative agent formulation should not mislead us into thinking that the individuals in this economy form a team. The objectives of individuals do not coincide, because in such models individuals care only about their own consumption. Consequently, even in representative agent models there are generally time-consistency problems.

We shall explore the precise nature of the time-consistency problem by using two classic illustrations of the problem: capital taxation and default on government debt. In Section 7.2 we shall analyze a variant of Fischer's

(1980) model of capital taxation; and in Section 7.3 we shall analyze Chari and Kehoe's (1987a) debt-default model. We shall define and characterize time-consistent equilibria for each of these examples.

Our formulation of time-consistent equilibria (based on Chari and Kehoe, 1987a,b) allows allocations and policies to depend on the entire history of past decisions by governments as well as on past aggregate (or per capita) allocations. Thus, policies and allocations are defined as *history-contingent* functions. This break from the general equilibrium tradition of considering equilibria that are state-contingent functions is essential in imposing the requirement of sequential rationality. Both governments and consumers must forecast how current decisions affect future outcomes. Allowing for history-contingent functions solves this forecasting problem.

For finite-horizon models, sequential rationality implies that this problem is solved by backward induction. For infinite-horizon models such a procedure is no longer available. Indeed, for infinite-horizon models there is typically a large set of time-consistent equilibria that are quite difficult to characterize. It turns out, however, that the set of allocations realized in time-consistent equilibria is fairly easy to characterize. In Section 7.2 we shall provide a simple set of inequalities that can be used to characterize such allocations for the capital taxation model. We shall show that with sufficiently little discounting, even the Ramsey allocations can be supported by some time-consistent equilibrium.

The policy plans and allocations rules used to support the large set of time-consistent allocations for the capital taxation model are closely related to "trigger" strategies of repeated games. (See, for example, Friedman, 1971.) Loosely speaking, for any given pair of policy and allocation sequences, the history-contingent policy and allocation rules used to support them specify continuation with these sequences as long as there has been no deviation. If there has been a deviation, the rules specify reversion to the single-period time-consistent equilibrium forever. Even though such rules resemble the trigger strategies of repeated games, it is important to point out that in our models, private agents behave competitively. In particular, private agents do not collude to "punish" the government. Rather, after a deviation, private agents choose the single-period time-consistent allocations because they forecast that the government will choose the single-period time-consistent policy. The government, in turn, takes the aggregate allocation rule for private agents as given and optimally chooses this policy. Because of this feature, some of our results differ from the related results in repeated games with only "large" players.

In Section 7.3 we shall extend the debt model of Lucas and Stokey (1983) to allow for default.[1] We shall model default by the government as a tax on debt. We shall consider a finite-horizon version of the model. As might be expected, the Ramsey allocations are not, in general, outcomes of a sustainable equilibrium, because the debt issues associated with a Ramsey allocation are positive at some dates. When the inherited debt is positive, the government has an incentive to default. Recognizing this, private agents will not buy such debt in previous periods. This result does not imply, however, that a sustainable equilibrium must have a continuously balanced budget. The government can smooth tax distortions over time by issuing negative debt, that is, by purchasing claims on private agents. Using a backward induction argument, Chari and Kehoe (1987a) show that time-consistent allocations solve a programming problem called the *constrained Ramsey problem.* The time-consistent allocations maximize the welfare of the representative consumer at date zero, subject to the budget constraint and a sequence of constraints that require that the present value of the government's surplus be nonpositive at all future dates.

We shall analyze the time-consistent equilibria in a series of examples. As we shall show, the Ramsey allocations are typically not time consistent, and hence there is a value to having a commitment technology. Under plausible assumptions, this value, as measured by the normalized difference between utility in a sustainable equilibrium and the Ramsey utility, can be made arbitrarily small by making the horizon sufficiently long and the discount factor sufficiently close to unity. Note that this result holds in a finite-horizon model and thus does not rely upon "trigger" strategies. Rather, the result holds because the ability to issue negative debt allows for almost as much tax smoothing as occurs in a Ramsey equilibrium.[2]

7.1. An Overview of the Time-Consistency Problem

In this section we shall formulate policy design as a simple social choice problem and shall use this framework to provide an overview of the time-consistency problem. We shall compare the equilibria of an environment with commitment with those of an environment without commitment. We shall formalize commitment as a particular timing scheme for decision making. Society first chooses a policy once and for all, and then private agents choose their actions. In the environment without commitment, decisions are made sequentially. Such a timing scheme in a multiperiod economy occurs when private agents first choose their first-period actions, then the government chooses its first-period policy, then private agents choose their second-period actions, and so on. For ease of exposition, we shall consider a one-period economy. In this case the two timing schemes are particularly simple. With commitment, the government first sets policy and then private agents make their decisions. Without commitment, private agents first make their decisions and then the government sets policy. It will be clear that all of the results extend to multiperiod economies.

Throughout this section, we shall consider special cases of the following environment. There is a society consisting of n private agents. Each agent i ($i = 1, \ldots, n$) chooses an action x_i from a set of actions X_i. The vector of actions $x = (x_1, \ldots, x_n)$ is called an *allocation*. Society chooses a policy π from a set of policies Π. The preferences of each private agent are given by a utility function $U^i(x,\pi)$, and society's preferences are given by $S(x,\pi)$. Initially we shall model allocations as the outcome of a Nash equilibrium and later as the outcome of a competitive equilibrium.

It turns out that the preferences of private agents and society together play a critical role in determining whether the allocations with and without commitment coincide—that is, in determining whether there is a time-consistency problem. We shall show that if all agents' preferences coincide with those of society, then there can be no time-consistency problem. We then shall give necessary conditions for there to be a time-consistency problem and illustrate these conditions in a simple model of inflation and unemployment.

7.1.1. Team Environments

A *team* is defined as a group of individuals who share a common objective. We shall show that in a team environment there can be no time-consistency problem. Specifically, suppose that each agent's preferences coincide with those of society. Let the utility function of each agent i over the vector x and the policy π be given by some strictly concave, twice-differentiable function $U(x,\pi)$. Let this function also be the social objective function. Notice that together the private agents and society form a team. Even though team members control only their own actions, they all choose these actions to achieve a common goal.

Under commitment, society chooses a policy π; and then, given this policy, private agents simultaneously choose their actions. First consider the choice of private agents, given some policy π. Each agent i, faced with a policy π and taking as given the decisions $x_{-i} = (x_1, \ldots, x_{i-1}, x_{i+1}, \ldots, x_n)$ of all other agents, solves

(7.1) $\max_{x_i} U(x, \pi).$

If we assume an interior solution, the first-order condition is

(7.2) $\dfrac{\partial U}{\partial x_i} = 0.$

For a given policy π, an equilibrium for private agents is a vector x such that for each i, x_i solves (7.1), given x_{-1}. For any such policy π, denote the resulting equilibrium allocations by $X(\pi)$. For simplicity, assume that for each π there is a unique equilibrium and that the resulting function $X(\cdot)$ is differentiable. This function $X(\cdot)$ is called the *outcome function*.

Society's problem, then, is to choose a policy π to maximize its objective function taking the outcome function $X(\cdot)$ as given. That is, society solves

(7.3) $\max_{\pi} U(X(\pi), \pi).$

If we assume an interior solution, the first-order condition for society is

(7.4) $\displaystyle\sum_{i=1}^{n} \frac{\partial U}{\partial x_i} \frac{\partial X_i}{\partial \pi} + \frac{\partial U}{\partial \pi} = 0.$

We can now define an equilibrium with commitment.

DEFINITION. An equilibrium with commitment is a policy π^* and an outcome function $X(\cdot)$ that satisfy

  (i) *Maximization for society*. Given $X(\cdot)$, the policy π^* solves society's problem (7.3).
  (ii) *Private equilibrium*. For each π, the outcome $X(\pi)$ is an equilibrium for private agents.

Notice that the private decisions actually taken in such an equilibrium are given by $x^* = X(\pi^*)$.

Without a commitment technology, the equilibrium is somewhat different. In particular, private agents first choose a vector x and then society chooses a policy π. Given some allocation x, the problem faced by society is

(7.5) $$\max_{\pi} U(x,\pi).$$

The first-order condition for society is

(7.6) $$\frac{\partial U}{\partial \pi} = 0.$$

Assume that for each vector x, the policy π defined by (7.6) is unique and that the resulting policy rule $\Pi(\cdot)$ is differentiable. In this equilibrium each private agent i takes the policy rule $\Pi(\cdot)$ and the decisions of other private agents x_{-i} as given and solves

(7.7) $$\max_{x_i} U(x,\Pi(x)).$$

The first-order condition for each agent i is

(7.8) $$\frac{\partial U}{\partial x_i} + \frac{\partial U}{\partial \pi} \frac{\partial \Pi}{\partial x_i} = 0.$$

(Notice that we let each private agent take account of the effect his action has on the policy chosen by society. When the number of private agents is large, this effect will be small; in the limit, it will be zero.) We can now define an equilibrium without commitment.

DEFINITION. An equilibrium without commitment is a vector of private decisions x^* and a policy rule $\Pi(\cdot)$ that satisfy

(i) *Private equilibrium.* Given x^*_{-i} and $\Pi(\cdot)$, x^*_i solves (7.7).
(ii) *Maximization for society.* For any x, the policy $\Pi(x)$ solves (7.5).

We can now compare the equilibrium outcomes with and without commitment. Combining (7.2) and (7.4), we have that the equilibrium outcome with commitment is completely characterized by

(7.9) $$\frac{\partial U}{\partial \pi} = 0 \quad \text{and} \quad \frac{\partial U}{\partial x_i} = 0, \qquad \text{for all } i.$$

Combining (7.6) and (7.8), we have that the equilibrium outcome without commitment is characterized by

(7.10) $\dfrac{\partial U}{\partial x_i} = 0,$ for all $i,$ and $\dfrac{\partial U}{\partial \pi} = 0.$

Notice that (7.9) and (7.10) are identical and that either set of equations are the first-order conditions to

$$\max_{x,\pi} U(x,\pi).$$

By strict concavity, the solution to this problem is unique, and hence we have established the following proposition.

PROPOSITION 7.1. *No Time-Consistency Problem in a Team Environment*
    If all agents have the same objective function as society has, the equilibrium allocations and policies with and without commitment are identical.

    Thus for there to be a time-consistency problem, there needs to be some conflict of interests either between society and private agents or among private agents themselves.

7.1.2. Benevolent Agents and a Self-Interested Society

A variety of papers in the literature have examined situations in which the preferences of society do not coincide with those of private agents. In our framework we shall model such a situation by letting each private agent's objective function be $U(x,\pi)$ and letting society's objective function be some other function, say, $S(x,\pi)$. For this specification, an equilibrium with commitment is summarized by

$$\frac{\partial U}{\partial x_i} = 0, \qquad \text{for all } i$$

and

$$\sum_{i=1}^{n} \frac{\partial S}{\partial x_i} \frac{\partial X_i}{\partial \pi} + \frac{\partial S}{\partial \pi} = 0.$$

Likewise, an equilibrium without commitment is summarized by

$$\frac{\partial S}{\partial \pi} = 0$$

and

$$\frac{\partial U}{\partial x_i} + \frac{\partial U}{\partial \pi} \frac{\partial \Pi}{\partial x_i} = 0, \quad \text{for all } i.$$

It is clear that, in general, the solutions to these two sets of equations will be different.

One justification for assuming that the preferences of society do not coincide with those of its constituent agents is that policy choices are made by a self-interested government. As we have seen, the discrepancy in objectives between such a government and the members of society induces a conflict of interests that can lead to a time-consistency problem. It is not clear to us why the preferences of society do not reflect the preferences of its constituents. Thus the time-consistency problems just described do not seem an interesting way to model social choice in democratic societies.

7.1.3. Self-Interested Agents and a Benevolent Society

Consider an environment in which the preferences of each private agent can differ. In particular, let the preferences of agent i be given by $U^i(x, \pi)$. Notice that since each agent's utility is affected by other agents' decisions, this economy has external effects. We model society as being benevolent in the sense that it solves a Pareto problem by maximizing

$$\sum_{i=1}^{n} \lambda_i U^i(x, \pi)$$

for some set of welfare weights $\lambda = (\lambda_1, \ldots, \lambda_n)$.

With commitment, the first-order condition for each agent is

$$\frac{\partial U^i}{\partial x_i} = 0$$

and the first-order condition for society is

$$\sum_{i=1}^{n} \lambda_i \left[\sum_{j=1}^{n} \frac{\partial U^i}{\partial x_j} \frac{\partial X_j}{\partial \pi} + \frac{\partial U^i}{\partial \pi} \right] = 0.$$

Likewise, without commitment the first-order condition for society is

$$\sum_{i=1}^{n} \lambda_i \frac{\partial U^i}{\partial \pi} = 0$$

and the first-order condition for an agent i is

$$\frac{\partial U^i}{\partial x_i} + \frac{\partial U^i}{\partial \pi} \frac{\partial \Pi}{\partial x_i} = 0.$$

Notice that, in general, these two solutions will differ; consequently, when there are externalities, typically there is a time-consistency problem.

7.1.4. Representative Agent Models

A particularly interesting class of social choice problems arises in competitive equilibrium models with a representative agent. It turns out that such problems can be represented in our general social choice framework. For this class of problems, the objective functions of agents are

$$U^i(x,\pi) = U(x_i,\bar{x},\pi),$$

where $\bar{x} = \sum_{i=1}^{n} x_i/n$ denotes the aggregate per capita allocations. The objective function of society is

$$S(x,\pi) = \sum_{i=1}^{n} U(x_i,\bar{x},\pi).$$

Modeling private agents as being competitive amounts to assuming that each agent i takes both the aggregate allocation $\bar{x}$ and the policy π as given. Furthermore, the policy rule Π used by society when there is no commitment is constrained to depend only on the aggregate allocation $\bar{x}$. In the case with commitment, the first-order conditions reduce to

$$\frac{\partial U^i}{\partial x_i} = 0, \qquad \text{for all } i$$

and

$$\sum_{i=1}^{n} \frac{\partial U^i}{\partial \bar{x}} \frac{\partial \bar{X}}{\partial \pi} + \frac{\partial U^i}{\partial \pi} = 0.$$

In the case without commitment, the first-order conditions are

$$\sum_{i=1}^{n} \frac{\partial U^i}{\partial \pi} = 0$$

and

$$\frac{\partial U^i}{\partial x_i} = 0, \qquad \text{for all } i.$$

It is clear that, in general, the solutions to these problems are different. Notice that if the utility functions did not depend on the aggregate allocation $\bar{x}$, then the solutions to these problems would be the same. Dependence of the utility functions on aggregate allocations induces a subtle source of conflict among agents. The nature of this conflict can be illustrated in a simple model of inflation. More complicated examples will be considered in Sections 7.2 and 7.3.

7.1.5. Conflict among Agents in a Simple Model of Inflation

Perhaps the most widely used example in the time-consistency literature is a Phillips curve model of inflation and unemployment. Kydland and Prescott (1977) first used this model to illustrate the problem of time consistency. Barro and Gordon (1983) and Rogoff (1987; and Chapter 6) have elaborated on the basic model. The idea is that unanticipated inflation provides benefits to society, whereas anticipated inflation is costly. Within our social choice framework, we can model these features as follows.

Each private agent chooses the (log of) his nominal wage x_i. Society, which here is identified with the monetary authority, chooses the (log of) the price level π. The aggregate $\bar{x} = \sum_{i=1}^{n} x_i/n$ is the average nominal wage in the economy. The utility function of private agents is given by

$$U^i(x,\pi) = U(x_i - \pi, \bar{x} - \pi, \pi)$$

while the utility function of the monetary authorities is given by

$$S(x,\pi) = \sum_{i=1}^{n} U(x_i - \pi, \bar{x} - \pi, \pi).$$

As usual, we shall consider two kinds of commitment technologies. The first-order conditions with commitment reduce to

$$U_1(x_i - \pi, \bar{x} - \pi, \pi) = 0, \quad \text{for all } i$$

and

(7.11) $$\sum_{i=1}^{n} [U_2(x_i - \pi, \bar{x} - \pi, \pi) \left(\frac{\partial \bar{X}}{\partial \pi} - 1 \right) + U_3(x_i - \pi, \bar{x} - \pi, \pi)] = 0.$$

The first-order conditions without commitment reduce to

$$U_1(x_i - \pi, \bar{x} - \pi, \pi) = 0$$

and

(7.12) $$\sum_{i=1}^{n} [U_3(x_i - \pi, \bar{x} - \pi, \pi) - U_2(x_i - \pi, \bar{x} - \pi, \pi)] = 0.$$

In this type of model it is common to assume that for a fixed price level π and aggregate nominal wage $\bar{x}$, the utility of agent i is maximized by setting the nominal wage equal to the price level plus a constant k. Thus $U_1(\cdot) = 0$ when the first argument equals k. One rationalization for this is that a real wage higher than the one given by the constant k leads to lower employment and hence lower utility.

Since $U_1(\cdot) = 0$ when the real wage $x_i - \pi$ equals k, then in an equilibrium with commitment, $\partial \bar{X}/\partial \pi = 1$. It follows from Equations (7.11) and (7.12) that the solutions to the two problems are different. Notice that it is crucial for society to care about the second argument $\bar{x} - \pi$, that is, the *average* real wage in the economy. If the utility functions of private agents or society did not depend upon this argument, then the solutions would be identical. Barro (1985) and Rogoff (1987; and Chapter 6) recognized the importance of this assumption. They argued that unanticipated inflation provides social benefits if the natural rate of unemployment exceeds the socially optimal level as a result of the presence of externalities or distorting taxation. Since these features are not modeled, it is hard to assess the validity of the argument. Suffice it to say, some such force must be present if this model is to generate a time-consistency problem.

7.1.6. Summary

We have made three main points in this section: First, time-consistency problems cannot arise in a team environment. Second, time-consistency problems typically arise whenever governments do not maximize the welfare of private agents. Third, even if governments are benevolent, conflicts among private agents can cause time-consistency problems. In the sections that follow we shall consider two examples that investigate how the interactions between external effects and the timing of decisions generate time-consistency problems.

7.2. The Capital Taxation Model

In this section we shall consider a version of Fischer's (1980) capital taxation model, modified along the lines of Chari and Kehoe (1987b). Initially we consider a one-period version of the model.

Consider an economy with a large number of identical consumers and a government. There is a linear production technology for which the marginal product of capital is a constant $R > 1$ and the marginal product of labor is 1. Consumers make decisions at two distinct points in time, the *first stage* and the *second stage*. They make consumption–investment decisions at the first stage and consumption–labor supply decisions at the second stage. In particular, at the first stage, consumers are endowed with ω units of the consumption good from which they consume c_1 and save k. At the second stage, they consume c_2 and work l units. Second-stage income, net of taxes, is $(1 - \delta)Rk + (1 - \tau)l$, where δ and τ denote the tax rates on capital and labor respectively. For simplicity we assume that first-stage consumption is a perfect substitute for second-stage consumption. A consumer, confronted with tax rates δ and τ, chooses $(c_1, k; c_2, l)$ to solve

(7.13) $\max\ U(c_1 + c_2, l)$

s.t. $c_1 + k \leq \omega$

$c_2 \leq (1 - \delta)Rk + (1 - \tau)l.$

If the tax rate on capital δ is set so that $(1 - \delta)R = 1$, the consumer is indifferent about the timing of consumption. We assume that in such a case, the consumer saves his entire endowment.

The government sets proportional tax rates on capital and labor income to finance an exogenously given amount of second-stage per capita government spending G. The government's budget constraint is

(7.14) $G \leq \delta RK + \tau L,$

where K and L denote the per capita (or aggregate) levels of capital and labor. We assume that $G > R\omega$, so even if consumers save their entire endowments and the tax on capital is set equal to one, the government still needs to tax labor.

In what follows we shall adopt the notational convention that lowercase letters denote individual variables and uppercase letters denote aggregate variables. This notation is used to emphasize what various agents take as given.

7.2.1. Capital Taxation with Commitment

In an economy with commitment, the government sets tax rates before private agents make their decisions. In this setup it is straightforward to define an equilibrium. Let $x_1 = (c_1, k)$ and $x_2 = (c_2, l)$ denote an individual consumer's first- and second-stage allocations and let $X_1 = (C_1, K)$ and $X_2 = (C_2, L)$ denote the corresponding aggregate allocations. Let $\pi = (\delta, \tau)$ denote government policy. We can now define a competitive equilibrium.

DEFINITION. A competitive equilibrium is an individual allocation (x_1, x_2), an aggregate allocation (X_1, X_2), and a tax policy π that satisfy

   (i) *Consumer maximization.* Given the tax policy π, the individual allocations solve the consumer's problem (7.13).
   (ii) *Government budget constraint.* At the aggregate allocation (X_1, X_2), the policy π satisfies the government budget constraint (7.14).
   (iii) *Representativeness.* The individual and aggregate allocations coincide; that is, $(x_1, x_2) = (X_1, X_2)$.

Given that the individual and aggregate allocations coincide. we can refer to such an equilibrium as a (π, X) pair, where $X = (X_1, X_2)$. Let E denote the set of policies π for which an equilibrium exists. Assume that for each π in E there is a unique equilibrium allocation $X(\pi)$ associated with π. Let $S(\pi, X(\pi))$ denote the equilibrium value of utility under the policy π so that

$$S(\pi, X(\pi)) = U(C_1(\pi) + C_2(\pi), L(\pi)).$$

We say that a pair (π,X) is a *Ramsey equilibrium* if π solves

$$\max_{\pi \in E} S(\pi,X(\pi))$$

and $X = X(\pi)$. We then have

PROPOSITION 7.2.   *The Single-Period Ramsey Equilibrium*
    The Ramsey equilibrium (π,X) has first-stage allocations $C_1 = 0$ and $K = \omega$ and a capital tax rate $\delta = (R - 1)/R$.

Proof. If the tax on capital is such that $(1 - \delta)R \geq 1$, then consumers save their entire endowments, while if $(1 - \delta)R < 1$, consumers save nothing. Thus the tax on capital acts like a lump-sum tax when it is selected at any level less than or equal to $(R - 1)/R$. Clearly it is optimal to raise as much revenue as possible from this tax. Since $G > R\omega$, government spending is greater than the maximal possible revenues from this capital tax, so it is optimal to set $\delta = (R - 1)/R$. Faced with this tax, consumers save their entire endowments. The tax rate on labor is then set at a level sufficient to raise the rest of the needed revenues.   ◊

7.2.2. Capital Taxation without Commitment

Formally, the lack of commitment is modeled by assuming that the government does not set policy until after consumers have made their first-stage decisions. The timing is (1) consumers make first-stage decisions, (2) the government sets tax policy, and (3) consumers make second-stage decisions. In this setup the government's tax rates depend on the aggregate first-stage decisions. Thus a government policy is no longer a pair of tax rates $\pi = (\delta,\tau)$ but a specification of tax rates for every possible X_1, say, $\sigma(X_1) = (\delta(X_1),\tau(X_1))$. To keep the distinction between these clear, we call the function σ a *policy plan* and we call a specific set of tax rates π simply a *policy*.

Each consumer's second-stage decisions depend on the first-stage decisions x_1, the aggregate first-stage decisions X_1, and the tax policy selected. Thus, a consumer's second-stage decisions are described by a pair of functions, say $f_2(x_1,X_1,\pi) = [c_2(x_1,X_1,\pi),l(x_1,X_1,\pi)]$. We call f_2 a second-stage *allocation rule* to distinguish it from a particular second-stage *allocation* x_2. Likewise, the aggregate allocation rule F_2 is defined as a function of the aggregate first-stage decision X_1 and the policy π and is denoted by $F_2(X_1,\pi)$.

An equilibrium in this environment is defined recursively. First, a second-stage competitive equilibrium is defined, given the history of past decisions by consumers and the government. We then consider symmetric histories (x_1,X_1,π) for which the individual allocation x_1 equals the aggregate allocation X_1. The resulting allocation rules are used to define the problem facing the government. Next, the first-stage competitive equilibrium is defined. Combining all of these gives an equilibrium that we call a *time-consistent equilibrium*. We define a second-stage competitive equilibrium as follows.

DEFINITION. A competitive equilibrium at the second stage, given the history (x_1,X_1,π), is a set of individual and aggregate allocation rules f_2 and F_2 that satisfy

(i) *Consumer maximization.* Given the history (x_1,X_1,π), the individual allocation rule $f_2(x_1,X_1,\pi)$ solves

$$\max_{c_2,l} U(c_1 + c_2,l)$$

$$\text{s.t.} \quad c_2 \leq (1 - \delta)Rk + (1 - \tau)l.$$

(ii) *Representativeness.* $f_2(X_1,X_1,\pi) = F_2(X_1,\pi)$.

Since this equilibrium is defined for each history, we can summarize it by the function $F_2(X_1,\pi)$.

Next consider the situation of the government. Given the past aggregate decisions X_1 and knowing that future decisions are selected according to the rule $F_2(X_1,\pi)$, the government selects a policy, say, $\pi = \sigma(X_1)$, that maximizes consumer welfare. The government's objective function is

(7.15) $S(\sigma,F_2;X_1) = U(C_1 + C_2(X_1,\pi),L(X_1,\pi))$

where $\pi = \sigma(X_1)$. Given X_1 and F_2, the government must select a policy $\sigma(X_1)$ that satisfies its budget constraint:

(7.16) $G \leq \delta(X_1)RK + \tau(X_1)L(X_1,\sigma(X_1))$.

Let $\Sigma(F_2;X_1)$ denote the set of all policies $\sigma(X_1)$ that satisfy (7.16). The problem of the government is to pick a plan σ such that for every F_1, $\sigma(X_1)$ maximizes utility (7.15) over the set of feasible policies $\Sigma(F_2;X_1)$.

Finally, consider the consumer's problem at the first stage. Each consumer chooses an individual allocation for the first stage, $x_1 = (c_1, k)$, together with an allocation rule f_2 for taking actions at the second stage. Each consumer takes as given that the current aggregate allocation is some X_1, that future policy is set according to the plan σ, and that future aggregate allocations are set according to some rule F_2. Given these assumptions, the definition of the first-stage competitive equilibrium is analogous to that of the second-stage competitive equilibrium, so the first-stage competitive equilibrium is summarized by (σ, X_1, F_2).

We have recursively defined the consumer's and the government's problems. Combining these gives an equilibrium with sequential rationality built in for both the private agents and the government. Because of this, we say the equilibrium is time consistent. Formally, we have

DEFINITION. A time-consistent equilibrium is a triple (σ, X_1, F_2) that satisfies

   (i) *Sequential rationality by consumers.* The triple (σ, X_1, F_2) is a first-stage competitive equilibrium and, for every history (π', X_1'), the allocation rule $F_2(\pi', X_1')$ is a second-stage competitive equilibrium.
  (ii) *Sequential rationality by the government.* Given F_2, the policy plan σ solves the government's problem for every history X_1'.

We then have

PROPOSITION 7.3. *The Single-Period Time-Consistent Equilibrium*
   The single-period time-consistent equilibrium has first-stage allocations $C_1 = \omega$ and $K = 0$ and a capital tax plan $\delta(X_1) \equiv 1$.

Proof. Consider first the policy plan σ. For any given first-stage aggregate allocation $X_1 = (C_1, K)$, it is clearly optimal for the government to raise as much revenue as possible from taxing the given amount of capital. By assumption, $G > R\omega$, so even if all the endowments are saved and the resulting capital is fully taxed, the revenues fall short of government spending. Thus, $\delta(X_1) \equiv 1$. Faced with such a tax, it is optimal for consumers to save nothing and consume all of their endowments. ◇

It is easy to verify that the utility level of each consumer in the time-consistent equilibrium is strictly lower than the level in the Ramsey equilibrium.

But an important question still remains: What is the source of the conflict in this example? To investigate this question we cast our model in the general social choice framework considered in Section 7.1. To accomplish this we need to embed the budget constraints of consumers and the government into preferences. Let the preferences of each private agent be given by

$$U(\omega - k + (1 - \delta)Rk + (1 - \tau)l,l) + W(K,L,\delta,\tau),$$

where the function W equals zero if its arguments (K,L,δ,τ) satisfy the government's budget constraint, $G \leq \delta RK + \tau L$, and W equals some large negative number otherwise. Let the government's preferences be

$$U(\omega - K + (1 - \delta)RK + (1 - \tau)L,L) + W(K,L,\delta,\tau).$$

Since we have assumed that consumers are competitive, in the sense that they regard aggregates as being unaffected by their decisions, this model is a special case of the representative agent model considered in Section 7.1.4. Thus the source of conflict is that each private agent cares more about his own allocation than about other private agents' allocations.

7.2.3. A Finite-Horizon Model of Capital Taxation

Consider a finite repetition of the capital taxation model. To keep things simple, we assume that capital cannot be stored between periods, that there is no borrowing and lending across periods, and that government spending is constant. With commitment, the government chooses a sequence of tax rates once and for all at the beginning of time. A competitive equilibrium is a sequence of individual and aggregate allocations that maximize consumer welfare and that satisfy the government budget constraint and representativeness. The Ramsey equilibrium in this multiperiod model is simply the one-period Ramsey equilibrium repeated finitely many times.

Without commitment, the problem is more complicated because all decisions must be sequentially rational. Consumers must forecast how future tax rates will be chosen, and the government must forecast how its current choices influence future decisions of consumers. Following Chari and Kehoe (1987a,b), we resolve this forecasting problem by making allocations and policies functions of the *history* of past decisions. Formally, the history of an individual consumer at the first stage of period t is

$$h_{1t} = (x_s, X_s, \pi_s | s = 0, \ldots, t - 1),$$

and the aggregate history at the first stage is

$$H_{1t} = (X_s, \pi_s | s = 0, \ldots, t - 1).$$

Likewise, the aggregate history confronting the government after consumers have made their first-stage decisions in period t is

$$H_t = (X_s, \pi_s | s = 0, \ldots, t - 1) \cup X_{1t}.$$

At the second stage, an individual consumer's history is given by

$$h_{2t} = (h_{1t}, x_{1t}, X_{1t}, \pi_t)$$

and the aggregate history by

$$H_{2t} = (H_{1t}, X_{1t}, \pi_t).$$

In keeping with the assumption that tax rates cannot be altered by the decisions of any single consumer, aggregate histories do not include individual allocations.

Allocations and policies are defined as functions of the histories. Let $f_t = (f_{1t}, f_{2t})$ denote individual allocation functions that map first- and second-stage individual histories into decisions at the respective stages. Let $F_t = (F_{1t}, F_{2t})$ denote the corresponding aggregate allocation function that maps aggregate histories into aggregate allocations. Let σ_t denote the government's policy function that maps histories H_t into decisions at t.

Now in order to define a time-consistent equilibrium, we need to explain how allocation and policy functions induce future histories. In what follows, we consider only symmetric histories. Let $f^t = (f_t, f_{t+1}, \ldots)$ denote a sequence of individual allocation rules from time t onward. Let F^t and σ^t denote the corresponding objects for the aggregate allocation rules and policy plans. Given a history h_{1t}, the functions f^t, F^t, and σ^t induce individual histories

$$h_{2t} = \{h_{1t}, f_{1t}(h_{1t}), F_{1t}(H_{1t}), \sigma_t(H_{1t}, F_{1t}(H_{1t}))\}$$

$$h_{1t+1} = \{h_{2t}, f_{2t}(h_{2t}), F_{2t}(H_{2t})\}$$

and so on. Likewise, from any initial aggregate history, say, H_{1t}, the functions F^t and σ^t induce future histories $(H_t, H_{2t}, H_{1t+1}, \ldots)$ in a similar fashion.

Consider the first stage of period t. Given some history h_{1t}, an individual consumer chooses a contingency plan f^t. Each consumer takes it as given that future aggregate allocations and policies will evolve according to the histories induced by F^t and σ^t. Recalling that we only consider symmetric histories, we have

DEFINITION. A competitive equilibrium at the first stage of t, given a history H_{1t}, is a set of contingency plans f^t, F^t, and σ^t that satisfy

(i) *Consumer maximization.* Given H_{1t}, F^t, and σ^t, the individual allocation rules f^t maximize

$$\sum_{s=t}^{T} \beta^{s-t} U(c_{1s}(h_{1s}) + c_{2s}(h_{2s}), l_s(h_{2s}))$$

s.t. $c_{1s}(h_{1s}) \leq \omega - k_s(h_{1s})$
$c_{2s}(h_{2s}) \leq [1 - \delta_s(H_s)]Rk_s(h_{1s}) + [1 - \tau_s(H_s)]l_s(h_{2s})$

where for all $s \geq t$, the future histories are induced by f^t, F^t, and σ^t.

(ii) *Representativeness.* $f^t = F^t$.

We can refer to this equilibrium as a pair (σ^t, F^t). Likewise, a competitive equilibrium at the second stage of t, given a history H_{2t}, is a set of contingency plans (f_{2t}, f^{t+1}), (F_{2t}, F^{t+1}), and σ^{t+1} that satisfy conditions similar to those above. We refer to this equilibrium as $(\sigma^{t+1}, F_{2t}, F^{t+1})$.

Next consider the situation of the government in period t. Given some history H_t and taking as given that future aggregate allocations evolve according to (F_{2t}, F^{t+1}), the government selects a policy plan σ^t that maximizes consumer welfare. The government's objective function is

(7.17) $S_t(\sigma^t, F_{2t}, F^{t+1}; H_t) = U(C_{1t} + C_{2t}(H_{2t}), L_t(H_{2t}))$

$$+ \sum_{s=t+1}^{T} \beta^{s-t} U(C_{1s}(H_{1s}) + C_{2s}(H_{2s}), L_s(H_{2s})).$$

Given the history H_t and the allocation rules (F_{2t}, F^{t+1}), the government must select a policy plan that not only satisfies its current budget constraint

$$G \leq \delta_t(H_t)RK_t + \tau_t(H_t)L_t(H_{2t})$$

but that also satisfies its future budget constraints

$$G \leq \delta_s(H_s)RK_s(H_{1s}) + \tau_s(H_s)L_s(H_{2s})$$

for all aggregate histories induced by (F_{2t}, F^{t+1}) and σ^t. Let $\Sigma_t(F_{2t}, F^{t+1}; H_t)$ be the set of all policy plans σ^t that satisfy these budget constraints. The problem of the government at t, then, is to pick a plan σ^t that maximizes consumer welfare (7.17) over the set of all feasible policies $\Sigma_t(F_{2t}, F^{t+1}; H_t)$.

Combining these various definitions gives a type of equilibrium that will not break down as time evolves, since by construction the various contingency plans will be carried out for any possible set of histories. We then have

DEFINITION. A time-consistent equilibrium is a pair (σ, F) that satisfies

(i) *Sequential rationality by consumers.* For every history H_{1t}, (σ^t, F^t) is a first-stage competitive equilibrium, and for every history H_{2t}, the triple $(\sigma^{t+1}, F_{2t}, F^{t+1})$ is a second-stage competitive equilibrium.

(ii) *Sequential rationality by the government.* For every history H_t, the plan σ^t maximizes consumer welfare over the set of feasible plans $\Sigma(F_{2t}, F^{t+1}; H_t)$.

We abbreviate notation and let $S_0(\sigma, F)$ denote the value of utility at time zero in a time-consistent equilibrium.

It is easy to characterize the time-consistent equilibria by using backward induction. At the second stage of the last period, the consumer's decision problem depends only upon current tax rates and the current capital stock; it is independent of the rest of the history. Consequently, the government's decision problem depends only upon the current capital stock. It follows that the equilibrium in the last period is identical with the single-period equilibrium and is independent of the history. Next consider the problem in period $T - 1$. Clearly, neither the government's decisions nor private agents' decisions have any effect on outcomes in period T. Hence, the period $T - 1$ problem is also static and the outcomes are identical to those in the single-period case. It follows by repetition of this argument that for the finite-horizon case, the time-consistent equilibrium is unique and is simply the sequence of the single-period time-consistent equilibria.

7.2.4. An Infinite-Horizon Model of Capital Taxation

With commitment, the characterization of equilibrium is straightforward. The infinite-horizon Ramsey equilibrium is simply the one-period Ramsey equilibrium of Proposition 7.2, repeated forever. Notice that this equilibrium is the limit of a sequence of finite-horizon Ramsey equilibria.

Without commitment, the way to characterize the set of equilibria is not obvious. One way to proceed is simply to take the limits of a sequence of finite-horizon time-consistent equilibria. This technique will indeed yield a time-consistent equilibrium. However, there are many other time-consistent equilibria that are not the limits of *any* sequence of finite-horizon equilibria. In fact, the set of time-consistent equilibria is very large and difficult to characterize. However, it is relatively easy to characterize the policies and allocations induced by time-consistent equilibria.

Recall that, in general, a time-consistent equilibrium (σ, F) is a sequence of functions that specify policies and allocations for all possible histories. Starting from the null history at date 0, a time-consistent equilibrium induces a particular sequence of policies and allocations—say, (π, X). We call this *the outcome induced by the time-consistent equilibrium.*

The technique for characterizing the set of such outcomes builds on Abreu's (1984) seminal work on repeated games. In our models, however, agents behave competitively rather than strategically, and thus we need to reformulate Abreu's arguments. We shall prove that a sequence of policies and allocations can be induced by some time-consistent equilibrium if and only if the sequence can be induced by a particular time-consistent equilibrium called the *revert-to-autarky equilibrium.* We shall then use this result to show that an arbitrary sequence is an outcome of a time-consistent equilibrium if and only if it satisfies two conditions: first, the sequence is a competitive equilibrium at date 0; second, the sequence must satisfy some simple inequalities.

We shall proceed in three steps. First, we shall define the autarky equilibrium and the revert-to-autarky equilibrium. Second, we shall prove that an arbitrary sequence of policies and allocations can be induced by some time-consistent equilibrium if and only if it can be induced by the revert-to-autarky equilibrium. Third, we shall use this result to provide a simple characterization of time-consistent policies and allocations.

The autarky equilibrium (σ^a, F^a) is defined as follows. For the government, the plan $\sigma_t^a(H_t)$ specifies the single-period time-consistent plan of Proposition 7.3 regardless of the history up until time t. For private agents, the allocation rules $F_{1t}^a(H_{1t})$ and $F_{2t}^a(H_{2t})$ specify the single-period time-consistent allocation rules regardless of the history up until time t. It is easy to verify that these policy plans and allocation rules constitute a time-consistent equilibrium. Chari and Kehoe (1987b) proved the following proposition.

PROPOSITION 7.4. *Autarky Is the Worst Time-Consistent Equilibrium*
Any time-consistent equilibrium (σ, F) must have a utility level $S(\sigma, F)$ greater than or equal to the utility level $S(\sigma^a, F^a)$ of the autarky equilibrium.

Proof. We shall sketch the proof here. To establish the proposition, one shows that, for an arbitrary equilibrium (σ, F), the following inequalities hold:

$$S(\sigma, F) \geq S(\sigma^a, F) \geq S(\sigma^a, F^a).$$

Both inequalities rely on a fact about competitive equilibria. That is, for any period t, the second-stage labor supply and consumption decisions solve the same static problem. From this fact it follows that a deviation by the government from σ to σ^a is feasible in that σ^a satisfies the government budget constraint for any equilibrium allocation rule F. Sequential rationality by the government then yields the first inequality.

Next, if the allocation rule F specifies positive savings at some date t, then the second equality holds, because distorting taxes are being replaced by lump-sum taxes. If the rule F specifies zero savings for all dates, then the resulting allocations under F and F^a are identical.   ◇

The next proposition uses a modified version of the autarky plans called the revert-to-autarky plans. For an arbitrary sequence of policies and allocations (π, X), the revert-to-autarky plans (σ^r, F^r) specify continuation with the candidate sequences (π, X) as long as they have been chosen in the past; otherwise, they specify revert to the autarky plans (σ^a, F^a). Thus, for example, at time t given a history H_t, this policy plan specifies: Choose the tax rates π_t specified by π if the tax rates $(\pi_0, \ldots, \pi_{t-1})$ have been chosen according to π and the allocations $(X_0, X_1, \ldots, X_{t-1})$ and X_{1t} have been chosen according to X. If they have not, then revert to the autarky tax rule σ^a. The revert-to-autarky allocation rules F^r are similarly defined.

Consider, then, some arbitrary sequences (π, X) and the associated revert-to-autarky plans. It will be useful to define the single-period utility when the government reverts to autarky. Given that the first-stage allocations X_{1t} at time t have been chosen according to X, let $U^d(X_{1t})$ be the maximized value of utility under the autarky rule. It is easy to show that

$$U^d(X_{1t}) = \max_{(\tau, C_2, L)} U(C_{1t} + C_2, L)$$

$$\text{s.t.} \quad C_2 \leq (1 - \tau)L$$

$$\frac{U_l}{U_c} = (1 - \tau)$$

$$G \leq RK_t + \tau L.$$

We then have

PROPOSITION 7.5. *Time-Consistent Equilibrium Outcomes*
An arbitrary pair of sequences (π, X) is the outcome of a time-consistent equilibrium if and only if

(i) The pair (π, X) is a competitive equilibrium at date 0.
(ii) For every t, the following inequality holds:

$$(7.18) \qquad \sum_{s=t}^{\infty} \beta^{s-t} U(X_s) \geq U^d(X_{1t}) + \frac{\beta}{1 - \beta} U(X^a)$$

where X^a denotes the autarky equilibrium allocation.

Proof. Suppose first that (π, X) is the outcome of a time-consistent equilibrium (σ, F). Sequential rationality by consumers requires that (π, X) be a competitive equilibrium at date 0. By an argument similar to the one in Proposition 7.4, a deviation by the government to the autarky plan σ^a is feasible. Also, by Proposition 7.4, the autarky equilibrium is the worst equilibrium. Clearly, then, the utility of the government must be at least as large as the right-hand side of (7.18) for every period t.

Next, suppose some arbitrary pair of sequences (π, X) satisfies (i) and (ii) of Proposition 7.5. We need to show that the associated revert-to-autarky plans (σ^r, F^r) constitute a time-consistent equilibrium. Consider histories under which there have been no deviations from (π, X) up until t. Since (π, X) is a competitive equilibrium at date 0, it is clear that its continuation from date t is also a competitive equilibrium. Thus sequential rationality by consumers is satisfied for such histories. Now consider the situation of the government when it is confronted with allocation rules F^r. The highest utility it can obtain from any deviation is given by the right-hand side of (7.18). We have proved that σ^r is sequentially rational for the government for such histories.

Next, consider histories for which there has been a deviation before time t. The revert-to-autarky rules (σ^r, F^r) specify autarky from then on. Clearly, the autarky policies and allocations constitute a competitive equilibrium at t. Finally, faced with the autarky allocation rule, the government finds it optimal to choose the autarky policy. Thus (σ^r, F^r) is a time-consistent equilibrium.   ◊

An immediate corollary to this proposition is a result that resembles the folk theorem for repeated games (see, for example, Fudenberg and Maskin, 1986).

PROPOSITION 7.6.   *Supporting Ramsey Allocations*
There is some discount factor $\beta \in (0,1)$ such that for all $\beta \in (\underline{\beta},1)$ the Ramsey allocations can be supported by a time-consistent equilibrium.

Proof. Recall that the Ramsey allocations are the same in all periods. Denote the Ramsey allocation of any period by X^*. By Proposition 7.5 we need only verify that inequality (7.18) is satisfied by X^*. Rearranging terms, we need to show

$$(7.19) \qquad \frac{\beta}{1 - \beta} [U(X^*) - U(X^a)] \geq [U^d(X_1^*) - U(X^*)].$$

Since the Ramsey allocations yield a strictly higher level of utility than the autarky allocations do, the left-hand side of (7.19) is positive. Since the left-hand side of (7.19) increases monotonically to infinity as the discount factor approaches one, the proposition follows.   ◊

Propositions 7.5 and 7.6 have shown that the set of time-consistent equilibria for the infinite horizon is much larger than the limit of the finite-horizon equilibria. The result depends critically on the fact that both policy and allocation rules were allowed to depend on histories. If either of these rules were restricted so as not to depend on the history prior to the current period, then the unique time-consistent equilibrium would be the limit of the finite-horizon equilibrium. We see no compelling reason to restrict attention to such rules.

Results similar to ours are well known for repeated games. Our models, however, differ from repeated games in an important aspect: private agents behave competitively rather than strategically. For example, in the revert-to-autarky equilibrium, consumers do not "punish" the government when it deviates; rather, they choose the autarky allocations, because taking the future aggregate allocations and policies as beyond their control, it is *optimal* to choose these allocations.

7.3. A Finite-Horizon Model of Debt and Default

In the multiperiod capital taxation model of Section 7.2, it was assumed that capital depreciated completely between periods and that agents could not borrow or lend. Technically, this implied that there were no state variables, like capital or debt, connecting one period to the next. In addition, we assumed a linear production function so that the calculation of equilibrium prices would be trivial. These features helped make our analysis of the model simple, and thus the model served as a useful introduction to multiperiod models with time-consistency problems. In most macroeconomic models of interest, however, there are physical state variables and the calculation of equilibrium prices is nontrivial. The main goal of this section is to provide an introduction to such models and to highlight some of the issues that arise. We shall accomplish this by studying a simple model of debt and default. A secondary goal is to show that even in this simple model it is a nontrivial problem to determine whether or not there is a time-consistency problem. In particular, we shall show that while the conflicts among agents of the type considered in Section 7.1 are necessary for a time-consistency problem, they are not sufficient.

We shall consider a finite-horizon model of debt similar to the models of Prescott (1977), Barro (1979), and Lucas and Stokey (1983). In the model, government consumption fluctuates over time and the revenues to finance this consumption are raised through distortionary taxation of labor. The government is also allowed to tax debt. Any tax on debt is interpreted as a partial default and a 100% tax is interpreted as a complete default. For simplicity, we assume there is no capital.

In the commitment equilibrium, the government uses debt to smooth distortions from labor taxation over time. With a fluctuating stream of government consumption, optimality implies that the Ramsey policy will *not* have the budget balanced in each period. In the no-commitment equilibrium, it is this lack of budget balance that drives the time-consistency problem. In particular, without commitment, whenever the outstanding government debt is positive, the government has an incentive to default on the debt in order to decrease the amount of distortionary labor taxation. When the outstanding debt is negative, however, the government has no incentive to default. Chari and Kehoe (1987a) use this fact to show that the time-consistent equilibria solve a certain programming problem called the *constrained Ramsey problem*. This problem is to maximize the welfare of a representative consumer at date 0, subject to the budget constraint and a sequence of constraints that require that the present value of the government's surplus be nonpositive at all future dates.

7.3.1. Debt and Default with Commitment

Consider an economy populated by a large number of identical agents who live for $T + 1$ periods. In each period there are two goods: labor and a consumption good. A constant returns-to-scale technology is available to transform one unit of labor into one unit of output. The output can be used for private consumption or for government consumption. The per capita level of government consumption in each period, denoted G_t, is exogenously specified. Let c_t and l_t denote the individual levels of consumption and labor, and let C_t and L_t denote the aggregate (or per capita) values of these variables. An aggregate allocation $(C,L) = \{C_t,L_t\}_{t=0}^T$ is feasible if it satisfies

(7.20) $C_t + G_t = L_t.$

The preferences of each agent are given by

(7.21) $\displaystyle\sum_{t=0}^{T} \beta^t U(c_t,l_t),$

where U is increasing, concave, and bounded, and where $0 < \beta < 1$.

Let p_t denote the price of the consumption good at time t in an abstract unit of account; and denote the vector of prices by $p = \{p_t\}_{t=0}^T$. Since the constant returns-to-scale technology transforms a unit of labor into one unit of output, the wage rate equals the price of the consumption good. We assume that revenues can be raised only through a proportional tax on labor income. Let τ_t denote the tax rate on the labor income earned in period t, and let $\tau = \{\tau_t\}_{t=0}^T$ denote the sequence of such tax rates. The budget constraint of the representative consumer is then

(7.22) $\displaystyle\sum_{t=0}^{T} p_t[c_t - (1 - \tau_t)l_t] = 0.$

Notice that we have written the consumer's budget constraint in date-0 or present-value form. Implicit in this constraint is a sequence of government debt held by consumers. One can understand the government's incentives to tax (or to default on the) debt by explicitly writing out this sequence.

Following Lucas and Stokey (1983), we allow for government debt of all maturities. In each period t the government has outstanding net claims denoted $_{t-1}B = \{_{t-1}B_s\}_{s=t}^{T}$ where $_{t-1}B_s$ is a claim to goods at time s. At time t the issue of new debt claims by the government results in a net debt position of $_tB$. (One can think of $_tB$ as a single bond with time-varying coupon payments.) We model default as a tax on outstanding debt. Let $\delta_t \in [0,1]$ denote the tax on debt outstanding in period t. Let $_tq_s$ be the price at time t of the debt claim maturing in period s. The value of the outstanding debt at time t, prior to the tax $(1 - \delta_t)$, is given by $\Sigma_{s=t}^{T} {}_tq_s {}_{t-1}B_s$. The government's budget constraint at time t is

$$(7.23) \qquad p_t[\tau_t L_t - G_t] + \sum_{s=t+1}^{T} {}_tq_s {}_tB_s = (1 - \delta_t) \sum_{s=t}^{T} {}_tq_s {}_{t-1}B_s$$

where $_{-1}B \equiv 0$.

The analogous sequential budget constraints for the aggregate allocations $\{C_t, L_t\}_{t=0}^{T}$ are

$$(7.24) \qquad p_t[C_t - (1 - \tau_t)L_t] + \sum_{s=t+1}^{T} {}_tq_s {}_tB_s = (1 - \delta_t) \sum_{s=t}^{T} {}_tq_s {}_{t-1}B_s$$

where $_{-1}B \equiv 0$. Obviously, in a competitive equilibrium there is an arbitrage relation between the prices of the consumption goods and the prices of the debt claims, namely, $_tq_t = p_t$, and for all $s \geq t + 1$

$$(7.25) \qquad {}_tq_s = p_s(1 - \delta_{t+1})(1 - \delta_{t+2}) \ldots (1 - \delta_s).$$

In this economy an individual agent's allocation is a vector of consumption and labor, denoted by $x = \{x_t\}_{t=0}^{T}$, where $x_t = (c_t, l_t)$. An aggregate allocation is defined analogously and denoted by $X = \{X_t\}_{t=0}^{T}$, where $X_t = (C_t, L_t)$. A policy for the government is a sequence of tax rates on labor, tax rates on debt, and debt issues, denoted by $\pi = \{\pi_t\}_{t=0}^{T}$, where $\pi_t = (\tau_t, \delta_t, {}_tB)$. We then have

DEFINITION. A competitive equilibrium is a set of individual allocations x, an aggregate allocation X, price systems p and q, and a policy π that satisfy

(i) *Consumer maximization.* Given π, p, q, and X, the individual allocation x maximizes (7.21) subject to (7.22).
(ii) *Sequential constraints for aggregate allocations.* The aggregate allocation X satisfies (7.24) for each t.
(iii) *Sequential constraints for government policies.* The policy π satisfies (7.23) for each t.
(iv) *No arbitrage.* The price systems p and q satisfy (7.25) for all t.
(v) *Representativeness.* $x = X$.

Notice that the sequential constraints (7.23) and (7.24) imply the feasibility condition (7.20).

We shall comment briefly on the no-arbitrage condition and the sequence of constraints for aggregate allocations. We can derive these conditions from consumer maximization by including the sequence of period budget constraints for each of the consumers. In these period budget constraints are the debt claims held on other consumers as well as on the government. Consumer maximization then implies the no-arbitrage condition. Market clearing in private debt and representativeness then imply the sequence of constraints for aggregate allocations. For notational convenience we have simply imposed these conditions as part of the definition of equilibrium.

In any equilibrium the individual and aggregate allocations coincide, so we refer to such a competitive equilibrium as (π,X,p,q). Let E denote the set of policies for which an equilibrium exists. Assume that for each π in E there is a unique allocation $X(\pi)$. (A sufficient condition for this to be true is that consumption and leisure are normal goods.) The equilibrium value of utility under a policy π is given by

$$S(\pi,X(\pi)) = \sum_{t=0}^{T} \beta^t U(C_t(\pi),L_t(\pi)).$$

We say (π,X,p,q) is a *Ramsey equilibrium* if π solves $\max_{\pi\in E} S(\pi,X(\pi))$ and $X = X(\pi)$, $p = p(\pi)$, and $q = q(\pi)$.

In this model we have allowed government to tax labor and debt. As we shall see in the no-commitment equilibrium, the incentive to use the tax on debt to renege on claims drives the time-inconsistency problem. However, interestingly enough, in the Ramsey equilibrium the ability to tax debt is irrelevant; and, in terms of allocations, all that really matters is the tax on labor. Specifically, the Ramsey equilibrium for this economy coincides with the Ramsey equilibrium considered by Lucas and Stokey (1983) in which governments are not allowed to tax debt. The reason for this is that letting the government tax debt does not expand the set of allocations attainable under a government policy. We then have

PROPOSITION 7.7. *The Ramsey Equilibrium of the Debt Model*
The consumption and labor allocations C and L in the Ramsey equilibrium solve

$$\max \sum_{t=0}^{T} \beta^t U(C_t, L_t)$$

subject to

(7.26) $C_t + G_t = L_t$

(7.27) $\sum_{t=0}^{T} \beta^t R_t = 0$

where $R_t \equiv U_c C_t + U_l L_t$ is the government surplus in period t in units of marginal utility.

Proof. First, the set of allocations attainable is the same as those in an economy where the government sets the tax on debt identically equal to zero. One can see this by noting that if (π, X, p, q) is an equilibrium with δ_t possibly positive for some t, then so is $(\hat{\pi}, X, p, \hat{q})$ with $\hat{\tau}_t = \tau_t$, $\hat{\delta}_t = 0$, $_t\hat{B}_s = {}_tB_s(1 - \delta_{t+1}) \ldots (1 - \delta_s)$, and $_t\hat{q}_s = p_s$, for all s and t with $s \geq t + 1$. Next, notice that in any competitive equilibrium, the consumer's first-order conditions imply

(7.28) $p_t = \beta^t U_c(C_t, L_t)$

and

(7.29) $(1 - \tau_t) = -U_l(C_t, L_t)/U_c(C_t, L_t)$.

Substituting (7.28) and (7.29) into the consumer's budget constraint (7.22) gives (7.27). Clearly there are many debt sequences $\{_tB\}_{t=0}^{T}$ and debt taxes $\{\delta_t\}_{t=0}^{T}$ that satisfy the sequential budget constraints (7.23) and (7.24).   ◇

The first-order conditions for the Ramsey problem are (7.26), (7.27), and for all t,

$$(7.30) \qquad (1 + \lambda_0)(U_c + U_l) + \lambda_0[C_t(G_t)(U_{cc} + U_{cl}) + L_t(G_t)(U_{cl} + U_{ll})]$$

$$= 0$$

where λ_0 is the Lagrangian multiplier on (7.27). Clearly the allocations that solve this problem depend on only the current value of government consumption G_t and the multiplier λ_0. Suppressing the multiplier, we let $R(G_t)$ denote the value of the government surplus (in marginal utility units) under the Ramsey allocations.

In the Ramsey plan, the government optimally smooths distortions over time. We shall provide a parametric example for which this smoothing of distortions is accomplished by having tax rates constant over time.

Example 7.1. Let U be given by

$$U(C,L) = \frac{C^{1-\alpha_1}}{1 - \alpha_1} - \alpha_3 \frac{L^{1-\alpha_2}}{1 - \alpha_2}.$$

Note that $\alpha_3 \geq 0$ and that from concavity we have $\alpha_1 \geq 0$ and $\alpha_2 \leq 0$. Given the additive separability of U, we can manipulate the first-order conditions (7.30) to get

$$(1 + \lambda_0)\tau_t + \lambda_0 \left[\frac{C_t U_{cc}}{U_c} - (1 - \tau_t) \frac{L_t U_{ll}}{U_l} \right] = 0,$$

where we have suppressed dependence on G_t and have let $\tau_t = 1 + U_l/U_c$. Substituting for the derivatives of U in this equation, we see that tax rates are constant over time and independent of the current level of government consumption. Furthermore, it is easy to show that the surplus under the Ramsey plan, $R(G_t)$, will be decreasing in G_t if $\alpha_1(1 - \alpha_1) \geq \alpha_2(1 - \alpha_2)$. We shall exploit this feature of the Ramsey plan in some later examples.

7.3.2. Debt and Default without Commitment

In an environment without commitment, we can no longer retain the fiction that all agents make decisions once and for all at the beginning of time and then simply execute those decisions at the appropriate time. Indeed, we need to ensure that these decisions are sequentially rational. In terms of the timing of decisions, we model the sequential decision making by assuming that governments in each period choose a policy at the beginning of the period and then consumers choose their consumption and labor supply decisions. As in Section 2, governments choose policies as a function of the aggregate history, which for this model consists of the past aggregate consumption, labor, and debt-holding decisions and the past policies. Thus an aggregate history confronting the government at time t is

$$H_t = (X_s, \pi_s | s = 0, \ldots, t - 1).$$

Consumers make their choices over consumption, labor, and their debt holdings at date t as functions of their individual histories. Such a history includes the policy choice π_t as well as the past individual decisions, past aggregate decisions, and past policy choices. The individual history is given by

$$h_{1t} = (x_s, X_s, \pi_s | s = 0, \ldots, t - 1) \cup \pi_t$$

and the aggregate history H_{1t} is given by

$$H_{1t} = (X_s, \pi_s | s = 0, \ldots, t - 1) \cup \pi_t.$$

In keeping with the representative agent model used, only symmetric histories are considered.

For this environment, a time-consistent equilibrium consists of an individual allocation rule f, an aggregate allocation rule F, a policy plan σ, and price systems p and q that satisfy certain sequential rationality conditions. An individual allocation rule is a sequence of functions $f = \{f_t\}_{t=0}^T$, where f_t maps each individual history h_{1t} into an agent's current choice of consumption and labor. Likewise, an aggregate allocation rule is a sequence of functions $F = \{F_t\}_{t=0}^T$, where F_t maps each aggregate history H_{1t} into an aggregate amount of consumption and labor. A policy plan σ is a sequence of functions $\sigma = \{\sigma_t\}_{t=0}^T$, where σ_t maps each history H_t into current taxes on labor and debt and new debt issues. Finally, price systems p and q are sequences of functions $p = \{p_t\}_{t=0}^T$ and $q = \{_t q\}_{t=0}^T$, where p_t maps each history H_{1t} into a price for the consumption good at t and where $_t q$ maps each history H_{1t} into a vector of debt prices $\{_t q_s\}_{s=t}^T$. Now just like the functions in Section 7.2, given any individual history h_{1t}, the contingency plans f^t, F^t, and σ^t induce future individual histories. For example, an agent's history at time $t + 1$ is

$$h_{1t+1} = \{h_{1t}, f_t(h_{1t}), F_t(H_{1t}), \sigma_t(H_t), \sigma_{t+1}(H_{1t}, F_t(H_{1t}))\}$$

and so on. In a similar fashion, given any aggregate history, the contingency plans F^t and σ^t induce future aggregate histories in the obvious way.

In a time-consistent equilibrium, sequential rationality by consumers is modeled by assuming that the policy plans, allocation rules, and price functions form a competitive equilibrium for each aggregate history. In this equilibrium each consumer is assumed to act competitively in that he assumes the evolution of policies and prices is not influenced by his actions. In particular, since future policies and prices are determined by aggregate histories, acting competitively implies that each consumer believes his actions have no effect on aggregate histories.

The problem of the consumer at time t, for some given functions F^t, σ^t, p^t and history h_{1t}, is to choose f^t to maximize

$$(7.31) \qquad \sum_{s=t}^{T} \beta^{s-t} U(c_s(h_{1s}), l_s(h_{1s}))$$

subject to the budget constraint

$$(7.32) \qquad \sum_{s=t}^{T} p_s(H_{1s})\{c_s(h_{1s}) - [1 - \tau_s(H_s)]l_s(h_{1s})\}$$
$$= [1 - \delta_t(H_t)] \sum_{s=t}^{T} {}_t q_s(H_t)_{t-1} B_s.$$

In such a competitive equilibrium, the allocation rule F^t must satisfy the sequence of constraints: for all $s \geq t$,

$$(7.33) \qquad p_s(H_{1s})\{C_s(H_{1s}) - [1 - \tau_s(H_s)]L_s(H_{1s})\} + \sum_{r=s+1}^{T} {}_s q_r(H_{1s})_s B_r(H_{1s})$$
$$= [1 - \delta_s(H_{1s})] \sum_{r=s}^{T} {}_s q_r(H_{1s})_{s-1} B_r(H_{1s-1}).$$

We then have

DEFINITION. A sequence of individual and aggregate allocation rules f^t and F^t, price functions p^t and q^t, and policy plans σ^t are sequentially rational for consumers at time t, given a history H_t, if it satisfies

   (i) *Consumer maximization.* Taking F^t, p^t, q^t, and σ^t as given, f^t solves the consumers' problem of maximizing (7.26) subject to (7.27).

   (ii) *Sequential constraints for aggregate allocations.* F^t satisfies (7.24) for all $s \geq t$.

(iii) *No arbitrage.* The price systems p^t and q^t satisfy

$$_sq_r(H_{1s}) = p_r(H_{1r})[1 - \delta_{s+1}(H_{s+1})] \ . \ . \ . \ [1 - \delta_r(H_r)]$$

and $_sq_s(H_{1s}) = p_s(H_{1s})$ for all r, s with $r \geq s \geq t + 1$.
(iv) *Representativeness.* $f^t = F^t$.

It is important to note that in this definition the future histories h_{1s}, H_{1s}, and H_s are induced by σ^t, f^t, and F^t. Since representativeness is part of the definition of sequential rationality, we summarize these functions by $(\sigma^t, F^t, p^t, q^t)$.

Next consider the problem of the government. At time t the government, faced with an aggregate history H_t, takes as given that the future aggregate allocations and prices evolve according to the functions F^t, p^t, and q^t. It is important to note that in contrast to individual consumers, the government can influence the future allocations and prices by affecting the aggregate history. The objective function of the government at t is given by the utility of the representative agent from t onward under F^t and σ^t; namely,

$$(7.34) \qquad S_t(\sigma^t, F^t; H_t) = \sum_{s=t}^{T} \beta^s U(C_s(H_{1s}), L_s(H_{1s})).$$

The government choice set at time t, given a history H_t, is the set of policy plans σ^t from t onward that satisfy the government budget constraints

$$(7.35) \qquad p_s(H_{1s})[\tau_s(H_s)L_s(H_s) - G_s] + \sum_{r=s+1}^{T} {}_sq_r(H_{1s})_sB_r(H_s)$$

$$= [1 - \delta_s(H_s)] \sum_{r=s}^{T} {}_sq_r(H_{1s})_{s-1}B_r(H_{s-1})$$

for all $s \geq t$, where the future histories are induced from H_t by σ^t and F^t. We denote this choice set by $\Sigma(F^t, p^t, q^t; H_t)$. We then have

DEFINITION. A time-consistent equilibrium is a (σ, F, p, q) that satisfies

(i) *Sequential rationality by consumers.* For every history H_{1t}, the sequence of functions $(\sigma^t, F^t, p^t, q^t)$ are sequentially rational for consumers.

(ii) *Sequential rationality by the government.* For every history H_t, the policy plan σ^t maximizes consumer welfare (7.34) over the set $\Sigma(F^t,p^t,q^t;H_t)$.

We can characterize the time-consistent equilibria of this model using a backward induction argument. Recall that for the capital taxation model of Section 7.2, we used such an argument to reduce the multiperiod time-consistent equilibrium to a sequence of static equilibria. The key to the reduction was that there were no state variables connecting the periods. In this model, government debt is such a state variable. This feature, together with the fact that government consumption fluctuates over time, implies that the time-consistent equilibrium does not reduce so simply. Rather, the backward induction argument can be used to show that the time-consistent equilibrium solves a constrained Ramsey problem in which debt issues are constrained to be nonpositive. Specifically, Chari and Kehoe (1987a) show that if debt of all maturities is allowed, the following proposition holds.

PROPOSITION 7.8. *The Time-Consistent Equilibrium for the Debt Model*
The allocations in the unique time-consistent equilibrium solve the constrained Ramsey problem: Choose $\{C_t,L_t\}_{t=0}^T$ to solve

$$\max \sum_{t=0}^T \beta^t U(C_t,L_t)$$

$$\text{s.t.} \quad C_t + G_t = L_t$$

$$\sum_{t=0}^T \beta^t [U_c C_t + U_l L_t] = 0$$

and for all $s = 0, 1, \ldots, T$,

(7.36) $$\sum_{s=t}^T \beta^s [U_c C_s + U_l L_s] \leq 0.$$

Notice that this problem is simply the Ramsey problem of Proposition 7.7 with the extra constraints (7.36). These constraints ensure that debt issues at each date are nonpositive.

The reason that the time-consistent equilibrium solves such a problem is fairly intuitive. Consider the last period T. If the government inherits positive debt, it clearly has an incentive to default in order to minimize the amount of revenue it must collect through a distortionary labor tax. However, if the government inherits negative debt, so that the government holds claims on private agents, it has no incentive to tax the debt. By induction it follows that for any period t, regardless of the history, the government will default on positive debt but not tax negative debt. From the no-arbitrage condition, it follows that if the government ever issues positive debt, it will have a zero price. Using this fact, the consumer's first-order conditions, and the government's sequence of budget constraints, we can recursively derive constraints (7.36).

We shall present some examples that illustrate the nature of the time-consistent equilibrium. For these we let the horizon be infinite. (As Chari and Kehoe, 1987a, showed, even with an infinite horizon, the solutions to the constrained Ramsey problem are sustainable outcomes.) In Example 7.2, the Ramsey allocations are time consistent.

Example 7.2. Let $T = \infty$. Let $G_t = 0$ for t even and $G_t = \gamma$ for t odd. Let $R(G_t)$ denote the surplus function for the Ramsey plan. Let U be like U in Example 7.1 (Section 7.3.1), so that $R(G_t)$ is decreasing. It immediately follows that under the Ramsey plan, the budget is balanced over each two-period cycle; thus,

$$R(0) + \beta R(\gamma) = 0.$$

Since $R(G_t)$ is decreasing, $R(0)$ is positive and $R(\gamma)$ is negative. For t even, $\sum_{r=t}^{\infty} \beta^r R(G_r) = 0$ and for t odd, $\sum_{r=t}^{\infty} \beta^r R(G_r) = R(\gamma) < 0$. Since the debt issues are negative, the Ramsey allocations solve the constrained Ramsey problem. Thus the Ramsey allocations are time consistent.

The next example is a slight variant of Example 7.2. In it there is a time-consistency problem; however, the value of a commitment technology is not very large.

Example 7.3. Let $T = \infty$. Let $G_t = \gamma$ for t even and $G_t = 0$ for t odd. Let U be like U in Example 7.1. Let $R(G_t)$ denote the surplus function for this pattern of government consumption. Again, under the Ramsey plan, the budget is balanced over each two-period cycle:

$$R(\gamma) + \beta R(0) = 0.$$

For t even, $\sum_{r=t}^{\infty} \beta^r R(G_r) = R(0) > 0$ and for t odd, $\sum_{r=t}^{\infty} \beta^r R(G_r) = 0$. Thus the Ramsey allocations do not solve the constrained Ramsey problem, so there is a time-consistency problem. We can compute an upper bound for the welfare loss due to the time-consistency problem as follows. Consider the policy of balancing the budget in period 0 and then following the constrained Ramsey allocations from date 1 on. From Example 7.2 we know that from date 1 on, this policy gives the Ramsey allocations of that example. The utility difference between this plan and the Ramsey plan is at most the utility lost from balancing the budget in the first period.

In Example 7.3, the value of a commitment technology is bounded above by the utility lost in a single period. Chari and Kehoe (1987a) examined the value of a commitment technology when government spending is stochastic. They measured this value by the expected utility difference between the Ramsey allocations and the constrained Ramsey allocations, where this difference is normalized by dividing by $\sum_{t=0}^{T} \beta^t$. This normalization converts the measure into a type of average discounted utility.

In the comparison of the Ramsey and the constrained Ramsey allocations, two assumptions are used. The first assumption is on the stochastic process for government consumption.

ASSUMPTION 7.1. Government consumption follows a stationary Markov process with strictly positive elements. Furthermore, it is persistent in that $\text{Prob}\{G_{t+1} \leq \gamma | G_t\}$ is a decreasing function of G_t for all γ.

Note that the persistence condition requires that higher values of government consumption at t give stochastically larger values of government consumption at $t + 1$.

The second assumption is on the surplus function $R(G_t)$ from the Ramsey plan.

ASSUMPTION 7.2. $R(G_t)$ is decreasing in G_t.

This assumption requires that the value of tax revenues is smoother than the value of government consumption. Recall that the parametric utility function of Example 7.1 satisfies this assumption. Chari and Kehoe (1987a) proved the following proposition.

PROPOSITION 7.9. *The Value of a Commitment Technology*
    Given Assumptions 7.1 and 7.2, for any $\varepsilon > 0$ there is some horizon length $T < \infty$ and some discount factor $\beta < 1$ such that the difference in the normalized value of utilities under the Ramsey and the constrained Ramsey allocations is at most ε.

This proposition implies that for an interesting class of economies, the value of a commitment technology (measured in units of normalized utility) is not very large.

To sum up, in this section we have shown (1) how the introduction of state variables complicates the computation of time-consistent equilibria, (2) that the presence of conflict among agents does not guarantee there is a time-consistency problem, and (3) that the value of a commitment technology may be quite small in the debt-default model.

7.4. Conclusions

There is a large and growing body of literature on the time-consistency problem and its implications for macroeconomic policy. In this chapter we have sought to provide a perspective on the issue of time consistency rather than to survey the literature. In our view, conflict among agents plays a central role in creating time-consistency problems. Because much of the literature has used representative agent models, the nature of this conflict has been obscured. We have shown how two representative agent models (of capital taxation and of debt and default) can be cast into a social choice theoretic framework in which the nature of this conflict among agents is made explicit. Optimal taxation models, where revenues are raised through distorting taxes, have the feature that each agent is better off by forcing others to bear a larger share of the burden of providing public goods. This conflict plays an essential role in establishing that the timing of policies matters for allocations.

We have also provided a careful definition of time-consistent equilibria for the capital taxation and debt and default models. Correctly defining a time-consistent equilibrium requires that we consider history-contingent allocation and price functions. These are essential to ensure that the forecasting problems of policymakers and agents are well defined. In particular, this way of defining an equilibrium ensures that we do not fall into the trap of thinking about policy as a sequence of "announcements" of future plans, each of which is fully believed by private agents. The problem with this approach to modeling sequential rationality can be understood by examining the debt and default model. In each period the government would default on the inherited debt and announce it will never do so again in the future. If private agents believe such announcements, they will buy the debt issued by the government and invariably be disappointed in the future. With this approach, therefore, no equilibrium can exist. With history-contingent functions we avoid such problems.

We should reemphasize that in no sense can societies *choose* between commitment or time-consistent equilibria. Commitment technologies are like technologies for making shoes in an Arrow-Debreu model—they are either available or not. In particular, commitment technologies are not objects of choice. This fact has important implications for the debate over rules versus discretion.

There is a temptation to view rules as describing policies chosen under commitment and discretion as describing policies chosen without commitment. Under our interpretation, society cannot choose between commitment and no commitment. Consequently, society cannot choose between rules and discretion. However, we think there are deeper issues in this debate. We have described policies here as being chosen by society, but actual policy choices must necessarily be delegated to specific institutions or individuals. Society's problem, then, is more than choosing from alternative policy rules; rather, the problem is designing the *process* by which policies are chosen. Formally, this is a problem in mechanism design. (See, for example, Hurwicz, 1973; Myerson, 1979; and Harris and Townsend, 1981.) From this perspective, the debate over rules versus discretion is actually a debate about how much authority should be delegated to policymakers. Research directed at integrating the issues of mechanism design into aggregative models is essential if we are to progress further in this debate.

Acknowledgments

The views expressed in this chapter are those of the authors and not necessarily those of the Federal Reserve Bank of Minneapolis or the Federal Reserve System.

Notes

1. For some further work using the model of Lucas and Stokey, see Alesina and Tabellini (1987); Persson and Svensson (1984); Persson, Persson, and Svensson (1987); and Rogers (1987).
2. In an interesting paper, Bulow and Rogoff (1988) have investigated the implications of allowing for negative debt in an open economy setting.

References

Abreu, D. 1984. Infinitely Repeated Games with Discounting: A General Theory. Discussion paper 1083, Harvard University.

Alesina, A., and G. Tabellini. 1987. A Positive Theory of Fiscal Deficits and Government Debt. Unpublished paper, Carnegie-Mellon University.

Barro, R. J. 1979. On the Determination of the Public Debt. *Journal of Political Economy* 87 (5, pt. 1): 940–971.

—— 1985. Recent Developments in the Theory of Rules versus Discretion. Working paper 12, University of Rochester.

Barro, R. J., and D. B. Gordon. 1983. Rules, Discretion, and Reputation in a Model of Monetary Policy. *Journal of Monetary Economics* 12(1): 101–121.

Bulow, J., and K. Rogoff. 1988. Sovereign Debt: Is to Forgive to Forget? Unpublished paper, Stanford University.

Calvo, G. A. 1978. On the Time Consistency of Optimal Policy in a Monetary Economy. *Econometrica* 46(6): 1411–28.

Chari, V. V., and P. J. Kehoe. 1987a. Sustainable Plans and Debt. Research Department working paper 354, Federal Reserve Bank of Minneapolis.

—— 1987b. Sustainable Plans. Research Department working paper 377, Federal Reserve Bank of Minneapolis.

Fischer, S. 1980. Dynamic Inconsistency, Cooperation, and the Benevolent Dissembling Government. *Journal of Economic Dynamics and Control* 2(1): 93–107.

Friedman, J. W. 1971. A Non-cooperative Equilibrium for Supergames. *Review of Economic Studies* 38(113): 1–12.

Fudenberg, D., and E. Maskin. 1986. The Folk Theorem for Repeated Games with Discounting or with Incomplete Information. *Econometrica* 54(3): 533–554.

Harris, M., and R. M. Townsend. 1981. Resource Allocation under Asymmetric Information. *Econometrica* 49(1): 33–64.

Hurwicz, L. 1973. The Design of Mechanisms for Resource Allocation. *American Economic Review* 63(2): 1–30.

Kydland, F. E., and E. C. Prescott. 1977. Rules Rather Than Discretion: The Inconsistency of Optimal Plans. *Journal of Political Economy* 85(3): 473–491.

Lucas, R. E., Jr., and N. L. Stokey. 1983. Optimal Fiscal and Monetary Policy in an Economy without Capital. *Journal of Monetary Economics* 12(1): 55–93.

Myerson, R. B. 1979. Incentive Compatibility and the Bargaining Problem. *Econometrica* 47(1): 61–73.

Persson, M., T. Persson, and L. E. O. Svensson. 1987. Time Consistency of Fiscal and Monetary Policy. *Econometrica* 55(6): 1419–31.

Persson, T., and L. E. O. Svensson. 1984. Time-Consistent Fiscal Policy and Government Cash-Flow. *Journal of Monetary Economics* 14(3): 365–374.

Prescott, E. C. 1977. Should Control Theory Be Used for Economic Stabilization? *In* K. Brunner and A. H. Meltzer (eds.), *Optimal Policies, Control Theory and Technology Exports*, Carnegie-Rochester Conference Series on Public Policy 7. Amsterdam: North-Holland, pp. 13–38.

Ramsey, F. P. 1927. A Contribution to the Theory of Taxation. *Economic Journal* 37: 47–61.

Rogers, C. A. 1987. Debt Restructuring with a Public Good. Unpublished paper, Georgetown University.

Rogoff, K. 1987. Reputational Constraints on Monetary Policy. *In* K. Brunner and A. H. Meltzer (eds.), *Bubbles and Other Essays*, Carnegie-Rochester Conference Series on Public Policy 26. Amsterdam: North-Holland, pp. 141–182. (A version of this paper appears in this volume.)

Strotz, R. H. 1955. Myopia and Inconsistency in Dynamic Utility Maximization. *Review of Economic Studies* 23: 165–180.

8   Some Alternative Monetary Models and Their Implications for the Role of Open-Market Policy

Neil Wallace

In this chapter I shall survey some alternative monetary models from the point of view of their implications for the effects of different open-market policies—that is, different portfolio strategies available to a government. The models examined share the feature that default-free securities with positive nominal interest and government money with zero nominal interest can coexist. In other words, there can be rate-of-return dominance of government money. The devices used for generating such rate-of-return dominance are not novel; they are money in the utility function, cash-in-advance constraints, and legal restrictions. I shall examine these devices in the context of two prototypical models: one with infinitely lived representative agents and the other with overlapping generations. Although these devices for generating rate-of-return dominance of government money have often been criticized, the models I shall survey continue to be used because they, and closely related models, seem to be the only ones available that are simple and coherent enough to permit economists to describe the welfare consequences of alternative open-market policies.

Before I summarize those welfare consequences, I must describe more precisely the class of policies studied. In models with rate-of-return dominance, different government portfolio strategies imply different streams of profits on the portfolio or, equivalently, different streams of government interest payments. That being so, a complete description of a policy requires a description of how these profits are used. I shall examine different portfolio strategies while holding constant real government consumption and real direct taxes and, hence, the real net-of-interest deficit.[1] Among this class of policies, the higher the earnings on the government's portfolio, the greater the rate of decrease in outstanding government liabilities and, therefore, through lower inflation, the higher the real return on government money.

I have focused on this class for three reasons. First, since policies in this class have been studied in only some of the models I shall survey, some common implications of all the models have not been emphasized. Second, since these policies do not call for adjusting direct taxation, their implementation requires only voluntary exchanges between the government and the public. Third, this class of policies allows the government, through its own lending, to arbitrage between its money and higher-yield assets and, by so doing, drive down the yield differential.[2] Such arbitrage is an obvious kind of policy to study in these models because it resembles what private agents or intermediaries would do on their own if the models allowed privately issued liabilities to play the role that the models assign to government money—that is, if the models allowed privately supplied liabilities to yield utility or allowed such liabilities to serve as cash in cash-in-advance models, or if they excluded legal restrictions.

I shall further limit policy by imposing two restrictions. First, I impose a nonnegative real net-of-interest deficit, which rules out deflation financed by direct taxation. Second, I assume a positive initial nominal stock of outside money and require that policies be consistent with a positive value of this stock; this is a way of requiring that the existing monetary system be maintained.

Although this is a volume on business cycles, I shall conduct the analysis entirely in terms of stationary and nonstochastic models and stationary policies because such an analysis is sufficient to highlight the main similarities and differences among the models. In particular, I shall not address questions concerning time consistency, a topic dealt with elsewhere in this volume.

In all the models I shall examine, a difference between the rate of return on nonmonetary assets and that on money is distorting. In the representative agent models, although utility of the agent is higher the lower this rate-of-return difference, my two restrictions do not allow the difference to be completely eliminated. For such models I shall show that policies with some government lending dominate a policy without such lending. In the overlapping-generations models, the results are similar but less straightforward for two reasons. First, in those models, policies in the class studied have distribution effects. Second, policy effects depend in part on whether or not the model allows steady-state equilibrium interest rates to be nonpositive.

For the class of policies studied here, the qualitative results do not seem to depend on the way rate-of-return dominance is produced in the different models. That should not, however, be taken to mean that how one accounts for rate-of-return dominance is in general unimportant. For other policy issues, the different models may have quite different implications. Also, the common conclusions concerning the effects of different government portfolios could conceivably be the result of a common flaw in the way all the models produce rate-of-return dominance. This matter will be discussed briefly in the conclusion.

8.1. Money, Bonds, and Steady-State Seigniorage

Many of the results reported below are directly traceable to the government's possibilities for earning revenue by manipulating its portfolio. I begin here by discussing such possibilities in terms of the government's cash flow constraint and some general features of the steady-state demands for two kinds of government-issued liabilities: money and bonds.

I write the government's cash flow constraint as

(8.1) $D = p_t(M_{t+1} - M_t) + p_t(S_t B_{t+1} - B_t),$

where

D = the constant per capita nonnegative real net-of-interest deficit

p_t = the price of a unit of money at t in terms of the single time t consumption good

M_t = the per capita stock of money at the beginning of date t

$M_{t+1} - M_t$ = the time t per capita addition to the stock

S_t = the price in terms of money of a bond (which is a default-free promise to one unit of money at $t + 1$)

$S_t^{-1} - 1$ = the time t nominal interest rate

B_t = the per capita face value in units of time t money of the bonds that mature at date t.

Throughout, I take D as given, let $t = 1$ be the initial date, and treat M_1 and B_1 as the given initial conditions that satisfy $M_1 + B_1 > 0$.

Suppose I let $m_t = p_t M_{t+1}$ and $b_t = p_t S_t B_{t+1}$ be the real per capita values of money and bonds, respectively, and let $r_t^m = p_{t+1}/p_t$ and $r_t = p_{t+1}/p_t S_t$ be the real returns on money and bonds. Then constant values of these variables for $t \geq 1$, denoted without subscripts, satisfy (8.1) for all $t \geq 1$ if and only if they satisfy

(8.2) $D = m + b - p_1(M_1 + B_1),$

(8.3) $D = (1 - r^m)m + (1 - r)b,$

where, for such constant sequences, (8.2) is equivalent to (8.1) for $t = 1$ and (8.3) is equivalent to (8.1) for $t \geq 2$. It follows that such constant values can be a monetary equilibrium only if they satisfy (8.3) and imply a positive value of p_1 by way of (8.2).

In the stationary (no growth) models discussed, a stationary equilibrium (one in which m_t, b_t, r_t, and r_t^m are constant) is Pareto optimal if and only if the returns satisfy

(8.4) $r^m = r \geq 1.$

In (8.4) the equality is the familiar condition that the yield on money be equal to the yield on other assets, and the inequality is the familiar condition that the rate of interest be at least as high as the growth rate.

One can quickly draw some conclusions about the possible consistency and inconsistency of (8.2)–(8.4) and $p_1 > 0$. The assumptions $D \geq 0$ and $M_1 + B_1 > 0$ and the requirement $p_1 > 0$ imply, by way of (8.2), that $m + b > D \geq 0$. These last inequalities and (8.3) are consistent with (8.4) only if $r = 1$. In the infinitely lived representative agent models, r exceeds one in a stationary equilibrium, so (as noted above) no policy in the class studied will permit (8.2)–(8.4) to be satisfied. Nevertheless, through sufficient government lending, $r - r^m$ can be made small. In some versions of overlapping-generations models, (8.2)–(8.4) are mutually consistent.

8.2. Prototype Infinitely Lived Representative Agent Models

For my purpose of extracting the implications of different monetary models for open-market operations, it is enough to use quite simple prototypes of the different models. Here I use what to me seem the simplest money-in-the-utility-function and cash-in-advance models that are consistent with equality between returns on money and returns on other assets being necessary for optimality.

8.2.1. *Money in the Utility Function*

Here I use a pure exchange (no production) economy in which the representative agent has preferences given by $\Sigma_{t=1}^{\infty}\beta^t u(c_t,m_t)$, where c_t is time t consumption of the model's single good, m_t is real balances held from t to $t + 1$, and $\beta \in (0,1)$. For u, I assume there is a satiation level of m_t, denoted m^*, such that for all (c_t,m_t), $u(c_t,m^*) \geq u(c_t,m_t)$. For $c_t > 0$ and $m_t \in (0,m^*]$, u is differentiable, increasing [except that $u_2(c_t,m^*) = 0$], strictly concave with $v(c_t,m_t) \equiv u_2(c_t,m_t)/u_1(c_t,m_t) \rightarrow \infty$ as $m_t \rightarrow 0$ for any fixed c_t and $v_2 < 0$. (The reader will be able to determine how the results noted below are affected if u is increasing in m_t for all m_t.) The agent is endowed with a constant amount of the consumption good, denoted w, at each date and enters date 1 with a positive nominal stock of money.

Throughout, I assume that behavior is competitive. Here the agent maximizes discounted utility by choice of sequences for c_t, m_t, and b_t (real loans at t to be repaid at $t + 1$) subject, for $t \geq 1$, to

$$(8.5) \qquad c_t + m_t + b_t \leq w + r_{t-1}^m m_{t-1} + r_{t-1}b_{t-1},$$

taking as given the right-hand side of (8.5) for $t = 1$ and taking as given positive and bounded sequences for r_t^m and r_t, which are the real gross returns on money and loans, respectively. In addition, to keep the constraint set compact, I restrict the choices of m_t and b_t to be from bounded sets; however, the sets can be chosen so that the bounds turn out to be nonbinding.

I define an equilibrium to be sequences for c_t, m_t, b_t, p_t, S_t, M_{t+1}, and B_{t+1}, for $t \geq 1$, that are appropriately bounded and nonnegative except for b_t and B_{t+1}, and such that the sequences for c_t, m_t, and b_t are utility maximizing for the agent, that (8.1) is satisfied, and that, for $t \geq 1$, the following market-clearing conditions hold: $c_t = w - D$, $m_t = p_t M_{t+1}$, and $b_t = p_t S_t B_{t+1}$. I can now describe some stationary equilibria and their dependence on the government's portfolio.

Subject to the bounds on m_t and b_t being nonbinding, the following standard first-order conditions are necessary and sufficient for a maximum solution to the agent's choice problem: condition (8.5) at equality and

$$(8.6) \qquad c_t: \quad \beta^t u_1(c_t,m_t) = \lambda_t,$$

$$(8.7) \qquad m_t: \quad \beta^t u_2(c_t,m_t) = \lambda_t - \lambda_{t+1}r_t^m,$$

$$(8.8) \qquad b_t: \quad 0 = -\lambda_t + \lambda_{t+1}r_t,$$

where λ_t is the positive multiplier associated with (8.5). Upon dividing (8.7) by (8.6) and using (8.8) to substitute for λ_t/λ_{t+1}, one sees that (8.6)–(8.8) imply

(8.9) $v(c_t, m_t) = 1 - r_t^m/r_t.$

It follows by construction that there is a stationary equilibrium corresponding to any constants $m > 0$, $r^m > 0$, and b that satisfy $v(w - D, m) = 1 - r^m/r$ [(8.9) with $c_t = w - D$], (8.3), $r = 1/\beta$, and $m + b > D$. The inequality is the condition for a positive initial value of money p_1, which is obtained from (8.2).

In general, if D is too big, then there will be no such equilibria. Therefore, I shall proceed by assuming that there is a stationary equilibrium for $b = 0$ and showing that a consequence is the existence of other, higher utility equilibria for some $b < 0$. Formally, I shall prove the following.

PROPOSITION 8.1. Assume there is a stationary monetary equilibrium with $b = 0$, and let $\theta = b/m$. Then there exists $a \in (0,1)$ such that there is a stationary equilibrium for any $\theta \in (-a,0]$. Moreover, the maximum equilibrium values of m and of utility are decreasing in θ on this interval.

Proof. I begin by rewriting (8.3) as

(8.10) $1 - \dfrac{r^m}{r} = \dfrac{r-1}{r} + \dfrac{D}{mr} + \left(\dfrac{r-1}{r}\right)\theta \equiv g(m,\theta,r),$

where $\theta \equiv b/m$. Then, m and b satisfy $v(w - D, m) = 1 - r^m/r$, (8.10), and $r = 1/\beta$ if and only if they satisfy

(8.11) $v(w - D, m) = g(m,\theta,1/\beta).$

I treat θ as a parameter and first consider solutions to (8.11) for $\theta \in (-1,0]$.

Figure 8.1 shows $v(w - D, m)$ for $m \in (0, m^*]$, the relevant interval. Since $g(m,0,1/\beta) > 0$, it follows that, if there is a solution to (8.11) with $\theta = 0$, then there is a largest one and it is less than m^*. Moreover, in the neighborhood of that solution, $g_1 > v_2$. Since $g_2 > 0$ and since $g(m,\theta,1/\beta) > 0$ for $\theta \in (-1,0]$, it follows that the existence of a solution for $\theta = 0$ implies the existence of a solution for all such θ's and that the maximum solution is decreasing in θ.

I now consider the subset of these maximum solutions that satisfy $m + b > D$. Figure 8.2 shows the maximum solution to (8.11) as a function of θ. The maximum solution for $\theta = 0$ is shown as exceeding D in accord

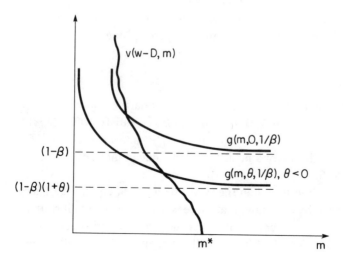

Figure 8.1   Solutions to Equation (8.11) for fixed θ.

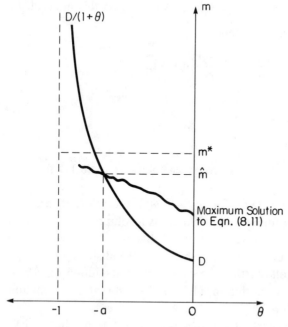

Figure 8.2   Solutions to Equation (8.11) and $m + b > D$.

with the hypothesis that there is a solution for $\theta = 0$. Figure 8.2 also shows the curve $m + b = D$, which is equivalent to $m = D/(1 + \theta)$. The region to the right and above this latter curve satisfies the inequality $m + b > D$. It follows that the interval $(-a,0]$ is as shown in Figure 8.2.

Note that since utility is increasing in m for all solutions to (8.11), utility corresponding to $(c_t,m_t) = (w - D,\hat{m})$ is the least upper bound on utility consistent with stationary equilibria under our policies. Moreover, there are stationary equilibria that get arbitrarily close to this upper bound. By Equation (8.2), arbitrary closeness to $\hat{m}$ implies an initial value of money p_1 that is arbitrarily close to zero.   ◊

With equilibria indexed by θ, there seems to be a possibility of multiple solutions to (8.11) for a given θ. However, it is easy to avoid this. Policy can be described directly in terms of a magnitude of $1 - r^m/r = 1 - S$, where S is a constant value of S_t. In other words, the policy that uniquely determines a given equilibrium m can be expressed by a choice of a nominal interest rate: the government simply announces a willingness to lend (and borrow) at a given nominal interest rate. Expressing policy this way does not, of course, get around the fact that there is no best policy. In particular, if $D = 0$, then utility is increasing in S for $S \in (\beta,1)$, but a monetary stationary equilibrium does not exist for $S = 1$ (a zero nominal interest rate).

8.2.2. Cash-in-Advance Constraints

Here I shall use a model in which the representative agent again maximizes discounted instantaneous utility. Now, however, instantaneous utility depends on consumption of a (purchased) good, denoted c_t at time t, and on leisure, denoted $w - y_t$ at t, where w is the agent's constant endowment of labor measured in units of potential production and y_t is time t production. Thus, the agent has preferences given by $\sum_{t=1}^{\infty} \beta^t u(c_t,w - y_t)$, where $\beta \in (0,1)$; where u is increasing, strictly concave, and twice differentiable; and where $v(x_1,x_2) \equiv u_2(x_1,x_2)/u_1(x_1,x_2)$ and is increasing in x_1 and decreasing in x_2 and satisfies $v(x_1,x_2) \to 0$ as $x_1 \to 0$ for any fixed $x_2 > 0$ and $v(x_1,x_2) \to \infty$ as $x_2 \to 0$ for any fixed $x_1 > 0$.

The model's cash-in-advance feature is that the agent cannot use the proceeds from selling production at date t to finance purchases of the consumption good at date t. Instead, following Helpman (1981) and Lucas (1982), I assume that the agent faces three constraints:

$$(8.12) \qquad \tilde{m}_t + b_t \leq r^m_{t-1}m_{t-1} + r_{t-1}b_{t-1},$$

$$(8.13) \qquad c_t \leq \tilde{m}_t,$$

$$(8.14) \qquad m_t \leq y_t + (\tilde{m}_t - c_t).$$

The first of these inequalities is the constraint in a money-securities market that occurs at the start of each date. (Note that $\tilde{m}_t$ denotes the value of money held at the close of the money-securities market.) After the market's close, shopping for the consumption good is undertaken subject to (8.13), and the selling of production and accumulation of money carried into period $t + 1$, denoted m_t, is undertaken subject to (8.14). Implicit in (8.14) is the symmetry condition that the price faced while shopping is the same as that faced while selling. To keep the constraint set compact, I again assume that the agent faces sequences of positive and bounded returns and is constrained to choose $\tilde{m}_t$, b_t, and m_t sequences that are bounded.

A symmetric equilibrium for this model consists of sequences for c_t, y_t, $\tilde{m}_t$, m_t, b_t, p_t, S_t, M_{t+1}, and B_{t+1}, for $t \geq 1$, that are appropriately bounded and that, except for b_t and B_{t+1}, are nonnegative and are such that c_t, y_t, $\tilde{m}_t$, m_t, and b_t are utility maximizing subject to (8.12)–(8.14), that (8.1) holds, and that the following market-clearing conditions hold: $c_t = y_t - D$, $m_t = p_t M_{t+1}$, and $b_t = p_t S_t B_{t+1}$. As before, I shall describe some stationary equilibria and their dependence on the government's portfolio.

Subject to the bounds on quantity choices being nonbinding, the following first-order conditions are necessary and sufficient for a maximum solution to the agent's problem: constraints (8.12)–(8.14) and

$$(8.15) \qquad c_t: \quad \beta^t u_1(c_t, w - y_t) = \lambda_{2t} + \lambda_{3t},$$

$$(8.16) \qquad y_t: \quad \beta^t u_2(c_t, w - y_t) = \lambda_{3t},$$

$$(8.17) \qquad b_t: \quad -\lambda_{1t} + r_t \lambda_{1,t+1},$$

$$(8.18) \qquad \tilde{m}_t: \quad -\lambda_{1t} + \lambda_{2t} + \lambda_{3t} = 0,$$

$$(8.19) \qquad m_t: \quad r^m_t \lambda_{1,t+1} - \lambda_{3t} = 0,$$

where λ_{1t}, λ_{2t}, and λ_{3t} are nonnegative multipliers associated with (8.12), (8.13), and (8.14), respectively. Upon eliminating the multipliers in (8.15)–(8.19), I obtain

(8.20) $\qquad v(c_t, w - y_t) = r_t^m/r_t.$

Here again, by construction, there is a stationary equilibrium in which (8.12)–(8.14) hold at equality corresponding to any constants $r^m > 0$ and $m = y > 0$ that satisfy $v(y - D, w - y) = r^m/r < 1$ [the equality being (8.20) with $c_t = y - D$], (8.3), $r = 1/\beta$, and $m + b > D$.

To avoid making additional assumptions about v, I again assume the existence of a stationary equilibrium for $b = 0$ and prove that a consequence is the existence of other stationary equilibria for $b < 0$. In fact, the wording of Proposition 8.2 is identical to that of Proposition 8.1.

PROPOSITION 8.2. Assume there is a stationary equilibrium with $b = 0$, and let $\theta = b/m$. Then there exists $a \in (0,1)$ such that there is a stationary equilibria for any $\theta \in (-a,0)$. Moreover, the maximum equilibrium values of m and of utility are decreasing in θ on this interval.

Proof. It is immediate that $y = m$, $r = 1/\beta$, (8.3), and $v(y - D, w - y) = r^m/r$ are satisfied for a given θ if and only if m satisfies

(8.21) $\qquad v(m - D, w - m) = 1 - g(m,\theta,1/\beta)$

$\qquad\qquad\qquad\qquad\quad = 1 - \beta D/m - (1 + \theta)(1 - \beta).$

Since $g(m,\theta,1/\beta) > 0$ for any $\theta > -1$ (or $m + b > 0$), any solution of (8.21) consistent with $m + b > D$ implies $r^m/r < 1$. Therefore, I can proceed essentially as I did for the money-in-the-utility-function model, by analyzing maximum solutions to (8.21) for m that also satisfy $m + b > D$.

Figure 8.3 depicts the left- and right-hand sides of (8.21). Since $1 - g(m, \theta, 1/\beta)$ is decreasing in θ, the existence of a solution with $m > 0$ for $\theta = 0$ implies that there is at least one solution to (8.21) for any $\theta \in (-1,0)$.[3] It also follows that the maximum solution is larger the smaller θ is.

These results imply that Figure 8.2 is applicable to this model, except that m^* must now be interpreted as the solution to $v(m^* - D, w - m^*) = 1$ and the curve labeled "maximum solution to (8.11)" must be relabeled "maximum solution to (8.21)." This reinterpretation shows that there are solutions to (8.21) and $m + b > D$ for any $\theta \in (-a,0)$ for some $a \in (0,1]$.

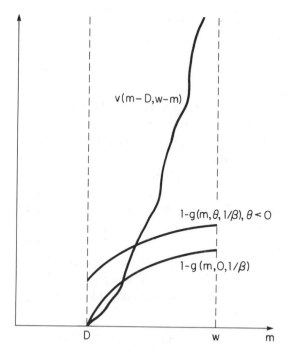

$v(m-D,w-m)$

$1-g(m,\theta,1/\beta), \theta<0$

$1-g(m,0,1/\beta)$

D   w   m

Figure 8.3   Solutions to Equation (8.21) for fixed θ.

Moreover, since the maximum solution to (8.21) is decreasing in θ on this interval and since $u(m-D,w-m)$ is increasing in m for $m \in (0,m^*]$, it immediately follows that utility corresponding to the maximum solution to (8.21) is decreasing in θ. (As in the money-in-the-utility-function model, this maximum solution can be achieved by stating policy in terms of a nominal interest rate.)   ◊

Thus, in both the money-in-the-utility-function model and the cash-in-advance model, more government lending gives rise to a lower inflation rate (a higher real return on money) and a higher initial price level. In these models, the initial price level is irrelevant to anyone's welfare, whereas the higher real return on money improves welfare.

8.3. Overlapping-Generations Models

Overlapping-generations models without bequest motives allow for a richer set of possible outcomes than the representative agent models, because in the overlapping-generations models different policies generally give rise to distribution effects, at least across generations. One consequence is that even in very simple, pure exchange versions of such models, steady-state real interest rates can depend on the government's portfolio. Moreover, as is well known, in some versions real interest rates can be negative. I shall review some simple versions in which rate-of-return dominance is produced by money in the utility function, by cash-in-advance constraints, and by legal restrictions.

8.3.1. Money in the Utility Function

Consider a stationary, pure exchange, one-good-per-date, overlapping-generations model defined over dates $t \geq 1$ in which agents live for two periods. Each two-period-lived agent has preferences given by $U(c_1,c_2,m) = u(c_1,c_2) + v(m)$, where c_i is consumption in the ith period of life and m is real money holdings carried from the first period of life into the second. (The assumption that U is additively separable in this way simplifies the analysis.) I assume that u is differentiable, increasing, and strictly quasi-concave with both c_1 and c_2 being normal goods; that v is differentiable; and that there exists $m^* > 0$ such that $v(m^*) \geq v(m)$ for all m and $v'(m) > 0$ for $m \in [0,m^*)$. Each such agent is endowed with $w_i > 0$ units of the consumption good at the ith period of life. At $t = 1$, each agent who is in the second period of life is endowed with w_2 units of the date-1 good and with $M_1 > 0$ units of money and wants to maximize consumption of the date-1 good.

For any $t \geq 1$, a two-period-lived agent can be viewed as choosing (c_1,c_2,m,b), where b is real lending, to maximize U subject to

(8.22) $c_1 + m + b \leq w_1,$

(8.23) $c_2 \leq w_2 + r_t^m m + r_t b,$

and to nonnegativity constraints, except on b. Since b is unconstrained, this pair of constraints is equivalent in the way it constrains the arguments of U to the following single constraint,

(8.24) $c_1 + c_2/r_t \leq w_1 + w_2/r_t - m(1 - r_t^m/r_t).$

The following first-order conditions and (8.24) at equality are necessary and sufficient for maximization of U, subject to (8.24):

(8.25) c_1: $u_1(c_1,c_2) = \lambda_t,$

(8.26) c_2: $u_2(c_1,c_2) = \lambda_t/r_t,$

(8.27) m: $v'(m) = \lambda_t(1 - r_t^m/r_t),$

where λ_t is the nonnegative multiplier associated with (8.24).

As before, I shall discuss how stationary equilibria depend on the government's portfolio. Here, however, I shall consider only $D = 0$ and demonstrate only that there are equilibria in which money balances are close to the satiation level m^*. Note that with $D = 0$, a stationary equilibrium consists of scalars (c_1,c_2), r, r^m, m, b, and p_1 (all positive except for b) such that (c_1,c_2,m) maximizes U subject to (8.24); such that (8.1) holds; and such that $c_1 + c_2 = w_1 + w_2$. The following proposition considers two cases: (a) the negative real interest case and (b) the nonnegative real interest case.

PROPOSITION 8.3. Let $D = 0$. Case (a): If $u_1(w_1,w_2)/u_2(w_1,w_2) < 1$, then there is an equilibrium with $m_t = m^*$ for all t. Case (b): If $u_1(w_1,w_2)/u_2(w_1,w_2) \geq 1$, then there are equilibria with $m_t = m < m^*$ and m arbitrarily close to m^*.

Proof. For this model, the requirement that the equilibrium be monetary, $m + b > 0$, is by (8.22), equivalent to $c_1 < w_1$. This requirement and market clearing, $c_1 + c_2 = w_1 + w_2$, imply that any monetary stationary equilibrium is on the slope -1 line and is northwest of the endowment, as depicted in Figure 8.4.

Case (a). There is an equilibrium with $r = r^m = 1$ and $(c_1,c_2,m) = (c_1^*,c_2^*,m^*)$, where (c_1^*,c_2^*) is the unique solution to $u_1(c_1,c_2)/u_2(c_1,c_2) = 1$ and $c_1 + c_2 = w_1 + w_2$. The corresponding b is chosen to satisfy (8.22) at equality. It follows then that (8.25)–(8.27) hold, that (8.23) holds at equality, and, by summing (8.22) and (8.23), that (8.3) holds. The initial value of money is obtained from (8.2).

Case (b). Let $(\bar{c}_1,\bar{c}_2)$ satisfy $\bar{c}_1 < w_1$ and $\bar{c}_1 + \bar{c}_2 = w_1 + w_2$. Then, by assumption, $\bar{r} = u_1(\bar{c}_1,\bar{c}_2)/u_2(\bar{c}_1,\bar{c}_2) > 1$, a condition that implies that $\bar{c}_1 + \bar{c}_2/\bar{r} < \bar{w}_1 + \bar{w}_2/\bar{r}$. I can now show that if $\bar{c}_1$ is sufficiently close to w_1, then for $(c_1,c_2,r) = (\bar{c}_1,\bar{c}_2,\bar{r})$, there are corresponding constant values of m_t and r_t^m that satisfy (8.24) at equality and (8.27) and that these are an

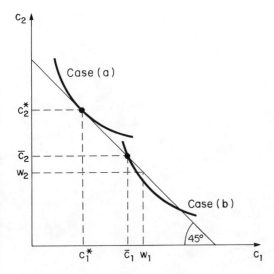

Figure 8.4 Possible consumption preferences for an overlapping-generations model.

equilibrium. I proceed using Figure 8.5 and letting $x_t = (1 - r_t^m/\bar{r})$. For fixed $(\bar{c}_1, \bar{c}_2, \bar{r})$, the locus of pairs (x_t, m_t) satisfying $m_t > 0$ and (8.24) at equality is a rectangular hyperbola that approaches the axes as $\bar{c}_1 \rightarrow w_1$. The locus of pairs satisfying (8.27) [and (8.25)] is shown in Figure 8.5. Therefore, as $\bar{c}_1 \rightarrow w_1$, the loci intersect at an $m_t \rightarrow m^*$. Given m_t and x_t, b is chosen to satisfy (8.22) at equality. As in Case (a), it follows that (8.23) holds at equality. Then (8.22) and (8.23) imply that (8.3) holds. ◇

The argument used in Case (b) could be used to show that any $(\bar{c}_1, \bar{c}_2)$ satisfying $\bar{c}_1 + \bar{c}_2 = w_1 + w_2$, $\bar{c}_1 < w_1$, and $u_1(\bar{c}_1, \bar{c}_2)/u_2(\bar{c}_1, \bar{c}_2) \equiv \bar{r} > 1$ can be supported as an equilibrium, provided that the locus determined by $v'(m_t) = \lambda x_t$ is somewhere above the locus determined by $m_t x_t = (w_1 - \bar{c}_1) + (w_2 - \bar{c}_2)/\bar{r}$. Such a qualification did not arise in my discussion of the representative agent model with money in the utility function, because there I simply assumed that an equilibrium with $b = 0$ exists and then showed that there were equilibria with $b < 0$. That kind of argument would apply here if u were assumed to be such that $u_1(c_1, w_1 + w_2 - c_1)$ is decreasing in c_1.

Policies in this model are able to affect the real rate of interest because the equilibrium consumption allocation is not fixed by the given endow-

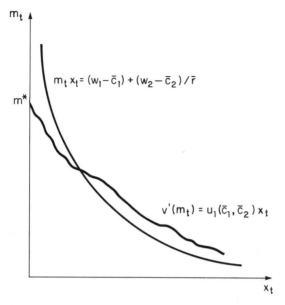

Figure 8.5   Solution to Equations (8.24)–(8.27).

ment. The presence of young and old at each date allows for distribution effects. These effects, in turn, produce noncomparability among all the equilibria that produce nonnegative real interest rates. In particular, although the lifetime utility of each two-period-lived agent is increasing for moves southeast along the line $c_1 + c_2 = w_1 + w_2$ (in Figure 8.4) toward (c_1^*, c_2^*) in Case (a) or toward (w_1, w_2) in Case (b), the consumption of the time-1 good by the initial old person is decreasing. This reduced consumption is brought about by a lower value of the initial money stock, a lower value that in this model affects an agent's utility.

8.3.2. Cash-in-Advance Constraints

Woodford (1987) presented an overlapping-generations, cash-in-advance model with many identical three-period-lived agents per generation. Each agent has preferences given by $u(w - y, c_1, c_2, c_3)$, where c_i is consumption of a (purchased) good in the ith period of life, w is an endowment of leisure in the first period of life, and y is output of a produced good, which the individual does not consume, in the first period. There are no intertemporal technologies. For my purpose, it is enough to suppose that u is increasing and strictly quasi-concave.

The cash-in-advance aspect of the model is the same as that in the representative agent, cash-in-advance model described in Section 8.2.2. In particular, at each date, trade proceeds subject to (8.12)–(8.14). That is, first there is a market in which money and loans are traded subject to (8.12). Then shopping for the consumption good occurs subject to (8.13), and sales of the produced good and acquisition of money for the next period occurs subject to (8.14). Although the young, middle-aged, and old are subject to these constraints at each date, the endowment and age patterns of the participants imply somewhat special patterns of demands.

For the young, the right-hand side of (8.12) is zero. Therefore, because of (8.13), they must incur debts or borrow at least enough to finance their desired consumption when young. The old cannot borrow and do not want to lend. Thus, any borrowing by the young must be matched by lending by the middle-aged or the government.

I again impose $D = 0$ and mainly discuss the role of government lending in supporting the allocation that maximizes sustainable lifetime utility and the consequences for steady states of alternative policies. Here, however, it must be remembered that steady states are not equilibria except for certain initial conditions. In particular, if this economy is defined over dates $t \geq 1$, a specific steady state is an equilibrium only for a specific corresponding initial distribution of wealth among the people who are middle-aged and old at $t = 1$ and, in the case of nonseparable utility, a particular realized (y, c_1) for the middle-aged.

Let $(y_1^*, c_1^*, c_2^*, c_3^*) = z^*$ be the solution to the following problem: maximize u subject to $y = c_1 + c_2 + c_3$, for $y \in [0, w]$ and $c_i \geq 0$. Also, let M be the nominal stock of outside money—that is, the stock that would exist if there were no government borrowing and lending—and let p^* be such that $p^* M = c_2^* + 2c_3^*$. If the government stands ready to borrow and lend at a zero nominal interest rate, then it is easy to see that $p_t = p^*$, $r_t = 1$, and z^* is a steady state for the model. At nominal and real interest rates of zero, the market constraints facing a young person—(8.12)–(8.14) at each period of life—are equivalent to $y \geq c_1 + c_2 + c_3$. Therefore, z^* is a utility-maximizing choice. If repeated date after date, such a choice also clears the goods market. It turns out that there are many individual portfolios that support z^* and are market clearing. One of these is to have each young person borrow c_1^*/p^* units of money from the government (repaying when middle-aged) and to have each middle-aged person neither borrow nor lend. Another possibility is to have each young person borrow c_3^*/p^* from a middle-aged person and borrow $(c_1^* - c_3^*)/p^*$ from the government. More generally, the amount of government lending can be anything greater than or equal to this last quantity.

If the government does not lend and if $c_1^* < c_3^*$, then, as just explained, $p_t = p^*$, $r_t = 1$, and z^* is a steady state. If $c_1^* > c_3^*$, then $p_t = p^*$ and $r_t = 1$ cannot be a steady state if there is no government lending. Faced with such returns, desired lending by a middle-aged person is no greater than c_3^*/p^*, while desired borrowing by a young person is no less than c_1^*/p^*. If a steady state is to exist under these circumstances, it must have a constant value of money ($r_t^m = 1$) and a constant $r_t > 1$, implying a positive nominal interest rate. With $r_t^m = 1$, the higher is r_t, the more expensive is c_1 in terms of leisure and the cheaper is c_3 in terms of leisure; the terms of trade between c_2 and leisure are determined by r_t^m. In particular, like the agents in the representative agent, cash-in-advance model, at any positive nominal interest rate, agents see themselves as able to trade a unit of leisure for less than a unit of current consumption.

Since any steady state satisfies $y = c_1 + c_2 + c_3$, the lifetime utility implied by any steady state different from z^* is less than that of z^*. This conclusion is analogous to the result I found in the overlapping-generations model with money in the utility function. There, however, each steady state was a stationary equilibrium for the same arbitrary initial condition, a result that allowed us to conclude that steady states with nonnegative real interest rates are noncomparable equilibria. Here, the analogous result would be that starting from a given initial condition, different policies give rise to noncomparable equilibria. I suspect this is the case for policies that give rise to equilibria that converge to steady states with nonnegative nominal and real interest rates.

Finally, the Woodford model can easily be converted to one with implications similar to those of the nonnegative interest rate version of the overlapping-generations model with money in the utility function. If the middle-aged, in addition to the young, are endowed with productive leisure, then the model can be a naturally nonnegative real interest rate economy. In such a version, a zero nominal interest rate could not be achieved by government lending. In this regard, such a version would resemble the representative agent, cash-in-advance model.

8.3.3. Legal Restrictions

In several papers, the overlapping-generations intertemporal framework has been combined with a legal-restrictions explanation of money dominated in rate of return. (See, for example, Wallace, 1983.) It turns out that for a given set of legal restrictions consistent with rate-of-return dominance, legal-restrictions models have implications for the role of different government portfolios that are similar to the implications of models relying on natural explanations for rate-of-return dominance. I shall discuss this similarity by comparing the implications of two models that use the legal-restrictions explanation with the implications of the money-in-the-utility-function and cash-in-advance overlapping-generations models previously described.

Bryant and Wallace (1984) described a model basically like the money-in-the-utility-function, overlapping-generations model in Section 8.3.1, except that money is not an argument of the utility function. In their model, the legal restriction is that members of a single generation, assumed to be identical, cannot intermediate among themselves and, as a result, cannot share large-denomination bonds issued by the government. Since they cannot intermediate, arbitrage does not rule out the possible coexistence of money with zero nominal interest and bonds with positive interest.

Bryant and Wallace showed that if a positive deficit can be financed with zero government borrowing, $b_t = 0$, then there are Pareto-superior stationary equilibria that involve the issue of bonds. The bonds, as just noted, are large-denomination securities whose presence along with divisible money implies that savers face a nonconstant return schedule on savings, that is, a schedule increasing in the amount saved. This feature allows schemes with bonds to dominate the solutions with money financing alone. Such Pareto-superior equilibria have yields on bonds that are negative but higher than the yield on money. The equilibria are Pareto superior in that they give higher utility to each two-period-lived person and also give more consumption to the initial old by way of a higher value of initial money holdings. The higher value comes about through higher equilibrium values of $m + b$ in (8.2).

I suspect that the same kind of result can show up in versions of the money-in-the-utility-function and cash-in-advance overlapping-generations models. In the money-in-the-utility-function model, a comparable situation would be one in which for a positive net-of-interest deficit and no government borrowing, there is an equilibrium with a negative real interest rate. Then there will be stationary equilibria with some government borrowing and with both higher utility and additional savings by each two-period-lived person. The additional savings imply additional consumption by the initial old. Matters are less clear-cut in Woodford's model because steady states are not equilibria for given initial conditions. However, with a positive net-of-interest deficit and without government borrowing, Woodford's model can have steady states with a negative real interest rate on securities. It would then seem that there are other steady states with some government borrowing that give higher utility to each three-period-lived person. The crucial common feature at work is that some bonds can be sold at a negative real interest rate.

Sargent and Wallace (1982) looked at a somewhat different legal restriction in a model with a special kind of within-generation diversity. They assumed that the legal restriction prevents private borrowers from issuing claims in a small size—a kind of denomination restriction—and that there is a group of poor savers who are thereby restricted to holding government-issued money. There are also other savers who are not constrained by the restriction. These others, along with private borrowers, interact in a private credit market that, for some parameters and some policies, gives rise to a positive nominal interest rate in a credit market completely separate from the market for government-issued money.

In a stationary version of the Sargent-Wallace model (the original version had a periodic endowment for borrowers), it is easy to show that different equilibria with differing real returns on both money and bonds can be generated by policies in the class I have been examining.[4] Government lending tends to reduce the real interest rate in the credit market and to increase the real return on money. These effects are accompanied by the obvious distribution effects on market participants; the greater the amount of government lending, the better off are borrowers and money-holders and the worse off are lenders in the credit market. As in the other overlapping-generations models, whether a policy in this class can eliminate the difference in returns in the two markets depends on whether the economy is or is not a nonnegative interest rate economy.

The effects of different policies that show up in the Sargent-Wallace model would also appear in versions of money-in-the-utility-function and cash-in-advance overlapping-generations models with diversity, so that some people end up borrowing and some lending at most interest rates.

Thus, in the Sargent-Wallace model the important role of the government's portfolio should not be attributed to the model's legal-restriction feature. Instead, it should be attributed to the presence of diversity, which allows for a rich set of distribution effects.

8.4. Concluding Remarks

Now that I have examined a small set of models from the perspective of their implications for policies in a particular class, I would like to review the policies examined and comment on the models.

Examining alternative government portfolios while holding the real net-of-interest deficit constant is one way to discuss the role of monetary policy while holding fiscal policy constant. An alternative that is, perhaps, more standard involves holding constant the real gross-of-interest deficit. According to that alternative, any change in the government's portfolio is accompanied by a change in direct taxes that offsets the implied change in the flow of government interest payments. If lump-sum taxes can be levied, then that kind of experiment is a very simple one. In fact, then open-market operations are irrelevant in the models examined here, in the sense that, given an equilibrium with some government borrowing or lending, there is another equilibrium with no government borrowing or lending and a different stream of lump-sum taxes that leaves unchanged all the variables affecting welfare. If, however, lump-sum taxes are not permitted, then such an experiment is not simple. But the simplicity of holding the net-of-interest deficit constant should also be qualified. If there are direct taxes being held fixed in the background, then it would seem that those taxes can only be lump-sum taxes; if there were other taxes, their effects and the revenue they raise would depend on the government's portfolio. Subject to that qualification, the class of policies examined amounts to one way of isolating the role of the government's portfolio. In general, it is not possible to study monetary policy (in the sense of open-market operations) in isolation from fiscal policy.

The models examined share two features that make them convenient for the analysis of open-market policies: money and bonds are distinct assets and there is a centralized market in which money and bonds are traded. Obviously, in models in which money and bonds are not distinct assets, open-market operations do not matter at all. And, no less obviously, in models without a centralized market in money and bonds, open-market operations cannot be conducted. Although one seems to "see" both features—that money and bonds are distinct and that markets exist in which they are traded—there are reasons to be skeptical about the coincidence of these features in the models examined here.[5]

A long-standing point of view in monetary theory is that the role of "money" is to be understood in the context of settings in which trade or exchange is difficult to accomplish. Such difficulty is implicit in the notion of an absence of double coincidence of wants—a notion that presumes something like pairwise, isolated meetings rather than centralized markets. Consistent with that point of view is the useful concept of a spectrum of alternative models or environments, ranging from ones in which exchange is very difficult to accomplish (for example, Harris, 1979) to ones in which exchange is accomplished so easily that money and bonds cannot be distinct assets (for example, Wallace, 1981).

There should be skepticism about money-in-the-utility-function and cash-in-advance models because they seem to adopt some features from environments where exchange is difficult—for example, the distinct role of "money"—and some features from environments in which exchange is easy to carry out—for example, the centralized market in "money" and bonds. The few explicit attempts to study models in which exchange is difficult to accomplish (Harris, 1979; Townsend, 1980; Freeman, 1985) do not display both features.

The legal-restrictions theory is in part inspired by such findings and by the related failure of the money-in-the-utility-function and cash-in-advance models to address the following kinds of questions: Is the "money" in the money-in-the-utility-function model necessarily a government-supplied object, or could it instead be a privately issued object? In a cash-in-advance model, what prevents private arrangements in the money-securities market from supplanting the need for government-issued money? These questions are pertinent because when those models give rise to a positive nominal interest rate, there seem to be profits to be made by private intermediation that takes the form of lending in the money-securities market and borrowing by issuing claims that compete with the zero-interest government currency in the models. The legal-restrictions theory takes the extreme view that such privately supplied claims could compete perfectly with government-supplied money. There is skepticism about this theory because it asserts that the relevant model is the extreme one in which exchange is accomplished so easily that money and bonds cannot be distinct, except insofar as explicit legal restrictions interfere.

All such skepticism aside, the implications for open-market operations of the models examined here follow from the fact that in all of them the government has a monopoly on money. Subject to two qualifications, all of the models say that the government should supply that money cheaply by lending it at a low nominal interest rate. By doing so it is able, in effect, to replace outside money that does not bear interest by inside money that does. One qualification concerns the net-of-interest deficit. If there is such a deficit, then the requirement that it be financed limits the extent to which the replacement can be accomplished, because the deficit requires outside money to be taxed. The other qualification concerns distribution effects, discussed earlier.

Finally, regarding the potential cyclical role of monetary policy, I have shown that variations in the government's portfolio while holding the net-of-interest deficit constant affect real rates of returns. Thus, there is scope for different deterministic policies in that class to have cyclical effects. That scope is limited in the prototypical models examined because, for the most part, those were pure exchange models. Given that real returns can be affected in such models, however, it is obvious that production will respond to such policies in more general models. (Such a response is present in the cash-in-advance model.) Thus these models provide no basis for taking as a kind of benchmark the conclusion that alternative deterministic monetary policies are neutral.

Acknowledgments

I am indebted to colleagues at the University of Minnesota and the Federal Reserve Bank of Minneapolis and to graduate students at the University of Minnesota for helpful comments on an earlier draft. I am also indebted to the Federal Reserve Bank of Minneapolis for financial support. The views expressed in this chapter are my own and not necessarily those of the Federal Reserve Bank of Minneapolis or the Federal Reserve System.

Notes

1. For a discussion of some consequences of alternative specifications, see Waldo (1985).
2. This class includes policies in which the government attempts to finance interest on money through earnings on its portfolio. See Friedman (1960) and Sargent and Wallace (1985).
3. Notice that the only role of the hypothesis of Proposition 8.2 (existence for $b = 0$) is to assure that the function $1 - g(m,0,1/\beta) > v(m - D, w - m)$ for

some $m > D$. Since at $m = D$, $1 - g(m,0,1/\beta) = 0$ and has a negative second derivative with respect to m (as shown in Figure 8.3), that hypothesis could be replaced by assumptions about the shape of v in the neighborhood of $v(0,w - D)$—for example, by the assumption that $v'' > 0$.

4. The original version can be used to study a policy (within the class of those studied here) in which the central bank eliminates a deterministic fluctuation in the nominal interest rate (a seasonal fluctuation) and earns zero, averaged over time, on its portfolio.

5. Not everyone assumes the existence of a centralized market in which money and bonds are traded. One often comes across the comment that in some countries, open-market operations cannot be conducted because there is no such centralized market.

References

Bryant, J., and N. Wallace. 1984. A Price Discrimination Analysis of Monetary Policy. *Review of Economic Studies* 51(2): 279–288.

Freeman, S. 1985. Transactions Costs and the Optimal Quantity of Money. *Journal of Political Economy* 93(1): 146–157.

Friedman, M. 1960. *A Program for Monetary Stability*. New York: Fordham University Press.

Harris, M. 1979. Expectations and Money in a Dynamic Exchange Model. *Econometrica* 47(6): 1403–19.

Helpman, E. 1981. An Exploration in the Theory of Exchange-Rate Regimes. *Journal of Political Economy* 89(5): 865–890.

Lucas, R. E., Jr. 1982. Interest Rates and Currency Prices in a Two-Country World. *Journal of Monetary Economics* 10(3): 335–359.

Sargent, T. J., and N. Wallace. 1982. The Real-Bills Doctrine versus the Quantity Theory: A Reconsideration. *Journal of Political Economy* 90(6): 1212–36.

——— 1985. Interest on Reserves. *Journal of Monetary Economics* 15(3): 279–290.

Townsend, R. M. 1980. Models of Money with Spatially Separated Agents. *In* J. H. Kareken and N. Wallace (eds.), *Models of Monetary Economies*. Minneapolis: Federal Reserve Bank of Minneapolis, pp. 265–303.

Waldo, D. G. 1985. Open Market Operations in an Overlapping Generations Model. *Journal of Political Economy* 93(6): 1242–57.

Wallace, N. 1981. A Modigliani-Miller Theorem for Open-Market Operations. *American Economic Review* 71(3): 267–274.

——— 1983. A Legal Restrictions Theory of the Demand for "Money" and the Role of Monetary Policy. *Federal Reserve Bank of Minneapolis Quarterly Review* 7(1): 1–7.

Woodford, M. 1987. Credit Policy and the Price Level in a Cash-in-Advance Economy. *In* W. A. Barnett and K. J. Singleton (eds.), *New Approaches to Monetary Economics*. New York: Cambridge University Press, pp. 52–66.

Contributors

Index

Contributors

Robert J. Barro
Department of Economics, Harvard University

V. V. Chari
Research Department, Federal Reserve Bank of Minneapolis

Sanford J. Grossman
Department of Economics, Princeton University

Robert E. Hall
Hoover Institution *and* Department of Economics, Stanford University

Patrick J. Kehoe
Department of Economics, University of Minnesota, *and* Research
    Department, Federal Reserve Bank of Minneapolis

Bennett T. McCallum
School of Industrial Administration, Carnegie-Mellon University

Edward C. Prescott
Department of Economics, University of Minnesota, *and* Research
    Department, Federal Reserve Bank of Minneapolis

Kenneth Rogoff
Department of Economics, University of Wisconsin, Madison

Paul M. Romer
Department of Economics, University of Chicago

Neil Wallace
Department of Economics, University of Minnesota, *and* Research
    Department, Federal Reserve Bank of Minneapolis

Index